Current Trends in Natural Language Processing (NLP) and Human Language Technology (HLT)

Current Trends in Natural Language Processing (NLP) and Human Language Technology (HLT)

Editor

Florentina Hristea

Basel • Beijing • Wuhan • Barcelona • Belgrade • Novi Sad • Cluj • Manchester

Editor
Florentina Hristea
University of Bucharest
Bucharest
Romania

Editorial Office
MDPI
St. Alban-Anlage 66
4052 Basel, Switzerland

This is a reprint of articles from the Special Issue published online in the open access journal *Mathematics* (ISSN 2227-7390) (available at: https://www.mdpi.com/si/mathematics/NLP_HLT).

For citation purposes, cite each article independently as indicated on the article page online and as indicated below:

Lastname, A.A.; Lastname, B.B. Article Title. *Journal Name* **Year**, *Volume Number*, Page Range.

ISBN 978-3-7258-0085-8 (Hbk)
ISBN 978-3-7258-0086-5 (PDF)
doi.org/10.3390/books978-3-7258-0086-5

© 2024 by the authors. Articles in this book are Open Access and distributed under the Creative Commons Attribution (CC BY) license. The book as a whole is distributed by MDPI under the terms and conditions of the Creative Commons Attribution-NonCommercial-NoDerivs (CC BY-NC-ND) license.

Contents

About the Editor vii

Preface ix

Jesus-German Ortiz-Barajas, Gemma Bel-Enguix and Helena Gómez-Adorno
Sentence-CROBI: A Simple Cross-Bi-Encoder-Based Neural Network Architecture for Paraphrase Identification
Reprinted from: *Mathematics* **2022**, *10*, 3578, doi:10.3390/math10193578 1

Gabriel Bercaru, Ciprian-Octavian Truică, Costin-Gabriel Chiru and Traian Rebedea
Improving Intent Classification Using Unlabeled Data from Large Corpora
Reprinted from: *Mathematics* **2023**, *11*, 769, doi:10.3390/engproc2023030004 17

Wejdan Alkaldi and Diana Inkpen
Text Simplification to Specific Readability Levels
Reprinted from: *Mathematics* **2023**, *11*, 2063, doi:10.3390/math11092063 37

Valentin Barriere and Alexandra Balahur
Multilingual Multi-Target Stance Recognition in Online Public Consultations
Reprinted from: *Mathematics* **2023**, *11*, 2161, doi:10.3390/math11092161 49

Minhyeok Lee
A Mathematical Interpretation of Autoregressive Generative Pre-Trained Transformer and Self-Supervised Learning
Reprinted from: *Mathematics* **2023**, *11*, 2451, doi:10.3390/math11112451 69

Jani Dugonik, Mirjam Sepesy Maučec, Domen Verber and Janez Brest
Reduction of Neural Machine Translation Failures by Incorporating Statistical Machine Translation
Reprinted from: *Mathematics* **2023**, *11*, 2484, doi:10.3390/math11112484 88

Andrei-Marius Avram, Verginica Barbu Mititelu, Vasile Păiș, Dumitru-Clementin Cercel and Ștefan Trăușan-Matu
Multilingual Multiword Expression Identification Using Lateral Inhibition and Domain Adaptation
Reprinted from: *Mathematics* **2023**, *11*, 2548, doi:10.3390/math11112548 110

Ze Shi, Hongyi Li, Di Zhao and Chengwei Pan
Research on Relation Classification Tasks Based on Cybersecurity Text
Reprinted from: *Mathematics* **2023**, *11*, 2598, doi:10.3390/math11122598 128

Yunho Mo, Joon Yoo and Sangwoo Kang
Parameter-Efficient Fine-Tuning Method for Task-Oriented Dialogue Systems
Reprinted from: *Mathematics* **2023**, *11*, 3048, doi:10.3390/math11143048 144

Yanbing Xiao, Guorong Chen, Chongling Du, Lang Li, Yu Yuan, Jincheng Zou and Jingcheng Liu
A Study on Double-Headed Entities and Relations Prediction Framework for Joint Triple Extraction
Reprinted from: *Mathematics* **2023**, *11*, 4583, doi:10.3390/math11224583 158

Adrian-Gabriel Chifu and Sébastien Fournier
Sentiment Difficulty in Aspect-Based Sentiment Analysis
Reprinted from: *Mathematics* **2023**, *11*, 4647, doi:10.3390/math11224647 171

Mihailo Škorić, Miloš Utvić and Ranka Stanković
Transformer-Based Composite Language Models for Text Evaluation and Classification
Reprinted from: *Mathematics* **2023**, *11*, 4660, doi:10.3390/math11224660 . . . . **204**

José Antonio García-Díaz, Ronghao Pan and Rafael Valencia-García
Leveraging Zero and Few-Shot Learning for Enhanced Model Generality in Hate Speech Detection in Spanish and English
Reprinted from: *Mathematics* **2023**, *11*, 5004, doi:10.3390/math11245004 . . . . **229**

About the Editor

Florentina Hristea

Florentina Hristea, Ph.D., is currently a Full Professor in the Department of Computer Science at the University of Bucharest, Romania. At this same institution, she received both her B.S. degree in Mathematics and Computer Science and her Ph.D. in Mathematics in 1984 and 1996, respectively. She received her habilitation in Computer Science from this same university in 2017 with the habilitation thesis "Word Sense Disambiguation with Application in Information Retrieval". Her current field of research is artificial intelligence, with specialization in knowledge representation, natural language processing (NLP), human language technologies (HLT), and computational linguistics, as well as computational statistics and data analysis with applications in NLP. She has been a principal investigator of several national and international interdisciplinary research development projects and is an expert evaluator of the European Commission in the fields of NLP and HLT. Professor Hristea is the author or co-author of nine books, two chapters in books, and various scientific papers, of which 32 comprise articles in peer-reviewed scholarly journals. She is the author of an outlier detection algorithm which is named after her (Outlier Detection, Hristea Algorithm. Encyclopedia of Statistical Sciences, Second Edition, Vol. 9, N. Balakrishnan, Campbell B. Read, and Brani Vidakovic, Editors-in-Chief. Wiley, New York, p. 5885–5886, 2005) and is an elected member of the ISI (International Statistical Institute). She is also a member of the GWA (Global WordNet Association). Professor Hristea was a Fulbright Research Fellow at Princeton University, USA, an Invited Professor at the University of Toulouse, France, and has been a visiting scientist at Heidelberg Institute for Theoretical Studies, Germany; the University of Toulouse Paul Sabatier III, France; Institut de Recherche en Informatique de Toulouse, France; and L' école Polytechnique "Polytech Montpellier", France.

Preface

As often noted, AI-powered text processing continues to represent a strong trend in artificial intelligence (AI), primarily due to the genuine explosion of texts on the World Wide Web. Natural language processing (NLP) is one of the most important technologies in use today, especially due to the large and growing amount of online text, which needs to be understood in order for its enormous value to be fully asserted. NLP can make sense of the unstructured data that are produced by social platforms and other social data sources and can help organize them into a more structured model that supports various types of tasks and applications. Human language technology (HLT) poses a significant challenge for computing, requiring advanced NLP and the availability of big data to create large-scale systems and applications. The large size, unrestrictive nature, and ambiguity of natural language have led to substantial developments in the NLP field in various ways and from different perspectives, all of which were of interest to this Special Issue. Although numerous machine learning models have been developed for NLP applications, recently, deep learning approaches have achieved notable results across many NLP tasks. This Special Issue also contributes to the use and exploration of current advances in machine learning and deep learning for a great variety of NLP topics, belonging to a broad spectrum of research areas that are concerned with computational approaches to natural language and, specifically, with processing human language in the form of text.

The paper authored by Ortiz-Barajas et al. (2022) represents a first approach that combines bi-encoder and cross-encoder representations for sentence pair tasks. It proposes a simple language model-based architecture that combines cross-encoders and bi-encoders to compute a vector representation, suggesting that the model's performance in sentence pair tasks could thus be improved without any auxiliary technique. The success of the proposed model does not rely on adding more pre-training tasks, modifying the transformer architecture, or creating new fine-tuning algorithms. The model is easy to implement using existing tools, and it is possible to adapt it to different tasks by performing minor changes only.

The paper authored by Bercaru et al. (2023) examines the problem of intent classification as part of a conversational agent pipeline. The authors propose a novel pipeline for efficiently analyzing large, unlabeled corpora and extracting examples similar to a user-supplied query. The aim is to minimize the retrieval time while maintaining a high similarity between the query and the retrieved example. Moreover, the authors examine how the proposed example retrieval system improves the intent classification accuracy in several few-shot learning scenarios, where intent examples are scarce. The experimental results show that using the proposed corpus augmentation methods enables an increase in text classification accuracy in few-shot settings. Specifically, the gains in accuracy increase up to 16% when the number of labeled examples is very low (e.g., two examples). We believe that the proposed method is important for any natural language processing (NLP) or natural language understanding (NLU) task in which labeled training data are scarce or expensive to obtain.

The paper authored by Alkaldi and Inkpen (2023) introduces a system that uses deep learning techniques to simplify texts in order to match a reader's level. Text simplification (TS) techniques that are currently available do not use the readability level as a required feature for the output text. Instead, they typically simplify the given text to whatever readability level it can reach. In contrast with this current trend, the model proposed here takes a complex text with a low readability level and produces a simplified version of the text that considers a required readability level. This ensures that every simplified text will be readable and understandable by its targeted audience. This research brings novelty in the area of TS in the way the deep learning models are trained, using augmented data, and in the way the reinforcement learning loop is performed, using a readability classifier. The proposed text simplification models achieve better performance than state-of-the-art techniques for this task.

The paper authored by Barriere and Balahur (2023) aims to contribute to the field of multilingual stance recognition by addressing the challenges and opportunities presented when analyzing online multilingual debates. Specifically, the paper focuses on developing models and methods for recognizing the stance of users in different languages on a given topic and how to make use of the cross-lingual information present in the debates. The proposed setting makes the task of stance detection more difficult due to the high variability in terms of topics and languages. The research addresses the problem of ternary stance classification, i.e., whether a comment is *pro*, *against*, or *other* towards the proposal it is commenting on. It additionally proposes a series of methods to learn with a limited number of labels, by pre-training over similar datasets and leveraging information from non-annotated data with the help of self-training methods.

The paper authored by Lee (2023) represents a mathematical examination of generative pre-trained transformer (GPT) models and their autoregressive self-supervised learning mechanisms. The author formalizes key concepts, definitions, assumptions, and theorems to provide a rigorous understanding of these models' underlying mechanisms. The study starts by defining natural language space and knowledge space, which are two key concepts for understanding the dimensionality reduction process in GPT-based large language models (LLMs). By exploring projection functions and their inverses, a framework for analyzing the language generation capabilities of these models is established. The GPT representation space is investigated afterward, with the author examining its implications for the models' approximation properties. The proposed exploration of GPT, as an approximation of the projection function and its inverse, has potential implications for the development of more efficient, effective, and robust LLMs, hopefully driving future advancements in the fields of language understanding and generation.

The paper authored by Dugonik et al. (2023) proposes a hybrid machine translation (HMT) system that improves the quality of neural machine translation (NMT) by incorporating statistical machine translation (SMT). The main contributions of the paper are to improve NMT translation quality by using SMT and to represent the source sentence and both translations as vectors in the same vector space, using a multilingual language model—in this case, mBERT—that supports over 100 languages. The translation, in both directions, between English and the highly inflected language Slovene is examined. However, the suggested framework is language-independent and can be applied to other languages supported by the multilingual language model as well. The proposed method of combining SMT and NMT in the hybrid system is novel.

The paper authored by Avram et al. (2023) deals with the issue of correctly identifying multiword expressions (MWEs), which represents an important task for most natural language processing systems. This work leverages the knowledge developed in the two research areas (i.e., MWEs and multilingual NLP) to improve the results obtained with the PARSEME 1.2 shared task. The authors have analyzed the performance of MWE identification in a multilingual setting, training the mBERT model on the combined PARSEME 1.2 corpus, using all of the 14 languages found in its composition. In addition, to boost the performance of their system, they have employed lateral inhibition and language adversarial training in their methodology, intending to create embeddings that are as language independent as possible and to improve their capabilities in identifying multiword expressions. We note here that this research is the first to experiment with and show the advantages of lateral inhibition in multilingual adversarial training. The approach employed in this research achieves better results compared to the best system of the PARSEME 1.2 competition, MTLB-STRUCT, on 11 out of 14 languages for global MWE identification and on 12 out of 14 languages for unseen

MWE identification.

The paper authored by Shi et al. (2023) concentrates on relation classification, which represents a classical problem within the domain of relation extraction and a crucial task in natural language processing. Specifically, the paper focuses on investigating the task of relation classification in the field of cybersecurity. To address this issue, the authors first construct a manually annotated cybersecurity dataset called CS13K. This research proposes a new relation classification model that achieves exceptional performance on the SemEval-2010 task 8 dataset, surpassing previous approaches with a remarkable F1 value of 92.3%.

The paper authored by Mo et al. (2023) is concerned with task-oriented dialogue (TOD) systems and proposes PEFTTOD, a novel structure for solving TOD systems using a large-scale pre-trained language model. The proposal leverages the parameter-efficient fine-tuning method (PEFT), which incorporates an adapter layer and prefix tuning into the pre-trained language model. It significantly reduces the overall parameter count used during training and efficiently transfers dialogue knowledge. We note that, despite utilizing only around 4% of the parameters compared to the baseline model, notable efficiency gains were achieved, including a 20% improvement in training speed and an approximately 96% reduction in storage space requirements.

The paper authored by Xiao et al. (2023) addresses a fundamental procedure in knowledge graph construction, namely that of relational triple extraction. The authors propose a double-headed entities and relations prediction (DERP) framework, which divides the entity recognition process into two stages—head entity recognition and tail entity recognition—using the obtained head and tail entities as inputs. By utilizing the corresponding relation and the corresponding entity, the DERP framework further incorporates a triple prediction module to improve the accuracy and completeness of the joint relation triple extraction. A good foundation is constructed for subsequent natural language processing and knowledge graph construction efforts. An extensive empirical evaluation is organized: experiments were conducted on two English datasets and two Chinese datasets, with the English dataset's experimental results being compared with those derived from ten baseline models. The experimental results demonstrated the effectiveness of the proposed DERP framework for triple extraction.

The paper authored by Chifu and Fournier (2023) initiates the discussion around the definition of sentence difficulty in the context of aspect-based sentiment analysis. Two strategies for defining sentence difficulty are proposed and a great number of experiments are carried out in order to better understand where the difficulties lie in the sentiment classification task based on aspects. Thorough experiments are conducted on three well-known aspect-based sentiment analysis datasets, testing more than 20 classification models on two different textual representations: TF-IDF and BERT. In studying performance enhancement, fine-tuned BERT representations are considered and ensemble learning (majority vote) is also applied. Although difficulty detection is a key area of research, the notion of difficulty in aspect-based sentiment analysis has not been studied so far. From this perspective, the paper raises a new, important research question and initiates a discussion that should be both promising and challenging for future research.

The paper authored by Škorić et al. (2023) aims to present the advantages of using composite language models in the processing and evaluation of texts written in highly inflective and morphologically rich natural languages, particularly in Serbian. The performed investigation employs the most common intrinsic metric used in computational linguistics, perplexity, which ultimately represents a measure of how much the model is surprised by seeing new input text. The paper describes a comparative analysis of calculated perplexities in order to measure the classification capability of different models on two binary classification tasks: low-quality sentence detection and machine translation detection. On both tasks, the improvements achieved using composite language models (built upon the perplexity outputs of several language models) over the accuracy of standalone models, which is taken as the baseline, were tested. In conclusion, composite models were shown to improve upon the accuracy of standalone models for classification tasks, with a composite language model based on a stacked classifier architecture that uses properties extracted from perplexity vectors as features being singled out as the best option for the detection of both machine translations and low-quality sentences. Other contributions of this research pertain to the development of a perplexity-based dataset for the testing and validation of composite and standalone language models using existing models and parallel language corpora, as well as the creation of composite Serbian language models that can be used in natural language processing tasks, including document classification and text evaluation. We especially note the development of a detailed model of the composite systems for the parallel unification of created models which can be applied to both future models and other languages. This study opens new research avenues, since the question of whether the composition of a few smaller models is better than a large standalone model in terms of both training and execution speed, as well as in terms of accuracy, still remains.

The paper authored by García-Díaz et al. (2023) explores the advantages of zero and few-shot learning over supervised training, with a particular focus on hate speech detection datasets covering different domains and levels of complexity. The generalization capabilities of generative models such as T5, BLOOM, and Llama-2 are evaluated on both Spanish and English datasets. The conducted investigation offers insight into their cross-lingual applicability and versatility, thus contributing to a broader understanding of generative models in natural language processing. The obtained results highlight the potential of generative models to bridge the gap between data scarcity and model performance across languages and domains. These research efforts have equally provided valuable insights into the evolving field of hate speech detection strategies. The obtained results suggest that the selection of the best strategy for hate speech detection is highly dependent on the dataset and model. Therefore, further research should be conducted to determine the similarities and differences of the evaluated linguistic models and strategies.

This Special Issue presents innovative research in the domain of NLP and HLT while opening new, challenging research avenues for future investigations. We note the large range of research topics that have been covered, showing the diversity and the dynamic of a permanently evolving field, which is giving one of the most important technologies in use today. It is our hope that the presented research results will contribute to fostering future research in NLP and inspiring future studies in all related fields.

As the Guest Editor of this Special Issue, I would like to express my gratitude to the 43 authors who contributed their articles. I am equally grateful to a great number of wonderful reviewers whose valuable comments and suggestions helped improve the quality of the submitted manuscripts, as well as to the dedicated MDPI editorial staff who helped greatly during the entire process of creating this Special Issue.

Florentina Hristea
Editor

Article

Sentence-CROBI: A Simple Cross-Bi-Encoder-Based Neural Network Architecture for Paraphrase Identification

Jesus-German Ortiz-Barajas [1], Gemma Bel-Enguix [2,*] and Helena Gómez-Adorno [3]

[1] Posgrado en Ciencia e Ingeniería de la Computación, Universidad Nacional Autónoma de México, Mexico City 04510, Mexico
[2] Instituto de Ingeniería, Universidad Nacional Autónoma de México, Mexico City 04510, Mexico
[3] Instituto de Investigaciones en Matemáticas Aplicadas y en Sistemas, Universidad Nacional Autónoma de México, Mexico City 04510, Mexico
* Correspondence: gbele@iingen.unam.mx

Abstract: Since the rise of Transformer networks and large language models, cross-encoders have become the dominant architecture for various Natural Language Processing tasks. When dealing with sentence pairs, they can exploit the relationships between those pairs. On the other hand, bi-encoders can obtain a vector given a single sentence and are used in tasks such as textual similarity or information retrieval due to their low computational cost; however, their performance is inferior to that of cross-encoders. In this paper, we present Sentence-CROBI, an architecture that combines cross-encoders and bi-encoders to obtain a global representation of sentence pairs. We evaluated the proposed architecture in the paraphrase identification task using the Microsoft Research Paraphrase Corpus, the Quora Question Pairs dataset, and the PAWS-Wiki dataset. Our model obtains competitive results compared with the state-of-the-art by using model ensembles and a simple model configuration. These results demonstrate that a simple architecture that combines sentence pair and single-sentence representations without using complex pre-training or fine-tuning algorithms is a viable alternative for sentence pair tasks.

Keywords: paraphrase identification; transformers; cross-encoders; bi-encoders

MSC: 68-04

1. Introduction

"Paraphrase" refers to sentences that have the same meaning as other sentences but use different words [1]. The problem of paraphrase identification is a binary classification task in which, given two texts S_1 and S_2, it must be determined whether they have the same meaning or not. Developing paraphrase identification systems is challenging because defining what constitutes a paraphrase is complex. Previous works define the paraphrase as an approximate equivalence between texts; in addition, there are different types of paraphrasing based on the level of changes that the texts could have [2]: the low paraphrase, which consists of substituting synonyms, hypernyms, hyponyms, meronyms and holonyms; and the high paraphrase, which consists of the realization of the phenomena of the low paraphrase, in addition to the morphological, lexical, semantic, syntactic and discursive phenomena. Because of the above, one option is to develop deep-learning-based approaches, which allow us to identify paraphrases of any type without extracting complex linguistic features to define text pairs.

The Transformer architecture [3] introduced a new era of Natural Language Processing (NLP) with the rise of pre-trained large language models. As a result of pre-training, they can learn universal representations of language that can be fine-tuned to specific tasks, without the need to train each model from scratch [4].

The cross-encoder model is one of the most popular approaches based on pre-trained language models. This model encodes the two texts together and applies full self-attention

to both texts at once [5]. Another pre-trained language model approach is the bi-encoder model. This approach applies self-attention separately for each text using a Siamese network and then compares them using a similarity metric [6].

Following the introduction of the BERT model [7], many approaches have emerged to increase its performance, from the modification of the pre-training stage [8] to modifications to the attention mechanisms [9], knowledge distillation [10], and other complex approaches. Our work proposes Sentence-CROBI, a simple architecture that combines the representations of cross-encoders and bi-encoders for sentence pair tasks. The results show competitive performance with state-of-the-art models when using model assembly and when using a simple approach, which offers a simple alternative for these types of tasks.

The structure of the paper is the following. In Section 2, we describe related work, where we consider previous BERT-based approaches applied to the paraphrase identification task. Section 3 describes the corpora that we used to train and evaluate the Sentence-CROBI architecture. In Section 4, we explain the proposed architecture and the experimental setup. Finally, in Sections 5 and 6, we present the results and conclusions, respectively.

2. Related Work

The Transformer network [3] is an architecture that can encode texts in parallel by using attention mechanisms instead of a sequential mechanism such as Recurrent Neural Networks. This feature enables researchers to train models with large amounts of text efficiently, marking the beginning of a new era in the artificial intelligence field where pre-trained large language models are used to solve several Natural Language Processing tasks [4].

The BERT model [7] is the most well-known language model based on the Transformer architecture using a cross-encoder approach, and it has obtained state-of-the-art results in a wide variety of tasks [11]. It consists of two versions: the base version and the large version, made up of 12 and 24 Transformer encoder blocks, respectively. The pre-training of the model consists of two tasks. The first task is the Masked Language Model, in which the [MASK] token replaces a portion of the input tokens, and the model learns to predict the actual values of those tokens. The second task is the Next Sentence Prediction, in which, from two texts A and B, the model must identify whether B is the text that comes after A or not. After pre-training, the model can be fine-tuned for any NLP problem by appending an additional layer to the top of the model, using a small number of epochs and a low learning rate. After the emergence of the BERT model, the NLP community proposed different approaches to improve the performance of large language models based on the Transformer architecture using the two-stage scheme: pre-training and fine-tuning. There are four axes for these approaches.

The first axis consists of modifying the pre-training stage. The RoBERTa model [8] was proposed as an optimized configuration of BERT. The modifications consist of performing dynamic masking of the input tokens to the model in each epoch, eliminating the auxiliary loss function for the Masked Language Model task, using longer sequences and a more extensive dataset, and training for more epochs. Similarly, the StructBERT [12] model adds two tasks to this stage to learn the structure of the language both at the word level and the sentence level. The first task consists of changing the order of the masked tokens to predict the correct word order. The second task consists of changing the order of the statements in the Next Sentence Prediction task to predict the order of the statements. The last example in this axis is the Ernie 2.0 model [13]. The authors propose a continuous multi-task learning framework to learn lexical, syntactic, and semantic information in this work. This framework allows the use of the knowledge of previous tasks for new tasks during the pre-training phase. To check the effectiveness of the proposed model, they propose a set of seven pre-training tasks divided into three sets. The first set consists of word-level tasks. The first task is knowledge masking, in which the [MASK] token replaces some named entities and phrases of the text, and the model predicts its actual value. The second task is to predict whether a word begins with a capital letter, and, finally, the last task of this set consists of predicting whether a token appears in other document segments or not. The second set consists of structure-level tasks. These tasks are sentence reordering and sentence distance prediction. Sentence reordering consists of finding the correct order of segment permutations of the original text. Sentence distance prediction is a multi-class classification problem. The model predicts whether two text segments are adjacent in a document, whether they are in the same document but not adjacent, or whether they do not belong to the same document. The last set consists of semantic-level tasks, where the model predicts the semantic relationship of two texts and the relevance of a text in an information retrieval system.

The second axis of modifications consists of reducing the size of the models. The ALBERT model [14] uses the factorized embedding parameterization technique. This technique splits the model vocabulary into two matrices: one for the embedding layer's vocabulary and the other for the hidden layer's vocabulary. ALBERT also implements parameter sharing between layers to prevent the model's growth in depth. Another proposed approach for model reduction is the BORT model [10]. It is an optimal sub-architecture of BERT obtained using a fully polynomial time approximation scheme based on three evaluation metrics: inference time, model size, and error rate. However, since the resulting model is 95% smaller than the large BERT, it is more prone to overfitting. Therefore, the authors use the Agora algorithm [15], which combines data augmentation and knowledge distillation techniques, for the fine-tuning stage.

The third axis consists of modifying the fine-tuning stage of the model to achieve better performance in the target tasks. The SMART algorithm [16] was proposed as an alternative when target task data are limited. The method uses a smoothness-inducing adversarial regularization technique to control the capacity of the model and its high complexity by adding a small perturbation to the input data. In addition, to prevent the aggressive model's parameter update, the authors present a class of Bregman proximal point optimization techniques. These methods use a confident-region-based regularization; therefore, the model updates its parameters only based on a small neighborhood of the previous iteration. The authors apply the proposed algorithm to fine-tune the RoBERTa [8] and MT-DNN [17] models to evaluate their performance in ensemble and single model approaches.

Finally, the fourth axis consists of modifications to the Transformer architecture. In the DeBERTa model [9], the authors propose a new attention mechanism that encodes the words in two vectors: the first vector encodes the word, and the other encodes its relative location. In contrast, the vanilla Transformer architecture encodes the words by summing the content vector and the position vector. The attention mechanism calculates the attention weights in separate arrays based on both representations by separating the words into content and relative position vectors. In addition, the authors incorporate the absolute position information for the Masked Language Model task; therefore, the model takes into account the content of the word, its relative position, and its absolute position to predict the actual value of the masked token. In the same field, the Funnel-Transformer model [18] was proposed to reduce the computational cost of pre-training a language model on a vast dataset. The authors add a pooling layer after some Transformer encoder blocks to achieve this goal, reducing the hidden representations' size by half. In the case of token-level tasks such as the Masked Language Model task during the pre-training stage, the authors add a decoder to reconstruct the final vector to the original size. In the case of sentence-level tasks, the decoder is unnecessary, and the fine-tuning process only applies to the encoder.

Additionally, there is a different axis where researchers use pre-trained large language models to obtain sentence-level representations from texts and combine them with features that do not rely on neural network models. The Lexical, Syntactic, and Sentential Encodings (LSSE) learning model [19] is a unified framework that incorporates Relational Graph Convolutional Networks (R-GCNs) to obtain different features from local contexts through word encoding, position encoding, and full dependency structures, as well as sentence-level representations obtained using the BERT model. The authors use the [CLS] token as the sentence pair representation, while the graph network learns the syntactic context by capturing the dependency structure and word order. Each context vector is compared using a distance metric and is concatenated to the sentence pair vector to obtain the global representation.

Unlike the works described above, there is another approach based on pre-trained language models called bi-encoders. For example, in sentence pair tasks, each text is encoded by a Siamese neural network [20] separately. The Sentence-BERT model [21] uses two instances of the BERT model with shared weights, where each text is encoded independently. At the output of each BERT instance, a pooling operation is applied to the last hidden state to obtain the vectors of each text; the global representation for the sentence pair consists of some combination of the individual vectors. Although this is a more efficient approach, its performance is lower than that of cross-encoder-based approaches [5,6].

In this work, we propose Sentence-CROBI, a simple architecture that combines cross-encoder and bi-encoder approaches for sentence pair tasks.

3. Corpora

This section describes the characteristics of the corpora that we used to evaluate our architecture. We selected these datasets based on the Papers with Code (https://paperswithcode.com/ accessed on 1 February 2022) platform. It is possible to search research papers based on the task that they solve, the datasets that they use, or the proposed approach. We selected the three datasets with the highest citations for the paraphrase identification task: the Microsoft Research Paraphrase Corpus (MRPC) [22], the Quora Question Pairs (QQP) corpus, and the PAWS corpus [23].

The Microsoft Research Paraphrase Corpus (MRPC) [22] consists of 5801 sentence pairs, collected over two years from various news websites and manually classified into two classes: Paraphrase and No Paraphrase. The corpus is partitioned into train and test subsets. The training set contains 4076 sentence pairs, where 2753 examples are paraphrases—that is, 67.5% of the pairs correspond to the Paraphrase class—and the remaining 1323 pairs of this set are non-paraphrase examples. On the other hand, the testing set consists of 1725 sentence pairs, where 66.5% are paraphrases—that is, 1147 sentence pairs. The remaining 578 pairs are non-paraphrase examples. Besides the paraphrase identification task, this corpus has been used in various tasks, such as sentence embedding computation using contrastive learning [24], zero-shot learning techniques [25], and the explainability of pre-trained language models [26].

The Quora Question Pairs (QQP) corpus consists of 795,241 question pairs labeled in a binary manner as Duplicated or Not Duplicated. It is divided into three subsets: the training set contains 363,846 question pairs, the validation set 40,430, and the testing set 390,965. The validation and training subsets have a distribution of 37% for duplicate questions and 63% for non-duplicate questions; the distribution of the test set is unknown because its labels are not publicly available. Therefore, the evaluation was performed using the GLUE Benchmark [27] server by uploading the output of our model on the test set using a specific format. To ensure the consistency of our results, we downloaded the corpus version provided by the GLUE Benchmark on their website (https://gluebenchmark.com/tasks accessed on 1 April 2022). This dataset has been used in tasks such as adversarial reprogramming [28] and model pre-training with limited resources [29].

The PAWS corpus [23]—specifically, the PAWS-Wiki subset—contains sentence pairs from Wikipedia (https://dumps.wikimedia.org accessed on 5 February 2022). It consists of 65,401 sentence pairs divided into three subsets: the training set with 49,401 instances and validation and testing sets with 8000 instances each. The distribution of the corpus includes 44% of examples labeled as Paraphrase and 56% labeled as No Paraphrase. This corpus contains examples with high lexical overlap, even for non-paraphrase sentence pairs. This characteristic makes it a challenging corpus when evaluating paraphrase detection models. Although it has been recently created, this dataset has been used in tasks such as in-context learning [30], condescending language detection [31], and intent detection [32].

Table 1 displays the statistics of the datasets described above.

Table 1. Statistics for the MRPC, QQP, and PAWS-Wiki datasets.

Corpus	Paraphrase Instances	Non-Paraphrase Instances	Total Instances
MRPC (train)	2753	1323	4076
MRPC (test)	1147	578	1725
QQP (train)	134,623	229,223	363,846
QQP (val)	14,959	25,471	40,430
QQP (test)	-	-	390,965
PAWS-Wiki (train)	21,829	27,572	49,401
PAWS-Wiki (val)	3539	4461	8000
PAWS-Wiki (test)	3536	4464	8000

Additionally, we used the Multi-Genre NLI corpus [33], which consists of labeled sentence pairs with textual entailment information in three classes: Neutral, Contradiction, and Entailment. It is composed of two subsets of training and testing. The training set contains 391,164 examples, with 130,375 examples for the Neutral class, 130,379 for the Contradiction class, and 130,411 for the Entailment class; the testing set is composed of 9714 pairs of statements, with 3094 examples of the class Neutral, 3180 for Contradiction, and 3440 labeled as Entailment. Following a two-stage fine-tuning approach, [34], we used this dataset to perform an intermediate fine-tuning stage for the proposed architecture before tuning the model in the target task.

4. Methodology

This section describes in detail the proposed architecture, the preprocessing steps that we performed to train and evaluate the model, and, finally, the experimental configuration.

4.1. Text Preprocessing

The preprocessing performed on the sentence pairs is detailed below. We converted each text to a sequence of IDs based on the BERT model [7] vocabulary. Similarly, we converted the sentence pairs to a sequence of IDs based on the ROBERTa model vocabulary [8]. Then, after encoding each text and the sentence pair, we added the classification [CLS] token and the separation [SEP] token. Following the preprocessing process, we added padding for individual texts and sentence pairs to normalize inputs to a single size. Finally, we obtained the attention mask for each text and sentence pair. This mask allows the model to distinguish between word tokens and padding tokens.

4.2. Model

In this section, we present the Sentence-CROBI architecture and its implementation. The bi-encoder component of our approach is based on the Sentence-BERT model [21]; we use a modification of the BERT model through a Siamese neural network [20] that is capable of obtaining individual vectors of fixed size from each text. We apply a pooling operation to the last hidden state of the BERT model to obtain a sentence vector for each text. We represent these sentence vectors as u and v, respectively. We use an instance of the RoBERTa model for the cross-encoder component. This model receives the joint encoding of the sentence pair. To obtain the final representation of the sequence, we use the classification token [CLS].

After obtaining the individual representation of each text and its joint representation, we compute the Euclidean distance D between the vectors u and v. Finally, we obtain the global vector representation of the sentence pair by concatenating the classification token [CLS] from the cross-encoder representation, the vectors u and v, and the Euclidean distance D. This vector is the input to a classifier composed of two fully connected networks.

We use the BERT base version composed of 12 Transformer blocks for the bi-encoder component of our architecture. Meanwhile, we use the RoBERTa large version composed of 24 Transformer blocks for the cross-encoder component.

Figure 1 shows the structure of the Sentence-CROBI architecture.

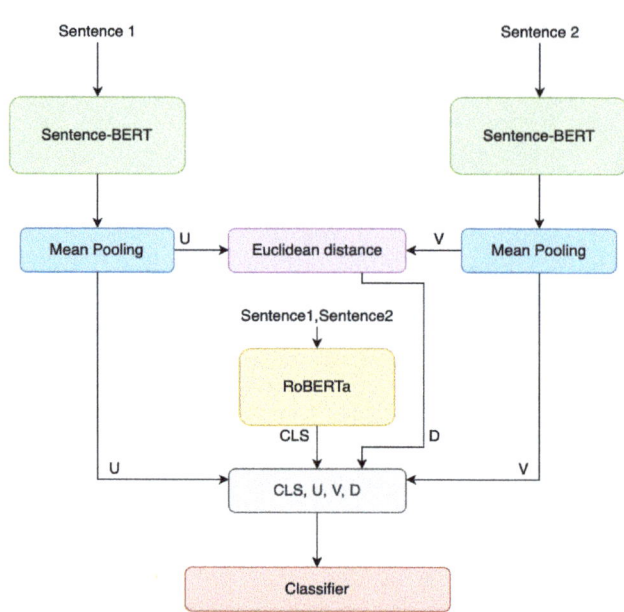

Figure 1. Diagram of the Sentence-CROBI model. CLS corresponds to the classification token of the cross-encoder component. U and V correspond to the individual vector representations of each text, denoted by Sentence 1 and Sentence 2, respectively. D is the Euclidean distance between vectors U and V.

The Siamese component of the Sentence-CROBI architecture produces contextual word vectors. We obtain sentence vectors by applying a mean pooling operation to the contextual word embedding matrix, where each row represents a word in the input text. The proposed architecture takes the last hidden state of BERT as contextual word embeddings.

The final component of our proposed model is the classifier. It is a fully connected network with two layers. First, it receives the global sentence pair representation as input, and a dropout layer is applied with a probability of 0.1. Dropout is a regularization technique to avoid overfitting of the network; it consists of randomly setting some values of its input to zero. Then, it passes through a fully connected layer of 1793 units with a hyperbolic tangent as the activation function. Finally, the output layer consists of 2 neurons with a linear function as an activation function.

We use the cross-entropy as a loss function during the training of the Sentence-CROBI architecture. The function's objective is to compare the probability of the predicted class to that of the actual class of the training instance. The model's prediction is then penalized based on the distance from the actual value. Equation (1) defines the cross-entropy function, where

- y^i is the actual label;
- $\hat{y}^i$ denotes the probability predicted by the model;
- N is the size of the test set.

$$CE = \sum_{i=1}^{N} y^i \log(\hat{y}^i) + (1 - y^i) \log(1 - \hat{y}^i) \tag{1}$$

4.3. Fine-Tuning

To fine-tune the model, we use two approaches. The first is the original approach proposed for the BERT model: it consists of initializing the model's parameters based on the pre-training stage and training the model for a few epochs on the target task using a small learning rate. However, one of the issues with this approach is that when the target task dataset is small, the model is prone to overfitting [35]. Because the Microsoft Research Paraphrase Corpus has only 4076 training examples, we apply a second approach by using an intermediate-related target task to fine-tune the model. The intermediate target task has more labeled data [34] and allows the model to increase its robustness and effectiveness. In this work, we use the Multi-Genre NLI described in Section 3 for intermediate training of the Sentence-CROBI architecture before fine-tuning on the Microsoft Paraphrase corpus.

4.4. Ensemble Learning

To improve the classifier's performance in the paraphrase identification task, we use the Bagging technique [36], which reduces the generalization error by combining several models. This technique consists of training different models separately and combining each output set to vote on test data and obtain the final prediction.

In the case of neural networks, differences in random initialization or in batch generation cause independent errors in each member of the ensemble; therefore, the ensemble will perform significantly better than its members [37].

In this work, we perform the ensemble learning technique by fine-tuning several instances of the Sentence-CROBI architecture using different random seeds to initialize each model. After the fine-tuning stage, we compute the output probabilities of each test example for each independent instance of the Sentence-CROBI model. We obtain k output matrices, where k is the number of independent instances of the model, and the dimension of each matrix is $N \times 2$, where N is the number of examples on the test set, and 2 corresponds to the number of classes. We compute the probability average of the k predictions, and the classification is based on the class with the highest probability.

4.5. Training Details

Following the fine-tuning procedure in the ROBERTa model [8], we train our models with a batch size in the range of {16,32}. We use a learning rate in the range of {1×10^{-5}, 2×10^{-5}, 3×10^{-5}} with the Adam optimizer, with a warm-up ratio of 0.06 and a linear decay to zero. We train all models for a maximum of 10 epochs and perform pseudo early stopping to use the model with the best performance on the validation data. The maximum length is 35 for individual texts and 128 for text pairs. We use HuggingFace's Transformers library to implement the Sentence-CROBI model [38]. Our code implementation is publicly available on Github (https://github.com/jgermanob/Sentence-CROBI created on 14 September 2022).

5. Results

We present the Sentence-CROBI model's results for the corpora described in Section 3 and their comparison with the state-of-the-art models described in Section 2. The evaluation metrics used are Accuracy and F1-score in the Paraphrase class.

Tables 2 and 3 report the results obtained from each paper for the BORT, StructBERT, Funnel-Transformer, ALBERT, and Ernie 2.0 models. In the case of the SMART algorithm, we use the results reported by the authors when fine-tuning the RoBERTa and MT-DNN models using their approach.

Tables 4 and 5 report the results that we obtained using the public implementation for each model in the state-of-the-art. We report the average of five runs using different random seeds.

Table 2 shows the state-of-the-art results obtained from the GLUE Benchmark leaderboard on the Microsoft Research Paraphrase Corpus and the results with the Sentence-CROBI architecture. We order the different approaches based on the F1-score metric in descending order. The state-of-the-art results correspond to some ensemble learning approaches; nevertheless, the authors do not provide details on their ensemble learning process.

For the case of the Sentence-CROBI architecture, we use 15 different models for the Bagging algorithm as an ensemble learning technique. All models correspond to an independent run using different random seeds. Five models correspond to fine-tuning the model on the MRPC corpus after performing intermediate fine-tuning of the model on the MNLI corpus—that is, we initialize the model's weights based on the pre-training stage, fine-tune the model on the intermediate task, and finally fine-tune the model on the target task. Another five models are analogous but use the PAWS-Wiki dataset as the intermediate task. The remaining five models correspond to the MRPC corpus's fine-tuning without any intermediate fine-tuning. After completing all runs, we average the output probabilities to obtain the final prediction.

Our model obtains competitive results in comparison to the state-of-the-art. There is only a difference of 1.23 in Accuracy and 0.75 in F1-score with the BORT model [10].

Table 2. Results on the Microsoft Research Paraphrase Corpus obtained from the GLUE Benchmark leaderboard.

Model	Accuracy	F1-Score	Difference Compared with Sentence-CROBI (Accuracy/F1-Score)
BORT [10]	92.30	94.10	1.23/0.75
MT-DNN SMART [16]	91.60	93.70	0.53/0.35
RoBERTa SMART [16]	91.60	93.70	0.53/0.35
StructBERTRoBERTa [12]	91.50	93.60	0.43/0.25
Funnel-Transformer [18]	91.20	93.40	0.13/0.05
ALBERT [14]	91.20	93.40	0.13/0.05
Sentence-CROBI	**91.07**	**93.35**	-
Ernie 2.0 [13]	87.40	90.20	$-3.67/-3.15$

Table 3 shows the state-of-the-art and the Sentence-CROBI results in the Quora Question Pairs dataset. Our proposed model obtains competitive results. However, there is a more significant gap compared to the best approach, with a difference of 0.6 in Accuracy and 1.6 in F1-score. The main difference with this corpus is the evaluation process, because all the state-of-the-art approaches follow a single-task fine-tuning approach. We use the Bagging algorithm as an ensemble learning technique and five runs with different random seeds to obtain the final prediction. In addition, the dataset is challenging because of the difference between the distributions in the subsets.

Table 3. Results on the Quora Question Pairs dataset obtained from the GLUE Benchmark leaderboard.

Model	Accuracy	F1-Score	Difference Compared with Sentence-CROBI (Accuracy/F1-Score)
Funnel-Transformer [18]	90.70	75.40	0.6/1.6
StructBERTRoBERTa [12]	90.70	74.40	0.6/0.6
ALBERT [14]	90.50	74.20	0.4/0.4
RoBERTa SMART [16]	90.01	74.00	$-0.09/0.2$
MT-DNN SMART [16]	90.20	73.90	0.1/0.1
Ernie 2.0 [13]	90.10	73.80	0.0/0.0
Sentence-CROBI	**90.10**	**73.80**	-
BORT [10]	85.90	66.00	$-4.2/-7.8$

Table 4 shows the results for the PAWS-Wiki corpus. The authors do not originally use this corpus in their work; for this reason, we use the public implementation of each of the state-of-the-art models. In this configuration, we do not use any intermediate fine-tuning task, and we report the mean over five runs with different random seeds. Our proposed model obtains the second-best performance using this dataset, with a small difference of 0.13 in both Accuracy and F1-score.

Figure 2 displays a bar chart showing each model's best performance on the Microsoft Research Paraphrase Corpus and Quora Question Pair dataset. We obtain these performance metrics from the GLUE Benchmark leaderboard for the state-of-the-art models. The Sentence-CROBI model corresponds to the ensemble learning technique described above in the case of MRPC and a single fine-tuning approach for the QQP dataset. All models achieve a higher F1-score than 90 in MRPC. However, in the QQP dataset, only the BORT model obtained an F1-score lower than 70. The difference in the BORT model's performance on both datasets suggests instability in its fine-tuning algorithm because of the model's size.

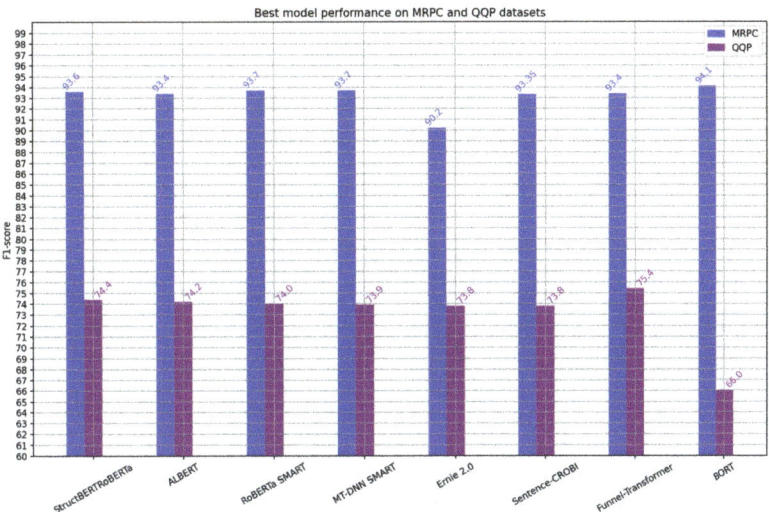

Figure 2. Best performance metrics of the proposed architecture and the state-of-the-art on the Microsoft Research Paraphrase Corpus and the Quora Question Pairs dataset using intermediate fine-tuning and ensemble learning techniques.

Table 4. Results on the PAWS-Wiki dataset.

Model	Accuracy	F1-Score	Difference Compared with Sentence-CROBI (Accuracy/F1-Score)
RoBERTa SMART [16]	94.93	94.34	0.13/0.13
Sentence-CROBI	**94.80**	**94.21**	-
DeBERTa [9]	94.69	94.12	$-0.11/-0.09$
ALBERT [14]	94.70	94.08	$-0.1/-0.13$
MT-DNN SMART [16]	94.16	93.52	$-0.64/-0.69$
Ernie 2.0 [13]	93.86	93.18	$-0.94/-1.03$
StructBERT [12]	93.13	92.41	$-1.67/-1.8$

Finally, Table 5 shows the results obtained in the Microsoft Paraphrase corpus with a simple model configuration—that is, without intermediate fine-tuning tasks or ensemble learning strategies. We report the mean over five runs with different random seeds. Under these conditions, the Sentence-CROBI architecture obtains the third-best performance compared to state-of-the-art models. The difference regarding the best performance, obtained by the DeBERTa model [9], is 0.21 in Accuracy and 0.08 in F1-score.

Table 5. Results on the Microsoft Research Paraphrase Corpus following a single-model approach.

Model	Accuracy	F1-Score	Difference Compared with Sentence-CROBI (Accuracy/F1-Score)
DeBERTa [9]	89.30	91.96	0.21/0.08
Ernie 2.0 [13]	89.11	91.89	0.02/0.01
Sentence-CROBI	**89.09**	**91.88**	-
RoBERTa SMART [16]	88.83	91.75	−0.26/−0.13
MT-DNN SMART [16]	87.71	90.84	−1.38/−1.04
ALBERT [14]	87.58	90.83	−1.51/−1.05
StructBERT [12]	86.56	90.06	−2.53/−1.82

Figure 3 displays a bar chart showing each model's average performance over five runs using different random seeds on the Microsoft Research Paraphrase Corpus and PAWS-Wiki corpus. The configuration for all the models is a single fine-tuning approach, without any intermediate task or ensemble learning technique. BORT and Funnel-Transformer do not appear in this chart because there is no public implementation. The Sentence-CROBI architecture is 0.56 above the average in F1-score for MRPC, which is 91.31. In the same corpus, 4 of 7 models, our approach included, have performance higher than 91. Meanwhile, the average F1-score for the PAWS-Wiki dataset is 93.69, and our proposed model achieves a value 0.51 above this. Similar to MRPC, our model is one of the four models with an F1-score higher than 94.

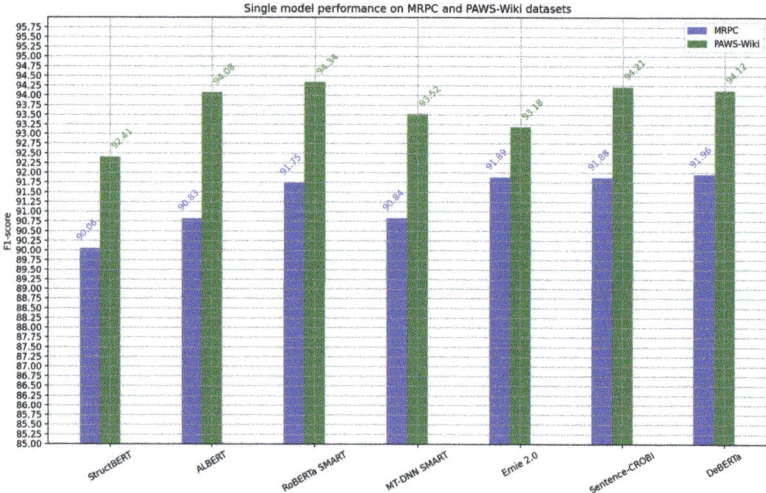

Figure 3. Average performance metrics over five runs with different random seeds of the proposed architecture and the state-of-the-art on the Microsoft Research Paraphrase Corpus and the PAWS-Wiki corpus, using a single-model configuration without intermediate fine-tuning and ensemble learning techniques.

5.1. Statistical Significance Tests

We perform a statistical significance test to compare the performance of the Sentence-CROBI architecture with the state-of-the-art. We select the non-parametric Wilcoxon signed test [39] because the distribution of our data is unknown [40]. To compute the significance tests, we use the Python library SciPy [41]. The null hypothesis is that the differences follow a symmetric distribution around zero. First, the absolute values of the differences are ranked. Then, each rank is given a sign according to the sign of the difference. The threshold that we use to accept or reject the null hypothesis is $\alpha = 0.05$. We use the MRPC and PAWS-Wiki corpora to perform this test, without intermediate fine-tuning or ensemble learning. Table 6 shows the results of the Wilcoxon signed test between the proposed architecture and the state-of-the-art methods. It is possible to observe that none of the comparisons is statistically significant, since the p-values of all the comparisons are not less than the threshold α.

Table 6. Significance tests using the Wilcoxon signed test between the proposed architecture and the state-of-the-art models. We compare the p-values with a threshold $\alpha = 0.05$ to accept or reject the null hypothesis.

Model 1	Model 2	MRPC p-Value	PAWS-Wiki p-Value
	ALBERT [14]	0.0625	0.3125
	Ernie 2.0 [13]	0.8125	0.0625
Sentence-CROBI	StructBERT [12]	0.0625	0.0625
	RoBERTa SMART [16]	0.3125	0.3125
	MT-DNN SMART [16]	0.0625	0.0625

Additionally, we performed a statistical significance test using the Wilcoxon signed test with the methods described in the state-of-the-art. As in the tests with the Sentence-CROBI architecture, we used a threshold of $\alpha = 0.05$ to accept or reject the null hypothesis. The datasets used are MRPC and PAWS-Wiki. Following the same approach as the significance tests with our model, we do not perform any intermediate fine-tuning stage or ensemble learning strategy. Table 7 shows the results of the tests. In the same way, it is possible to observe that, for the two datasets used, there is no significant difference between the results.

Table 7. Significance tests using the Wilcoxon signed test between the state-of-the-art models. We compare the p-values with a threshold $\alpha = 0.05$ to accept or reject the null hypothesis.

Model 1	Model 2	MRPC p-Value	PAWS-Wiki p-Value
	DeBERTa [9]	0.0625	1.0
	Ernie 2.0 [13]	0.0625	0.0625
ALBERT [14]	StructBERT [12]	0.1875	0.0625
	RoBERTa SMART [16]	0.0625	0.0625
	MT-DNN SMART [16]	1.0	0.0625
	Ernie 2.0 [13]	0.8125	0.0625
DeBERTa [9]	StructBERT [12]	0.0625	0.0625
	RoBERTa SMART [16]	0.4375	0.125
	MT-DNN SMART [16]	0.0625	0.0625
	StructBERT [12]	0.0625	0.0625
Ernie 2.0 [13]	RoBERTa SMART [16]	0.8125	0.0625
	MT-DNN SMART [16]	0.0625	0.125
StructBERT [12]	RoBERTa SMART [16]	0.0625	0.0625
	MT-DNN SMART [16]	0.0625	0.0625
RoBERTa SMART [16]	MT-DNN SMART [16]	0.0625	0.0625

Since there is no statistical significance between our proposed approach and the state-of-the-art models, the Sentence-CROBI architecture has an advantage due to two factors. The first one is its implementation facility that relies only on using two pre-trained models, one with a cross-encoder approach and the other with a bi-encoder approach, and combining both representations to obtain a global vector; there are no modifications to the pre-trained models' architecture or during the pre-training stage. The second one is the fine-tuning procedure: our model takes the most straightforward scheme, with only a few epochs and a low learning rate, to adjust the model to the target task, using a standard loss function as the cross-entropy for classification tasks.

5.2. Error Analysis

We perform a quantitative error analysis of our architecture's performance on the Microsoft Research Paraphrase Corpus, which we report in Table 2; in this setting, we perform ensemble learning by using the Bagging technique and 15 instances of our model with different random seeds. Five correspond to an intermediate fine-tuning stage using the MNLI corpus; five correspond to an intermediate fine-tuning stage using the PAWS-Wiki corpus, and the remaining instances correspond to fine-tuning the model on MRPC without using intermediate tasks. Figure 4 shows the confusion matrix obtained by our model using the configuration described above. The Sentence-CROBI model correctly predicts 1081 of 1147 paraphrase instances, corresponding to 94.24% of the examples of this class. On the other hand, it correctly predicts 490 of 578 non-paraphrase samples, corresponding to 84.77% instances of this class.

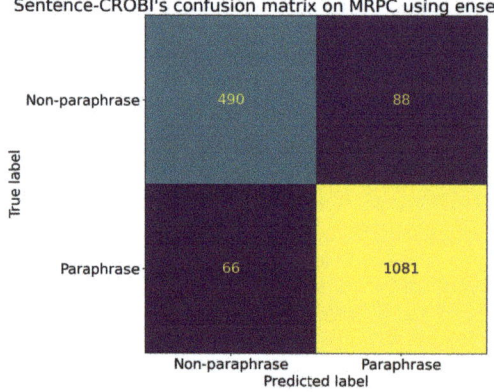

Figure 4. Sentence-CROBI's confusion matrix on the Microsoft Research Paraphrase Corpus using an intermediate-task fine-tuning approach and ensemble learning.

We also perform a qualitative error analysis based on the first five false positive and false negative examples predicted by the Sentence-CROBI model.

Table 8 shows the false positive examples. In general, it is possible to notice that all examples share the subject. For instance, in the first pair is "Ballmer". In the second pair, the first sentence refers to a female subject, while the second refers to a person who plays a schoolgirl character, and both subjects go to see a specialist because they are sick. The difference between the sentences in the third to fifth pairs is the specificity in describing the performed actions, but the subjects are the same.

Table 8. False positive examples predicted by the Sentence-CROBI model. False positives correspond to non-paraphrase instances classified by the model as paraphrases.

Text 1	Text 2
Ballmer has been vocal in the past warning that Linux is a threat to Microsoft.	"In the memo, Ballmer reiterated the open-source threat to Microsoft".
"She first went to a specialist for initial tests last Monday, feeling tired and unwell".	"The star, who plays schoolgirl Nina Tucker in Neighbours, went to a specialist on 30 June feeling tired and unwell".
"Garner said the self-proclaimed mayor of Baghdad, Mohammed Mohsen al-Zubaidi, was released after two days in coalition custody".	Garner said self-proclaimed Baghdad mayor Mohammed Mohsen Zubaidi was released 48 h after his detention in late April.
"It appears from our initial report that this was a textbook landing considering the circumstances", " Burke said".	"Said Mr. Burke: It was a textbook landing considering the circumstances".
"Powell recently changed the story, telling officers that Hoffa's body was buried at his former home, where the search was conducted Wednesday".	"Powell changed the story earlier this year, telling officers that Hoffa's body was buried at his former home, where the aboveground pool now sits".

Table 9 shows the false negative examples predicted by our model. Our approach struggles with sentences with a high word overlapping rate between them. For instance, in the first pair, the first sentence talks about the possibility of a man becoming sick, while the second talks about the fact that there is only a sick man. The third pair is different because of the number of bodies that they refer to. Finally, in the fourth and fifth examples, the model cannot identify correctly that the subjects are different.

Table 9. False negative examples predicted by the Sentence-CROBI model. False negatives correspond to paraphrase instances classified by the model as non-paraphrases.

Text 1	Text 2
"A Washington County man may have the countys first human case of West Nile virus, the health department said Friday".	The countys first and only human case of West Nile this year was confirmed by health officials on 8 September.
"Snow's remark "has a psychological impact", said Hans Redeker, head of foreign-exchange strategy at BNP Paribas".	"Snow's remark on the dollar's effects on exports "has a psychological impact", said Hans Redeker, head of foreign-exchange strategy at BNP Paribas".
"Another body was pulled from the water on Thursday and two seen floating down the river could not be retrieved due to the strong currents, local reporters said".	"Two more bodies were seen floating down the river on Thursday, but could not be retrieved due to the strong currents, local reporters said".
"Amgen shares gained 93 cents, or 1.45 percent, to $65.05 in afternoon trading on Nasdaq".	Shares of Allergan were up 14 cents at $78.40 in late trading on the New York Stock Exchange.
"In his speech, Cheney praised Barbour's accomplishments as chairman of the Republican National Committee".	Cheney returned Barbour's favorable introduction by touting Barbour's work as chair of the Republican National Committee.

6. Conclusions

We present the Sentence-CROBI model, a simple language-model-based architecture that combines cross-encoders and bi-encoders to compute a vector representation in sentence pair tasks. Our model works by combining the output representations of cross-encoders and bi-encoders. Therefore, it does not rely on complex architecture modifications, adding more tasks to the pre-training stage, reducing the model's size, or modifying the fine-tuning algorithm.

Our proposed architecture achieved competitive results with the state-of-the-art models in all the evaluated datasets. The most significant difference is when we evaluate the Quora Question Pairs dataset. The Funnel-Transformer model outperforms our model by 1.6 regarding the F1-score. On the other hand, the least significant difference is concerning the PAWS-Wiki dataset, where the RoBERTa model fine-tuned using the SMART algorithm outperformed our model by 0.13 in terms of the F1-score.

The proposed model performs best when no intermediate fine-tuning tasks or ensemble learning techniques are used. These results suggest that combining cross-encoders and bi-encoders could improve the model's performance in sentence pair tasks without any auxiliary technique. Moreover, there is no statistical significance between our proposed approach and the state-of-the-art models. These results represent our model's advantage, because its success does not rely on adding more pre-training tasks, modifying the Transformer architecture, or creating new fine-tuning algorithms. In the same way, it is easy to implement using existing tools, and it is possible to adapt the model to different tasks with minor changes. The changes only consist of replacing the combination strategy of the cross-encoder and bi-encoder representations, the last layer on the model, and the loss function. This configuration follows the current paradigm of the Natural Language Processing field, where pre-trained models are adapted to a wide variety of tasks without designing each model from scratch.

This paper is the first approach that combines bi-encoder and cross-encoder representations for sentence pair tasks. Therefore, future work includes exploring different combinations of these two models and measuring their impact on the current state-of-the-art datasets and new scenarios.

Author Contributions: Conceptualization, J.-G.O.-B.; methodology, J.-G.O.-B., G.B.-E. and H.G.-A.; software, J.-G.O.-B.; validation, G.B.-E. and H.G.-A.; formal analysis, J.-G.O.-B.; investigation, J.-G.O.-B.; resources, J.-G.O.-B.; data curation, J.-G.O.-B., G.B.-E., and H.G.-A.; writing—original draft preparation, J.-G.O.-B.; writing—review and editing, G.B.-E. and H.G.-A.; visualization, J.-G.O.-B.; supervision, G.B.-E. and H.G.-A.; project administration, G.B.-E. and H.G.-A.; funding acquisition, G.B.-E. and H.G.-A. All authors have read and agreed to the published version of the manuscript.

Funding: This research was partially funded by PAPIIT projects TA400121 and TA101722, CONACYT CB A1-S-27780, and CONACYT PNPC scholarship with No. CVU 1086461.

Data Availability Statement: Publicly available datasets were used in this study: The Microsoft Research Paraphrase Corpus (https://www.microsoft.com/en-us/download/details.aspx?id=52 398 accessed on 1 March 2022), the Quora Question Pairs Corpus (https://gluebenchmark.com/tasks accessed on 1 March 2022), the PAWS-Wiki Corpus (https://github.com/google-research-datasets/paws accessed on 1 March 2022), and the Multi-Genre NLI Corpus (https://cims.nyu.edu/~sbowman/multinli/ accessed on 1 March 2022).

Acknowledgments: The authors thank CONACYT for the computing resources provided through the Plataforma de Aprendizaje Profundo para Tecnologías del Lenguaje of the Laboratorio de Supercómputo del INAOE.

Conflicts of Interest: The authors declare no conflict of interest. The funders had no role in the design of the study; in the collection, analyses, or interpretation of data; in the writing of the manuscript; or in the decision to publish the results.

References

1. Bhagat, R.; Hovy, E. What is a Paraphrase? *Comput. Linguist.* **2013**, *39*, 463–472. [CrossRef]
2. Montoya, M.M.; da Cunha, I.; López-Escobedo, F. Un corpus de paráfrasis en español: Metodología, elaboración y análisis. *Rev. Lingüíst.Teor. Apl.* **2016**, *54*, 85–112. [CrossRef]
3. Vaswani, A.; Shazeer, N.; Parmar, N.; Uszkoreit, J.; Jones, L.; Gomez, A.N.; Kaiser, Ł.; Polosukhin, I. Attention is All You Need. *Adv. Neural Inf. Process. Syst.* **2017**, *30*, 6000–6010.
4. Qiu, X.; Sun, T.; Xu, Y.; Shao, Y.; Dai, N.; Huang, X. Pre-trained models for natural language processing: A survey. *Sci. China Technol. Sci.* **2020**, *63*, 1872–1897. [CrossRef]
5. Humeau, S.; Shuster, K.; Lachaux, M.A.; Weston, J. Poly-encoders: Architectures and pre-training strategies for fast and accurate multi-sentence scoring. *arXiv* **2019**, arXiv:1905.01969.
6. Peng, Q.; Weir, D.; Weeds, J.; Chai, Y. Predicate-argument based Bi-encoder for paraphrase identification. In Proceedings of the 60th Annual Meeting of the Association for Computational Linguistics (Volume 1: Long Papers), Dublin, Ireland, 22–27 May 2022; Association for Computational Linguistics: Dublin, Ireland, 2022; pp. 5579–5589. [CrossRef]
7. Devlin, J.; Chang, M.W.; Lee, K.; Toutanova, K. BERT: Pre-training of deep bidirectional transformers for language understanding. In Proceedings of the 2019 Conference of the North American Chapter of the Association for Computational Linguistics: Human Language Technologies, Volume 1 (Long and Short Papers), Minneapolis, MN, USA, 2–7 June 2019; Association for Computational Linguistics: Minneapolis, MN, USA, 2019; pp. 4171–4186. [CrossRef]
8. Liu, Y.; Ott, M.; Goyal, N.; Du, J.; Joshi, M.; Chen, D.; Levy, O.; Lewis, M.; Zettlemoyer, L.; Stoyanov, V. RoBERTa: A robustly optimized BERT pretraining approach. *arXiv* **2019**, arXiv:1907.11692.
9. He, P.; Liu, X.; Gao, J.; Chen, W. DeBERTa: Decoding-enhanced Bert with disentangled attention. *arXiv* **2020**, arXiv:2006.03654.
10. de Wynter, A.; Perry, D.J. Optimal subarchitecture extraction for bert. *arXiv* **2020**, arXiv:2010.10499.
11. Rogers, A.; Kovaleva, O.; Rumshisky, A. A Primer in bertology: What we know about how bert works. *Trans. Assoc. Comput. Linguist.* **2020**, *8*, 842–866. [CrossRef]
12. Wang, W.; Bi, B.; Yan, M.; Wu, C.; Xia, J.; Bao, Z.; Peng, L.; Si, L. StructBERT: Incorporating language structures into pre-training for deep language understanding. *arXiv* **2020**, arXiv:1908.04577.
13. Sun, Y.; Wang, S.; Li, Y.; Feng, S.; Tian, H.; Wu, H.; Wang, H. Ernie 2.0: A Continual Pre-training framework for language understanding. In Proceedings of the AAAI Conference on Artificial Intelligence, New York, NY, USA, 7–12 February 2020; Volume 34, pp. 8968–8975.
14. Lan, Z.; Chen, M.; Goodman, S.; Gimpel, K.; Sharma, P.; Soricut, R. ALBERT: A lite BERT for Self-supervised learning of language representations. *arXiv* **2020**, arXiv:1909.11942.
15. de Wynter, A. An Algorithm for Learning Smaller Representations of Models with Scarce Data. *arXiv* **2020**, arXiv:2010.07990.
16. Jiang, H.; He, P.; Chen, W.; Liu, X.; Gao, J.; Zhao, T. SMART: Robust and Efficient Fine-Tuning for Pre-trained Natural Language Models through Principled Regularized Optimization. In Proceedings of the 58th Annual Meeting of the Association for Computational Linguistics, Online, 5–10 July 2020; Association for Computational Linguistics: Stroudsburg, PA, USA, 2020; pp. 2177–2190. [CrossRef]

7. Liu, X.; He, P.; Chen, W.; Gao, J. Multi-task deep neural networks for natural language understanding. In Proceedings of the 57th Annual Meeting of the Association for Computational Linguistics, Florence, Italy, 28 July–2 August 2019; Association for Computational Linguistics: Florence, Italy, 2019; pp. 4487–4496. [CrossRef]
8. Dai, Z.; Lai, G.; Yang, Y.; Le, Q. Funnel-transformer: Filtering out sequential redundancy for efficient language processing. *Adv. Neural Inf. Process. Syst.* **2020**, *33*, 4271–4282.
9. Xu, S.; Shen, X.; Fukumoto, F.; Li, J.; Suzuki, Y.; Nishizaki, H. Paraphrase Identification with Lexical, Syntactic and Sentential Encodings. *Appl. Sci.* **2020**, *10*, 4144. [CrossRef]
10. Bromley, J.; Guyon, I.; LeCun, Y.; Säckinger, E.; Shah, R. Signature verification using a "Siamese" time delay neural network. *Adv. Neural Inf. Process. Syst.* **1993**, *6*, 737–744. [CrossRef]
11. Reimers, N.; Gurevych, I. Sentence-BERT: Sentence embeddings using siamese BERT-networks. In Proceedings of the 2019 Conference on Empirical Methods in Natural Language Processing and the 9th International Joint Conference on Natural Language Processing (EMNLP-IJCNLP), Hong Kong, China, 3–7 November 2019; Association for Computational Linguistics: Hong Kong, China, 2019; pp. 3982–3992. [CrossRef]
12. Dolan, W.B.; Brockett, C. automatically constructing a corpus of sentential paraphrases. In Proceedings of the Third International Workshop on Paraphrasing (IWP2005), Jeju Island, Korea, 14 October 2005.
13. Zhang, Y.; Baldridge, J.; He, L. PAWS: Paraphrase adversaries from word scrambling. In Proceedings of the 2019 Conference of the North American Chapter of the Association for Computational Linguistics: Human Language Technologies, Volume 1 (Long and Short Papers), Minneapolis, MN, USA, 2–7 June 2019; Association for Computational Linguistics: Minneapolis, MN, USA, 2019; pp. 1298–1308. [CrossRef]
14. Wei, J.; Bosma, M.; Zhao, V.; Guu, K.; Yu, A.W.; Lester, B.; Du, N.; Dai, A.M.; Le, Q.V. finetuned language models are zero-shot learners. *arXiv* **2022**, arXiv:2109.01652.
15. Gao, T.; Yao, X.; Chen, D. SimCSE: Simple contrastive learning of sentence embeddings. In Proceedings of the 2021 Conference on Empirical Methods in Natural Language Processing, Online, 7–11 November 2021; Association for Computational Linguistics: Punta Cana, Dominican Republic, 2021; pp. 6894–6910. [CrossRef]
16. Sinha, K.; Jia, R.; Hupkes, D.; Pineau, J.; Williams, A.; Kiela, D. Masked language modeling and the distributional hypothesis: order word matters pre-training for little. In Proceedings of the 2021 Conference on Empirical Methods in Natural Language Processing, Online, 7–11 November 2021; Association for Computational Linguistics: Punta Cana, Dominican Republic, 2021; pp. 2888–2913. [CrossRef]
17. Wang, A.; Singh, A.; Michael, J.; Hill, F.; Levy, O.; Bowman, S.R. GLUE: A multi-task benchmark and analysis platform for natural language understanding. In Proceedings of the 7th International Conference on Learning Representations, New Orleans, LA, USA, 6–9 May 2019.
18. Hambardzumyan, K.; Khachatrian, H.; May, J. WARP: word-level adversarial rePrograming. In Proceedings of the 59th Annual Meeting of the Association for Computational Linguistics and the 11th International Joint Conference on Natural Language Processing (Volume 1: Long Papers), Online, 1–6 August 2021; Association for Computational Linguistics: Stroudsburg, PA, USA, 2021; pp. 4921–4933. [CrossRef]
19. Izsak, P.; Berchansky, M.; Levy, O. How to train BERT with an academic budget. In Proceedings of the 2021 Conference on Empirical Methods in Natural Language Processing, Online, 7–11 November 2021; Association for Computational Linguistics: Punta Cana, Dominican Republic, 2021; pp. 10644–10652. [CrossRef]
20. Min, S.; Lewis, M.; Zettlemoyer, L.; Hajishirzi, H. MetaICL: Learning to learn in context. In Proceedings of the 2022 Conference of the North American Chapter of the Association for Computational Linguistics: Human Language Technologies, Seattle, WA, USA, July 2022; Association for Computational Linguistics: Seattle, WA, USA, 2022; pp. 2791–2809. [CrossRef]
21. Perez-Almendros, C.; Espinosa-Anke, L.; Schockaert, S. SemEval-2022 task 4: Patronizing and condescending language detection. In Proceedings of the 16th International Workshop on Semantic Evaluation (SemEval-2022), Seattle, WA, USA, 14–15 July 2022; Association for Computational Linguistics: Seattle, WA, USA, 2022; pp. 298–307. [CrossRef]
22. Dopierre, T.; Gravier, C.; Logerais, W. PROTAUGMENT: Unsupervised diverse short-texts paraphrasing for intent detection meta-learning. In Proceedings of the 59th Annual Meeting of the Association for Computational Linguistics and the 11th International Joint Conference on Natural Language Processing (Volume 1: Long Papers), Online, August 2021; Association for Computational Linguistics: Stroudsburg, PA, USA, 2021; pp. 2454–2466. [CrossRef]
23. Williams, A.; Nangia, N.; Bowman, S. A Broad-coverage challenge corpus for sentence understanding through Inference. In Proceedings of the 2018 Conference of the North American Chapter of the Association for Computational Linguistics: Human Language Technologies, Volume 1 (Long Papers), New Orleans, LA, USA, 1–6 June 2018; Association for Computational Linguistics: Stroudsburg, PA, USA, 2018; pp. 1112–1122.
24. Phang, J.; Févry, T.; Bowman, S.R. Sentence Encoders on STILTs: Supplementary training on intermediate labeled-data tasks. *arXiv* **2018**, arXiv:1811.01088.
25. Chen, Y.; Kou, X.; Bai, J.; Tong, Y. Improving BERT with self-supervised attention. *IEEE Access* **2021**, *9*, 144129–144139. [CrossRef]
26. Breiman, L. Bagging predictors. *Mach. Learn.* **1996**, *24*, 123–140. [CrossRef]
27. Goodfellow, I.; Bengio, Y.; Courville, A. *Deep Learning*; MIT Press: Cambridge, MA, USA, 2016. Available online: http://www.deeplearningbook.org (accessed on 15 June 2022).

38. Wolf, T.; Debut, L.; Sanh, V.; Chaumond, J.; Delangue, C.; Moi, A.; Cistac, P.; Rault, T.; Louf, R.; Funtowicz, M.; et al. Transformers: State-of-the-Art natural language processing. In Proceedings of the 2020 Conference on Empirical Methods in Natural Language Processing: System Demonstrations, Online, 16–20 November 2020; Association for Computational Linguistics: Stroudsburg, PA, USA, 2020; pp. 38–45. [CrossRef]
39. Wilcoxon, F. Individual comparisons of grouped data by ranking methods. *J. Econ. Entomol.* **1946**, *39*, 269–270. [CrossRef] [PubMed]
40. Dror, R.; Baumer, G.; Shlomov, S.; Reichart, R. The Hitchhiker's guide to testing statistical significance in natural language processing. In Proceedings of the 56th Annual Meeting of the Association for Computational Linguistics (Volume 1: Long Papers), Melbourne, Australia, 15–20 July 2018; Association for Computational Linguistics: Melbourne, Australia, 2018; pp. 1383–1392. [CrossRef]
41. Virtanen, P.; Gommers, R.; Oliphant, T.E.; Haberland, M.; Reddy, T.; Cournapeau, D.; Burovski, E.; Peterson, P.; Weckesser, W.; Bright, J.; et al. SciPy 1.0: Fundamental algorithms for scientific computing in Python. *Nat. Methods* **2020**, *17*, 261–272. [CrossRef] [PubMed]

Article

Improving Intent Classification Using Unlabeled Data from Large Corpora

Gabriel Bercaru [1,2,*], Ciprian-Octavian Truică [1,2,*], Costin-Gabriel Chiru [1,2,*] and Traian Rebedea [2,*]

[1] SoftTehnica, RO-030128 Bucharest, Romania
[2] Computer Science and Engineering Department, Faculty of Automatic Control and Computers, University Politehnica of Bucharest, RO-060042 Bucharest, Romania
* Correspondence: gabriel.bercaru@upb.ro (G.B.); ciprian.truica@upb.ro (C.-O.T.); costin.chiru@upb.ro (C.-G.C.); traian.rebedea@upb.ro (T.R.)

Abstract: Intent classification is a central component of a Natural Language Understanding (NLU) pipeline for conversational agents. The quality of such a component depends on the quality of the training data, however, for many conversational scenarios, the data might be scarce; in these scenarios, data augmentation techniques are used. Having general data augmentation methods that can generalize to many datasets is highly desirable. The work presented in this paper is centered around two main components. First, we explore the influence of various feature vectors on the task of intent classification using RASA's text classification capabilities. The second part of this work consists of a generic method for efficiently augmenting textual corpora using large datasets of unlabeled data. The proposed method is able to efficiently mine for examples similar to the ones that are already present in standard, natural language corpora. The experimental results show that using our corpus augmentation methods enables an increase in text classification accuracy in few-shot settings. Particularly, the gains in accuracy raise up to 16% when the number of labeled examples is very low (e.g., two examples). We believe that our method is important for any Natural Language Processing (NLP) or NLU task in which labeled training data are scarce or expensive to obtain. Lastly, we give some insights into future work, which aims at combining our proposed method with a semi-supervised learning approach.

Keywords: intent classification; chatbot; few-shot learning; data augmentation; online clustering; data projection

MSC: 68T50

1. Introduction

In the present day, conversational agents (or chatbots) are a core component of many applications, ranging from online reservations to customer support. The quality of the chatbot replies depends on its ability to accurately understand the user query. To ensure that, the user intention must be understood. Thus, the chatbot designer has to provide multiple alternatives on how the user may formulate a query. This is often performed by specialists and it is a time-consuming task. Automating this process will highly benefit chatbot designers, reducing iteration time.

In order to obtain chatbot training examples in a semi or fully automated manner, one could leverage large volumes of unlabeled data available in various online corpora (e.g., movie subtitles, translation datasets, etc.). The only impediment is that the unlabeled corpora are usually large enough such that a simple search for semantically similar examples within them becomes unpractical. As a result, efficient retrieval of similar examples is highly desirable.

Driven by such motivation, we propose a novel pipeline for efficiently analyzing large, unlabeled corpora and extracting examples similar to a user-supplied query. We aim to

minimize the retrieval time while maintaining a high similarity between the query and the retrieved example. Moreover, we examine how the proposed example retrieval system improves the intent classification accuracy in several few-shot learning scenarios, where intent examples are scarce.

As the results of this research will show, our proposed method is highly beneficial in the few-shot intent classification scenario. In such a setup, the number of labeled examples is very small (e.g., 2, 3, 5, or 10 examples per class). Using our similar example retrieval pipeline, we expand the number of examples per class, while increasing the classification accuracy with significant rates, up to 16%. To our knowledge, at the time of writing this article, there is no open-source service that can be used to augment textual datasets based on online clustering of movie conversations. Our method allows relatively quick and cheap dataset augmentation, making use of only open-source components.

The research questions that guide our research can be summarized as follows:

(Q_1) How do existing chatbots perform in terms of intent classification?
(Q_2) How can we use unlabeled data to improve the intent detection phase of conversational agents?
(Q_3) How can we efficiently extract meaningful examples from large, unlabeled corpora?
(Q_4) To what extent does the proposed system benefit in a few-shot learning scenario?

Our objectives can be stated as follows:

(O_1) Analyze current intent classification performance for existing systems to address Q_1;
(O_2) Process large, unlabeled corpora such that they become suitable for our similarity-based example retrieval system to address Q_2;
(O_3) Achieve low example retrieval duration to address Q_3;
(O_4) Evaluate our example retrieval system in few-shot learning scenarios to address Q_4.

The contributions of this work can be summarized as follows:

(C_1) An analysis of standard intent detection systems and their performance;
(C_2) An efficient, similarity-based retrieval system that is used for augmenting intent classification datasets;
(C_3) An extensive experimental performance analysis of our proposed system in few-shot learning scenarios using real-world datasets.

The rest of this paper is structured as follows. Section 2 presents previous work done with respect to intent classification, in both standard and few-shot scenarios. Section 3 shows the general structure of a RASA-based conversational agent. Section 4 describes the experiments performed on the RASA NLU component, for analyzing Transformer models' accuracy in intent classification. Section 5 provides details on the work done for retrieving similar examples in a large corpus. Section 6 presents the evaluation methods and the results obtained for corpus clustering. Section 7 discusses our findings and their implications. Lastly, Section 8 summarizes and concludes our work and hints at possible future directions.

2. Related Work

The first component of our contribution consists of an analysis of existing Transformer embedders in the context of intent classification. Balakrishnan et al. [1] provided a similar analysis for disaster classification in tweets. As their results show, using Transformer-based embedders is beneficial and increases the accuracy, compared to other embedding options, e.g., bag-of-words, Word2Vec, GloVe, etc.

As already mentioned, one of the crucial aspects regarding the quality of a chatbot is related to the datasets that it uses. Related to this, Larson et al. [2] and Casanueva et al. [3] introduced two datasets for intent classification, namely CLINC150 and BANKING77. CLINC150 is designed for benchmarking models meant to distinguish in-domain queries from out-of-domain queries, thus its structure is more complex compared to BANKING77. CLINC150 queries span 150 intents over 10 different domains, while BANKING77 queries span 77 intents over a single domain, namely banking-related operations. In this paper, we use these two datasets to evaluate the performance of our models.

Another important aspect of a chatbot is the framework used for its development. In this sense, Liu et al. [4] presented an analysis of several conversational agents designing frameworks, including RASA. Their study focuses on a dataset created by the authors, which includes queries belonging to 21 domains, with 64 intents and 54 annotated entity types. The queries belonging to the mentioned dataset contain tasks that can be given to a house-cleaning robot. Compared to this dataset, the ones used in this paper contain more intents, namely 77 for BANKING77 and 150 for CLINC150.

Most of the current literature is centered around two axes: intent identification and data augmentation. Regarding intent identification, Ahmadvand et al. [5] performed dialogue act classification in the context of open-domain conversational agents. Unlike our subject, open-domain dialogue cannot divide the intents into well-defined classes simply by looking at the current utterance. Consequently, the authors tackled the problem by incorporating dialogue history information. The information is encoded by including features from the lexical, syntactic, and system state information layers. The information is captured through pre-trained Word2Vec embedding vectors. The training procedure is split across two distinct phases: (1) the dialogue act system is trained on human-to-human conversations, and (2) the human-to-machine conversations are fine-tuned. Their results, evaluated on Switchboard data and Alexa Prize data, show that the proposed Context-aware Dialogue Act Classification system outperforms state-of-the-art models trained on each dataset.

Zhan et al. [6] designed an out-of-scope (OOS) intent detection method, modeling the distribution of out-of-scope intents. Their work splits OOS intents into (1) 'hard' OOS intents that are close to the decision boundary, and (2) 'easy' intents that are distant from the in-scope intents. Their research is focused on a rather binary classification task, namely separating in-scope from out-of-scope intents. Nonetheless, the datasets used for carrying out the research include BANKING77 and CLINC150, the same as our work does. The authors tested their models by using only 25%, 50% or 75% of the classes (in three different setups), while leaving the rest of the classes unseen. The models are subsequently used to predict whether an example is in-scope or out-of-scope. The best results are obtained in the 75% seen–25% unseen classes setup, with 88.08% accuracy for CLINC150 and 81.07% accuracy for BANKING77.

In intent classification, out-of-scope intents can be further divided into two classes [7]: (1) in-distribution out-of-scope examples (ID-OOS), and (2) out-of-distribution out-of-scope examples (OOD-OOS). Zhang et al. [7] showed that pre-trained Transformer models (e.g., BERT, RoBERTa, etc.) are vulnerable to mispredicting OOD-OOS examples. However, existing intent classification datasets, such as CLINC150 and BANKING77 do not contain any ID-OOS data. Particularly, CLINC150 contains an OOS class, but most of the examples are easily distinguishable from the in-domain ones, thus OOD. Besides the performance analysis of pre-trained Transformer based models on the OOD-OOS examples, the authors contributed with two datasets for OOS intent detection. These datasets feature both ID-OOS and OOD-OOS data.

Liu et al. [8] tackled the problem of intent classification when the number of available examples per intent is limited. They reconstructed capsule network models (such as IntentCapsNet [9]) in order to include information regarding the possible polysemy of the words which contribute to the features of the semantic capsules. Moreover, their proposed method, IntentCapsNet-ZS, behaves better than previous models with respect to unseen intents, in the zero-shot setting.

Yan et al. [10] designed a Gaussian Mixture Model (GMM) method for out-of-domain intent detection. Their research shows that previous intent outlier detection methods project sentence embeddings into a latent space in which the class (intent) label is the centroid and all examples are scattered across a long and narrow domain. In such representation, detecting out-of-scope intents is error-prone. Their proposed method alleviates this problem by regularizing the projection space such that the class label remains the centroid, but the examples are distributed more evenly around it. The output of such a scenario can be paired with an anomaly detection algorithm in order to separate in-domain intents from unknown out-of-domain intents. Moreover, the authors demonstrated that their method (SEG—Semantic-Enhanced Gaussian Mixture Model) can be paired with previously developed zero-shot intent classification methods (i.e., ReCapsNet [11]), in order to improve their performance.

In terms of data augmentation, Chatterjee and Sengupta [12] performed a corpus clustering operation, with the goal of grouping together similar sentences in a corpus, for manual intent annotation. With their technique, the resulting corpus may be used for manually augmenting the dataset of any intent classification task. Their intent discovery pipeline comprises 4 main steps: (1) the extraction of conversation utterances using a pre-trained dialogue act classifier, (2) grouping together similar utterances, (3) manual labeling of the clusters, and (4) re-classifying utterances that have not been previously assigned to any cluster. The experimental results show that a clustering algorithm such as ITER-DBSCAN performs better than previous methods when it comes to intent coverage. Unlike their work, our proposed corpus augmentation method does not require any manual intervention of the designer of the conversational agent. Similarly, Kuchlous and Kadaba [13] performed intent classification in the context of a therapy and mental wellness-oriented chatbot. Their dataset is of rather limited size, containing only 4 classes (intents), with approximately 400 examples in total. The authors used this dataset to benchmark several non-neural based models: Multinomial Naïve Bayes, Logistic Regression, SVM, and Random Forest. Due to the limited dataset, the authors resorted to several processing steps, i.e., artificially augmenting the training set and building a custom English stop words list. By applying these steps, the accuracy of the classification is increased. Unlike their work, in our experiments, we use a standard English language stop words list.

Sahu et al. [14] designed a method of augmenting datasets for intent classification that employs large language models (such as GPT-3 [15]) for generating artificial training examples, given a context containing the original intents for a specific class. However, their method requires the execution of two expensive stages in the pipeline: (1) using a large language model for performing inference on all the available examples, and (2) the possibility of including a manual verification stage, in order to filter out unrelated, retrieved examples. Furthermore, the authors investigated the effect of their corpus augmentation method in few-shot learning scenarios. Compared to their method, our experiments do not require large language models to augment the corpus and the post-processing filtering is performed automatically.

3. RASA Components for Building Conversational Agents

RASA [16] is one of the most successful frameworks for building conversational agents. Its architecture is composed of several interconnected modules, which can function both independently or as a whole.

A powerful feature of RASA is the possibility to integrate state-of-the-art, pre-trained Transformer models, via the Huggingface library [17] (https://huggingface.co/ (last accessed on 7 November 2022)). These Transformers can increase the intent prediction accuracy, in the NLU phase, by providing their own embedding vectors for the supplied tokens, at the cost of a larger memory footprint.

In the context of task-oriented dialogue, RASA emerged as the preferred solution, due to its ability to handle both simple (query-answer) and complex (multiple turns needed to obtain the required information) conversational scenarios. Its structure is composed of two loosely coupled sub-systems: the natural language understanding (NLU) component and the dialogue management component.

The NLU component is responsible for extracting information at a single dialogue turn, e.g., the intent associated with the turn and possible entities in the sentence. This process is divided throughout a pipeline consisting of several stages: (1) a tokenizer (which splits the raw input text into tokens), (2) one or several featurizers (which encode and extract meaningful information from the tokens), and (3) a classification method, which produces the final intent and entities associated with the input sentence. One of the more important stages in the pipeline is the featurizer stage where multiple methods of encoding the tokens are available. The encoding mechanism can employ either 'standard' text-based metrics (TF-IDF scores) or embedding vectors obtained through neural models (e.g., word embeddings, Transformer-based models, etc.).

Furthermore, the dialogue management component dictates how the conversation evolves. This component utilizes three main policies which choose the next agent action, given the dialogue context:

(1) *Rule policy.* If the current user input matches one of the agent's known rules, the corresponding action is executed immediately, without taking into consideration the conversation history or the known scenarios.
(2) *Memorization policy.* Unless the current turn matches any rule, the agent tries to fit it inside one of the conversational scenarios. A scenario consists of several exchanges between the user and the agent.
(3) *TED policy (Transformer Embedding Dialogue policy)* [18]. When the input text does not match any of the predefined rules or scenarios, the agent attempts to choose the most probable of the known actions, given the context. This is achieved by (i) generating the embedding of the input text using a Transformer encoder, (ii) computing the similarity between the resulting embedding vector and known actions embeddings, and (iii) extracting any possible entities in the user text through a Conditional Random Field (CRF) layer.

4. RASA NLU Intent Classification

In RASA, the NLU and dialogue management components are loosely coupled—the RASA NLU component can function independently of the latter one. As a result, the intent classification experiments are conducted using only the NLU stage.

4.1. Datasets Used

There are many public datasets (https://github.com/clinc/nlu-datasets (last accessed on 7 November 2022)) available online for benchmarking the intent classification task. For our experiments, we use both CLINC150 and BANKING77 datasets.

CLINC150 [2] is a dataset proposed for evaluating the performance of out-of-scope classification systems. The main version of the dataset (*full*) contains 150 in-domain classes and one class for out-of-domain examples. Each of the 150 domain classes contains 100 training examples, 20 validation examples, and 30 test examples. The out-of-domain class is split into 100 training examples, 100 validation examples, and 1000 test examples.

Besides the *full* dataset, Larson et al. [2] proposed 3 more datasets as sub-samples of the original large one. The *small* version of CLINC150 follows the same class distribution. However, it contains fewer examples for training, i.e., 50 examples per class. The *imbalanced* version of the dataset poses additional challenges since training examples are no longer equally distributed across classes. Thus, intents have either 25, 50, 75, or 100 training examples. The *plus* version features more training examples per class, i.e, 250.

BANKING77 [3] is another dataset introduced for benchmarking text classification methods. However, this dataset contains only queries from the banking domain. These banking queries are divided across 77 in-scope classes. It is a balanced set, as all intents contain the same number of examples.

4.2. Intent Classification

Within the RASA framework, accurately classifying the intent encoded inside a user query is critical for a correct dialogue flow. Consequently, RASA provides numerous options for analyzing the input text and extracting meaningful features, which ultimately determine the intent.

While most of the RASA pipeline components are customizable, the used featurizers deserve more attention as choosing one type of featurizer may have implications beyond classification accuracy. The memory footprint of the featurizer and the overall response time of the system are also metrics to consider.

One of the simpler featurizers tested is the *CountVectorsFeaturizer* (https://rasa.com/docs/rasa/components/#countvectorsfeaturizer (last accessed on 7 November 2022)), which analyzes the user text and creates a bag-of-words representation based on it. The result is a sparse representation of the input sequence, which disregards token sequentiality. In the case of a task such as intent classification, sequentiality might not prove to be as important as for other NLP/NLU tasks (i.e., machine translation, named entity recognition, part of speech tagging), as in many cases the intent of a sentence is determined by a keyword irrespective to the position it is located. Sparse tokenizers are able to extract features at multiple n-gram granularity (standard n values range between 1 and 4), working either at word or character level. For evaluation, we featurize the text based on character n-grams with sizes between 2 and 4 characters. Note that n-gram extraction is performed on each word's lemma rather than on the original word.

In order to better capture semantic similarities between words, several types of dense featurizers can be used, e.g., featurizers that produce embedding vectors based on the user utterance. We test the following dense featurizers: (1) *SpacyFeaturizer*, and (2) multiple *LanguageModelFeaturizers*. In the case of *SpacyFeaturizer*, the intent classifier used is SklearnIntentClassifier (implemented through Scikit-learn [19]). SklearnIntentClassifier is based on a linear SVM classification algorithm for which the parameters are determined via GridSearchCV. The *LanguageModelFeaturizers* component allows embedding integration mechanisms from state-of-the-art Transformer-based language models. To this extent, our experiments employ 6 models: (1) BERT [20], (2) ConveRT [21], a Transformer-based encoder designed for conversations, (3) RoBERTa [22], (4) GPT [23], (5) GPT-2 [24], and (6) XLNet [25]. For all the language model featurizers, the extracted features are used as input for *DIETClassifier* [18], a multi-task model for intent classification and entity extraction. DIETClassifier uses a single Transformer model for both intent detection and entity extraction and it produces entities by processing a Transformer's output layer with a CRF layer.

For both CLINC150 and BANKING77, we use the training subset to fine-tune the models. The test subset is used to compute the accuracy metrics. In all our experiments, the models are fine-tuned for 50 epochs using the training set, except for the SpaCy embeddings setup where fine-tuning is performed for 100 epochs.

The results are presented separately, depending on the used classifier. For this set of experiments, we use the following hardware configuration: a system with an Intel(R) Core(TM) i7-9850H CPU @ 2.60GHz processor, 32 GB RAM, and a NVIDIA Quadro T1000 GPU with 4 GB VRAM. The results from Table 1 are obtained without using the Transformer architecture (SklearnIntentClassifier and MitieClassifier). For all the scores in Table 2, the DIETClassifier was used.

Table 1. Intent classification accuracy obtained through non-Transformer-based methods. Best performing models for each dataset have their results in bold.

	CLINC150	BANKING77
SpaCy Embeddings	**0.8271**	0.8867
CountVectorsFeaturizer	0.7418	**0.9026**

Table 2. Intent classification accuracy obtained by using different language model features extracted from the user input text. Best performing models for each dataset have their results in bold.

	CLINC150	BANKING77
BERT Embeddings	0.8104	**0.9282**
ConveRT Embeddings	**0.8242**	0.9237
RoBERTa Embeddings	0.7651	0.9192
GPT Embeddings	0.7956	0.9081
GPT-2 Embeddings	0.7656	0.9019
XLNet Embeddings	0.7627	0.9006

The accuracy rates obtained by the featurizer based on word counts are slightly lower than those obtained by the featurizers that use neural models pre-trained on English texts (both SpaCy and language model based featurizers).

To better understand classification accuracy and which types of examples are misclassified, we computed the precision, recall, and macro-F1 scores for the language model-based methods. The scores were computed for both individual intent classes and globally for all classes. Table 3 presents the average scores by metric for RASA NLU intent classification. A sample plot of the resulting scores obtained by using the BERT featurizer for the BANKING77 set is presented in Figure A1 in Appendix A.

Table 3. Recall, precision, and F1 classification scores obtained using different types of language model featurizers (LMF). Best performing models, in terms of macro-F1 average score, have their results in bold.

LMF	CLINC150			BANKING77		
	Recall	Precision	Macro-F1 (avg.)	Recall	Precision	Macro-F1 (avg.)
BERT	0.9455	0.8236	0.8735	0.9282	0.9317	**0.9283**
ConveRT	0.9475	0.8369	**0.8816**	0.9237	0.9277	0.9241
RoBERTa	0.9107	0.7856	0.8349	0.9191	0.9220	0.9192
GPT	0.9311	0.8169	0.8614	0.9081	0.9122	0.9084
GPT-2	0.9066	0.7868	0.8332	0.9019	0.9056	0.9018
XLNet	0.8986	0.7813	0.8272	0.9006	0.9052	0.9003

Similar to the accuracy scores presented in Table 2, the highest F1 scores are obtained by using the ConveRT (for CLINC150) and BERT (for BANKING77) language model featurizers. To check which intents are specifically mistaken for other intents, we plot the confusion matrix of the test set for the BANKING77 dataset when using the ConveRT featurizer (Figure 1). The full confusion matrix is presented in Figure A2 in Appendix B.

The confusion matrix reveals that some of the incorrectly classified examples, i.e., the light-purple hue, denote semantically similar intent labels, which in turn contain semantically similar examples in the training set. In this sense, some examples of similar intents are:

- *card_arrival* vs. *order_physical_card*;
- *pending_top_up* vs. *top_up_reverted*;
- *declined_transfer* vs. *declined_card_payment*;
- *balance_not_updated_after_bank_transfer* vs. *transfer_timing*;
- *virtual_card_not_working* vs. *card_not_working*.

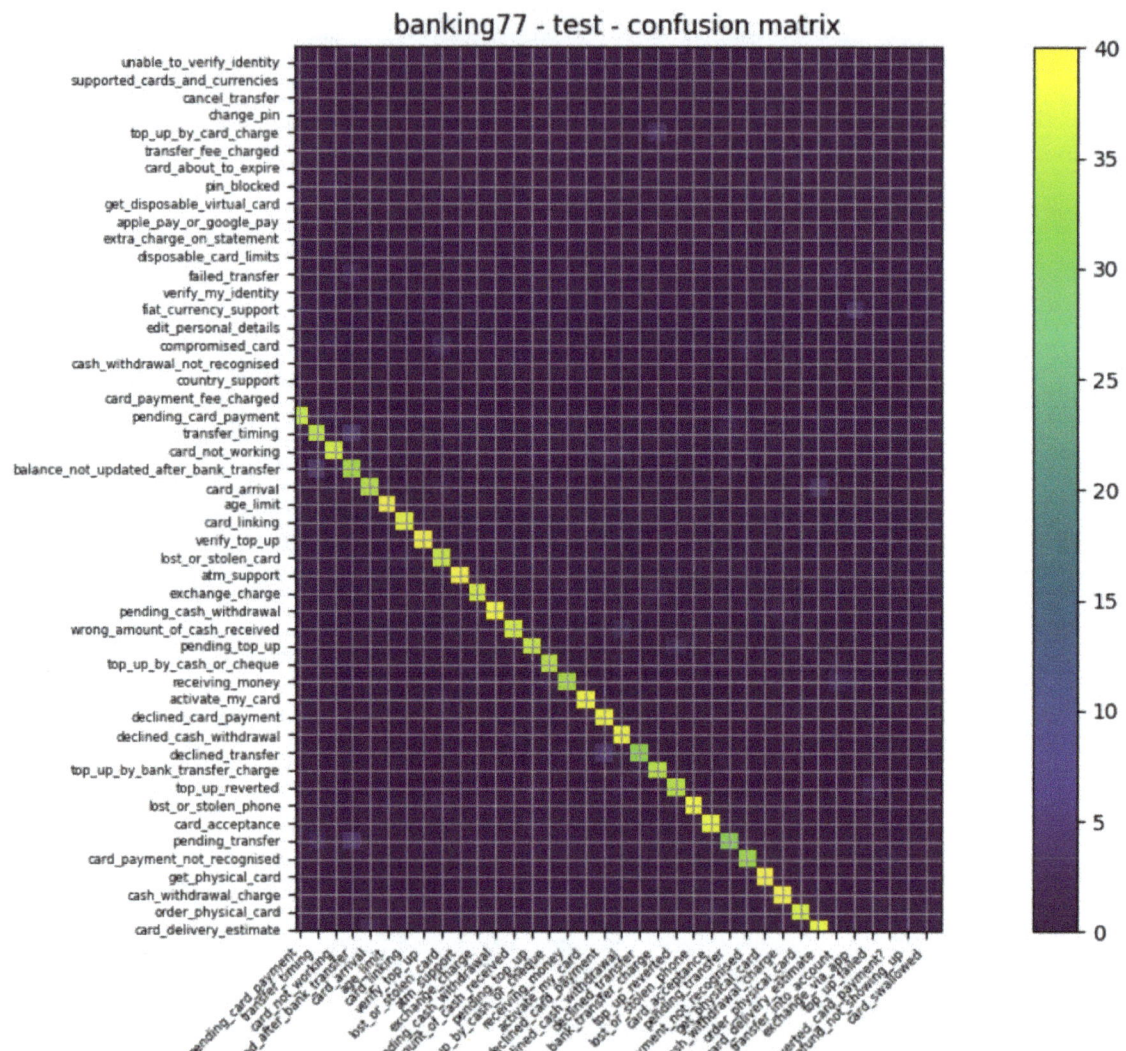

Figure 1. Selected section of the confusion matrix obtained for classifying BANKING77 test instances, with a model using the ConveRT language model featurizer. The yellow-green hue represents correctly classified test instances and it represents the main diagonal of the full matrix.

We do not include the confusion matrix for the CLINC150 test set, as the corresponding plot is not easily readable. However, it is plotted and interpreted with the help of a tool that renders it inside a scrollable webpage. Unlike BANKING77, where all test set classes contain exactly 40 instances, for CLINC150, the test set is unbalanced. There are many more *OOS* (out-of-scope) intents compared to the other ones (1000 vs. 30 for each other intent). As a result, most of the misclassifications occur when classifying an *OOS* example.

5. Corpus Clustering

As stated before, a standard RASA conversational agent relies on two distinct pipeline stages in order to converse with a user: (1) the NLU component and (2) the dialogue management component. At both levels, the chatbot designer has to provide multiple learning examples in terms of intents and conversational scenarios and, in order to obtain a robust agent, the examples must be as diverse and numerous as possible. Even though RASA automates to some extent the process of capturing training data through the RASA interactive mode, obtaining an adequate list of examples still remains a tedious and time-consuming task.

On the other hand, there exist many datasets containing conversations that could be used for acquiring the necessary data (e.g., *Cornell Movie-Dialogs Corpus* (https://www.cs.cornell.edu/~cristian/Cornell_Movie-Dialogs_Corpus.html (last accessed on 7 November 2022)) [26], *OpenSubtitles* (https://opus.nlpl.eu/OpenSubtitles-v2018.php (last accessed on 7 November 2022)) [27], etc.). Being able to process them in order to query for similar examples, given a designer's chosen example, would drastically reduce the chatbot design time.

The similarity could be exploited either at *local* level (utterance level) or at *global* level (conversation level), with the latter option being more difficult to tackle. Moreover, standard text similarity metrics (such as cosine distance) could be used to retrieve similar examples. The current impediment is given by the size of each such dataset, which makes a linear search prohibitively slow even for a single example. A possibility for an efficient example retrieval system would rely on pre-computations and searches performed within a subset of the complete dataset. Thus, offloading the intensive computations to a preprocessing step would ensure a smaller retrieval time for a single example.

5.1. Method Description

Our method can be regarded as a pipeline which processes raw transcripts, embeds individual sentences in order to obtain dense feature representations, and clusters them in order to shorten similar sentence retrieval time.

5.1.1. Data Preprocessing

The proposed system uses the subset of English subtitles from the OpenSubtitles [27] corpus as the training set. The subtitles are encoded as XML files. Each subtitle contains additional markdown data necessary for displaying specific parts of the subtitle at the correct moment. For this set of experiments, we only use the raw text of the subtitles. The timestamps are not necessary and, therefore, are discarded.

The initial set, including time annotations, contains 123 GB of data split across approximately 446,000 subtitle files. The first stage consists of aggregating the text of several files into larger 'record' files to ensure that dataset loading times are minimized. After this step, the dataset's size is reduced to approximately 11 GB of raw subtitles text split across 105 record files, each holding 100 MB of data. The total number of utterances in the resulting corpus is approximately 381 million and each file holds between 3.4 and 3.9 million examples. After manual examination, it was noticed that some movies contain multiple versions of the same transcript, which are most of the time identical. After filtering out duplicate subtitles, the final corpus is reduced to only 140,000 subtitle files, or 4 GB of raw text, split into 37 record files, approximately 100 MB of data each. The number of sentences per record remains unchanged. However, the total number of examples available is lowered to 131 million. The process of creating the record files considers that transcript lines being part of the same movie scene in the initial dataset to not be split across different record files.

5.1.2. Embedding, Clustering, and Data Projection

Local level similarity can be computed based on either sparse or dense features of the text. Following the success of the Transformer architecture in numerous NLP tasks, several types of embedding vectors obtained through the encoder modules of different Transformer models may be used. Two such options might be:

- A BERT [20] model from Huggingface (*bert-base-uncased*);
- An SBERT (Sentence BERT) [28] model (*all-mpnet-base-v2*).

The BERT model is used by Devlin et al. [20] to demonstrate that for a Named Entity Recognition (NER) task, state-of-the-art accuracy in terms of F1 score is obtained without fully fine-tuning a pre-trained BERT model on the training set at hand. However, the authors extracted contextual embeddings from several hidden layers and used them as input to two BiLSTM layers before applying the final classification layer. The results show that using embedding vectors obtained by concatenating the last four hidden layers produces the best results.

SBERT [28] is based on a pre-trained MPNet language understanding model [29] and fine-tuned on 1 billion pairs of sentences. The objective of pre-training is to predict to which pair a randomly given sentence belongs. In this case, the computed sentence-level embedding vectors have a lower dimensionality of 768 units compared to the solution offered by Devlin et al. [20]. This makes SBERT the preferred alternative when the dataset used is large, as in the case of OpenSubtitles, because precomputed embeddings would require at least four times less storage.

Given an input sentence x, retrieving semantically similar instances from a learning set $\mathcal{D}$ of N instances can be achieved by retrieving the sentence y, yielding the maximum cosine similarity between the corresponding embedding vectors:

$$y = \underset{t \in \mathcal{D}}{\mathrm{argmax}} \frac{emb_x \cdot emb_t}{\|emb_x\| \cdot \|emb_t\|} \quad (1)$$

From Equation (1), we observe that emb_x is compared against each instance in the dataset $\mathcal{D}$, which becomes unfeasible as the size N of $\mathcal{D}$ increases. In order to speed up the linear search by a constant factor K, the current approach proposes to divide all the N learning instances into K disjoint groups. Separation is performed based on embedding vectors emb_t of each sentence in $\mathcal{D}$. For small sizes of N, any standard clustering algorithm may be used to aggregate similar embedding vectors into the same cluster [30]. This becomes, however, impractical as N grows, due to large memory requirements in the clustering method. For instance, standard K-means clustering requires to have all data which are to be fitted in memory at once which, in turn, slows the algorithm performance [31]. Considering the dimensions of the gathered dataset, K-means would require $131 \times 10^6 \times 768 \times 4 \approx 375$ GB of memory (4 represents the size in bytes for a standard float).

Instead, *online* clustering algorithms could be used to cluster sentences. One such example is *mini-batch K-means* [32]. Similar to standard K-means, it optimizes the same non-convex objective function, while iteratively processing batches of the input data X. Equation (2) presents the *mini-batch K-means* optimization function, where X contains the embeddings of the instances in $\mathcal{D}$ and c_t represents the embedding of the centroid of the cluster where t is assigned.

$$\mathcal{L} = \sum_{t \in X} \|t - c_t\|^2 \quad (2)$$

Even though processing data in batches allows to construct and process of large amounts of embedding vectors, in a streaming manner, it might also have the disadvantage of possibly invalidating previous cluster assignments, e.g., t assigned to cluster c_t at timestep T might need to be reassigned to a different cluster after processing the next batch at timestep $T + 1$ since c_t might suffer significant modifications. However, depending on the sampled subset of instances, t might incorrectly remain assigned to the same cluster c_t. In practice, both standard K-means and mini-batch K-means converge to similar cluster assignments. During the cluster center update step, mini-batch K-means attempts to move the cluster centers as little as possible away from the previous cluster centers, by considering them as well in the update equation.

In the current implementation, fitting the data through mini-batch K-means is done for a fixed number of steps rather than until a given convergence criterion is met. After fitting the current examples, the embedding vectors and corresponding cluster labels are stored on the disk, to allow the processing of the next batch of embedding vectors. Furthermore, the fitted K-means object is also stored. Fitting the next batch of data must consider previously fitted data and the K-means object must also be persisted for later usage in the inference phase.

Having the instances from the learning set embedded and clustered, performing inference for a given test instance q consists of the steps described in Algorithm 1:

- Obtain the embedding vector emb_q for q based on the embedder E used for performing clustering (Line 1).
- Identify the closest cluster center c_q (bin) to emb_q, as computed through mini-batch K-means, i.e., compute the cosine similarity against all K clusters and return the most similar cluster center (bin) (Line 2).
- Identify the closest embedding vector to emb_q, in the current cluster c_q (bin), i.e., compute the cosine similarity against all learning examples assigned to cluster c_q (bin), and return the most similar example (Line 3). Note that the comparison is performed only within a restricted number of subsets of the initial data as we assume roughly uniform splitting of the initial N examples across the K clusters. Thus, the computations involve only $\frac{N}{K}$ cosine similarity computations.
- Lookup in the original corpus and retrieve p the natural language sentence paired with the index based on the embedding vector index (Lines 4 and 5).

Algorithm 1 Inference steps for a given test example q

Input: E embedder, q inference sentence
Output: p the <sentence, index> pair
1: $emb_q \leftarrow E(q)$ ▷ Obtain the embedding vector
2: $c_q \leftarrow$ closest cluster to emb_q ▷ Identify the closest cluster
3: $m_q \leftarrow$ closest example to emb_q in c_q
4: $p \leftarrow index(m_q)$ ▷ Index in the original corpus
5: **Return** p

Due to the online nature of the clustering algorithm and to counteract the possibility of early learning instances being assigned to a wrong bin, the second and third steps above can check more than one bin and example. This idea is inspired by *Beam Search*, a greedy decoding algorithm used in other NLP tasks (e.g., dialogue generation, machine translation, etc.), where multiple candidates in an implicit graph structure are explored in a breadth-first search manner. This might prove useful for detecting embedding vectors falling under a very similar bin, which might rank just below the closest bin in terms of cosine similarity to the inference embedding vector.

It is certain that not all of the sentences retrieved through the method described above would positively impact the quality of the corpus which is to be augmented. However, given a limited set of hand-chosen learning examples, one can train a *weak* classifier with the initial set of examples. The additional examples retrieved by the system can be filtered based on the classifier class output probabilities, i.e., if an example is assigned to a specific class with a probability greater than a threshold, then the example will be further considered for augmenting the corpus; otherwise, the low probability will lead to the dismissal of the example.

This initial technique of example filtering might not drastically improve classification accuracy, i.e., for high values of the confidence threshold (e.g., 0.9), the model might choose only examples which do not bring any additional information. A different approach would be to filter examples according to a semi-supervised approach, treating the initial learning set as labeled, and the set of retrieved examples as unlabeled. This idea is inspired by FixMatch, a method initially developed and applied for computer vision tasks [33].

While storing precomputed sentence embedding vectors decreases the lookup time, storage requirements are particularly high; i.e, the entire set of 131 million, 768-dimensional vectors requires approximately 390 GB of storage space. In order to reduce the amount of storage needed, dimensionality reduction algorithms can be used in order to downsample the embedding vectors. A different approach could be to use a different embedder, which produces lower dimensional embeddings. However, the main issue remains, as we do not know any embedder that might output vectors of only 32 or 64 dimensions, so we do not follow this path of experiments.

Similar to the clustering algorithm limitations, one requirement for the dimensionality reduction algorithm is that it must be able to process the data iteratively since they would not fit into the memory all at once. As a result, IPCA (Incremental PCA) is successfully used to downsample the set of vectors to 64 and 32 dimensions, while preserving semantic similarity [34]. The resulting sets take only 76 GB and 43 GB of storage, respectively.

5.2. Few-Shot Learning

A natural use case of this similar example retrieval system is the few-shot training scenario. Such a setup examines the performance of a model trained with a limited, small number of examples. Models may either make use of transfer learning or corpus augmentation techniques in order to increase the desired performance metric.

Considering a learning set $\mathcal{D}$ with C classes, each class has n_C examples. The augmentation process consists of retrieving $K \times L$ additional examples for each of the n_C examples, with K being the number of clusters to check and L being the 'beam' size in each cluster. The retrieved examples may be subject to further filtering or post-processing step, in order to minimize the noise introduced in the dataset. In our experiments, we test two different methods for filtering:

(1) Use a model trained on the initial data to classify the retrieved examples. The examples classified with confidence exceeding a fixed threshold (i.e., 0.8 or 0.9) are kept, while the others are discarded.
(2) Remove stop words from both the initial examples and the retrieved examples. Then, compute the set intersection over the tokens of a candidate sentence and the complete set of tokens of the initial examples. Only examples producing an intersection size over a given threshold (i.e., 1 or 2) are kept. Intuitively, this method forces to some extent the retrieved examples to be lexically similar to the initial examples.

6. Evaluation and Results

To evaluate the proposed similar sentence retrieval system, we use it to augment the intent classification training sets and, then, we evaluated the models trained with the augmented data on the unmodified test sets, using RASA's DIETClassifier. The first scenario aimed to verify to what extent does the number of clusters impact the classification accuracy. Thus, we experiment with 512 and 1024 clusters. In both setups, the complete training sets of BANKING77 and CLINC150 are used to train initial DIETClassifier models. These classifiers are subsequently used for classifying the additionally extracted examples. Only examples classified with at least 0.9 confidence are used for augmenting the training sets. For this set of experiments, we use the same hardware configuration as for the intent classification experiments (Section 4.2). For result reproducibility, we will make the code publicly available on GitHub, in the following repository: https://github.com/Gabriel-Bercaru/CorpusClustering.

For each example in the initial training sets, the top $K = 1$ cluster is inspected, retrieving the $L = 1$ similar example. In each setup, the initial training set sizes were 10,080 examples for BANKING77 and 15,251 examples for CLINC150. For augmentation, in the first phase 10,080 and 15,251 examples are retrieved. Out of these, only 3% and, respectively, 20% of them are classified with a confidence of at least 0.9 (294 for BANKING77 and 3043 for CLINC150), resulting in augmented set sizes of 10,374 and 18,294 examples. For each setup, 30 DIETClassifier models with different randomly initialized parameters are trained on the initial and augmented datasets. We measure the mean accuracy and the standard deviation for each setup (Table 4). We should note that for each setup, the BERT featurizer is kept fixed throughout all the experiments. Figure 2 presents the clustering results.

Table 4. Mean accuracy and standard deviation for the first augmentation method, in which a pretrained classifier is used for classifying additional examples. Bold text denotes the best performing model.

	CLINC150	BANKING77
Original data	0.8037 ± 0.0039	0.9305 ± 0.0031
Augmented data—1024 clusters	0.8036 ± 0.0046	0.9296 ± 0.0027
Augmented data—512 clusters	**0.8058 ± 0.0052**	**0.9305 ± 0.0022**

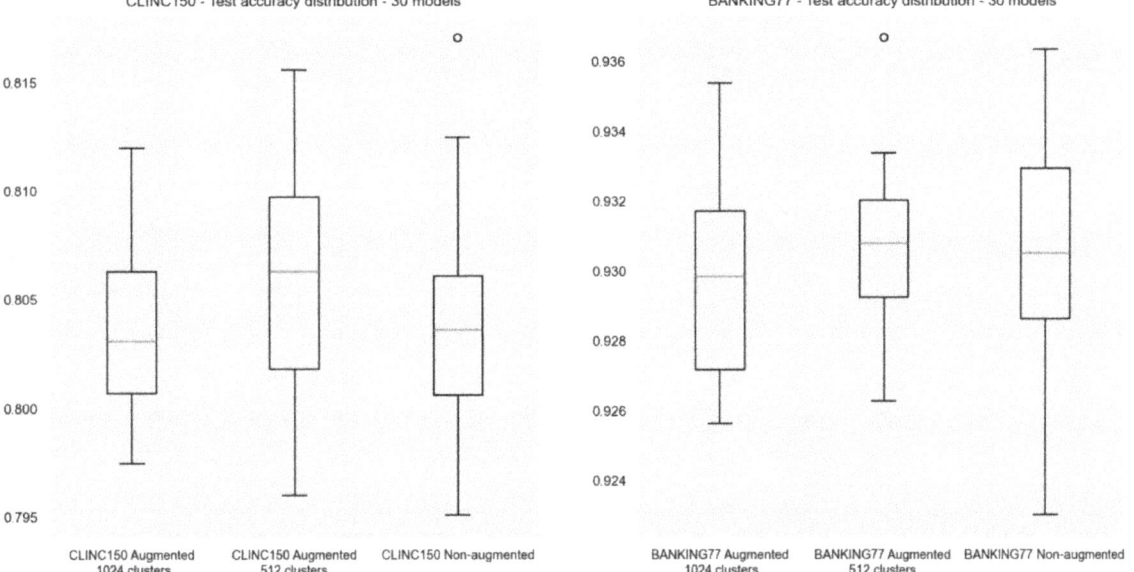

Figure 2. Box and whisker plots obtained when training an ensemble of 30 models for each combination of dataset and augmentation method. Augmented training sets do not improve the mean accuracy on the test set, but reduce variance across models. Whiskers extend from the lower to the upper quartile of the data.

As expected, the results are approximately the same because, firstly, the retrieved examples are selected to be as similar as possible to the ones already in the dataset and secondly, at least in the case of BANKING77, the number of retrieved examples is rather small. As already mentioned, a semi-supervised approach might help in future research to extract more meaningful examples out of the 'unlabeled' automatically retrieved set.

The second set of experiments is conducted to evaluate the sentence retrieval system in a few-shot scenario. In this setup, the training sets of BANKING77 and CLINC150 are sequentially restricted to only $k \in \{2, 3, 5, 10\}$ examples per class. The corpus clustering method is then used to artificially increase the number of examples available, based on the initial, limited number of examples. For each initial example x_i, a similar sentence y_i is retrieved. In the end, all retrieved y_i are aggregated and combined with the initial learning set and the duplicates are removed.

To minimize the number of noisy examples which are added to the learning set, the following heuristic is tested. When attempting to add a retrieved candidate y_i to a class C, first compute its set of unique tokens. Stop words are removed before set computation. Next, perform a set intersection with the set of tokens corresponding to all initial examples

x_i in the class C. Only add the example if the set intersection size exceeds a given threshold $t \in \{0, 1, 2\}$. This heuristic attempts to include only examples which are somewhat similar to the initial ones. During testing without the heuristic filtering, we observed that some unrelated examples are added to the learning set and, thus, we introduce this heuristic to avoid this issue. Evaluation of the few-shot setups is performed by training an ensemble of 10 different DIETClassifier models in each configuration. Table 5 presents the mean accuracy and its standard deviation.

Table 5. Mean accuracy and standard deviation obtained for the corpus augmentation method in the few-shot scenario. In each augmentation setup, t denotes the stop word (SW) filtering threshold. Note: bold marks the model with the highest mean accuracy.

Few-Shot-Scenario	Filtering	CLINC150	BANKING77
k = 2	no augmentation	0.2127 ± 0.0150	0.1983 ± 0.0205
	augmentation, t = 0	**0.3734 ± 0.0087**	**0.3336 ± 0.0169**
	augmentation, t = 1	0.2302 ± 0.0107	0.2618 ± 0.0216
	augmentation, t = 2	0.2347 ± 0.0123	0.2379 ± 0.0162
k = 3	no augmentation	0.3941 ± 0.0098	0.3875 ± 0.0155
	augmentation, t = 0	**0.4793 ± 0.0128**	**0.4562 ± 0.0157**
	augmentation, t = 1	0.4575 ± 0.0106	0.4371 ± 0.0115
	augmentation, t = 2	0.3850 ± 0.0236	0.4204 ± 0.0159
k = 5	no augmentation	0.5273 ± 0.0144	0.6007 ± 0.0145
	augmentation, t = 0	**0.5617 ± 0.0088**	**0.6199 ± 0.0130**
	augmentation, t = 1	0.5572 ± 0.0088	0.6140 ± 0.0117
	augmentation, t = 2	0.5491 ± 0.0094	0.6028 ± 0.0158
k = 10	no augmentation	0.6622 ± 0.0125	0.7667 ± 0.0074
	augmentation, t = 0	0.6570 ± 0.0063	0.7544 ± 0.0062
	augmentation, t = 1	0.6657 ± 0.0077	0.7648 ± 0.0059
	augmentation, t = 2	**0.6681 ± 0.0058**	**0.7669 ± 0.0086**

7. Discussion

Regarding the first set of experiments, in which we test different featurizers, it can be observed that embeddings provided by Transformer neural models help improve the intent classification accuracy, with BERT and ConveRT embeddings performing the best for both BANKING77 and CLINC150 datasets.

For the corpus clustering part, two sets of experiments are conducted. The first one consists in analyzing whether augmenting the training sets of BANKING77 and CLINC150 helps improve intent classification accuracy. As the results in Table 4 show, the method brings minor improvements in terms of classification mean accuracy, also with a reduction in variance. Moreover, the number of clusters used for grouping together similar examples seems to bring little influence, as in both cases, the classification means accuracy is approximately equal, with a small improvement when using 512 clusters.

For the second set of experiments regarding the few-shot scenario, we restrict the training sets of BANKING77 and CLINC150 to only 2, 3, 5, or 10 examples per intent. The corpus clustering method is then used to artificially increase the training set sizes. In the best-case scenario, the sizes are doubled. However, in most cases, duplicate similar examples are retrieved and, therefore, they are removed. Moreover, additional examples are removed according to the heuristic described in Section 6. In this setup, we observe that the proposed corpus clustering method helps improve the classification accuracy, in the best case leading to 16% accuracy increase for CLINC150 when $k = 2$ (Table 5) and a 14% accuracy increase for BANKING77 when $k = 2$ (Table 5). As more of the original training examples become available, the proposed method still increases the mean classification accuracy, but to a smaller extent. Including additional original training data will most likely result in even smaller improvements and will ultimately produce results similar to those presented in Table 4.

When interpreting the results, one should consider that they reflect the scores obtained when clustering based on reduced versions of the sentence embedding vectors, i.e., 32 dimensions, are used. The used sentence embedder (SBERT) produces 768-dimensional vectors. We hypothesize that using the full embedding vectors, with no dimensionality reduction applied, would lead to the retrieval of more meaningful examples, increasing the reported accuracy values. However, the retrieval time per example increases as well. In the 32-dimensional embedding vectors setup, the retrieval time per example is approximately 0.2–0.3 s, while for the 768-dimensional embeddings, the retrieval time is approximately 0.6 s. The exploration of this hypothesis is left as part of a future investigation.

8. Conclusions

In this work, we examine the problem of intent classification as part of a conversational agent pipeline. First, we discuss how existing systems perform in terms of intent classification—answering (Q_1) and achieving objective (O_1). Then, we define a method for clustering large corpora, to efficiently retrieve examples that are similar to a user-supplied query. Our method consists of several preprocessing stages, such as embedding movie transcripts, online clustering, and data projection. By making use of precomputations and data partitioning into clusters, we achieve low inference duration—answering (Q_2) and achieving objective (O_2). We automatically process 123 GB of raw movie subtitles data, available as part of the OpenSubtitles dataset—answering (Q_3) and achieving objective (O_3). The corpus clustering method is shown to bring minor improvements in terms of classification accuracy when the full training sets are available. Moreover, we also examine to what extent the method helps improve the accuracy when a limited number of examples are available. Our results have shown that the intent classification accuracy is raised by up to 16%, in the most favorable case, where only two labeled examples per class are available. Our proposed method achieves retrieval times as low as 0.2–0.3 s per example and is shown to bring statistically relevant improvements in intent classification scenarios in which training data are scarce—answering (Q_4) and achieving objective (O_4).

For tasks in which large datasets are available, our method does not introduce significant improvements; this is due to the fact that large datasets expose a high degree of example diversity and additional retrieved examples might not bring in additional useful information. However, for small datasets, our method helps improve the diversity of the examples, leading to larger accuracy scores, as shown by our research.

In future work, we plan to expand the corpus clustering method in order to further reduce the retrieval time per example. One such possibility would be to move to a hierarchical clustering approach. During the experiments, it was observed that some clusters are considerably larger than others; the loading time for such clusters becomes a bottleneck. A solution would be to identify the large clusters and further group their elements into smaller sub-clusters, in order to minimize the cluster loading time during the example retrieval phase.

Another possible direction that we will investigate is to use a semi-supervised learning approach in order to filter retrieved examples. In this work, we investigated the effect of filtering all the retrieved examples based on a pre-trained classifier confidence threshold. However, as the results show, this does not lead to major improvements in classification accuracy. Using a semi-supervised approach, in which the full set of retrieved examples is regarded as unlabeled, would possibly lead to better choices when filtering the examples, yielding more meaningful augmentations.

As a possible future application, we plan to evaluate how our proposed pipeline performs in augmenting real-world conversational scenarios. We plan to implement a conversational agent focused on the interaction during interviews. Its learning set is an ideal candidate for evaluating our data augmentation method. Since our method mainly deals with dataset augmentation, there is currently no plan to use it in a real-time scenario.

Author Contributions: Conceptualization, G.B., C.-O.T., C.-G.C. and T.R.; methodology, G.B., C.-O.T., C.-G.C. and T.R.; software, G.B.; validation, G.B., C.-O.T., C.-G.C. and T.R.; formal analysis, G.B., C.-O.T., C.-G.C. and T.R.; investigation, G.B., C.-O.T., C.-G.C. and T.R.; resources, G.B., C.-O.T., C.-G.C. and T.R.; data curation, G.B.; writing—original draft preparation, G.B., C.-O.T., C.-G.C. and T.R.; writing—review and editing, G.B., C.-O.T., C.-G.C. and T.R.; visualization, G.B.; supervision, C.-O.T., C.-G.C. and T.R.; project administration, C.-G.C. and T.R.; funding acquisition, T.R. All authors have read and agreed to the published version of the manuscript.

Funding: This work was funded by the Romanian Ministry of European Investments and Projects through the Competitiveness Operational Program (POC) project "HOLOTRAIN" (grant no. 29/221_ap2/07.04.2020, SMIS code: 129077).

Institutional Review Board Statement: Not applicable.

Informed Consent Statement: Not applicable.

Data Availability Statement: The CLINC150 and BANKING77 datasets used in this study are publicly available at https://github.com/clinc/nlu-datasets (last accessed 15 December 2022). The OpenSubtitles dataset is publicly available at https://opus.nlpl.eu/OpenSubtitles-v2018.php (last accessed 15 December 2022).

Conflicts of Interest: The authors declare no conflicts of interest.

Abbreviations

The following abbreviations are used in this manuscript:

BERT	Bidirectional Encoder Representations from Transformers
CRF	Conditional Random Field
DIET	Dual Intent-Entity Transformer
GPT	Generative Pre-Training
ID	In-Domain
LMF	Language Model Featurizer
NER	Named Entity Recognition
NLP	Natural Language Processing
NLU	Natural Language Understanding
OOD	Out-of-Domain
OOS	Out-of-Scope
RoBERTa	Robustly Optimized BERT pretraining Approach
SBERT	Sentence BERT
SVM	Support Vector Machines
SW	Stop Word
TED	Transformer Embedding Dialogue
TF-IDF	Term Frequency-Inverse Document Frequency

Appendix A. Intent Classification: Recall, Precision, and F1 Scores

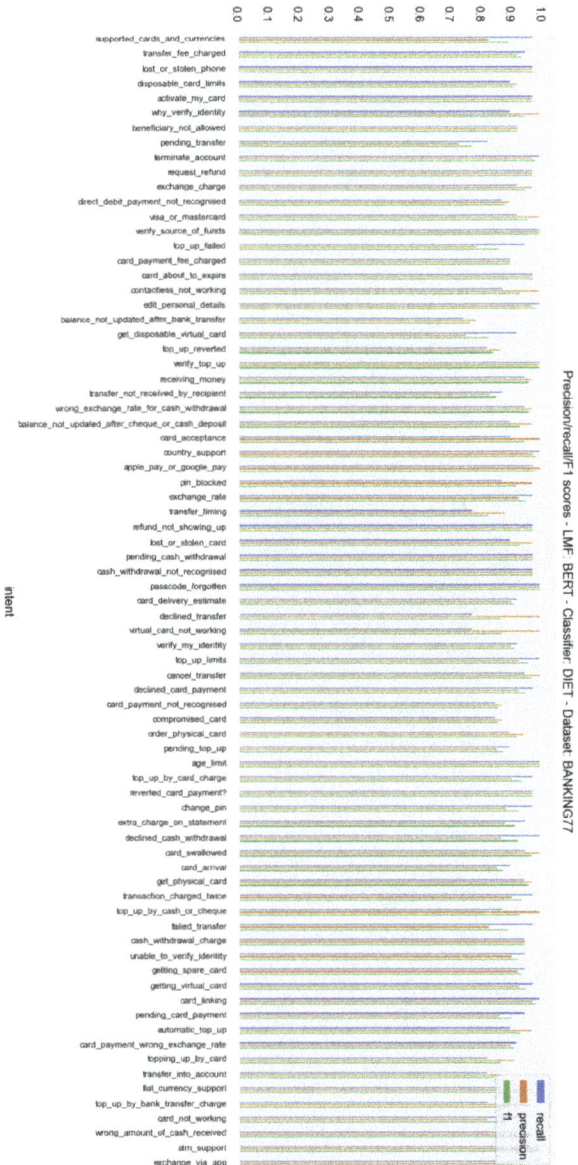

Figure A1. Recall, precision, and F1 scores obtained for intent classification on the BANKING77 test set using the BERT model as a language featurizer.

Appendix B. Intent Classification: Confusion Matrix

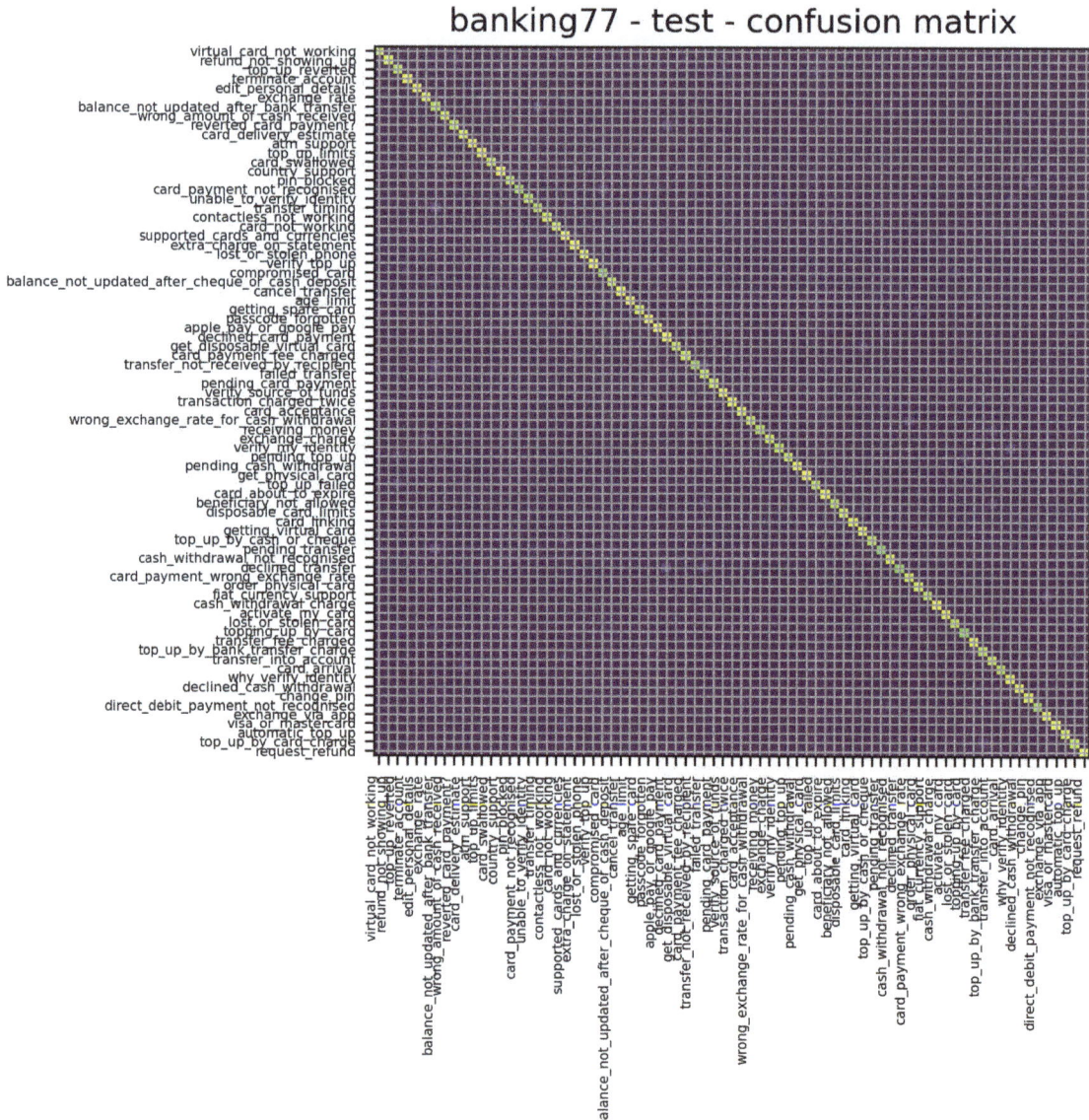

Figure A2. Full confusion matrix obtained for classifying BANKING77 test instances, with a model using the ConveRT language model featurizer. The yellow-green hue represents correctly classified test instances and it represents the main diagonal of the full matrix.

References

1. Balakrishnan, V.; Shi, Z.; Law, C.L.; Lim, R.; Teh, L.L.; Fan, Y.; Periasamy, J. A Comprehensive Analysis of Transformer-Deep Neural Network Models in Twitter Disaster Detection. *Mathematics* **2022**, *10*, 4664.
2. Larson, S.; Mahendran, A.; Peper, J.J.; Clarke, C.; Lee, A.; Hill, P.; Kummerfeld, J.K.; Leach, K.; Laurenzano, M.A.; Tang, L.; et al. An Evaluation Dataset for Intent Classification and Out-of-Scope Prediction. In Proceedings of the 2019 Conference on Empirical Methods in Natural Language Processing and the 9th International Joint Conference on Natural Language Processing (EMNLP-IJCNLP), Hong Kong, China, 3–7 November 2019; Association for Computational Linguistics: Stroudsburg, PA, USA, 2019; pp. 1311–1316. [CrossRef]
3. Casanueva, I.; Temčinas, T.; Gerz, D.; Henderson, M.; Vulić, I. Efficient Intent Detection with Dual Sentence Encoders. In Proceedings of the 2nd Workshop on Natural Language Processing for Conversational AI, Online, 9 July 2020; Association for Computational Linguistics: Stroudsburg, PA, USA, 2020; pp. 38–45. [CrossRef]
4. Liu, X.; Eshghi, A.; Swietojanski, P.; Rieser, V. *Benchmarking Natural Language Understanding Services for Building Conversational Agents*; Lecture Notes in Electrical Engineering; Springer: Singapore, 2021; pp. 165–183. [CrossRef]
5. Ahmadvand, A.; Choi, J.I.; Agichtein, E. Contextual Dialogue Act Classification for Open-Domain Conversational Agents. In Proceedings of the 42nd International ACM SIGIR Conference on Research and Development in Information Retrieval, Paris, France, 21–25 July 2019; pp. 1273–1276. [CrossRef]
6. Zhan, L.M.; Liang, H.; Liu, B.; Fan, L.; Wu, X.M.; Lam, A.Y. Out-of-Scope Intent Detection with Self-Supervision and Discriminative Training. In Proceedings of the 59th Annual Meeting of the Association for Computational Linguistics and the 11th International Joint Conference on Natural Language Processing (Volume 1: Long Papers), Virtual Event, 1–6 August 2021; Association for Computational Linguistics: Stroudsburg, PA, USA, 2021; pp. 3521–3532. [CrossRef]
7. Zhang, J.; Hashimoto, K.; Wan, Y.; Liu, Z.; Liu, Y.; Xiong, C.; Yu, P. Are Pre-trained Transformers Robust in Intent Classification? A Missing Ingredient in Evaluation of Out-of-Scope Intent Detection. In Proceedings of the 4th Workshop on NLP for Conversational AI, Dublin, Ireland, 22–27 May 2022; Association for Computational Linguistics: Stroudsburg, PA, USA, 2022; pp. 12–20. [CrossRef]
8. Liu, H.; Zhang, X.; Fan, L.; Fu, X.; Li, Q.; Wu, X.M.; Lam, A.Y. Reconstructing Capsule Networks for Zero-shot Intent Classification. In Proceedings of the 2019 Conference on Empirical Methods in Natural Language Processing and the 9th International Joint Conference on Natural Language Processing (EMNLP-IJCNLP), Hong Kong, China, 3–7 November 2019; Association for Computational Linguistics: Stroudsburg, PA, USA, 2019; pp. 4799–4809. [CrossRef]
9. Xia, C.; Zhang, C.; Yan, X.; Chang, Y.; Yu, P.S. Zero-shot user intent detection via capsule neural networks. In Proceedings of the 2018 Conference on Empirical Methods in Natural Language Processing, Brussels, Belgium, 31 October–4 November 2018; pp. 3090–3099. [CrossRef]
10. Yan, G.; Fan, L.; Li, Q.; Liu, H.; Zhang, X.; Wu, X.M.; Lam, A.Y. Unknown Intent Detection Using Gaussian Mixture Model with an Application to Zero-shot Intent Classification. In Proceedings of the 58th Annual Meeting of the Association for Computational Linguistics, Online, 5–10 July 2020; Association for Computational Linguistics: Stroudsburg, PA, USA, 2020; pp. 1050–1060. [CrossRef]
11. Fei, G.; Liu, B. Breaking the Closed World Assumption in Text Classification. In Proceedings of the 2016 Conference of the North American Chapter of the Association for Computational Linguistics: Human Language Technologies, San Diego, CA, USA, 12–17 June 2016; Association for Computational Linguistics: San Diego, CA, USA, 2016; pp. 506–514. [CrossRef]
12. Chatterjee, A.; Sengupta, S. Intent Mining from past conversations for Conversational Agent. In Proceedings of the 28th International Conference on Computational Linguistics, Barcelona, Spain (Online), 8–13 December 2020; International Committee on Computational Linguistics: Stroudsburg, PA, USA, 2020; pp. 4140–4152. [CrossRef]
13. Kuchlous, S.; Kadaba, M. Short Text Intent Classification for Conversational Agents. In Proceedings of the 2020 IEEE 17th India Council International Conference (INDICON), New Delhi, India, 11–13 December 2020; pp. 1–6. [CrossRef]
14. Sahu, G.; Rodriguez, P.; Laradji, I.; Atighehchian, P.; Vazquez, D.; Bahdanau, D. Data Augmentation for Intent Classification with Off-the-shelf Large Language Models. In Proceedings of the 4th Workshop on NLP for Conversational AI, Dublin, Ireland, 22–27 May 2022; Association for Computational Linguistics: Stroudsburg, PA, USA, 2022; pp. 47–57. [CrossRef]
15. Brown, T.; Mann, B.; Ryder, N.; Subbiah, M.; Kaplan, J.D.; Dhariwal, P.; Neelakantan, A.; Shyam, P.; Sastry, G.; Askell, A.; et al. Language models are few-shot learners. *Adv. Neural Inf. Process. Syst.* **2020**, *33*, 1877–1901. [CrossRef]
16. Bocklisch, T.; Faulkner, J.; Pawlowski, N.; Nichol, A. Rasa: Open source language understanding and dialogue management. *arXiv* **2017**, arXiv:1712.05181.
17. Wolf, T.; Debut, L.; Sanh, V.; Chaumond, J.; Delangue, C.; Moi, A.; Cistac, P.; Rault, T.; Louf, R.; Funtowicz, M.; et al. Transformers: State-of-the-Art Natural Language Processing. In Proceedings of the 2020 Conference on Empirical Methods in Natural Language Processing: System Demonstrations, Online, 16–20 November 2020; Association for Computational Linguistics: Stroudsburg, PA, USA, 2020. [CrossRef]
18. Vlasov, V.; Mosig, J.E.; Nichol, A. Dialogue transformers. *arXiv* **2019**, arXiv:1910.00486.
19. Pedregosa, F.; Varoquaux, G.; Gramfort, A.; Michel, V.; Thirion, B.; Grisel, O.; Blondel, M.; Prettenhofer, P.; Weiss, R.; Dubourg, V.; et al. Scikit-learn: Machine Learning in Python. *J. Mach. Learn. Res.* **2011**, *12*, 2825–2830.

20. Devlin, J.; Chang, M.W.; Lee, K.; Toutanova, K. BERT: Pre-training of Deep Bidirectional Transformers for Language Understanding. In Proceedings of the 2019 Conference of the North American Chapter of the Association for Computational Linguistics: Human Language Technologies, Volume 1 (Long and Short Papers), Minneapolis, MN, USA, 2–7 June 2019; Association for Computational Linguistics: Stroudsburg, PA, USA, 2019; pp. 4171–4186. [CrossRef]
21. Henderson, M.; Casanueva, I.; Mrkšić, N.; Su, P.H.; Wen, T.H.; Vulić, I. ConveRT: Efficient and Accurate Conversational Representations from Transformers. In Proceedings of the Findings of the Association for Computational Linguistics: EMNLP 2020, Online, 16–20 November 2020; Association for Computational Linguistics: Stroudsburg, PA, USA, 2020; pp. 2161–2174. [CrossRef]
22. Liu, Y.; Ott, M.; Goyal, N.; Du, J.; Joshi, M.; Chen, D.; Levy, O.; Lewis, M.; Zettlemoyer, L.; Stoyanov, V. Roberta: A robustly optimized bert pretraining approach. *arXiv* **2019**, arXiv:1907.11692.
23. Radford, A.; Narasimhan, K.; Salimans, T.; Sutskever, I. Improving language understanding by generative pre-training. *OpenAI Preprints* **2018**.
24. Radford, A.; Wu, J.; Child, R.; Luan, D.; Amodei, D.; Sutskever, I. Language models are unsupervised multitask learners. *OpenAI Blog* **2019**, *1*, 9.
25. Yang, Z.; Dai, Z.; Yang, Y.; Carbonell, J.; Salakhutdinov, R.R.; Le, Q.V. Xlnet: Generalized autoregressive pretraining for language understanding. *Adv. Neural Inf. Process. Syst.* **2019**, *32*. [CrossRef]
26. Danescu-Niculescu-Mizil, C.; Lee, L. Chameleons in Imagined Conversations: A New Approach to Understanding Coordination of Linguistic Style in Dialogs. In Proceedings of the 2nd Workshop on Cognitive Modeling and Computational Linguistics, Portland, OR, USA, 23 June 2011; Association for Computational Linguistics: Portland, OR, USA, 2011; pp. 76–87.
27. Lison, P.; Tiedemann, J. Opensubtitles2016: Extracting large parallel corpora from movie and tv subtitles. In Proceedings of the Tenth International Conference on Language Resources and Evaluation (LREC'16), Portorož, Slovenia, 23–28 May 2016; European Language Resources Association: Paris, France, 2016; pp. 923–929.
28. Reimers, N.; Gurevych, I. Sentence-BERT: Sentence Embeddings using Siamese BERT-Networks. In Proceedings of the 2019 Conference on Empirical Methods in Natural Language Processing and the 9th International Joint Conference on Natural Language Processing (EMNLP-IJCNLP), Hong Kong, China, 3–7 November 2019; Association for Computational Linguistics: Stroudsburg, PA, USA, 2019; pp. 3982–3992. [CrossRef]
29. Song, K.; Tan, X.; Qin, T.; Lu, J.; Liu, T.Y. Mpnet: Masked and permuted pre-training for language understanding. *Adv. Neural Inf. Process. Syst.* **2020**, *33*, 16857–16867.
30. Rădulescu, I.M.; Boicea, A.; Truică, C.O.; Apostol, E.S.; Mocanu, M.; Rădulescu, F. DenLAC: Density Levels Aggregation Clustering—A Flexible Clustering Method. In Proceedings of the International Conference on Computational Science (ICCS2021), Kraków, Poland, 16–18 June 2021; Springer International Publishing: Berlin/Heidelberg, Germany, 2021; pp. 316–329. [CrossRef]
31. Arthur, D.; Vassilvitskii, S. How slow is the k-means method? In Proceedings of the Twenty-Second Annual Symposium on Computational Geometry (SCG'06), Sedona, AZ, USA, 5–7 June 2006; ACM Press: New York, NY, USA, 2006; pp. 144–153. [CrossRef]
32. Sculley, D. Web-scale k-means clustering. In Proceedings of the 19th International Conference on World Wide Web (WWW'10), Raleigh, NC, USA, 26–30 April 2010; ACM Press: New York, NY, USA, 2010; pp. 1177–1178. [CrossRef]
33. Sohn, K.; Berthelot, D.; Carlini, N.; Zhang, Z.; Zhang, H.; Raffel, C.A.; Cubuk, E.D.; Kurakin, A.; Li, C.L. FixMatch: Simplifying Semi-Supervised Learning with Consistency and Confidence. *Adv. Neural Inf. Process. Syst.* **2020**, *33*, 596–608.
34. Radu, R.G.; Rădulescu, I.M.; Truică, C.O.; Apostol, E.S.; Mocanu, M. Clustering Documents using the Document to Vector Model for Dimensionality Reduction. In Proceedings of the 2020 IEEE International Conference on Automation, Quality and Testing, Robotics (AQTR), Cluj-Napoca, Romania, 21–23 May 2020. [CrossRef]

Disclaimer/Publisher's Note: The statements, opinions and data contained in all publications are solely those of the individual author(s) and contributor(s) and not of MDPI and/or the editor(s). MDPI and/or the editor(s) disclaim responsibility for any injury to people or property resulting from any ideas, methods, instructions or products referred to in the content.

Article

Text Simplification to Specific Readability Levels

Wejdan Alkaldi [1],* and Diana Inkpen [2],*

[1] Department of Information Technology, College of Computer and Information Sciences, King Saud University, Riyadh 11451, Saudi Arabia
[2] School of Electrical Engineering and Computer Science, University of Ottawa, 800 King Edward, Ottawa, ON K1N 6N5, Canada
* Correspondence: walkaldi@ksu.edu.sa (W.A.); diana.inkpen@uottawa.ca (D.I.); Tel.: +96-650-620-8504 (W.A.); +1-613-56258000 (ext. 6711) (D.I.)

Abstract: The ability to read a document depends on the reader's skills and the text's readability level. In this paper, we propose a system that uses deep learning techniques to simplify texts in order to match a reader's level. We use a novel approach with a reinforcement learning loop that contains a readability classifier. The classifier's output is used to decide if more simplification is needed, until the desired readability level is reached. The simplification models are trained on data annotated with readability levels from the Newsela corpus. Our simplification models perform at sentence level, to simplify each sentence to meet the specified readability level. We use a version of the Newsela corpus aligned at the sentence level. We also produce an augmented dataset by automatically annotating more pairs of sentences using a readability-level classifier. Our text simplification models achieve better performance than state-of-the-art techniques for this task.

Keywords: text simplification; deep learning; reinforcement learning; readability level; data augmentation

MSC: 68T50

Citation: Alkaldi, W.; Inkpen, D. Text Simplification to Specific Readability Levels. *Mathematics* **2023**, *11*, 2063. https://doi.org/10.3390/math11092063

Academic Editor: Catalin Stoean

Received: 23 March 2023
Revised: 16 April 2023
Accepted: 19 April 2023
Published: 26 April 2023

Copyright: © 2023 by the authors. Licensee MDPI, Basel, Switzerland. This article is an open access article distributed under the terms and conditions of the Creative Commons Attribution (CC BY) license (https://creativecommons.org/licenses/by/4.0/).

1. Introduction

The ultimate goal of writing a text is to communicate. Any written text must be readable and understandable to its targeted audience. However, readers might have a low level of reading skills and cannot understand a given text. The organization of the text and the vocabulary used affects the text readability level. Manipulating these features could increase the readability of the text to a certain level that allows poor literacy readers or children to read and understand the written text.

Text Simplification (TS) techniques available now do not use the readability level as a required feature for the output text. Instead, they typically simplify the given text to whatever readability level it can reach. For instance, consider readability levels from 1 to 4 (as used in Newsela dataset to classify documents to their readability level), where level 1 represents a very complex text to read and level 4 represents a very simple text to read. If a reader with reading level 3 wants to read a text with readability level 1, the text must be simplified to the reader's level at least, i.e., level 3 or 4. However, using the available simplification techniques, the original text could be simplified to a simple text with a readability level that cannot be controlled. In the example, if the output text readability is at level 2, then the text is still difficult for the reader to grasp and comprehend, despite being simplified from its original state. So, the original text must be re-simplified to represent the readability level of at least 3. Unfortunately, this scenario cannot be executed with the available techniques since the readability level of a text does not play a role in the present simplification models. To fill this gap, we create a novel state-of-the-art simplification model that is trained over aligned sentences from the Newsela dataset (https://newsela.com/data/ accessed on 6 November 2019) [1].

Also, we produce additional data in an automatic way, to improve the performance of the simplification. The model takes a complex text with a low readability level, and produces a simplified version of the text that considers the required readability level. This will ensure that every simplified text will be readable and understandable by its targeted audience.

We start with related works in Section 2, where we express simplification projects available in non-English languages, followed by deep learning techniques used in current TS projects. Then, we explain the framework of our simplification in Section 3. We start with the datasets used, the simplification models, and the evaluation measures applied. After that, we discuss the experiments in Section 4, including training and testing setup, examining samples of generated simplified sentences, and presenting the results for the experiments. Section 5 compares and analyses the performance of all the trained models on the same test set followed by the limitations we faced in Section 6. Finally, in Section 7, we conclude our paper and present directions for future work.

2. Related Work
2.1. Natural Language Simplification

In Natural Language Processing (NLP) applications, early Text Simplification (TS) systems are built based on statistical machine translation models like PBMT-R [2] and Hybrid [3]. While most TS researches are done for the English language, TS is also applied across many other languages. Every language has its own specific characteristics. It is non-trivial to re-implement existing TS techniques into other languages. Every language has different characteristics that need to be handled differently. Languages like Latin and Swedish, use complex verb conjugations; e.g. specific forms of verbs express passive voice sentences. While Mandarin Chinese, have unchangeable verb forms when expressing passive voice sentences. This means their verbs do not have any tenses. Several projects focus on re-implementing existing TS techniques and adapting them to their own language. TS is a major challenge in all languages. We found many projects and tools in TS for different languages. Most of them were developed to assist people with disabilities or learning difficulties.

The KURA project [4] is a Japanese project and one of the earliest works found in TS. It aims to simplify Japanese language text for deaf students by developing a lexico-structural paraphrasing engine. KURA introduced the concept of phrase-based simplification which identifies then simplifies complex terms [5]. SIMPLIFICA [6] is another tool for producing simplified texts in Portuguese. It helps authors write simple texts for poor literate readers. The author writes a text and receives a simplified version. SIMPLIFICA uses lexical and syntactic simplification features to assist the readability of the text targeting Brazilian Portuguese. The tool performs simplification on the sentence level. Similarly, the PorSimples project [7] developed text adaptation tools for Brazilian Portuguese. The tools developed serve both people with poor literacy levels and authors who produce texts for this audience. It is one of the largest TS projects with three main systems and many types of simplification techniques investigated in [8]. Its main purpose is to increase the comprehension of written texts through the simplification of their linguistic structure. It replaces uncommon words with more usual words. It also changes the sentence syntactic structure to an easier form to avoid ambiguity. The Simplext project [9] develops tools that produce a simplified text for the Spanish language. It has a particular focus on producing applications of TS for dyslexic readers [8].

Another work [10] developed a pioneering TS model that can control the sentence level. It trained a TS model on a corpus of sentences with tags referring to 11 grade levels (2–12) [11]. The trained model generates sentences of a desired level specified by a tag attached to the input. This model controls the syntactic complexity but often produces difficult words for the target grade level [12]. It uses the Naive Bayes classifier from scikit-learn toolkit [13] with extra few features which could be improved. To enhance this TS work, an Auto-Regressive Transformers (AR) model is proposed [12] that controls the lexical complexity using weights. The model is trained on a dataset with weights added to training loss according to the levels of words from [10]. Therefore, it generates only the words with the desired level. Both [10,12] use only Sequence-to-Sequence (Seq2Seq) model as the main TS component.

Later, EDITOR was proposed [14] which is a Non Auto-Regressive transformer (NAR) where the decoder layer is used to apply a sequence of edits on the initial input sequence. The sequence can be empty or has repositioning and insertion commands. The model never learns to delete tokens from the source, instead learning to delete tokens inserted by the model. An enhanced version of this work is found [15] that identifies complex words from the source that are too complex for the target grade. These words are deleted from the initial sequence before getting refined by EDITOR. All these models [10,12,14,15] focus on grades "2–12" as the main levels to simplify to. Focusing on only 4 simplified versions gives more balanced dataset to train on.

There are other TS works that are developed for a specific domain. One of these domains is medical and biomedical fields using TS across many languages like English, Spanish, and French [16–19]. Another domain is the legal field. TS can be used to simplify legal documents for individuals to help in understand and comprehend any required legal text [20–23].

2.2. Deep Learning in Text Simplification

Deep Learning (DL) is the state-of-the-art approach for solving many NLP problems. It uses neural networks as the central component to process and analyze written text, then produce the output results. There are only few tools that we found for TS using DL techniques. DRESS [24] is one of the few NLP systems that provides a reinforcement learning-based TS model. It allows only one level of simplification instead of several simplified levels of a given text, as we do in our task.

Another state-of-the-art sentence simplification system that uses DL methods is EditNTS [25]. Its model learns explicit edit operations (ADD, DELETE, and KEEP) via a neural programmer-interpreter approach. It is trained to predict a series of edit operations for each word of the original complex sentence. Then, using this series of operations, it generates the simplified sentence. EditNTS favors generating short sentences with big semantic deviation [26]. It produces only one level of simplification, as all other simplification systems except the one we are proposing in this paper. However, we are able to train EditNTS on our data for multiple levels for comparison purposes.

3. Simplification Framework

3.1. Dataset

We use the Newsela Corpus that contains 10,786 documents with readability levels varying from 0 to 4 that targets students of grades between 2 and 12. The corpus contains 2154 original complex documents labeled with Level 0 which means that they are not simplified and they are difficult to read. For every complex document, it provides four simplified versions written by expert editors. Each version represents a readability level that varies from Level 1 (representing the first level of simplification) to Level 4 (the most readable version of the document). The higher the readability level number, the simpler the document text.

We used sentence alignment on Newsela dataset as found in [27], which uses a neural CRF model. The aligned pairs of sentences are labeled with the readability level of the target sentence. We excluded pairs that had non-English words or consisted less than three words in a sentence (not a proper complete sentence) and obtained 464,555 pairs of Newsela Aligned Sentences (hereafter, the NAS dataset).

We also classified more sentences to enrich our dataset. Several works were put together to help determine the text readability level [6,28–37]. However, we decided to use a DL classifier that classifies text into five readability levels (0–4) found in [38]. We modified the document classification features from that system by removing paragraph features in order to be able to classify the simplicity level of a text at the sentence level. Then we trained and tested the modified sentence classifiers on the NAS dataset (split into 80% for training and 20% for test) to find the best classification model. Table 1 shows the classification results on the sentence level. Similar to the document classification results, the best sentence classification model was using CNN classifier with an accuracy of 85.52%. Using the trained classifier against Wikipedia Corpus and Mechanical Turk Corpus, we produced 238,019 pairs of automatically Classified Simplified Sentences (hereafter CSS). We used CSS to augment the NAS dataset and obtained 702,574 pairs of sentences as our Augmented Simplification Dataset (hereafter ASD), in order to be able to provide more training data for our models. All three datasets are divided into four categories (level 1 to level 4) based on the readability level of the target sentences (simple sentences). For every category, we split the datasets into 90% for training (10% of it for validation) and 10% for test.

Table 1. Sentence classifiers results using aligned sentences.

Dataset	Classifier Model	Accuracy
Training (xval)	CNN	**85.69%**
	SVM	81.02%
	Random Forest	85.64%
Test	CNN	**85.52%**
	SVM	80.68%
	Random Forest	85.48%

3.2. Simplification Models

3.2.1. Seq2seq Model with Attention

We use the model Seq2Seq with Attention layer (S2SA) as a base for our work. Seq2seq models are used in solving most of text-to-text generation problems, including TS. The model takes a sequence of items (words) as an input, and generates another sequence of items as an output. The model consists at least two Recurrent Neural Networks (RNNs), an Encoder, and a Decoder [39]. A simple illustration of S2SA model we used in this work is shown in Figure 1 with a simplification sentence example. Our model uses Gated Recurrent Units (GRU) as RNN units, since GRU requires less memory units than Long Short Term Memory (LSTM); thus, it trains faster. Besides, according to [40], when using long text and a small dataset, GRU performance surpassed that of LSTM. Therefore, using GRU is more appropriate for our work. Both the encoder and the decoder have an embedding layer with 256 dimensions, 256 hidden states, GRUs unites with dropout equals to 10%, and a linear layer to pass the output through. To enhance the performance when dealing with long sentences, we added an attention layer [41] to the decoder to find where to focus for better-predicted outputs. The layer contains two linear layers with 256 hidden dimensions. With this layer, our S2SA model can deal with all sentences of any length without forgetting the source input.

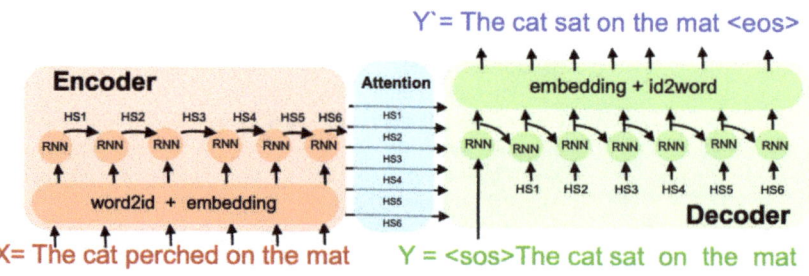

Figure 1. Illustration of S2SA model with a simple simplification example.

3.2.2. Reinforcement Learning

Reinforcement Learning (RL) is the state-of-the-art technology in DL for TS. To further boost our simplification model results, we used the S2SA model with Reinforcement Learning loop (S2SARL), Figure 2 shows a simple illustration of our RL model with an example. RL is a machine learning technique that enables an agent to learn in an interactive environment by trial and error using rewards earned from its own actions [42]. The main components of a RL system are the environment and the agent. We start the model by creating the vocabulary dictionary table using the words found in the dataset. Then for the agent, we set up our S2SA model introduced earlier in Section 3.2.1 to produce set of actions (words) using the dictionary table created. We initialized the reward, status, total loss, and the vocabulary dictionary table to zeros. Then we built a step function that uses the environment tools to perform a simplification for a given sentence (sequence of input words).

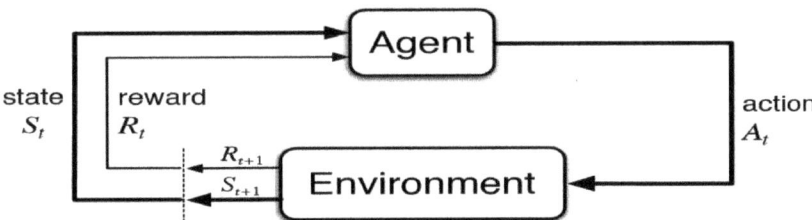

Figure 2. Simple Reinforcement Learning model.

After performing every step, the agent updates the reward, status, loss, and the vocabulary dictionary values with new values based on the predicted simplified sentence (sequence of actions).

To prepare the environment, we set up the *Target* Level number (1 to 4) and provide tools to help the agent during training like: observe current status, get all possible outputs for an action (predicted word), and give appropriate rewards based on a set of chosen actions (predicted simplified sentence). The reward value is determined by the readability level of the predicted sentence ($PrdS$). For every ($PrdS_t$), we use the adapted readability level classifier ($Rclf$) found in [38] to classify the $PrdS_t$ sentence into its readability level. Then we calculate the reward R_t as follows:

$$R_t = \begin{cases} -0.5 & \text{if } Rclf(PrdS_t) < Target \\ +2.0 & \text{if } Rclf(PrdS_t) == Target \\ +1.0 & \text{if } Rclf(PrdS_t) > Target \end{cases}$$

Using the reward function, if the predicted sentence readability level is less than the Targeted Level, the environment gives -0.5 as a penalty. This encourages the agent to predict simpler sentences for their next step. If the predicted sentence readability level matches the Targeted Level, the reward will be $+2.0$ to encourage the agent to keep this level of simplicity. However, if the output is too simple, i.e., the readability level is more than the Targeted Level, the reward will be only $+1.0$. Penalizing the agent with negative rewards for exceeding the Targeted Level did not improve the output. Yet giving a smaller reward like $+1.0$, improved the results.

Figure 3 shows the structure of our S2SARL model, with a simple simplification example. The RL loop aims to maximize the reward given to the agent at every step during training stage. Therefore, the agent chooses the actions that influence the environment to produce higher rewards. Our RL loop is different from the one in the DRESS system. It is designed specifically for our task of simplifying a sentence to a specified readability level.

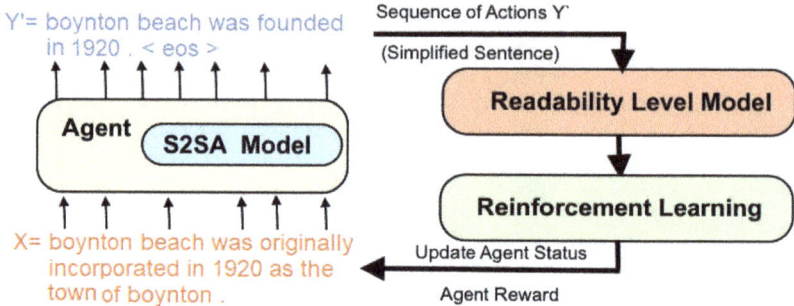

Figure 3. Illustration of S2SARL model with a simple simplification example.

3.3. Evaluation Method

To evaluate our work, we use EditNTS [25] as a notable simplification model to compare our work with. EditNTS uses DL to produce a series of edit operations (delete, keep, and add) to operate on the original sentence. The evaluation will consider 12 trained versions of each model: EditNTS, S2SA, and S2SARL. Each model will be trained against the datasets NAS, CSS, and ASD including the categories from Level 1 to Level 4 for each dataset.

After training each model, we report the results using System output Against References and against the Input sentence (SARI) and BiLingual Evaluation Understudy (BLEU) scores since they are popularly used in measuring the quality of TS models. SARI measures the simplicity of a sentence by focusing on the words added, deleted and kept [43]. While BLEU score is more related to the meaning preservation as shown in [44]. Then, we apply the 36 resulted trained models against one common test data. We choose the test part of the ASD dataset, Level 1 to Level 4, since they are not automatically classified and rather assigned by professional editors as mentioned in Section 3.1. We then compare the reported scores.

4. Experiments

4.1. Training and Testing

We train our simplification models S2SA and S2SARL along with EditNTS against every readability category, labeled from level 1 to level 4, from the training parts of NAS and CSS datasets. We also train them against ASD categories, which includes both NAS and CSS datasets as an augmented simplification dataset. To avoid memory problems due to the vocabulary dictionary size for each dataset, we use a batch size of 128 for training the models to level 1 and 4, and batch size of 64 for training the models to level 2 and 3. The number of epochs are set to 20 for training all the models over all four categories. We record SARI and BLEU scores for all the experiments to measure the simplification models' performance on the set aside test sets.

4.2. Examples of Generated Sentences

Examples of simplified sentences using the S2SARL model that was trained against NAS with targeted readability level 3 are shown in Table 2. Generated and target sentences could have the same words but with different word spelling, e.g., honour and honor. This is due to the available spelling found in the dictionary table during training phase. Also, some words are annotated as <unk> which means that the word was not present during training in the dictionary table.

Table 2. Simplified sentences using S2SARL trained against NAS and readability level set to 3.

Sentence	Text	Readability Level
Source	volterra is a town in the tuscany region of italy.	0
Target	volterra is a town in italy.	3
Predicted	volterra is a town in tuscany, <eos>	3
Source	he was appointed cbe in 1969.	0
Target	he was given the honour of cbe in 1969.	3
Predicted	he was given the honor of cbe in 1969. <eos>	3
Source	the seat of the district is the town of cossonay.	0
Target	the capital is the town of cossonay.	3
Predicted	the capital is the town of <unk>.<eos>	4
Source	punctuation, capitalization, and spacing are usually ignored, although some (such as "rats live on no evil star") include the spacing.	0
Target	rats live on no evil star.	3
Predicted	rats live on no evil star. <eos>	3

The S2SARL model aims to produce sentences with readability matching the target level. The table shows the readability level for the predicted sentences. Most of them are level 3 to match the target level as expected, but sometimes the sentence has higher readability level like level 4 in Table 2. That is due to the reward function in the RL loop introduced in Section 3.2.2. We did not penalize the agent for exceeding the target level, +2 for reaching target level and +1 when exceeding the level.

Comparing the performance of the two models S2SARL and S2SA, Table 3 shows the prediction of the two models using the CSS with readability level of 4. The table shows how S2SA sometimes produce sentences with lower readability level than we anticipated, which is level 4 in these sentences. This is because S2SA does not take into consideration the readability level when simplifying. Also, if we look at the Target sentences in Table 3 and compare it with the generated sentences, we see an improvement in the simplified sentences generated with S2SARL model compared with the ones generated with S2SA model.

Table 3. Simplification using S2SA and S2SARL with level 4 augmented data.

Sentence	Text	Readability Level
Source	thank you for your contributions.	
Target	thank you for your changes.	
S2SA	thank you for your changes. <eos>	4
S2SARL	thank you for your changes. <eos>	4
Source	the capital of the state is aracaju (pop 664,908).	
Target	the state 's capital is aracaju.	
S2SA	the capital of the state is . . <eos>	3
S2SARL	the capital of the state is aracaju. <eos>	4
Source	the birthstone for july would be a red ruby.	
Target	its birthstone is the ruby.	
S2SA	july 's birthstone is the ruby. <eos>	3
S2SARL	its birthstone is the ruby. <eos>	4
Source	boynton beach was originally incorporated in 1920 as the town of boynton.	
Target	boynton beach was founded in 1920.	
S2SA	boynton was part of the town of boynton. <eos>	4
S2SARL	boynton beach was founded in 1920. <eos>	4

4.3. Results

After training and validating the models, we apply them on the test data that was split from each dataset category. The results on the test data are shown in Tables 4–6. The tables show that S2SARL model always gives the best BLEU score compared with S2SA and EditNTS for all readability levels. However, when the dataset is small, like shown for level 1 and level 4 in Table 5, the S2SA model obtains better SARI scores. The model S2SARL gives better SARI results only when trained on a bigger dataset, and that is why we augmented the simplification dataset (to produce the ASD set). EditNTS prefers to generate short sentences with big semantic deviation. It usually deletes important information of the original sentences and generates shorter sentences, as discussed in [26]. This explains the low EditNTS scores in the tables.

Table 4. Test scores for TS models trained on Newsela Aligned Sentences (NAS) using NAS test data.

Dataset	Model	SARI	BLEU
To Level 1 5129 pairs	EditNTS S2SA S2SARL	26.48 **31.76** 31.57	65.23 65.61 **70.22**
To Level 2 9780 pairs	EditNTS S2SA S2SARL	20.62 27.18 **31.56**	46.81 53.95 **60.53**
To Level 3 13,922 pairs	EditNTS S2SA S2SARL	20.26 30.83 **32.27**	33.28 45.24 **53.85**
To Level 4 17,626 pairs	EditNTS S2SA S2SARL	23.21 31.69 **32.42**	23.97 42.60 **50.97**

Table 5. Test scores for TS models trained on Classified Simplified Sentences (CSS) using CSS test data.

Dataset	Model	SARI	BLEU
To Level 1 1350 pairs	EditNTS S2SA S2SARL	21.92 **28.12** 26.34	49.45 51.23 **67.67**
To Level 2 10,652 pairs	EditNTS S2SA S2SARL	21.89 30.97 **32.57**	49.30 65.79 **70.92**
To Level 3 9380 pairs	EditNTS S2SA S2SARL	17.12 31.56 **32.50**	35.13 59.26 **64.50**
To Level 4 2422 pairs	EditNTS S2SA S2SARL	21.60 **29.79** 29.36	27.35 65.78 **69.70**

Table 6. Test scores for TS models trained on Augmented Simplification Dataset (ASD) using ASD test data.

Dataset	Model	SARI	BLEU
To Level 1 6478 pairs	EditNTS S2SA S2SARL	25.32 **32.07** 30.75	61.25 69.18 **70.23**
To Level 2 20,432 pairs	EditNTS S2SA S2SARL	20.99 28.43 **32.30**	46.94 60.31 **65.22**
To Level 3 23,301 pairs	EditNTS S2SA S2SARL	19.89 30.67 **32.47**	33.77 50.24 **56.43**
To Level 4 20,048 pairs	EditNTS S2SA S2SARL	23.06 31.62 **32.62**	24.86 44.08 **51.10**

5. Comparison and Analysis

The TS models applied in this work (EditNTS, S2SA, and S2SARL) are trained on 12 different datasets: NAS (Level-1 to Level-4), CSS (Level-1 to Level-4), and ASD (Level-1 to Level-4). The experiments produced 36 trained models: 12 EditNTS, 12 S2SA, and 12 S2SARL models as shown in the Tables 4–6. To compare the performance of all those models, we test them on the same test data that should not include any automatically classified sentences as targets, i.e, CSS and ASD. Therefore, we tested all the models on the NAS test data (Level-1 to Level-4) since all its target sentences are classified and labeled by expert editors as explained in Section 3.1.

The test results are compared as shown in Table 7. Looking at the table, S2SARL model outperforms the other two simplification models across all readability levels. That is due to the involvement of the output sentence readability level during the training phase of the model (in the RL loop). As shown in Table 7, S2SARL models give the best BLEU scores across all four readability levels when trained with ASD since it is the largest simplification dataset (in term of the number of training sentence pairs) compared with NAS and CSS. However, for SARI scores, S2SARL models report the best scores throughout all four readability levels when trained against the CSS dataset. Although ASD is larger than CSS since it contains the CSS and the NAS datasets, training S2SARL model over ASD did not increase the SARI scores. This could be due to the alignment technique used for aligning Newsela sentences (NAS) in [27]. The alignment includes sentence splitting, merging, and paraphrasing with deletion which resulted in more meaningful sentences, while the sentences found in CSS do not include sentence splitting or merging.

To summarise the analysis, S2SARL gives better BLEU scores when trained with ASD (which includes CSS and NAS with sentence splitting, merging, and paraphrasing). That is because BLEU score focuses on grammar and meaning [18]. On the other hand, SARI score pays more attention to the lexical aspects of the sentences [43]. Therefore, S2SARL returns good SARI scores when trained against CSS only, where the lexical part is not changed as much compared with the NAS dataset.

Table 7. Testing 36 simplification models on ASD test data across all four readability levels. NAS: Newsela Aligned Sentences, CSS: Classified Simplified Sentences, and ASD: Augmented Simplification Dataset.

Test on NAS Level 1 (5129 Pairs)			
Trained on	Model	SARI	BLEU
NAS-Level1	EditNTS	26.48	65.23
	S2SA	31.76	65.61
	S2SARL	31.57	70.22
CSS-Level1	EditNTS	26.41	65.37
	S2SA	34.07	33.35
	S2SARL	**34.08**	36.25
ASD-Level1	EditNTS	26.81	65.70
	S2SA	31.36	73.11
	S2SARL	31.26	**76.47**
Test on NAS Level 2 (9780 pairs)			
Trained on	Model	SARI	BLEU
NAS-Level2	EditNTS	20.62	46.81
	S2SA	27.18	53.95
	S2SARL	31.56	60.53
CSS-Level2	EditNTS	15.66	46.15
	S2SA	31.36	35.07
	S2SARL	**32.51**	43.67
ASD-Level2	EditNTS	20.63	46.82
	S2SA	25.23	61.78
	S2SARL	31.73	**68.69**

Table 7. *Cont.*

Test on NAS Level 3 (13,922 pairs)			
Trained on	Model	SARI	BLEU
NAS-Leve3	EditNTS	20.26	33.28
	S2SA	30.83	45.24
	S2SARL	32.27	53.85
CSS-Leve3	EditNTS	15.72	32.36
	S2SA	33.23	23.30
	S2SARL	**33.24**	23.27
ASD-Leve3	EditNTS	20.52	33.77
	S2SA	32.21	52.96
	S2SARL	32.23	**61.88**
Test on NAS Level 4 (17,626 pairs)			
Trained on	Model	SARI	BLEU
NAS-Leve4	EditNTS	23.21	23.97
	S2SA	31.69	42.60
	S2SARL	32.42	50.97
CSS-Leve4	EditNTS	12.71	24.22
	S2SA	33.23	12.32
	S2SARL	**33.24**	12.41
ASD-Leve4	EditNTS	23.32	24.86
	S2SA	32.31	61.22
	S2SARL	32.32	**61.38**

6. Limitations

Working on a dataset that consists four levels of simplification was limited to the sentences available by Newsela dataset. Although we automatically augmented the dataset with more labeled simplified sentences, it would be more efficient if we work on a larger dataset labeled by expert users like Newsela. Also, applying reinforcement learning during training phase is time-consuming compared with a plain S2SA model. Therefore, we applied only one method to reward the agent using the output readability level.

7. Conclusions and Future Work

The goal of our simplification method was to produce simple sentences at a certain readability level using DL models. We used aligned sentences from the Newsela dataset (NAS) and augmented the corpus with automatically classified sentences from the Wikipedia and the Mechanical Turk datasets (CSS), creating a novel augmented simplification dataset (ASD) that we used later for simplification. Then we created the simplification models, S2SA and S2SARL, where the S2SARL model employs the readability level as part of the simplification process using the reinforcement learning loop to produce simplified sentence to the desired readability level. We trained EditNTS and the created models with the same datasets NAS, CSS, and ASD, to compare their performance. We found that S2SARL always outperform the other two models for every dataset used. We also compared all the simplification models (S2SA, S2SARL, and EditNTS), that were trained on different datasets, by testing them on the same test data, the test part of NAS. The results of SARI and BLEU scores were compared and analysed.

Our work brings novelty in the area of TS in the way we train our deep leaning models using augmented data, and in the way we perform the reinforcement leaning loop using a readability classifier.

In future work, other evaluation measures could be incorporated in the RL loop as a part of the reward function, for example the SARI score to measure simplicity, or the cosine between the generated and and the target sentences vectors to measure their similarity, in addition to the readability level given by the classifier. Also, the simplification models could be trained on paragraph level using the Newsela aligned paragraphs. Another direction of future work is to develop a similar system for other languages, for specific level of simplification targeted.

Author Contributions: W.A. wrote the article and implemented and tested the system. D.I. helped with the design and with revisions to the article. All authors have read and agreed to the published version of the manuscript

Funding: The first author was funded by the Research Center of College of Computer and Information Sciences, Deanship of Scientific Research in King Saud University; and the second author was funded by the Natural Science and Engineering Research Council of Canada (NSERC).

Data Availability Statement: We are making our dataset available to other researchers, upon request.

Conflicts of Interest: The authors declare no conflict of interest.

References

1. Newsela Inc. Newsela Dataset. 2019. Available online: http://newsela.com/data/ (accessed on 1 May 2020).
2. Wubben, S.; Van Den Bosch, A.; Krahmer, E. Sentence simplification by monolingual machine translation. In Proceedings of the 50th Annual Meeting of the Association for Computational Linguistics (Volume 1: Long Papers), Jeju Island, Republic of Korea, 8–14 July 2012; pp. 1015–1024.
3. Narayan, S.; Gardent, C. Hybrid simplification using deep semantics and machine translation. In Proceedings of the 52nd Annual Meeting of the Association for Computational Linguistics, Baltimore, MD, USA, 23–24 June 2014; pp. 435–445.
4. Takahashi, T.; Iwakura, T.; Iida, R.; Fujita, A.; Inui, K. KURA: A transfer-based lexico-structural para-phrasing engine. In Proceedings of the 6th Natural Language Processing Pacific Rim Symposium (NLPRS 2001) Workshop on Automatic Paraphrasing: Theories and Applications, Tokyo, Japan, 27–30 November 2001; pp. 37–46.
5. Inui, K.; Fujita, A.; Takahashi, T.; Iida, R.; Iwakura, T. Text Simplification for Reading Assistance: A Project Note. In Proceedings of the Second International Workshop on Paraphrasing-Volume 16, Sapporo, Japan, 11 July 2003; Association for Computational Linguistics: Stroudsburg, PA, USA, 2003; PARAPHRASE '03, pp. 9–16. [CrossRef]
6. Scarton, C.; de Oliveira, M.; Candido, A.; Gasperin, C.; Aluísio, S.M. SIMPLIFICA: A tool for authoring simplified texts in Brazilian Portuguese guided by readability assessments. In Proceedings of the NAACL HLT 2010 Demonstration Session, Los Angeles, CA, USA, 2 June 2010.
7. Aluisio, S.; Gasperin, C. PorSimples: Simplification of Portuguese Texts Fostering Digital Inclusion and Accessibility. In Proceedings of the NAACL HLT 2010 Young Investigators Workshop on Computational Approaches to Languages of the Americas, Los Angeles, CA, USA, 6 June 2010.
8. Shardlow, M. A Survey of Automated Text Simplification. *Int. J. Adv. Comput. Sci. Appl.* **2014**, *4*, 58–70. [CrossRef]
9. Saggion, H.; Gómez-Martínez, E.; Etayo, E.; Anula, A.; Bourg, L. Text Simplification in Simplext. Making Text More Accessible. *Proces. Leng. Nat.* **2011**, *47*, 341–342.
10. Scarton, C.; Specia, L. Learning simplifications for specific target audiences. In Proceedings of the 56th Annual Meeting of the Association for Computational Linguistics (Volume 2: Short Papers), Melbourne, Australia, 15–20 July 2018; pp. 712–718.
11. Xu, W.; Callison-Burch, C.; Napoles, C. Problems in Current Text Simplification Research: New Data Can Help. *Trans. Assoc. Comput. Linguist.* **2015**, *3*, 283–297. [CrossRef]
12. Nishihara, D.; Kajiwara, T.; Arase, Y. Controllable text simplification with lexical constraint loss. In Proceedings of the 57th Annual Meeting of the Association for Computational Linguistics: Student Research Workshop, Florence, Italy, 28 July–2 August 2019; pp. 260–266.
13. Pedregosa, F.; Varoquaux, G.; Gramfort, A.; Michel, V.; Thirion, B.; Grisel, O.; Blondel, M.; Prettenhofer, P.; Weiss, R.; Dubourg, V.; et al. Scikit-learn: Machine learning in Python. *J. Mach. Learn. Res.* **2011**, *12*, 2825–2830.
14. Xu, W.; Carpuat, M. EDITOR: An edit-based transformer with repositioning for neural machine translation with soft lexical constraints. *Trans. Assoc. Comput. Linguist.* **2021**, *9*, 311–328. [CrossRef]
15. Agrawal, S.; Xu, W.; Carpuat, M. A non-autoregressive edit-based approach to controllable text simplification. In Proceedings of the Findings of the Association for Computational Linguistics: ACL-IJCNLP 2021, Online Event, 1–6 August 2021; pp. 3757–3769.
16. Štajner, S. Automatic text simplification for social good: Progress and challenges. In Proceedings of the Findings of the Association for Computational Linguistics: ACL-IJCNLP 2021, Online Event, 1–6 August 2021; pp. 2637–2652.
17. Van, H.; Kauchak, D.; Leroy, G. AutoMeTS: The autocomplete for medical text simplification. *arXiv* **2020**, arXiv:2010.10573.
18. Van den Bercken, L.; Sips, R.J.; Lofi, C. Evaluating neural text simplification in the medical domain. In Proceedings of the World Wide Web Conference, San Francisco, CA, USA, 13–17 May 2019; pp. 3286–3292.
19. Cardon, R.; Grabar, N. French biomedical text simplification: When small and precise helps. In Proceedings of the 28th International Conference on Computational Linguistics, Online, 8–13 December 2020.
20. Collantes, M.; Hipe, M.; Sorilla, J.L.; Tolentino, L.; Samson, B. Simpatico: A text simplification system for senate and house bills. In Proceedings of the 11th National Natural Language Processing Research Symposium, Manila, Philippines, 24–25 April 2015; pp. 26–32.
21. Bhatia, V.K. Simplification v. easification—The case of legal texts1. *Appl. Linguist.* **1983**, *4*, 42–54. [CrossRef]

22. Garimella, A.; Sancheti, A.; Aggarwal, V.; Ganesh, A.; Chhaya, N.; Kambhatla, N. Text Simplification for Legal Domain:{I}nsights and Challenges. In Proceedings of the Natural Legal Language Processing Workshop, Abu Dhabi, United Arab Emirates, 8 December 2022; pp. 296–304.
23. Rubab, I. Investigating the Effect of Text Simplification to Speed the Justice in Pakistan. Ph.D. Thesis, Islamia University, Bahawalpur, Pakistan, 2018.
24. Zhang, X.; Lapata, M. Sentence Simplification with Deep Reinforcement Learning. In Proceedings of the 2017 Conference on Empirical Methods in Natural Language Processing, Copenhagen, Denmark, 7–11 September 2017; Association for Computational Linguistics: Copenhagen, Denmark, 2017; pp. 584–594. [CrossRef]
25. Dong, Y.; Li, Z.; Rezagholizadeh, M.; Cheung, J.C.K. EditNTS: An neural programmer-interpreter model for sentence simplification through explicit editing. *arXiv* **2019**, arXiv:1906.08104.
26. Lin, X.W.Z.; Wan, X. Neural sentence simplification with semantic dependency information. In Proceedings of the AAAI Workshop on Deep Learning on Graphs: Methods and Applications, Virtual, 28 February 2021.
27. Jiang, C.; Maddela, M.; Lan, W.; Zhong, Y.; Xu, W. Neural CRF model for sentence alignment in text simplification. *arXiv* **2020**, arXiv:2005.02324.
28. Kincaid, J.P.; Fishburne, R.P.J.; Rogers, R.L.; Chissom, B.S. *Derivation of New Readability Formulas (Automated Readability Index, Fog Count and Flesch Reading Ease Formula) for Navy Enlisted Personnel*; Technical Report; Institute for Simulation and Training, University of Central Florida: Millington, TN, USA, 1975.
29. Gunning, R. The Fog Index After Twenty Years. *J. Bus. Commun.* **1969**, *6*, 3–13.
30. Aluisio, S.; Specia, L.; Gasperin, C.; Scarton, C. Readability assessment for text simplification. In Proceedings of the NAACL HLT 2010 Fifth Workshop on Innovative Use of NLP for Building Educational Applications, Association for Computational Linguistics, Los Angeles, CA, USA, 5 June 2010; pp. 1–9.
31. Bessou, S.; Chenni, G. Efficient Measuring of Readability to Improve Documents Accessibility for Arabic Language Learners. *arXiv* **2021**, arXiv:2109.08648.
32. Marvin Imperial, J.; Ong, E. Under the Microscope: Interpreting Readability Assessment Models for Filipino. *arXiv* **2021**, arXiv:2110.00157.
33. Yeakel, K.; Tzeng, S. *Autograder: Classifying Documents to Grade School Level*; Stanford University: Stanford, CA, USA, 2019.
34. Štajner, S.; Ponzetto, S.P.; Stuckenschmidt, H. Automatic assessment of absolute sentence complexity. In Proceedings of the 26th International Joint Conference on Artificial Intelligence, Melbourne, Australia, 19–25 August 2017; Volume 17, pp. 4096–4102.
35. Larson, R.R. Introduction to Information Retrieval. *J. Am. Soc. Inf. Sci. Technol.* **2010**, *61*, 852–853.
36. Giovanelli, C.; Liu, X.; Sierla, S.; Vyatkin, V.; Ichise, R. Towards an aggregator that exploits big data to bid on frequency containment reserve market. In Proceedings of the IECON 2017-43rd Annual Conference of the IEEE Industrial Electronics Society, Beijing, China, 29 October–1 November 2017; pp. 7514–7519. [CrossRef]
37. Li, H. Deep learning for natural language processing: Advantages and challenges. *Natl. Sci. Rev.* **2018**, *5*, 24–26. [CrossRef]
38. Alkaldi, W.; Inkpen, D. Classifying Documents to Multiple Readability levels. In Proceedings of the AAAI 2021 Spring Symposium on Artificial Intelligence for K-12 Education, Virtual, 22–24 March 2021.
39. Sojasingarayar, A. Seq2Seq AI Chatbot with Attention Mechanism. *arXiv* **2020**, arXiv:2006.02767. Available online: http://xxx.lanl.gov/abs/2006.02767 (accessed on 1 January 2021).
40. Yang, S.; Yu, X.; Zhou, Y. LSTM and GRU Neural Network Performance Comparison Study: Taking Yelp Review Dataset as an Example. In Proceedings of the 2020 International Workshop on Electronic Communication and Artificial Intelligence (IWECAI), Shanghai, China, 12–14 June 2020; pp. 98–101. [CrossRef]
41. Luong, M.T.; Pham, H.; Manning, C.D. Effective approaches to attention-based neural machine translation. *arXiv* **2015**, arXiv:1508.04025.
42. Sutton, R.S.; Barto, A.G. *Reinforcement Learning: An Introduction*; MIT Press: Cambridge, MA, USA, 2018.
43. Alva-Manchego, F.; Martin, L.; Scarton, C.; Specia, L. EASSE: Easier Automatic Sentence Simplification Evaluation. In *Proceedings of the 2019 Conference on Empirical Methods in Natural Language Processing and the 9th International Joint Conference on Natural Language Processing (EMNLP-IJCNLP): System Demonstrations*; Association for Computational Linguistics: Hong Kong, China, 2019; pp. 49–54. [CrossRef]
44. Xu, W.; Napoles, C.; Pavlick, E.; Chen, Q.; Callison-Burch, C. Optimizing Statistical Machine Translation for Text Simplification. *Trans. Assoc. Comput. Linguist.* **2016**, *4*, 401–415. [CrossRef]

Disclaimer/Publisher's Note: The statements, opinions and data contained in all publications are solely those of the individual author(s) and contributor(s) and not of MDPI and/or the editor(s). MDPI and/or the editor(s) disclaim responsibility for any injury to people or property resulting from any ideas, methods, instructions or products referred to in the content.

Article

Multilingual Multi-Target Stance Recognition in Online Public Consultations

Valentin Barriere [1,*] and Alexandra Balahur [2]

1. Centro Nacional de Inteligencia Artificial, Santiago 4860, Chile
2. European Commission, Joint Research Center, 1050 Bruxelles, Belgium
* Correspondence: valentin.barriere@cenia.cl

Abstract: Machine Learning is an interesting tool for stance recognition in a large-scale context, in terms of data size, but also regarding the topics and themes addressed or the languages employed by the participants. Public consultations of citizens using online participatory democracy platforms offer this kind of setting and are good use cases for automatic stance recognition systems. In this paper, we propose to use three datasets of public consultations, in order to train a model able to classify the stance of a citizen within a text, towards a proposal or a debate question. We studied stance detection in several contexts: using data from an online platform without interactions between users, using multilingual data from online debates that are in one language, and using data from online intra-multilingual debates, which can contain several languages inside the same unique debate discussion. We propose several baselines and methods in order to take advantage of the different available data, by comparing the results of models using out-of-dataset annotations, and binary or ternary annotations from the target dataset. We finally proposed a self-supervised learning method to take advantage of unlabelled data. We annotated both the datasets with ternary stance labels and made them available.

Keywords: stancerecognition; multilingual models; online debates; public consultations; natural language processing; transformers

MSC: 68T50

Citation: Barriere, V.; Balahur, A. Multilingual Multi-Target Stance Recognition in Online Public Consultations *Mathematics* **2023**, *11*, 2161. https://doi.org/10.3390/math11092161

Academic Editor: Florentina Hristea

Received: 21 February 2023
Revised: 29 March 2023
Accepted: 14 April 2023
Published: 4 May 2023

Copyright: © 2023 by the authors. Licensee MDPI, Basel, Switzerland. This article is an open access article distributed under the terms and conditions of the Creative Commons Attribution (CC BY) license (https://creativecommons.org/licenses/by/4.0/).

1. Introduction

Stance recognition is a Natural Language Processing (NLP) task that has as its objective the automatic detection and classification of the opinions and attitudes expressed by users in different languages on a wide range of topics. The task has gained momentum in Natural Language Processing during the past few years. As such, different methods have been proposed to tackle it, and various corpora have been developed and employed to train and test stance recognition classification models. Additionally, the increasing availability of multilingual online platforms and social media platforms such as the *"Conference for the Future of Europe"* and other large-scale citizen consultation projects such as *Decidim* (https://decidim.org/, accessed on 20 February 2023) or *Make.org* (https://make.org/, accessed on 20 February 2023) have led to a growing need for methods to analyse and understand the attitudes and opinions expressed in multiple languages. These platforms provide a unique opportunity to study public opinion on political, societal, and economic issues, which are becoming increasingly important in the context of participatory democracy.

The analysis of multilingual online debates has the potential to provide valuable insights into the attitudes and opinions of citizens from different backgrounds, as well as to identify commonalities and differences among these attitudes across languages and cultures. Furthermore, it can also provide a means to identify and address potential language barriers in democratic processes, by fostering more significant participation in these processes with citizens from different geographical, sociological, and cultural backgrounds. Nevertheless, there remains a series of important aspects related to this task that have not yet been tackled in the literature. The work presented in this article and the corresponding contributions is motivated by the need to fill existing gaps in research on stance classification, in view of a real-life application of this task in a large-scale citizen consultation project.

Stance recognition algorithms are of interest for multiple reasons. They can be easily deployed on social media or debating platforms [1]. They are heavily used for misinformation and disinformation detection [2–4], but also to predict poll results [5], users polarisation [6], or in order to analyse citizen contributions in a consultation project [7]. Another essential aspect of stance detection is the use of rhetorical strategies, such as hedging, attributions, or denials, that can be used to display varying degrees of certainty or uncertainty [8]. These strategies are particularly relevant in the context of political discourse, where participants may use them to express their stance in a nuanced manner.

Many of the works have focused on data from Twitter, incorporating conversational and interactional context [9,10] in order to better classify the stances of the users in a thread of tweets or simply by taking the tweets in an independent way [11–14]. The SemEval-2017 task 8 [15] proposes to use the interactional context of Twitter threads, focusing on rumour-oriented stance classification, where the objective is to identify support towards a rumour and an entire statement, rather than individual target concepts.

Foundation works were made before Twitter, and hence based on online debate websites [16–18] or more rarely on Congress [19]. The authors proposed to model the text using linguistics features, crafted regarding the targets of the stances, that were fixed, pre-defined, and opposed, such as *"Windows vs. Mac"*. Typical debates were also created around hot social topics in the form of ideological debates on subjects such as *"public healthcare"* or *"gun control"* [17], but also on playful ones such as *"cats"* vs. *"dogs"* [20]. Most of those papers were about hybrid methods mixing statistical learning tools with high-level linguistic features [21,22]. Since then, the conversation has been integrated with graphical models that allow taking into account its dynamics [22–24] through the different successive speech turns of the participants. Neural networks [12,25–27] fall into this type of model and can even be pre-trained for the conversation setting [10] to understand better the conversational context to analyse stances in Twitter threads.

Recently, there have been a few efforts to tackle multilingual stance recognition. Lai et al. [28] presented a model for stance analysis over tweets using mainly high-level linguistic features scuh as stylistic, structural, affective, or contextual knowledge, but no dense contextual vectors. Hardalov et al. [29] proposed a few-shot cross-lingual neural model by aggregating different language datasets together. The TW-10 Referendum Dataset [30] contains tweets in Catalan and Spanish with stance annotation towards the independence of Catalonia. All of them are tweet datasets.

Stance-annotated datasets containing highly varying targets are rare. They usually focus on a set of defined targets or concepts [14,29]. Building on seminal work on stance, the SemEval 2016 task [11] was capable of targeting abstract concepts (e.g., *"atheism"* or *"abortion"*), as well as persons (e.g., *"Hillary Clinton"* or *"Donald Trump"*). One example of a dataset with highly varying targets is Stanceosaurus [31], which contains tweets in English, Hindi, and Arabic annotated with stance towards 251 misinformation claims over a diverse set of global and regional topics. Sobhani et al. [32] proposed multi-target stance classification that includes two targets per instance, such as classifying the stances of a tweet in relation to both Sanders and Trump. While the framework permits more than two targets, it is still limited to a specific and defined set of targets. It has been extended when the targets can be a written concept or proposal [12,33]. Finally, Deng et al. [34] proposed complex models for cross-target stance recognition, applied to a small set of specific targets.

In Vamvas and Sennrich [33], the authors proposed the X-stance dataset, containing 67k comments over 150 political issues in three languages. Their approach was to reformulate the target in a natural question in order to train one multilingual multi-target model on the entire dataset easily. Similarly, in the *procon* dataset, containing 6019 comments over 419 controversial issues, each target was also reformulated as a question [35]. This allows using the semantic knowledge encoded inside a pre-trained language model [36] and implicitly captures relationships between topics [25]. Hardalov et al. [37] combined this technique with label embedding [38] in order to train on 16 English datasets from various domains. However, none of these datasets contain interactional data from multilingual online political debates. On the contrary, Barriere et al. [39] presented the **Debating Europe (DE)** dataset, a multi-target, multi-lingual stance classification over online debates, integrating the interactional context inside a model. In all the presented works, the language of the comments and propositions is the same, which can be seen as *intra-monolingual*. Finally, Barriere and Jacquet [7] presented the **CoFE** dataset, which was collected from an online debating platform that contains 4.2k proposals and 20k comments in various languages. A particularity of this dataset is that the comments and the propositions in the same discussion can be written in different languages because of the use of a machine translation system on the online platform, making it *intra-multilingual*.

Another classical issue is that, when the labels are scarce because of the difficulty or time needed to annotate, it is possible to use several techniques to take advantage of the available resources [40]. Hardalov et al. [29] proposed a novel noisy sentiment-based stance detection pre-training leveraging Wikipedia data, for cross-language few-shot learning. Semi-supervised learning methods such as self-training [41], label propagation, or label spreading [42,43] are also profitable options. Giasemidis et al. [44] used the latter methods for rumour-related stance recognition over Twitter data. A recent work on the domain is that of [45], which used knowledge distillation on COVID tweets for the same type of task. On other types of data, Wei et al. [46] proposed an interesting self-training method for imbalanced images on CIFAR, but they assumed the distributions of the unlabelled and labelled datasets were the same, which is a strong assumption that is not true every time.

In this work, we focused on studying models that analyse the stances of a comment on a target formulated in natural language, not necessarily with the same language. This setting makes the task more difficult due to the high variability in terms of topics and in terms of languages. It is also important to note that restricting a dataset to one language could induce nationality or cultural bias. To the best of the authors' knowledge, having several different languages inside the same online debate is specific and could only be found in the literature in [7]. Here, we address the problem of ternary stance classification, i.e., whether a comment is *pro*, *against*, or *other* towards the proposal it is commenting on. Moreover, we propose to use two approaches to learn even with limited labels: a pre-training over other similar datasets [40] and a semi-supervised learning self-training method [41] to take advantage of large available datasets that are not annotated.

This research aimed to contribute to the field of multilingual stance recognition by addressing the challenges and opportunities presented by analysing online multilingual debates. In particular, the paper focuses on developing models and methods for recognising the stance of users in different languages on a given topic and how to make use of the cross-lingual information present in the debates. Section 2 refers to the three stance datasets mainly used in this work and especially the collection and annotation of two of them. Section 3 refers to the Machine Learning experiments and Section 4 to the results and discussions of these experiments.

2. Materials and Methods

In this section, we describe all the datasets we used in our experiments, the methods employed to collect and annotate them when applicable, as well as the details of the training models. The datasets used were the X-stance dataset [33], the Debating Europe dataset [39], and the CoFE dataset [7].

2.1. Debating Europe Dataset

We released the Debating Europe (DE) dataset, composed of online debates annotated with stance annotations at the comment level.

2.1.1. Data Extraction

The DE dataset consists of debates collected in September 2020 from the *"Debating Europe"* platform (https://www.debatingeurope.eu/, accessed on 20 February 2023). Most of the debates revolve around questions such as *"Should we have a European healthcare system?"* or *"Do the benefits of nuclear power outweigh the risks?"*, which can typically be rephrased as yes/no questions. Each debate includes a topic tag, a text paragraph providing the context of the debate, and comments about either the main context or previous comments.

We used a scraped version of the *"Debating Europe"* website containing all the debate questions with their associated presentation texts, comments, and replies to comments. Examples of conversations can be seen in Figure 1.

The dataset contains 125,798 comments for 1406 debates. Additional statistics are provided in Table 1. More information about the general distribution of the words is available in Appendix B, Table A1.

Table 1. Low-level statistics on the DE dataset, regarding the presence or absence of label annotation. μ_{com}/μ_{deb} is the average mean of the respective units (comments or words) at the comment/debate level.

Label	% DE	Unit	μ_{com}	μ_{deb}	Σ
✗	100%	Comments	∅	89.5	125,798
		Words	51.7	4623	6,499,625
✓	2.0%	Comments	∅	140	2523
		Words	33.4	4683	84,289

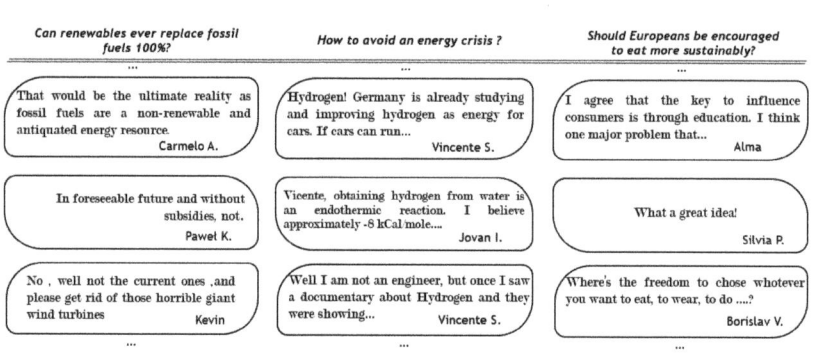

Figure 1. Examples of comments from 3 debates of the Debating Europe Dataset.

2.1.2. Annotation

Subset Selection

We annotated 18 debates from the entire dataset scraped from Debating Europe. The criteria for selecting these debates were the number of comments associated with each debate and their relevance to one or more of the new *"European Green Deal"* policy areas. These policy areas are biodiversity, from farm to fork, sustainable agriculture, clean energy, sustainable industry, building and renovating, sustainable mobility, eliminating pollution, and climate action. More information is available online (https://tinyurl.com/GreenDealEC, accessed on 20 February 2023).

To filter the debates, we used the metadata from the *"Debating Europe"* website, keeping only those with the *"Greener"* tag, resulting in 150 debates. Finally, we selected the ones with at least 25 comments. When necessary, the debate question was reformulated into a closed question to make it compatible with our framework. Additional information about the debates and policy areas can be found in the Appendix A.

Annotation Scheme

The annotation scheme and guidelines were developed to identify citizens' stance toward the debate question at the comment level. To achieve this, four labels were defined: *Yes*, *No*, *Neutral*, and *Not answering*. Each comment was annotated to indicate whether the user responded to the answer and, if so, whether they were in favour of, against, or neutral with respect to the original question. The questions of the annotated debates can be found in Appendix A. The annotation task was carried out by a single expert using the INCEpTION software [47].

Final Annotations

We obtained 2523 labels for the 18 debates, with four classes: *Yes* (40.1%), *No* (19.4%), *Neutral* (11.2%), and *Not answering* (29.3%). We included the last category to determine whether the commenter was interested in answering the debate question. In the following experiments, we merged the *Neutral* and *Not answering* classes into a single class to simplify the work [11,48]. Since a single expert performed the annotation, validating the dataset using classical inter-annotator agreement metrics was impossible. Instead, we validated the dataset by demonstrating its usefulness for cross-datasets, cross-topics, and cross-lingual transfer learning. The results are presented in Section 3.1.1. The annotated dataset consisted of 2523 comments, totalling 84,289 words. Additional information about the overall distribution of words can be found in Table 1 and in Appendix B, Table A1.

2.2. CoFE

We released the CoFE dataset, which is composed of multilingual online debates over contemporary hot topics. It has been partially annotated in stance at the comment level by the commenters themselves when they were posting their comments or by external coders afterwards. The text of the proposals and comments have been automatically translated so that participants can interact with each other in their native languages. Here, we present the data collection process and the annotation plus the validation of the annotation, used to create the several subdatasets used in this study: CF_S, CF_U, CF_{E-D}, and CF_{E-T}.

2.2.1. CoFE Participatory Democracy Platform

The raw data used in this study consisted of current questions being debated at the Conference on the Future of Europe (CoFE) (https://futureu.europa.eu/?locale=en, accessed on 20 February 2023). The CoFE is an online platform where users can write proposals in any of the EU24 languages (and more: Catalan and Esperanto have been observed to be used on the platform). Users can also comment on and endorse proposals or like other comments. All texts are automatically translated into any of the EU24 languages.

The dataset includes more than 20,000 comments on 4200 proposals in 26 languages, with English, German, and French being the most-commonly used languages on the platform. The language distribution is shown in Figure 2.

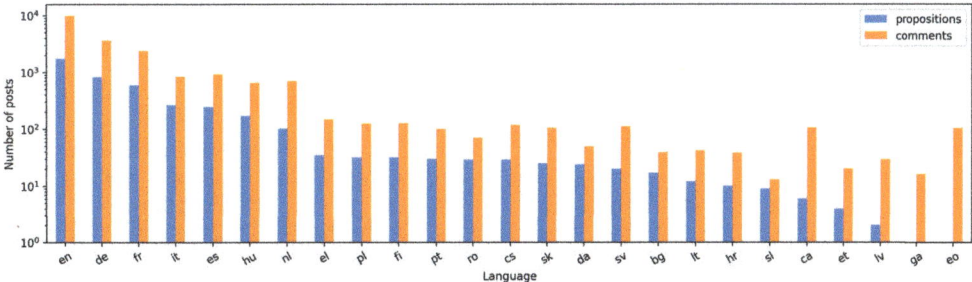

Figure 2. Number of posts and comments per language, using ISO 3166-1 (https://en.wikipedia.org/wiki/ISO_3166-1, accessed on 20 February 2023) alpha-2 country codes.

The proposals in the dataset have been dispatched into one of ten topics by the participants, as shown in Figure 3. As can be seen in the figure, some topics, such as *"European Democracy"* and *"Values, Rights, and Security"* have generated more discussion than others. The topic with the largest number of proposals is *"Climate Change and the Environment"*. Table 2 provides examples of the proposals, comments, and stance labels.

Table 2. Examples of comments and proposals with the associated stance (url links in the appendix).

Title	Topic	Proposal	Comment	Stance	Url
Focus on Anti-Aging and Longevity research	Health	The EU has presented their green paper on ageing, and correctly named the aging…	The idea of prevention being better than a cure is nothing new or revolutionary. Rejuvenation…	Pro	
Set up a program for returnable food packaging…	Climate change and the environment	The European Union could set up a program for returnable food packaging made from…	Bringing our own packaging to stores could also be a very good option. People would be…	Pro	
Impose an IQ or arithmetic-logic test to immigrants	Migration	We should impose an IQ test or at least several cognitive tests making sure immigrants have…	On ne peut pas trier les migrants par un simple score sur les capacités cognitives. Certains fuient la guerre et vous…	Against	
Un Président de la Commission directement élu…	European democracy	Les élections, qu'elles soient présidentielles ou législatives, sont au coeur du processus…	I prefer sticking with a representative system and have the President of the…	Against	
Europa sí, pero no así	Values and rights, rule of law, security	En los últimos años, las naciones que forman parte de la UE han visto como su soberanía ha sido…	Zdecydowanie nie zgadzam się z pomysłem, aby interesy indywidualnych Państw miały…	Against	

2.2.2. Online Debates with Intra-Multilingual Interactions

The CoFE dataset includes long debates with comments organised into threads, allowing for the study of interactions between users responding to each other in different languages. The full dataset consists of 4247 debates with a total of over 15,961 threads, including 1 to 4 comments in response to each other and 5085 threads with 2 or more comments. The distribution of threads by length is shown in Table 3. The debates have generated a range of interests among the participants, with 3576 debates containing 5 comments or fewer and 382 debates having 10 or more comments, reaching a total of 11,942 comments.

In terms of multilingual aspects, more than 40% of the proposal/comment pairs, as well as 46% of the threads include at least two languages, and 684 debates contain three or more distinct languages. Finally, the dataset also includes the number of likes and dislikes for each comment and the number of endorsements for each proposal (a user can endorse a proposal without commenting).

Table 3. Number of threads regarding their length in term of comments.

Length	1	2	3	4	All
Number	10,876	2365	1920	800	15,961

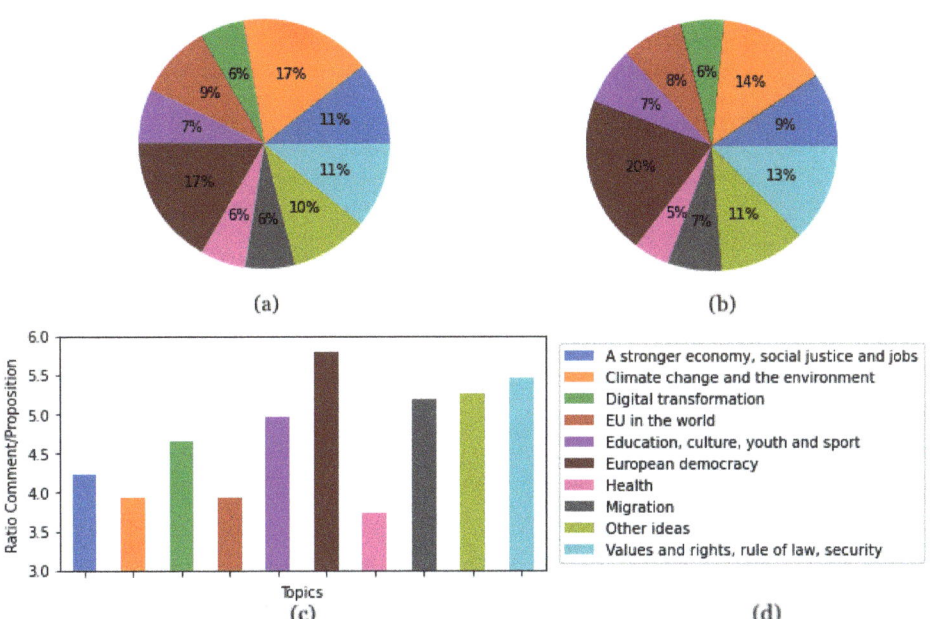

Figure 3. Topics' distribution in the propositions (**a**), comments (**b**), and the ratio of comments over propositions (**c**) regarding the differnt topics (**d**).

2.2.3. Annotation

A portion of the data (more than 7 k comments, in 24 languages) has already been annotated by the commenters with a self-tag assessing whether they are in favour of or against the proposal. We refer to this set as CF_S (as Self-annotated). Two other subparts of the data (without a self-tag) have been manually annotated: one to be used for testing purposes and another one to be used for training purposes. The subset of 1283 comments in six morphologically different languages (fr, de, en, el, it, hu) was tagged using the Inception platform [47]. We refer to this set as CF_{E-T} (as Externally annotated-Test). Another subset of 1500 comments in the most-common languages of the platform (fr, de, en, es) was tagged by using the Inception platform [47]. We refer to this set as CF_{E-D} (as Externally annotated-Test).

Annotation Scheme

Annotating the stance of a comment on an entire proposition can be challenging, in particular when the participant expresses multiple stances within his/her comment. To address this issue, we asked the coders to label not only the prominent stance of the comment, but also any secondary stance they believed to be present. This allows for the consideration of cases where multiple contradictory stances are present within the same comment in order to determine the stance that is most-commonly agreed upon by the coders. In the end, the secondary stances were used to aggregate in 1.0% of the cases.

For CF_{E-T}, we collected a total of 3814 annotations that were distributed among 15 different people. More than 95% of the examples were tagged three times, and the others were tagged two times only. For CF_{E-D}, we collected a total of 3500 annotations that were distributed among four different people. The French and English comments (1000 comments) were tagged three times, and the German and Spanish (300 + 200 comments) were tagged by only one annotator, which is reliable since they were not used for testing purposes. We manually removed four proposals that were not real debates and 61 of the 200 annotated Spanish comments that were judged of bad quality.

Annotation Validation and Aggregation

The inter-annotator agreement for a three-class stance annotation task was evaluated using Krippendorff's α [49] using only the prominent stance annotations. It yielded a value of 0.68 for $CF_{E\text{-}T}$, which is considered satisfactory for this type of task. It should be noted that the level of agreement among annotators can vary greatly depending on the specific target of the stance detection task and the annotators' confidence in their annotations [50]. For $CF_{E\text{-}D}$, the obtained Krippendorff's α was 0.61, which is less good. This is not a problem since these data are considered and used as the silver standard and not the gold standard.

The stances were aggregated through a majority vote using the primary stances. The secondary stances were included in cases where there was no consensus using the primary stance (3.4% of the time), and they helped to reach a consensus in 1.0% of cases. Comments without consensus in the annotations were discarded for both cases. A total of 1228 annotated comments were obtained for $CF_{E\text{-}T}$: 600 English, 241 French, 230 German, 88 Italian, 37 Hungarian, and 32 Greek. A total of 1414 comments were obtained for $CF_{E\text{-}D}$: 675 English, 300 French, 300 German, and 139 Spanish.

Final Datasets

We obtained three labelled datasets and one unlabelled dataset. The first labelled dataset, called CF_S, consists of 6985 stances with binary annotations that were self-annotated. The second and third labelled datasets, called $CF_{E\text{-}T}$ (this version is slightly bigger than the one from [7]) and $CF_{E\text{-}D}$ (as Test and as Development, respectively), consist of, respectively, 1226 and 1414 multilingual comments with ternary annotations that were externally annotated. The fourth dataset, called CF_U, is the remaining unlabelled comments.

2.3. Dataset Generalities

All the datasets used in this paper have common properties: they contain short texts written in the context of, or answering to, a controversial question of political range. In this layout, the targets of the stance are not a defined person or subject. They vary greatly and are expressed in the form of text in natural language. Table 4 compares the three datasets of stance recognition where the targets are political proposals or questions formulated as text. The CF datasets have the most targets, are intra-multilingual with many languages, and contain interactions between users in the form of threads.

Table 4. Comparison with other annotated datasets.

Dataset	X-Stance	DE	CF_S	CF_E	CF_U
Classes	2	3	2	3	∅
Languages	3	2	25	22	26
Targets	150	18	2724	757	4274
Comments	67,271	2523	6985	1206	12,024
Debate	✗	✓	✓	✓	✓
Intra Mult.	✗	✗	✓	✓	✓

2.4. X-Stance Dataset

The X-stance (XS) dataset [33] is a collection of 67,271 comments in French, German, and Italian on more than 150 political issues (referred to as *targets*) extracted from the Swiss application *Smartvote*. Each of the comments is associated with a label. To leverage the semantics information contained in a pre-trained model [51], the authors proposed incorporating the target into a natural language question, such as *"La Suisse devrait-elle conclure un accord de libre-échange avec les Etats-Unis?"*, which can be interpreted as a debate title. This allows the model to learn across targets and perform effectively in a zero-shot learning setting. Indeed, this approach in which the target can be viewed as a debate title enables the model to learn across targets, maintains efficiency in a zero-shot learning scenario, and leverages the knowledge transfer capability of transformer-based language models [51] (this method has also been used by others [25,37] for zero-shot stance classification).

The annotations from the annotators were consolidated into two classes: in *favour* of and *against* the proposition, which can be represented as *yes* or *no* when the proposition is phrased as a question.

3. Experiments

We ran two different sets of experiments of very similar model types, detecting the stances of comments toward a proposal formulated in natural language. The first set presented in Section 3.1 targeted the Debating Europe as the test dataset, focusing on cross-lingual transfer learning, integrating context and semi-supervised learning. The second set of experiments presented in Section 3.2 targeted the CoFE dataset as the test dataset, proposing several baselines on multilingual data.

3.1. Debating Europe

The three experiments below are complementary. The first experiment focused on transfer learning across topics, targets, and languages. The second one focused on the interactive aspect of online debates. The last experiment highlights the value of the unlabelled DE dataset, by presenting a self-training method handling unlabelled and imbalanced data.

3.1.1. Multilingual Stance Detection Using Transfer Learning

It is well known that when the source and target domains are dissimilar, standard transfer learning may fail and result in negative transfer [52]. Therefore, demonstrating that the small DE dataset can improve the performance on the 25-times larger non-English XS dataset through transfer learning across topics and languages is a way to validate the annotations. The XS dataset, which consists of multilingual comments responding to political debate questions from various topics, is an ideal candidate for transfer learning. The DE dataset consists of comments from the online debate forum Debating Europe, so the targets of the stances are closely related to those in the multilingual XS dataset. For these reasons, we first investigated the potential of using our labels to enhance performance across different topics and languages.

3.1.2. Data Augmentation with Semi-Supervised Learning

As mentioned in Section 2.1, we annotated only a small portion of the available DE dataset, leaving a large amount of data unlabelled, which could potentially be useful in improving model performance. To maximise the potential of this unlabelled data, we propose to use a self-training method [41]. The general principle we followed was to leverage some of the model's own predictions on unlabelled data by adding pseudo-examples to the training set in an iterative way. Typically, new unlabelled examples were selected regarding how confident the prediction of their label is, and they were added to the training set for the supervised step of the next iteration. We compared two classical methods: using a threshold on the model's class probability and selecting the k predictions with the highest probability (respectively referred to as *thresh* and *k-best* in Section 4.1.2). We are aware of the potential drawbacks of self-training, such as the inability of the model to correct its own mistakes and the amplification of errors [53]. Thus, if the unlabelled dataset is imbalanced, the classifier bias may be amplified by the pseudo-labels, exacerbating the class imbalance issue [46].

To mitigate this risk, we propose a technique that combines both methods by adding a definite and balanced number of k_{max} examples chosen randomly from those with a probability above the threshold, at each iteration of the ST algorithm. Our technique makes no assumptions about the label distribution of the unlabelled dataset and, at the same time, can help to prevent the training set from being flooded with pseudo-examples from outer domains.

3.2. Experiences on CoFE

3.2.1. Multilingual Stance Detection Using Transfer Learning

A set of several baselines is proposed over the CF_{E-T} dataset, which is the subpart that had been externally annotated to be used as a test set. X-stance and CF_S are big datasets annotated in a binary way. However, they cannot be used to train a model for a ternary classification. Moreover, the small size of the tri-class DE dataset makes it difficult to naively aggregate the datasets altogether (the model called *All-1 training*).

Several configurations were compared. First, we compared the models that do not use any comments from the CoFE dataset. Subsequently, we compared the models that use only binary annotation from the CoFE dataset and, finally, the models that use ternary annotations during the training. First, we trained a *cross-datasets* model that does not use any of the CoFE data during the training, and we compared it to two strong baselines trained on stance recognition from various domains: an English model [37] trained over 16 English stance datasets from various domains and a multilingual model [29] pre-trained over the same 16 English datasets and fine-tuned over 14 non-English datasets. Second, we present a *cross-debates* model trained on X-stance and the subpart of CF_S not containing debates from the test and two models that use the three datasets (*All-2 trainings* and *All-1 training*). Third, we present models trained with the CF_{E-D} dataset of ternary stance annotations from the CoFE, alone (CF_{E-D}-1 *training*) or with other data using a one-step (*All-1 training*) or a two-step (*All-2 trainings*) training process.

If not specified, all of our models were trained using a two-step training process: trained over binary data, then fine-tuned over ternary data. *Cross-datasets* was pre-trained over X-stances and fine-tuned with Debating Europe. *Cross-debates* was trained with X-stances and Debating Europe, plus CF_S minus all debates included in CF_E. *All-2 trainings* was trained over X-stances and CF_S, then Debating Europe (and CF_{E-D} when the case is warranted). *All-1 training* was trained over X-stances and CF_S and Debating Europe (and CF_{E-D} when the case is warranted).

3.2.2. Data Augmentation with Semi-Supervised Learning

As in Section 3.1.2, we ran experiments with self-supervised learning. We used the model that gave the best results of the transfer learning experiments, by adding the unlabelled CF_U dataset during the second step of the learning phase. We followed the same protocol as specified before.

3.3. Methodological Protocol

In our study, the protocol of [36,54] was followed for training transformers, which had previously been used for multilingual sentiment analysis and text classification. The transformers library [55] was used to access pre-trained models and to train our models. XLM-R [56] was employed as a multilingual learning model, referred to as XLM-R_{ft} when it had been previously trained on a dataset (as described in Section 3.1).

For optimisation, the Adam algorithm [57] with early stopping based on the training loss was used. The learning rate was set to 2×10^{-6} for the first training of the model on a stance task and to 5×10^{-7} when fine-tuning on another dataset for transfer learning. Performance on the development set was evaluated after each training epoch, and the model that achieved the best performance was kept. The batch size was set to 32. Unlike [33], no hyperparameter optimisation was performed on the development set, and a shorter maximum sequence length (128 instead of 512) was used to speed up training and evaluation.

The transformer encoding of the debate and comments was carried out according to the protocol of [33], in which each transformer was used as follows:

```
[CLS] Target [SEP] Comment [SEP]
```

For X-stance and Debating Europe, closed questions were used as the `target` text. For the CoFE, the debate title was simply used.

For the transfer learning, a multilingual pre-trained transformer XLM-R [56] was pre-trained on a 2-class dataset, then fine-tuned over a 3-class dataset with a different classification head in order to obtain a ternary classifier. For the ST, a maximum of five iterations was set out, with a probability threshold of 0.99 and 600 and 2000 as the maximum number of examples added at each iteration when applicable.

Metrics widely employed for this kind of task were computed in order to compare our models: the accuracy, precision, recall, as well as macro-F1 score, in order to reflect both the global and per-class model's performances and take into account class imbalance. The DE dataset was divided into three training/validation/test sets in a stratified way with a ratio of 75/5/20. To compare the results, the same partition as [33] was carried out for the XS dataset. CF_{E_T} was used as the test set for the CoFE. Experiments were run using Tensorflow 2.4.1 [58], transformers 3.5.1 [55], a GPU Nvidia RTX-8000, and CUDA 12.0.

4. Results and Discussion

This section presents the results of the experiments over the Debating Europe (Section 4.1) and CoFE datasets (Section 4.2). It highlights how models can take advantage of datasets, even though the regimes are cross-lingual, cross-topics, and even cross-tasks in the case of binary labelled data. It also shows the efficiency of multilingual self-supervised learning for this kind of data and task.

4.1. Results on Debating Europe

The experiments were complementary. The first one gave an insight into the effect of pre-training a classification model over a non-English multilingual dataset from another domain. The second experiment used a self-training method applicable to a dataset of unlabelled and imbalanced data.

4.1.1. Cross-Datasets Transfer Learning

Here, we investigated the effects of pre-training over one dataset before fine-tuning over another one. Table 5 shows the results of applying transfer learning from Debating Europe to X-stance, while Table 6 shows the results of applying transfer learning from X-stance to Debating Europe. The former gave an insight into the effect of pre-training over a non-English multilingual dataset from another domain. The latter gave an insight into the effect of pre-training on English and specialised data from an online debate.

Table 5. Results over X-stance dataset for a binary classification, best result in bold. The M-BERT results came from [33].

	Intra-Target			X-Question			X-Topic			X-Lingual
	DE	FR	Mean	DE	FR	Mean	DE	FR	Mean	IT
M-BERT [33]	76.8	76.6	76.6	68.5	68.4	68.4	68.9	70.9	69.9	70.2
XLM-R	76.3	78.0	77.1	71.5	72.9	72.2	71.2	73.7	72.4	73.0
XLM-R$_{ft}$	77.3	79.0	**78.1**	71.5	74.8	**73.1**	72.2	74.7	**73.4**	**73.9**

As can be seen in Tables 5 and 6, the transfer learning approach was efficient for both datasets, even though they had different languages, topics, and targets. Pre-training over Debating Europe allowed for reaching higher results on the X-stance dataset. It is important to note that this worked even if the DE dataset is very small compared to X-stance. Moreover, it is a way to validate the annotation that has been made by one expert only, without the possibility of calculating an inter-annotator agreement.

4.1.2. Self-Training Setting

The results of the ST setups are presented in Table 6. Analysing the results, we can see that not all settings led to satisfactory results. In order to understand the causes of this failure, we analysed the distribution of the pseudo-labels (see Figure 4), along with the number of pseudo-labels. By analysing the distribution, it is possible to gain an understanding of the weaknesses of each method and to conclude on the reason why our method performed well: it did not overwhelm the gold labels with weak labels and offered a balanced distribution.

Table 6. Results over the Debating Europe dataset for a 3-class classification using ST. k_{max} is the number of examples added at each iteration.

Unsupervised Method	Threshold	k_{max}	Balanced	Model	Prec.	Rec.	F1	Acc
✗	✗	✗	✗	XLM-R	68.6	69.3	68.9	70.1
				XLM-R$_{ft}$	70.7	69.9	**70.2**	**72.1**
thresh-0.99	0.99	✗	✗	XLM-R	68.6	69.8	69.1	70.7
				XLM-R$_{ft}$	68.9	69.6	69.0	70.9
k-best-2000	✗	2000	✗	XLM-R	67.5	68.3	67.8	69.3
				XLM-R$_{ft}$	70.4	69.9	69.8	71.9
k-best-600	✗	600	✗	XLM-R	69.4	68.5	68.0	69.5
				XLM-R$_{ft}$	72.5	70.3	71.1	73.3
our-2000	0.99	2000	✓	XLM-R	69.5	69.4	69.4	71.3
				XLM-R$_{ft}$	70.5	69.9	69.3	71.7
our-600	0.99	600	✓	XLM-R	70.9	71.6	71.1	72.7
				XLM-R$_{ft}$	71.5	71.5	**71.4**	**73.5**

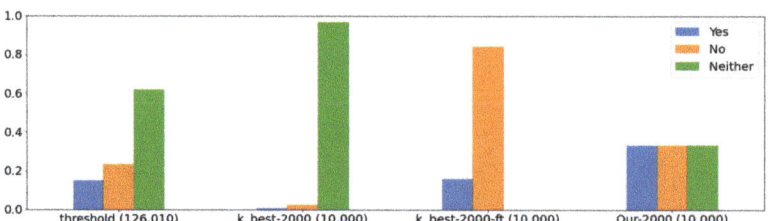

Figure 4. Distribution of the pseudo-labels.

The threshold method did not improve the model's performance due to the small size of our dataset and the lack of model calibration. Specifically, the non-calibration of the model led to the addition of too many pseudo-examples at each iteration (more than 30-times the number of labels in pseudo-labels in the end), which significantly decreased the model's performance. On the other hand, the k-best method was able to reduce the number of examples added at each iteration and performed well with the XLM-R$_{ft}$, as this latter model was trained on a larger number of examples and appeared to be more robust.

4.2. Results on CoFE

4.2.1. Baselines for Scarce Annotation Regimes

We present the results in a cross-datasets setting and without or with manually annotating data from the target dataset for the target task.

The results of the models trained without access to the three-class labelled data can be found in Table 7. We evaluated the performance of our proposed configurations using the F1, macro-F1, and accuracy metrics over the externally annotated dataset CF_{E-T}. The first column shows the different configurations we used, and the next columns show the annotation used during the training: OODataset means annotations Out-Of-Dataset; CoFE-2 means binary annotations from the CoFE; CoFE-3 means ternary annotations from the CoFE. The following columns show the results for each class (− for the negative class, ∼ for the neutral class, and + for the positive class), and the last columns show the accuracy and macro-F1 of the configurations.

Table 7. F1, macro-F1 and accuracy of the different baselines over the externally annotated dataset CF_{E-T}.

Model	Annotations Used			−	∼	+	Acc.	M-F1
	CoFE-3	CoFE-2	OODataset					
Hardalov et al. [37] + MT	✗	✗	✓	7.7	29.5	61.4	46.3	32.8
Hardalov et al. [29]	✗	✗	✓	20.7	19.1	58.9	43.2	32.9
Cross-datasets	✗	✗	✓	45.3	44.0	62.6	52.7	50.6
All-1 training	✗	✓	✓	56.8	00.6	77.9	62.9	45.1
Cross-debates	✗	✓	✓	54.3	41.4	77.3	63.0	57.6
All-2 trainings	✗	✓	✓	52.9	45.0	76.3	63.1	**58.1**
CF_{E-D}-1 training	✓	✓	✗	42.1	39.9	75.6	62.3	52.5
All-1 training	✓	✓	✓	57.9	30.0	78.5	65.4	55.5
All-2 trainings	✓	✓	✓	57.3	40.2	80.5	67.3	**59.3**

The first section of the table lists models that used only annotations from the Out-Of-Domain (OODataset) dataset. The first two models, Hardalov et al. [37] + MT and Hardalov et al. [29], both use only OODataset annotations from 16 English stance datasets and 10 multilingual stance datasets from various domains and had an accuracy of 46.3 and 43.2, respectively, with a macro-F1 of 32.8 and 32.9, respectively. The third model in this section, cross-datasets, also uses only OODataset annotations from X-stance and Debating Europe and had an accuracy of 52.7 and a macro-F1 of 50.6.

The table's second section lists models that add binary annotations from the target dataset (CoFE-2) in the training set. The first three models in this section, "All-1 training", cross-debates, and "All-2 trainings", use binary annotations from the target dataset. The first configuration, "All-1 training", showed an F1 of 59.7 for the negative class, 00.7 for the neutral class, and 79.5 for the positive class. The accuracy of this configuration was 65.5, and the macro-F1 was 46.6. The second configuration, "cross-datasets", showed an F1 of 54.3 for the negative class, 30.5 for the neutral class, and 73.9 for the positive class. The accuracy of this configuration was 59.6, and the macro-F1 was 52.9. The third configuration, "cross-debates", showed an F1 of 55.3 for the negative class, 40.4 for the neutral class, and 76.6 for the positive class. The accuracy of this configuration was 63.2, and the macro-F1 was 57.4. Finally, the fourth configuration, "All-2 trainings" showed an F1 of 55.4 for the negative class, 44.6 for the neutral class, and 77.3 for the positive class. The accuracy of this configuration was 64.3, and the macro-F1 was 59.1.

The last section of the table lists models that use ternary annotations from the target dataset (CoFE-3). The first two models in this section, CF_{E-D}-1 training and All-1 training, use ternary annotations from the target dataset and had accuracy scores of 62.3 and 65.4, respectively, with macro-F1 scores of 52.5 and 55.5, respectively. The last model in the table, "All-2 trainings", had the best macro-F1 score of 59.3 and the highest accuracy score of 67.3 among all models in the table.

4.2.2. Self-Training Setting

The results of the three-class classification using self-training with the CF_U dataset on the CF_{E-T} dataset are presented in Table 8. The model uses an unlabelled dataset, CF_U, to augment the training data through the ST process. The columns in the table represent the unsupervised method used, the threshold applied during the ST process, the maximum number of examples (k_{max}) added at each iteration, whether the distribution of pseudo-labels was balanced, and the precision results for the negative (−), neutral (∼), and positive (+) classes, as well as the overall accuracy (Acc) and the macro-weighted F1-score (m-F1). The results showed that using a balanced distribution of pseudo-labels led to better performance compared to the models without this balance. Specifically, the best results in terms of the macro-F1 were obtained by the unsupervised method with a threshold of 0.99, a maximum number of examples added of 2000, and a balanced distribution of pseudo-labels. This model achieved a macro-weighted F1-score of 63.2, which was the highest among the models compared.

Table 8. Results of the best model over the CF_{E-T} dataset for a 3-class classification using ST with the unlabelled CF_U dataset. k_{max} is the number of examples added at each iteration.

Unsupervised Method	Threshold	k_{max}	Balanced	−	∼	+	Acc	M-F1
✗	✗	✗	✗	57.3	40.2	80.5	67.3	59.3
thresh-0.99	0.99	✗	✗	43.6	55.8	77.3	65.2	58.9
k-best-2000	✗	2000	✗	59.6	42.6	79.9	66.2	60.4
k-best-600	✗	600	✗	51.8	50.4	78.8	66.4	60.3
our-2000	0.99	2000	✓	57.6	52.7	79.2	67.8	**63.2**
our-600	0.99	600	✓	56.8	51.5	76.4	65.1	61.6

4.3. Analysis of the Results

In this part, we focused our analysis on the experiments using the CoFE data. From the results, we can draw different conclusions regarding the three different parts of Table 7: using only out-of-dataset annotations, using binary annotations from the target dataset, or using ternary annotations from the target dataset. We also discuss the results of the self-training experiments briefly.

Cross-Datasets Data

Our cross-datasets model trained over X-stance and Debating Europe allowed results that were better than two strong cross-datasets baselines. The first baseline is a model trained on English data, using English as the pivot language and machine translation. It gave poor performances on the negative class. The second baseline is a multilingual model, also using the X-stance dataset during its learning phase, making the low results surprising. The gain in performance of our model must come from the training data, which are online debates on political topics.

Binary Labels' Annotations from CoFE

The first conclusion came from the poor performances of the "All-1 training" configuration on the neutral class (0.06): the two-step learning process is mandatory to obtain proper results on the neutral class when tackling ternary stance classification and using only the large binary labelled datasets available. The second conclusion is that it was possible to achieve better results with our method even if we completely dropped the examples from the target dataset (macro-F1 rising to 50.6). Third, the "cross-debates" configuration obtained far better results than the "cross-datasets"; hence, the adaptation towards the domain and languages, which are contained in the target dataset, seems to be important (50.6 to 57.6). Fourth, the results of the "cross-debates" configuration, which is zero-shot regarding the target, were still good compared to the model that had seen examples from the test debates (57.6 vs. 58.1). Finally, we can see that our last proposed configuration, "All-2 trainings", achieved the best performance, with the highest macro-F1 of 58.1. This suggested that the use of both debates and languages from the target dataset during the training improved the performance of the overall stance classification. Interestingly, it also improved the performance on the neutral class, even though the labels used during training were only binary.

Ternary Labels' Annotations from CoFE

We can draw two main conclusions from the last section of Table 7. The first one would be that the best results came from the model using the more annotated data ("All-2 trainings" with CoFE-3 reaching the highest macro-F1). The second conclusion came from looking at the performance of CF_{E-D}-1 training being a bit higher than the cross-datasets one (52.5 vs. 50.6). This gap between the two results means that, even if costly, annotating data from the target dataset in a ternary way is not enough to reach high performances.

The results of our model on the dataset used by [29,37] can be seen in Appendix C.

Self-Training

All the self-training methods allowed for the improvement of the results, contrary to the experiments on the Debating Europe dataset (Section 3.1.2). The threshold method was the only one that was harmful to the performances. As the model was not calibrated, the first iteration already pseudo-labelled almost all of the unlabelled data (15% of negative, 39% of neutral, and 46% of positive). Hence, the pseudo-labelling only depended on the network trained at the first iteration: all the biases were inserted in the pseudo-labelled data, which overflowed the real training data.

5. Conclusions and Future Work

In this work, we focused on the task of ternary stance recognition, using data from public consultations and digital democracy platforms. We addressed the issue of multi-target stance recognition as defined in [33], where the target can also be expressed like a comment, in natural language. We can point out several contributions. We define dthe concept of intra-multilinguality, where the target and the comment can come in different languages, by using a platform that automatically translates the textual content so that the users can interact in their native languages. We collected and annotated parts of the dataset presented and made them available online for two shared tasks [59,60]. Finally, we proposed a series of methods to learn with a limited amount of labels, by pre-training over similar datasets and leveraging information from non-annotated data with the help of self-training methods.

Future work in this context will include studying the interactions between the participants of the debates, firstly within the different debates, by studying conversation dynamics [6] in the form of the threads that are available in the CoFE dataset and, secondly, within the platform, by looking at the group of topics each user is interested in to cluster political views at the user level. Another interesting way to study political debates would be to use multimodal content in several forms. Within the CoFE dataset, some descriptions contain multimodal data such as photos or videos, making this integration possible. A step further would be to use virtual video conference meetings to add real-time multimodal content and interactions between the participants to study the dynamics of a real-time debate. Ultimately, an embodied conversational agent [61] could be used as a moderator of the multimodal debates [62]. Finally, it would be interesting to look at the cultural and national biases that we can find in this dataset, by analysing the data separately in a monolingual way both at the semantic and linguistic levels, to understand how these biases influence the quality of the data and the classification performances.

Author Contributions: Conceptualisation—DE, A.B. and V.B.; conceptualisation—CoFE, V.B.; methodology, V.B.; software, V.B.; validation, V.B.; formal analysis, V.B.; investigation, V.B.; writing—original draft preparation, V.B.; writing—review and editing, V.B. and A.B.; visualisation, V.B. All authors have read and agreed to the published version of the manuscript.

Funding: V.B. research was funded by the National Center for Artificial Intelligence CENIA FB210017, Basal ANID.

Data Availability Statement: The CoFE datasets CF_U, CF_S, and CF_{E-D} are already available in the context of the Touché Lab @ CLEF 2023 (https://touche.webis.de/clef23/touche23-web/multilingual-stance-classification.html (accessed on 20 February 2023)). The Debating Europe dataset will be available online after publication.

Acknowledgments: We would like to thank Brian Ravenet, Léo Hemamou, and Simon Luck for helping to annotate CF_{E-D} and Guillaume Jacquet for helping in managing the annotation phase performed at the Joint Research Center during the annotation process of a subpart of CF_{E-T}. We thank the Big Data Analytics Platform of the JRC.

Conflicts of Interest: The authors declare no conflict of interest.

Abbreviations

The following abbreviations are used in this manuscript:

ML	Machine Learning
NLP	Natural Language Processing
DA	Data Augmentation
SSL	Self-Supervised Learning
ST	Self-Training
CoFE	Conference on the Future of Europe
DE	Debating Europe

Appendix A. Targets of the Annotated Debates from Debating Europe

The debates chosen for the annotation are the ones below: *Should we consume less energy?*, *Should we make the cities greener?*, *Can renewables ever replace fossil fuels 100?*, *Should we invest more in clean energies to avoid an energy crisis?*, *Should we cut CO2 emission and invest into clean energies?*, *Should we think about the real cost of the food we eat?*, *Should all cars be electric by 2025?*, *Does organic food really make a difference?*, *Should Europeans be encouraged to eat more sustainably?*, *Sustainable agriculture: With or without pesticides?*, *Should all EU countries abandon nuclear power?*, *Should we stop flying to help the environment?*, *Should plastic packaging be banned?*, *Should we all eat less meat?*, *Should we invest in cheap and clean energies?*, *Should we move towards a low-carbon economy or invest into clean energies?*, *Should the European Union ban plastic bags?*, and *Should plastic water bottles be banned?*.

Appendix B. Statistics on Debating Europe Annotated Dataset

Statistics on the Debating Europe annotated dataset can be found in Table A1.

Table A1. Low-level statistics on the Debating Europe dataset. Here, μ represents the average mean, σ the standard deviation, med the median, and Σ the sum.

Aggregation-Level		Debate			Comment			All
Units	Label	μ	σ	Med	μ	σ	Med	Σ
Comments	All	140	99	101	1	0	1	2523
	Yes	56	37	39	1	0	1	1012
	No	29	39	14	1	0	1	489
	Neutral	18	18	11	1	0	1	282
	Not answering	41	23	35	1	0	1	740
Words	All	4683	2721	3794	33	60	16	84,289
	Yes	1933	1221	1772	34	74	13	34,790
	No	942	1157	554	33	43	19	16,012
	Neutral	814	808	478	46	73	23	13,023
	Not answering	1137	627	972	28	39	16	20,464

Appendix C. Results of the Stance Models over Other Datasets

This section contains the results of the cross-datasets model we trained over data related to political topics: pre-trained over X-stance and fine-tuned over Debating Europe. We applied them on the stance datasets used in [37]. We only used the datasets with three or two labels, so we could achieve hard mapping using our model, and we removed the scd dataset, which has no target.

Table A2. Results of our cross-datasets model over binary annotated English datasets from [37].

Model	Perspectrum	Poldeb	Snopes	Argmin	Ibmcs	All
Hardalov et al. [37]	29.6	22.8	29.28	34.16	72.93	37.8
Cross-dataset	63.8	46.3	52.3	61.6	20.3	**48.9**

Table A3. Results of our cross-datasets model over ternary annotated English datasets from [37].

Model	Iac1	Emergent	Mtsd	Semeval16	Vast	All
Hardalov et al. [37]	35.2	58.49	23.34	37.01	22.89	**35.4**
Cross-dataset	15.5	21.6	16.7	13.0	29.1	19.2

When analysing the results from the ternary annotated stance datasets, we noticed that our network was struggling to predict things other than the neutral class for all the ternary datasets, leading to very poor results (see Table A3). Nevertheless, in the binary setting, where we discarded the neutral class to keep only the positive and negative, we could obtain higher competitive results (see Table A2). This result is interesting since our network was trained on online debates, but tested on data not only from debates, but also from news (Snopes) or other sources (IBMCS and Argmin).

References

1. ALDayel, A.; Magdy, W. Stance detection on social media: State of the art and trends. *Inf. Process. Manag.* **2021**, *58*, 102597. [CrossRef]
2. Hardalov, M.; Arora, A.; Nakov, P.; Augenstein, I. A Survey on Stance Detection for Mis- and Disinformation Identification. *arXiv* **2021**, arXiv:2103.00242.
3. De Magistris, G.; Russo, S.; Roma, P.; Starczewski, J.T.; Napoli, C. An Explainable Fake News Detector Based on Named Entity Recognition and Stance Classification Applied to COVID-19. *Information* **2022**, *13*, 137. [CrossRef]
4. Yang, R.; Ma, J.; Lin, H.; Gao, W. *A Weakly Supervised Propagation Model for Rumor Verification and Stance Detection with Multiple Instance Learning*; Association for Computing Machinery: New York, NY, USA, 2022; Volume 1, pp. 1761–1772. [CrossRef]
5. Beauchamp, N. Predicting and Interpolating State-Level Polls Using Twitter Textual Data. *Am. J. Political Sci.* **2017**, *61*, 490–503. [CrossRef]
6. Sakketou, F.; Lahnala, A.; Vogel, L.; Flek, L. Investigating User Radicalization: A Novel Dataset for Identifying Fine-Grained Temporal Shifts in Opinion. In Proceedings of the LREC, Marseille, France, 20–25 June 2022; pp. 3798–3808.
7. Barriere, V.; Jacquet, G. CoFE: A New Dataset of Intra-Multilingual Multi-target Stance Classification from an Online European Participatory Democracy Platform. In Proceedings of the 2nd Conference of the Asia-Pacific Chapter of the Association for Computational Linguistics and the 12th International Joint Conference on Natural Language Processing, Online, 21–24 November 2022.
8. Gupta, A.; Blodgett, S.L.; Gross, J.H.; O'Connor, B. ExPRES: Examining Political Rhetoric with Epistemic Stance Detection. *arXiv* **2022**, arXiv:2212.14486v2.
9. Gorrell, G.; Bontcheva, K.; Derczynski, L.; Kochkina, E.; Liakata, M.; Zubiaga, A. RumourEval 2019: Determining rumour veracity and support for rumours. In Proceedings of the SemEval 2019, Minneapolis, MN, USA, 6–7 June 2019; pp. 845–854.
10. Matero, M.; Soni, N.; Balasubramanian, N.; Schwartz, H.A. MeLT: Message-Level Transformer with Masked Document Representations as Pre-Training for Stance Detection. In Proceedings of the Findings of the Association for Computational Linguistics, Findings of ACL: EMNLP 2021, Punta Cana, Dominican Republic, 7–11 November 2021; pp. 2959–2966. [CrossRef]
11. Mohammad, S.M.; Kiritchenko, S.; Sobhani, P.; Zhu, X.; Cherry, C. A Dataset for Detecting Stance in Tweets. In Proceedings of the Tenth International Conference on Language Resources and Evaluation (LREC'16), Portorož, Slovenia, 23–28 May 2016. [CrossRef]

12. Augenstein, I.; Rocktäschel, T.; Vlachos, A.; Bontcheva, K. Stance detection with bidirectional conditional encoding. In Proceedings of the EMNLP 2016—Conference on Empirical Methods in Natural Language Processing, Austin, TX, USA, 1–5 November 2016; pp. 876–885. [CrossRef]
13. Dos Santos, W.R.; Paraboni, I. Moral stance recognition and polarity classification from twitter and elicited text. In Proceedings of the International Conference Recent Advances in Natural Language Processing, RANLP, Varna, Bulgaria, 2–4 September 2019; pp. 1069–1075. [CrossRef]
14. Li, Y.; Sosea, T.; Sawant, A.; Nair, A.J.; Inkpen, D.; Caragea, C. P-Stance: A Large Dataset for Stance Detection in Political Domain. In Proceedings of the Findings of the Association for Computational Linguistics: ACL-IJCNLP 2021, Punta Cana, Dominican Republic, 1–6 August 2021; pp. 2355–2365. [CrossRef]
15. Derczynski, L.; Bontcheva, K.; Liakata, M.; Procter, R.; Hoi, G.W.S.; Zubiaga, A. SemEval-2017 Task 8: RumourEval: Determining rumour veracity and support for rumours. *arXiv* **2017**, arXiv:1704.05972.
16. Somasundaran, S.; Wiebe, J. Recognizing stances in online debates. In Proceedings of the ACL-IJCNLP 2009—Joint Conference of the 47th Annual Meeting of the Association for Computational Linguistics and 4th Internation Joint Conference on Natural Language Processing of the AFNLP, Singapore, 2–7 August 2009; pp. 226–234. [CrossRef]
17. Somasundaran, S.; Wiebe, J. Recognizing Stances in Ideological On-Line Debates. In Proceedings of the NAACL Workshop, Los Angeles, CA, USA, 2 June 2010.
18. Walker, M.A.; Anand, P.; Tree, J.E.; Abbott, R.; King, J. A corpus for research on deliberation and debate. In Proceedings of the 8th International Conference on Language Resources and Evaluation, LREC 2012, Istanbul, Turkey, 21–27 May 2012; pp. 812–817.
19. Thomas, M.; Pang, B.; Lee, L. Get out the vote: Determining support or opposition from Congressional floor-debate transcripts. In Proceedings of the COLING/ACL 2006—EMNLP 2006: 2006 Conference on Empirical Methods in Natural Language Processing, Sydney, Australia, 22–23 July 2006; pp. 327–335.
20. Anand, P.; Walker, M.; Abbott, R.; Tree, J.E.F.; Bowmani, R.; Minor, M. Cats Rule and Dogs Drool!: Classifying Stance in Online Debate. In Proceedings of the 2nd Workshop on Computational Approaches to Subjectivity and Sentiment Analysis (WASSA 2011), Portland, OR, USA, 24 June 2011; pp. 1–9.
21. Abbott, R.; Walker, M.; Anand, P.; Fox Tree, J.E.; Bowmani, R.; King, J. How can you say such things?!?: Recognizing disagreement in informal political argument. In Proceedings of the Workshop on Languages in Social Media, Portland, OR, USA, 23 June 2011; pp. 2–11.
22. Walker, M.A.; Anand, P.; Abbott, R.; Grant, R. Stance classification using dialogic properties of persuasion. In Proceedings of the NAACL HLT 2012—2012 Conference of the North American Chapter of the Association for Computational Linguistics: Human Language Technologies—Proceedings, Montreal, QC, Canada, 3–8 June 2012; pp. 592–596.
23. Sridhar, D.; Foulds, J.; Huang, B.; Getoor, L.; Walker, M. Joint Models of Disagreement and Stance in Online Debate. In Proceedings of the 53rd Annual Meeting of the Association for Computational Linguistics and the 7th International Joint Conference on Natural Language Processing, Beijing, China, 27–31 July 2015; pp. 116–125.
24. Barriere, V. Hybrid Models for Opinion Analysis in Speech Interactions. In Proceedings of the ICMI, Glasgow, UK, 13–17 November 2017; pp. 647–651.
25. Allaway, E.; McKeown, K. Zero-Shot Stance Detection: A Dataset and Model Using Generalized Topic Representations. *arXiv* **2020**, arXiv:2010.03640.
26. Villa-Cox, R.; Kumar, S.; Babcock, M.; Carley, K.M. Stance in Replies and Quotes (SRQ): A New Dataset For Learning Stance in Twitter Conversations. In Proceedings of the AAAI, New York, NY, USA, 7–12 February 2020.
27. Hazarika, D.; Poria, S.; Zimmermann, R.; Mihalcea, R. Emotion Recognition in Conversations with Transfer Learning from Generative Conversation Modeling. *arXiv* **2019**, arXiv:1910.04980.
28. Lai, M.; Cignarella, A.T.; Hernández Farías, D.I.; Bosco, C.; Patti, V.; Rosso, P. Multilingual stance detection in social media political debates. *Comput. Speech Lang.* **2020**, *63*, 101075. [CrossRef]
29. Hardalov, M.; Arora, A.; Nakov, P.; Augenstein, I. Few-Shot Cross-Lingual Stance Detection with Sentiment-Based Pre-Training. *arXiv* **2022**, arXiv:2109.06050.
30. Zotova, E.; Agerri, R.; Nuñez, M.; Rigau, G. Multilingual stance detection: The catalonia independence corpus. In Proceedings of the LREC 2020—12th International Conference on Language Resources and Evaluation, Marseille, France, 11–16 May 2020; pp. 1368–1375.
31. Zheng, J.; Baheti, A.; Naous, T.; Xu, W.; Ritter, A. STANCEOSAURUS: Classifying Stance Towards Multicultural Misinformation. In Proceedings of the EMNLP, Abu Dhabi, United Arab Emirates, 7–11 December 2022.
32. Sobhani, P.; Inkpen, D.; Zhu, X. A Dataset for Multi-Target Stance Classification. In Proceedings of the 15th Conference of the European Chapter of the Association for Computational Linguistics, Valencia, Spain, 3–7 April 2017; Volume 2, pp. 551–557.
33. Vamvas, J.; Sennrich, R. X-stance: A Multilingual Multi-Target Dataset for Stance Detection. In Proceedings of the SwissText, Zurich, Switzerland, 23–25 June 2020.
34. Deng, R.; Panl, L.; Clavel, C. Domain Adaptation for Stance Detection towards Unseen Target on Social Media. In Proceedings of the 2022 10th International Conference on Affective Computing and Intelligent Interaction, ACII 2022, Nara, Japan, 18–21 October 2022. [CrossRef]
35. Hosseinia, M.; Dragut, E.; Mukherjee, A. Stance Prediction for Contemporary Issues: Data and Experiments. *arXiv* **2020**, arXiv:2006.00052.

36. Barriere, V.; Jacquet, G. How does a pre-trained transformer integrate contextual keywords? Application to humanitarian computing. In Proceedings of the International ISCRAM Conference, Blacksburg, VA, USA, May 2019 2021; pp. 766–771.
37. Hardalov, M.; Arora, A.; Nakov, P.; Augenstein, I. Cross-Domain Label-Adaptive Stance Detection. In Proceedings of the EMNLP, Virtual, 7–11 November 2021; Volume 19.
38. Augenstein, I.; Ruder, S.; Søgaard, A. Multi-Task learning of pairwise sequence classification tasks over disparate label spaces. In Proceedings of the NAACL HLT 2018—2018 Conference North American Chapter of the Association for Computational Linguistics: Human Language Technologies, New Orleans, LA, USA, 1–6 June 2018; Volume 1, pp. 1896–1906.
39. Barriere, V.; Balahur, A.; Ravenet, B. Debating Europe: A Multilingual Multi-Target Stance Classification Dataset of Online Debates. In Proceedings of the First Workshop on Natural Language Processing for Political Sciences (PoliticalNLP), LREC, Marseille, France, 20–25 June 2022; European Language Resources Association: Marseille, France, 2022; pp. 16–21.
40. Bai, F.; Ritter, A.; Xu, W. Pre-train or Annotate? Domain Adaptation with a Constrained Budget. In Proceedings of the EMNLP 2021—2021 Conference on Empirical Methods in Natural Language Processing, Virtual, 7–11 November 2021; pp. 5002–5015.
41. Yarowsky, D. Unsupervised word sense disambiguation rivaling supervised methods. In Proceedings of the ACL, Cambridge, MA, USA, 26–30 June 1995; pp. 189–196. [CrossRef]
42. Zhu, X.; Ghahramani, Z. *Learning from Labeled and Unlabelled Data with Label Propagation*; Technical Report; Technical Report CMU-CALD-02-107; Carnegie Mellon University: Pittsburgh, PA, USA, 2002.
43. Zhou, D.; Bousquet, O.; Navin Lal, T.; Weston, J.; Schölkopf, B. Learning with Local and Global Consistency. In Proceedings of the Advances in Neural Information Processing Systems, Vancouver, Canada, 8–13 December 2003. [CrossRef]
44. Giasemidis, G.; Kaplis, N.; Agrafiotis, I.; Nurse, J.R. A Semi-Supervised Approach to Message Stance Classification. *IEEE Trans. Knowl. Data Eng.* 2020, 32, 1–11. [CrossRef]
45. Glandt, K.; Khanal, S.; Li, Y.; Caragea, D.; Caragea, C. Stance Detection in COVID-19 Tweets. In Proceedings of the ACL-IJCNLP, Virtual, 1–6 August 2021; pp. 1596–1611. [CrossRef]
46. Wei, C.; Sohn, K.; Mellina, C.; Yuille, A.; Yang, F. CReST: A Class-Rebalancing Self-Training Framework for Imbalanced Semi-Supervised Learning. In Proceedings of the CVPR, Nashville, TN, USA, 20–25 June 2021.
47. Klie, J.C.; Bugert, M.; Boullosa, B.; de Castilho, R.E.; Gurevych, I. The INCEpTION Platform: Machine-Assisted and Knowledge-Oriented Interactive Annotation. In Proceedings of the International Conference on Computational Linguistics, Santa Fe, NM, USA, 20–26 August 2018; pp. 5–9.
48. Küçük, D.; Fazli, C.A. Stance detection: A survey. *ACM Comput. Surv.* 2020, 53, 1–37. [CrossRef]
49. Krippendorff, K. *Content Analysis: An Introduction to Its Methodology*; SAGE Publications: Los Angeles, CA, USA, 2013. [CrossRef]
50. Joseph, K.; Shugars, S.; Gallagher, R.; Green, J.; Mathé, A.Q.; An, Z.; Lazer, D. (Mis)alignment Between Stance Expressed in Social Media Data and Public Opinion Surveys. In Proceedings of the EMNLP 2021—2021 Conference on Empirical Methods in Natural Language Processing, Virtual, 7–11 November 2021; pp. 312–324. [CrossRef]
51. Yin, W.; Hay, J.; Roth, D. Benchmarking zero-shot text classification: Datasets, evaluation and entailment approach. In Proceedings of the EMNLP-IJCNLP 2019, Hong Kong, China, 3–7 November 2019; pp. 3914–3923. [CrossRef]
52. Rosenstein, M.T.; Marx, Z.; Kaelbling, L.P.; Dietterich, T.G. To transfer or not to transfer. In Proceedings of the NIPS 2005 Workshop Transfer Learning, Vancouver, BC, Canada, 5–8 December 2005; Volume 898, p. 3.
53. Ruder, S. Neural Transfer Learning for Natural Language Processing. Ph.D. Thesis, University of Galway, Galway, Ireland, 2019 .
54. Barriere, V.; Balahur, A. Improving Sentiment Analysis over non-English Tweets using Multilingual Transformers and Automatic Translation for Data-Augmentation. In Proceedings of the COLING, Barcelona, Spain, 12 December 2020.
55. Wolf, T.; Debut, L.; Sanh, V.; Chaumond, J.; Delangue, C.; Moi, A.; Cistac, P.; Rault, T.; Louf, R.; Funtowicz, M.; et al. HuggingFace's Transformers: State-of-the-art Natural Language Processing. *arXiv* 2019, arXiv:1910.03771.
56. Conneau, A.; Khandelwal, K.; Goyal, N.; Chaudhary, V.; Wenzek, G.; Guzmán, F.; Grave, E.; Ott, M.; Zettlemoyer, L.; Stoyanov, V. Unsupervised Cross-Lingual Representation Learning at Scale. *arXiv* 2020, arXiv:1911.02116. [CrossRef]
57. Kingma, D.; Ba, J. Adam: A Method for Stochastic Optimization. In Proceedings of the International Conference on Learning Representations, Banff, AB, Canada, 14–16 April 2014; pp. 1–13. http://arxiv.org/abs/1412.6980 .
58. Abadi, M.; Barham, P.; Chen, J.; Chen, Z.; Davis, A.; Dean, J.; Devin, M.; Ghemawat, S.; Irving, G.; Isard, M.; et al. TensorFlow: A system for large-scale machine learning. In Proceedings of the 12th USENIX Symposium on Operating Systems Design and Implementation, OSDI 2016, Savannah, GA, USA, 2–4 November 2016; pp. 265–283.
59. Bondarenko, A.; Fröbe, M.; Kiesel, J.; Schlatt, F.; Barriere, V.; Ravenet, B.; Hemamou, L.; Luck, S.; Reimer, J.H.; Stein, B.; et al. Overview of Touché 2023: Argument and Causal Retrieval. In Proceedings of the ECIR, Dublin, Ireland, 2–6 April 2023.
60. Mirzakhmedova, N.; Kiesel, J.; Alshomary, M.; Heinrich, M.; Handke, N.; Cai, X.; Barriere, V.; Dastgheib, D.; Ghahroodi, O.; Sadraei, M.A.; et al. The Touché23-ValueEval Dataset for Identifying Human Values behind Arguments. *arXiv* 2023, arXiv:2301.13771.

61. Pelachaud, C. Multimodal Expressive Embodied Conversational Agents. In Proceedings of the 13th annual ACM International Conference on Multimedia, Singapore, 6–11 November 2005; pp. 683–689. [CrossRef]
62. Argyle, L.P.; Busby, E.; Gubler, J.; Bail, C.; Howe, T.; Rytting, C.; Wingate, D. AI Chat Assistants can Improve Conversations about Divisive Topics. *arXiv* **2023**, arXiv:2302.07268v1.

Disclaimer/Publisher's Note: The statements, opinions and data contained in all publications are solely those of the individual author(s) and contributor(s) and not of MDPI and/or the editor(s). MDPI and/or the editor(s) disclaim responsibility for any injury to people or property resulting from any ideas, methods, instructions or products referred to in the content.

Article

A Mathematical Interpretation of Autoregressive Generative Pre-Trained Transformer and Self-Supervised Learning

Minhyeok Lee

School of Electrical and Electronics Engineering, Chung-Ang University, Seoul 06974, Republic of Korea; mlee@cau.ac.kr

Abstract: In this paper, we present a rigorous mathematical examination of generative pre-trained transformer (GPT) models and their autoregressive self-supervised learning mechanisms. We begin by defining natural language space and knowledge space, which are two key concepts for understanding the dimensionality reduction process in GPT-based large language models (LLMs). By exploring projection functions and their inverses, we establish a framework for analyzing the language generation capabilities of these models. We then investigate the GPT representation space, examining its implications for the models' approximation properties. Finally, we discuss the limitations and challenges of GPT models and their learning mechanisms, considering trade-offs between complexity and generalization, as well as the implications of incomplete inverse projection functions. Our findings demonstrate that GPT models possess the capability to encode knowledge into low-dimensional vectors through their autoregressive self-supervised learning mechanism. This comprehensive analysis provides a solid mathematical foundation for future advancements in GPT-based LLMs, promising advancements in natural language processing tasks such as language translation, text summarization, and question answering due to improved understanding and optimization of model training and performance.

Keywords: generative pre-trained transformer; GPT; ChatGPT; self-supervised learning; deep learning; natural language processing; NLP

MSC: 68T27

Citation: Lee, M. A Mathematical Interpretation of Autoregressive Generative Pre-Trained Transformer and Self-Supervised Learning. *Mathematics* **2023**, *11*, 2451. https://doi.org/10.3390/math11112451

Academic Editor: Florentina Hristea

Received: 29 April 2023
Revised: 23 May 2023
Accepted: 23 May 2023
Published: 25 May 2023

Copyright: © 2023 by the author. Licensee MDPI, Basel, Switzerland. This article is an open access article distributed under the terms and conditions of the Creative Commons Attribution (CC BY) license (https://creativecommons.org/licenses/by/4.0/).

1. Introduction

The recent advent of generative pre-trained transformer (GPT) models [1–4], a class of large-scale deep learning models, has led to an increasing focus on their applications in the field of natural language processing (NLP) [5–11] and artificial intelligence (AI) [12–15]. These GPT-based models, including notable instances such as ChatGPT [2], have demonstrated remarkable capabilities in generating human-like text and understanding intricate linguistic patterns. As a result, their potential to transform various domains, ranging from machine translation to question-answering systems, has garnered significant attention from both academia and industry. Despite the widespread interest in GPT-based large language models (LLMs) and their impressive performance [16,17], the mathematical underpinnings of these models and their training methods, specifically autoregressive self-supervised learning, remain relatively unexplored.

This paper aims to bridge the gap between the empirical success of GPT-based LLMs and the theoretical understanding of their fundamental properties. To this end, we delve into the mathematical framework that underlies GPT models and autoregressive self-supervised learning [18–20], seeking a mathematical interpretation of the mechanisms that contribute to their impressive language generation capabilities. By providing a formal analysis of GPT-based LLMs, we hope to lay the groundwork for a more systematic exploration of their properties, limitations, and potential improvements.

In order to establish a comprehensive mathematical foundation, we begin by defining the concept of a natural language space, which encompasses all possible human language expressions. We then introduce the notion of a knowledge space, a lower-dimensional space containing abstract representations of the information conveyed by expressions in the natural language space. By considering projection functions and their inverses, we develop a framework for understanding the process of dimensionality reduction in the context of GPT-based LLMs while preserving the meaning of linguistic expressions.

Furthermore, we examine the representation space of GPT models, which is used to encode input sentences or expressions as high-dimensional vectors. We discuss the smoothness of this space and its implications for the functionality of GPT models as approximations of projection functions. By considering the interplay between the natural language space, the knowledge space, and the GPT representation space, we provide insights into the inner workings of these models and their capacity to capture and manipulate linguistic information.

Additionally, we address the challenges and limitations of GPT models and autoregressive self-supervised learning, focusing on the trade-offs between model complexity and generalization capabilities. We also investigate the implications of incomplete inverse projection functions, which may hinder the ability of GPT-based models to accurately represent certain types of knowledge or meaning.

Given the context, this paper is dedicated to exploring several critical research aspects:

- First, it seeks to formally define the natural language space and the knowledge space to foster an understanding of the dimensionality reduction process in GPT-based LLMs.
- Second, it aims to elucidate the role of projection functions and their inverses in the language generation capabilities of these models.
- Third, it endeavors to identify the properties of the GPT representation space and analyze how these properties affect the models' approximation capabilities.
- Lastly, it contemplates the limitations and challenges of GPT models and autoregressive self-supervised learning, with a special focus on aspects such as model complexity, generalization capabilities, and the completeness of inverse projection functions.

Through this comprehensive analysis, we hope to contribute to the ongoing discourse surrounding GPT-based LLMs and provide a solid mathematical foundation for future advancements in the field.

2. Preliminaries

In this section, we establish a solid foundation on the underlying principles and mechanics of deep learning and GPT models, which is vital for readers who may not be intimately familiar with these concepts. This understanding is indispensable for the more advanced discourse that follows in the subsequent sections, where we delve into the functional intricacies of GPT models in the context of autoregressive self-supervised learning. We introduce formalized definitions and concepts, which are instrumental in these discussions, to provide a rigorous, mathematical depiction of how GPT-based models work. This includes a thorough understanding of how GPT models, comprised of stacked non-linear neural network layers with attention mechanisms, map the natural language space into the knowledge space via the intermediate layers, thus enabling these models to effectively capture and represent the semantic essence of natural language.

2.1. Deep Learning Models

Deep learning models are a class of machine learning models that consist of multiple layers of interconnected artificial neurons [21]. These models are designed to learn hierarchical representations from input data by minimizing a loss function that quantifies the discrepancy between the model's predictions and the ground truth. A deep learning model $f : \mathcal{X} \to \mathcal{Y}$ is a function that maps input data from a space $\mathcal{X}$ to a target space $\mathcal{Y}$. The model is composed of L layers, and each layer $l \in \{1, \ldots, L\}$ consists of a set of neurons $N^l = \{n_1^l, \ldots, n_{k_l}^l\}$, where k_l is the number of neurons in layer l.

Definition 1 (Activation function [21]). *An activation function $\sigma : \mathbb{R} \to \mathbb{R}$ is a non-linear function applied element-wise to the output of a neuron. It is assumed to be differentiable and monotonic.*

For each neuron $n_i^l \in N^l$, let a_i^l denote its pre-activation value and z_i^l denote its post-activation value. The pre-activation value is a linear combination of the outputs from the neurons in the previous layer, and the post-activation value is obtained by applying the activation function to the pre-activation value:

$$a_i^l = \sum_{j=1}^{k_{l-1}} w_{ij}^l z_j^{l-1} + b_i^l, \tag{1}$$

$$z_i^l = \sigma(a_i^l), \tag{2}$$

where w_{ij}^l is the weight connecting neuron n_j^{l-1} to neuron n_i^l, and b_i^l is the bias term for neuron n_i^l. In this context, $\sigma(\cdot)$ represents the activation function as defined in Definition 1.

A deep learning model can be viewed as a composition of functions $f = f^L \circ \cdots \circ f^1$, where each function $f^l : \mathbb{R}^{k_{l-1}} \to \mathbb{R}^{k_l}$ represents the operation performed by layer l. The model's parameters, $\Theta = \{W^l, b^l\}_{l=1}^L$, where $W^l \in \mathbb{R}^{k_l \times k_{l-1}}$ is the weight matrix for layer l and $b^l \in \mathbb{R}^{k_l}$ is the bias vector for layer l, are optimized by minimizing a loss function $\mathcal{L}(\Theta; \mathcal{D})$, where $\mathcal{D}$ denotes the training dataset.

Remark 1. *The backpropagation algorithm computes the gradient of the loss function with respect to the model's parameters, $\nabla_\Theta \mathcal{L}(\Theta; \mathcal{D})$, by applying the chain rule of differentiation. This gradient is used to update the model's parameters iteratively via gradient-based optimization methods, such as stochastic gradient descent (SGD) or variants thereof.*

Theorem 1 (Universal Approximation Theorem [22]). *Let $\sigma : \mathbb{R} \to \mathbb{R}$ be a continuous and nonconstant activation function. Given any continuous function $g : \mathbb{R}^d \to \mathbb{R}$ defined on a compact set $\mathcal{C} \subseteq \mathbb{R}^d$ and any $\epsilon > 0$, there exists a feedforward neural network with one hidden layer and width k_1, using activation function $\sigma(\cdot)$, such that the neural network can approximate $g(\cdot)$ with an error less than ϵ, i.e.,*

$$\sup_{\mathbf{x} \in \mathcal{K}} |f(\mathbf{x}) - g(\mathbf{x})| < \epsilon. \tag{3}$$

Theorem 1 states that a sufficiently wide neural network with a single hidden layer can approximate any continuous function with arbitrary accuracy. This theorem highlights the expressive power of deep learning models.

2.2. Generative Pre-Trained Transformer

A GPT model is composed of several layers of neural network modules, each consisting of layer normalization, multi-head attention, and dropout functionalities. The model integrates L number of transformer blocks, each of which houses a residual module encapsulating layer normalization, multi-head attention, dropout, and a fully connected layer. This systematic arrangement and interaction of modules and layers contribute to the robust performance of the GPT model. Figure 1 illustrates the architecture of the GPT model, and Definition 2 provides a formal description of the GPT model.

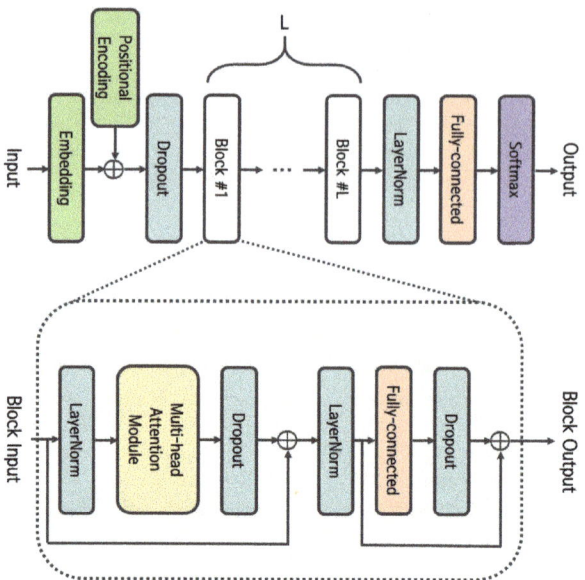

Figure 1. Neural Network Architecture of GPT.

Definition 2 (Generative Pre-trained Transformer (GPT) [4]). *A GPT is an autoregressive self-supervised learning model that employs the Transformer architecture for natural language processing tasks. Given an input sequence of tokens $\mathbf{x} = (x_1, x_2, \ldots, x_T)$, where $x_t \in \mathcal{X}$ for $t = 1, 2, \ldots, T$, the GPT model learns a probability distribution $P(x_t|x_{<t})$ over the vocabulary $\mathcal{X}$, which is conditioned on the preceding tokens $x_{<t} = (x_1, x_2, \ldots, x_{t-1})$. The conditional probability distribution $P(x_t|x_{<t})$ esimated by a GPT can be represented by*

$$P(x_t|x_{<t}) = f_\Theta(x_t|x_{<t}), \quad \forall t = 1, 2, \ldots, T. \tag{4}$$

In the GPT model, the position information of tokens in the input sequence is crucial for maintaining the autoregressive property and capturing the sequential dependencies between tokens. To incorporate this information, the GPT model utilizes a technique called positional encoding, which adds a fixed sinusoidal encoding to the input embeddings.

Definition 3 (Positional Encoding [23]). *The positional encoding function $\mathrm{PE} : \mathbb{N} \times \mathbb{N} \to \mathbb{R}$ computes the position encoding for each position $p \in \mathbb{N}$ and each dimension $i \in \mathbb{N}$ in the input embedding space as follows [24,25]:*

$$\mathrm{PE}(p, i) = \begin{cases} \sin\left(\dfrac{p}{10000^{\frac{2i}{d}}}\right) & \text{if } i \text{ is even}, \\ \cos\left(\dfrac{p}{10000^{\frac{2i-1}{d}}}\right) & \text{if } i \text{ is odd}. \end{cases} \tag{5}$$

The positional encoding function incorporates a 10,000 constant, which serves as a hyperparameter. This value was determined empirically during the original development of the Transformer model. It is designed to create a balance between the higher and lower frequency components of the positional encoding. To facilitate the optimization process, the GPT model employs layer normalization, which is applied to the input of both the multi-head self-attention and position-wise feedforward sublayers. Layer normalization helps alleviate the vanishing and exploding gradient problems and accelerates training.

Definition 4 (Layer Normalization [26]). *Given an input matrix $H \in \mathbb{R}^{T \times d}$, layer normalization computes the normalized output matrix $\hat{H} \in \mathbb{R}^{T \times d}$ as follows:*

$$\hat{H}_{ij} = \frac{H_{ij} - \mu_j}{\sqrt{\sigma_j^2 + \epsilon}}, \tag{6}$$

where $\mu_j = \frac{1}{T} \sum_{i=1}^{T} H_{ij}$ and $\sigma_j^2 = \frac{1}{T} \sum_{i=1}^{T} (H_{ij} - \mu_j)^2$ are the mean and variance of the j-th feature across all positions, respectively, and $\epsilon > 0$ is a small constant for numerical stability.

Definition 5 (Scaled Dot-Product Attention [23]). *The scaled dot-product attention function Attention : $\mathbb{R}^{T \times d} \times \mathbb{R}^{T \times d} \times \mathbb{R}^{T \times d} \to \mathbb{R}^{T \times d}$ takes as input a query matrix $Q \in \mathbb{R}^{T \times d}$, a key matrix $K \in \mathbb{R}^{T \times d}$, and a value matrix $V \in \mathbb{R}^{T \times d}$, and it computes the output as follows:*

$$\text{Attention}(Q, K, V) = \text{softmax}\left(\frac{QK^\top}{\sqrt{d}}\right) V, \tag{7}$$

where $\sqrt{d}$ is a scaling factor that prevents the dot products from becoming too large.

In addition to the scaled dot-product attention mechanism, the GPT model employs the multi-head attention mechanism to capture different aspects of the input sequence. By having multiple attention heads, the model can learn different types of relationships between tokens in parallel.

The GPT model consists of a stack of L identical layers, each containing a multi-head self-attention mechanism, followed by position-wise feedforward networks. The self-attention mechanism computes a weighted sum of the input embeddings, where the weights are determined by the compatibility between input tokens.

Definition 6 (Multi-Head Attention [23]). *The multi-head attention function MultiHead : $\mathbb{R}^{T \times d} \times \mathbb{R}^{T \times d} \times \mathbb{R}^{T \times d} \to \mathbb{R}^{T \times d}$ takes as input a query matrix $Q \in \mathbb{R}^{T \times d}$, a key matrix $K \in \mathbb{R}^{T \times d}$, and a value matrix $V \in \mathbb{R}^{T \times d}$, and it computes the output as follows [27,28]:*

$$\text{MultiHead}(Q, K, V) = \text{Concat}(\text{head}_1, \text{head}_2, \ldots, \text{head}_h) W^O, \tag{8}$$

where $\text{head}_i = \text{Attention}(QW_i^Q, KW_i^K, VW_i^V)$ for $i = 1, 2, \ldots, h$, with $W_i^Q, W_i^K, W_i^V \in \mathbb{R}^{d \times \frac{d}{h}}$ being learnable weight matrices, h being the number of attention heads, and $W^O \in \mathbb{R}^{d \times d}$ being a learnable output weight matrix.

Beyond the attention mechanism, the GPT model utilizes position-wise feedforward networks (FFNs) within each layer. These FFNs consist of two linear layers with a non-linear activation function in between, which allows the model to learn complex non-linear transformations of the input sequence.

Definition 7 (Position-wise Feedforward Networks [23]). *Given an input matrix $H \in \mathbb{R}^{T \times d}$, the position-wise feedforward network computes the output matrix $H' \in \mathbb{R}^{T \times d}$ as follows:*

$$H' = \sigma_H(HW^1 + b^1)W^2 + b^2, \tag{9}$$

where $W^1 \in \mathbb{R}^{d \times d'}$, $W^2 \in \mathbb{R}^{d' \times d}$ are learnable weight matrices, and $b^1 \in \mathbb{R}^{d'}$, $b^2 \in \mathbb{R}^d$ are learnable bias vectors. The activation function σ_H introduces non-linearity.

The GPT model is trained to maximize the likelihood of the target tokens given the context tokens. The objective function is the negative log-likelihood of the target tokens:

$$\mathcal{L}(\Theta; \mathcal{D}) = - \sum_{(\mathbf{x}, \mathbf{y}) \in \mathcal{D}} \sum_{t=1}^{T} \log P(y_t | x_{<t}; \Theta), \tag{10}$$

where $\mathcal{D}$ is the dataset of input-target pairs $(\mathbf{x}, \mathbf{y})$ with $\mathbf{y} = (y_1, y_2, \ldots, y_T)$ being the target sequence.

A multitude of research endeavors have been undertaken to investigate the architecture of GPT models and their practical applications. However, the majority of these studies' pursuits emphasize the exploration of architectural alterations and the development of fine-tuning methodologies that enhance empirical results [1,3,4,29].

For instance, Radford et al. [4] revealed that language models, when subjected to training on a novel dataset consisting of millions of webpages, exhibit an inherent ability to learn specific tasks without the need for any explicit supervision. They identified the significance of the language model's capacity in the success of zero-shot task transfer, with performance improving in a log-linear fashion across tasks. Their most extensive model, GPT-2, showcased an unparalleled performance on a majority of tested language modeling datasets, underscoring the potential of language processing systems that learn to perform tasks via naturally occurring demonstrations.

Similarly, Brown et al. [3] discovered that scaling up language models substantially enhances task-agnostic, few-shot, and GPT-3. They trained an autoregressive language model with a large parameter set, which was significantly larger than any previous non-sparse language model, and tested its performance in the few-shot setting. Despite acknowledging certain areas where GPT-3's few-shot learning struggles, their findings attest to the remarkable performance of GPT-3 across a range of NLP tasks.

Kaplan et al. [29] investigated the empirical scaling laws pertinent to language model performance on the cross-entropy loss, observing that the loss scales as a power-law with model, dataset size, and the amount of computation used in the training process. They noted the minimal effects of other features such as network width, despite the fact that larger models are significantly more sample-efficient.

However, notwithstanding the compelling empirical results of these studies, there exists a conspicuous gap in our understanding of the model's behavior from a mathematical perspective. This gap is exactly what our research aspires to fill. We aim to provide a functional analysis of GPT, contributing to a deeper comprehension of the model's properties and elucidating the mechanisms that drive its performance.

2.3. Autoregressive Self-Supervised Learning

Definition 8 (Autoregressive Self-Supervised Learning [4]). *Autoregressive self-supervised learning is a learning paradigm in which a model is trained to predict the next token in a sequence, given the preceding tokens, without using any labeled data [19]. The model learns a probability distribution $P(x_t | x_{<t}; \Theta)$ over the vocabulary $\mathcal{X}$, conditioned on the context tokens $x_{<t} = (x_1, x_2, \ldots, x_{t-1})$, where Θ denotes the model's parameters.*

Definition 9 (Token Probability Estimation [4]). *In autoregressive self-supervised learning, token probability estimation refers to the process of computing the probability of a token $x_t \in \mathcal{X}$ given the context tokens $x_{<t}$. Given a model with parameters Θ, the token probability estimation can be defined as:*

$$\hat{P}(x_t | x_{<t}; \Theta) = f_\Theta(x_{<t}), \tag{11}$$

where f_Θ is a function parameterized by Θ that maps the context tokens $x_{<t}$ to the estimated probability distribution over the vocabulary $\mathcal{X}$.

In the context of autoregressive self-supervised learning, the function f_Θ in Definition 9 is often implemented using deep neural networks, such as transformers or recurrent neural networks (RNNs). These architectures are designed to capture complex dependencies between tokens and are capable of representing a wide range of probability distributions over the vocabulary $\mathcal{X}$. In particular, the choice of the function f_Θ and its parameterization can have a significant impact on the model's ability to learn the true underlying data-generating process.

Assumption 1 (Markov Assumption). *For autoregressive self-supervised learning, it is assumed that the conditional probability of a token x_t depends only on a fixed number of preceding tokens $x_{<t}$. This is also known as the Markov assumption, which simplifies the modeling of the joint probability distribution over token sequences.*

Assumption 2 (Smoothness). *For autoregressive self-supervised learning, we assume that the function f_Θ in Definition 9 is smooth with respect to the model parameters Θ. This implies that small changes in the model parameters will result in small changes in the estimated probability distribution over the vocabulary $\mathcal{X}$.*

A key implication of Assumption 2 is that the optimization landscape of the autoregressive self-supervised learning problem is characterized by a continuous and differentiable space with respect to the model parameters Θ. This property allows the use of gradient-based optimization techniques, such as Adam and RMSProp, to iteratively update the model parameters and minimize the objective function in Equation (15). Furthermore, under appropriate conditions, convergence to a local minimum or stationary point can be guaranteed.

Definition 10 (Token Context Window [4]). *A token context window of size $w \in \mathbb{N}$ is a fixed-size sliding window that captures the w most recent tokens in a sequence. Given a sequence $\mathbf{x} = (x_1, x_2, \ldots, x_T)$, the token context window $C_t^w(\mathbf{x})$ at position $t \in 1, \ldots, T$ is defined as $C_t^w(\mathbf{x}) = (x_{t-w+1}, x_{t-w+2}, \ldots, x_t)$, where $1 \leq t - w + 1$.*

Remark 2. *In practice, the token context window size w is often chosen to balance the trade-off between computational complexity and the capacity to capture long-range dependencies in the input sequences.*

It is important to note that the choice of the token context window size w in Definition 10 can be influenced by the inherent structure and dependencies in the data. A larger context window can potentially capture longer-range dependencies, but it may also increase the computational complexity of the model and lead to overfitting. Conversely, a smaller context window reduces computational complexity but may fail to capture important dependencies between tokens. In practice, the optimal context window size is often determined using model selection techniques, such as cross-validation.

Definition 11 (Token Autocorrelation). *Token autocorrelation is a measure of the dependency between tokens at different positions in a sequence. Given a sequence $\mathbf{x} = (x_1, x_2, \ldots, x_T)$, the token autocorrelation at lag $k \in 1, 2, \ldots, T - 1$ is defined as:*

$$\rho_k(\mathbf{x}) = \frac{\sum_{t=k+1}^{T}(x_t - \bar{x})(x_{t-k} - \bar{x})}{\sum_{t=1}^{T}(x_t - \bar{x})^2}, \tag{12}$$

where $\bar{x}$ denotes the mean of the sequence $\mathbf{x}$.

Remark 3. *The token autocorrelation can be used to analyze the statistical dependencies between tokens in a sequence, which can inform the choice of the token context window size w in Definition 10.*

Token autocorrelation, as defined in Definition 11, can also provide insights into the appropriate choice of the function f_Θ in Definition 9. For example, if the token autocorrelation decays rapidly with increasing lag, it may indicate that a simpler model, such as an RNN with a small hidden state, could be sufficient to capture the dependencies between tokens. On the other hand, if the token autocorrelation decays slowly or exhibits periodic patterns, more complex models, such as transformers with multiple layers and attention mechanisms, might be necessary to accurately represent the underlying data-generating process.

Definition 12 (Conditional Entropy [30]). *The conditional entropy $H(X_t|X_{<t})$ is a measure of the uncertainty in a random variable X_t given the values of $X_{<t}$. The conditional entropy is defined as*

$$H(X_t|X_{<t}) = -\sum_{x_t \in \mathcal{X}} \sum_{x_{<t} \in \mathcal{X}^{t-1}} P(x_t, x_{<t}) \log P(x_t|x_{<t}), \quad (13)$$

where $P(x_t, x_{<t})$ denotes the joint probability of observing the sequence $(x_{<t}, x_t)$, and $P(x_t|x_{<t})$ represents the conditional probability of x_t given $x_{<t}$.

Definition 13 (Perplexity [31]). *Perplexity is a measure of the average uncertainty in predicting the next token in a sequence given the context tokens. The perplexity of a probability distribution $P(x_t|x_{<t}; \Theta)$, given the context tokens $x_{<t}$, is defined as the exponential of the conditional entropy:*

$$\text{Perplexity}(P(x_t|x_{<t}; \Theta)) = \exp(H(X_t|X_{<t})), \quad (14)$$

where $H(X_t|X_{<t})$ denotes the conditional entropy as defined in Definition 12.

Remark 4. *Lower perplexity values indicate a better model fit, as the model assigns higher probabilities to the observed sequences. Perplexity is often used as a performance metric for autoregressive self-supervised learning models.*

Given Definition 8, Assumption 1, and Definition 10, the objective function for training an autoregressive self-supervised learning model can be formulated as follows:

$$\mathcal{L}(\Theta; \mathcal{D}) = -\sum_{\mathbf{x} \in \mathcal{D}} \sum_{t=1}^{T} \log P(x_t|C_t^w(\mathbf{x}); \Theta), \quad (15)$$

where $\mathcal{D}$ is the dataset of input sequences $\mathbf{x}$ and Θ denotes the model's parameters.

Proposition 1. *Under the Markov assumption in Assumption 1 and given a token context window of size w as in Definition 10, the autoregressive self-supervised learning objective in Equation (15) converges to the true conditional probability distribution of the underlying data-generating process as the size of the dataset $\mathcal{D}$ goes to infinity, provided that the model has sufficient capacity and appropriate optimization techniques are employed.*

Proposition 2. *The conditional entropy $H(X_t|X_{<t})$ of the true data-generating process is upper-bounded by the logarithm of the size of the vocabulary $\mathcal{X}$, i.e., $H(X_t|X_{<t}) \leq \log |\mathcal{X}|$.*

Proof. The conditional entropy $H(X_t|X_{<t})$ is a function of the joint probability distribution $P(x_t, x_{<t})$ and the conditional probability distribution $P(x_t|x_{<t})$. By definition, $0 \leq P(x_t|x_{<t}) \leq 1$, and the maximum value of the conditional entropy occurs when $P(x_t|x_{<t}) = \frac{1}{|\mathcal{X}|}$ for all $x_t \in \mathcal{X}$. In this case, the conditional entropy becomes $H(X_t|X_{<t}) = \log |\mathcal{X}|$. Therefore, $H(X_t|X_{<t}) \leq \log |\mathcal{X}|$. □

It is worth noting that the bound on the conditional entropy in Proposition 2 has important implications for the optimization of autoregressive self-supervised learning models. Since the conditional entropy is upper-bounded by the logarithm of the size of the vocabulary $\mathcal{X}$, it follows that the perplexity, as defined in Definition 13, is also upper-bounded by $|\mathcal{X}|$. This provides an absolute reference point for comparing the performance of different models as well as a theoretical limit on the achievable perplexity. In practice, however, the true conditional entropy of the data-generating process may be much lower than the bound, and the choice of an appropriate model and optimization technique can lead to significant improvements in perplexity over a naïve uniform distribution over the vocabulary.

Definition 14 (GPT Autoregressive Self-Supervised Learning [4]). *Let $\mathcal{G}$ be a GPT model as defined in Definition 2. The autoregressive self-supervised learning of $\mathcal{G}$ is the process of training* the model by optimizing the objective function in Equation (15), where Θ represents the parameters of $\mathcal{G}$ and $\mathcal{D}$ is the dataset of input sequences.

Assumption 3 (Stationary Data-generating Process). *We assume that the dataset $\mathcal{D}$ is generated by a stationary data-generating process; i.e., the joint probability distribution of the tokens in the sequences does not change over time.*

Remark 5. *Assumption 3 simplifies the analysis of the convergence properties of autoregressive self-supervised learning. In practice, the data-generating process may be non-stationary, and the model may need to adapt to the changing distribution over time.*

Proposition 3. *Under the Markov assumption in Assumption 1 and given a token context window of size w as in Definition 10, the GPT autoregressive self-supervised learning process in Definition 14 converges to the true conditional probability distribution of the underlying data-generating process as the size of the dataset $\mathcal{D}$ goes to infinity, provided that the model has sufficient capacity and appropriate optimization techniques are employed.*

Proof. Given Definition 8 and Definition 14, the objective function for training a GPT model using autoregressive self-supervised learning can be formulated as in Equation (15). The proof of Proposition 3 follows directly from Proposition 1. □

Example 1 (GPT and Autoregressive Self-Supervised Learning). *Let $\mathcal{G}$ be a GPT model and $\mathcal{D}$ be a dataset of text sequences. We can train $\mathcal{G}$ using autoregressive self-supervised learning, as described in Definition 14. By optimizing the objective function in Equation (15), we can learn a conditional probability distribution over the vocabulary $\mathcal{X}$ that captures the statistical dependencies between tokens in the input sequences. Consider a GPT model, $\mathcal{G}$, trained on the dataset $\mathcal{D}$ that contains English sentences. When the model encounters the sentence "The quick brown fox jumps over the lazy dog", it predicts the next word in the sentence given the previous words. For example, after processing "The quick brown fox jumps", the model predicts "over" as the most likely next word. This demonstrates the use of autoregressive self-supervised learning, where the model learns the conditional probability distribution over the vocabulary that captures the statistical dependencies between words in a sentence.*

3. Natural Language Space

Definition 15 (Natural Language Space). *The natural language space L is a high-dimensional space that contains all possible human language sentences or expressions, where each point in the space corresponds to a unique sentence or expression. Each point can be represented as a vector in a high-dimensional space with d_L being the dimensionality of the natural language space.*

Definition 16 (Vector Representation of Sentences). *A vector representation function $f : L \to \mathbb{R}^{d_L}$ maps sentences or expressions in the natural language space L to points in a high-dimensional space, typically $\mathbb{R}^{d_L}$, where each point is represented as a unique vector. The function f ensures that each sentence or expression $s \in L$ has a corresponding vector $v_s \in \mathbb{R}^{d_L}$.*

Definition 17 (Knowledge Space). *The knowledge space $\mathcal{K}$ is a lower-dimensional space that contains abstract representations of the information or meaning conveyed by sentences or expressions in the natural language space L. Each point in the knowledge space can be represented as a vector in a relatively lower-dimensional space with $\mathcal{D}_\mathcal{K} < \mathcal{D}_L$ being the dimensionality of the knowledge space.*

Assumption 4 (Smoothness of Natural Language Space). *We assume that the natural language space L is smooth, meaning that small changes in the coordinates of a point in the space correspond to small changes in the meaning or information content of the corresponding sentence or expression.*

Assumption 5 (Smoothness of Knowledge Space). *We assume that the knowledge space $\mathcal{K}$ is smooth, meaning that small changes in the coordinates of a point in the space correspond to small changes in the underlying information or meaning represented by the point.*

Assumption 6 (Locality of Projection Function). *We assume that the projection function $p : L \to \mathcal{K}$ is local, meaning that if two sentences or expressions $s_1, s_2 \in L$ are similar in meaning or information content, then their projections $p(s_1), p(s_2) \in \mathcal{K}$ are also similar in their abstract representations of information or meaning.*

Definition 18 (Projection Function). *A projection function $p : L \to \mathcal{K}$ maps points in the natural language space L to points in the knowledge space $\mathcal{K}$, such that the information or meaning conveyed by a sentence or expression in L is preserved as an abstract representation in $\mathcal{K}$.*

Lemma 1 (Existence of a Projection Function). *There exists a projection function $p : L \to \mathcal{K}$ that maps points in the natural language space L to points in the knowledge space $\mathcal{K}$, preserving the information or meaning conveyed by the corresponding sentence or expression.*

Proof. Under Assumptions 4 and 5, both the natural language space L and the knowledge space $\mathcal{K}$ are smooth. Thus, it is possible to define a continuous mapping between these spaces. Furthermore, since the dimensionality of the knowledge space is lower than that of the natural language space, there exists a projection function $p : L \to \mathcal{K}$ that maps points in L to points in $\mathcal{K}$ while preserving the information or meaning conveyed by the corresponding sentence or expression. □

This lemma establishes the foundational existence of the projection function, facilitating Lemma 2, which discusses the composition of this projection function and its inverse.

Example 2 (Projection of Natural Language Space to Knowledge Space). *Consider a sentence in the natural language space L. Let $s \in L$ represent a specific sentence or expression, with vector representation $v_s \in \mathbb{R}^{d_L}$. We can define a projection function $p : L \to \mathcal{K}$ that maps the sentence s to a point $k \in \mathcal{K}$, with vector representation $v_k \in \mathbb{R}^{d_\mathcal{K}}$, such that $v_k = p(v_s)$. Consider the sentence "London is the capital of England" in the natural language space L. This sentence or expression $s \in L$ can be represented as a vector $v_s \in \mathbb{R}^{d_L}$. Using a projection function $p : L \to \mathcal{K}$, we map this sentence to a point $k \in \mathcal{K}$ in the knowledge space, which is, indeed, challenging to illustrate, but it might be a set of relationships of ("London", "is capital of", "England"). This illustrates how a projection function can convert a sentence from the natural language space to a more formal representation in the knowledge space.*

Definition 19 (Similarity Metric [32]). *A similarity metric $d : \mathcal{K} \times \mathcal{K} \to \mathbb{R}_{\geq 0}$ is a function that measures the similarity between two points in the knowledge space $\mathcal{K}$. It satisfies the following properties for all $k_1, k_2, k_3 \in \mathcal{K}$:*

1. *$d(k_1, k_2) \geq 0$ (non-negativity);*
2. *$d(k_1, k_2) = 0$ if and only if $k_1 = k_2$ (identity of indiscernibles);*
3. *$d(k_1, k_2) = d(k_2, k_1)$ (symmetry); and*
4. *$d(k_1, k_3) \leq d(k_1, k_2) + d(k_2, k_3)$ (triangle inequality).*

Remark 6. *Under the smoothness Assumptions 4 and 5, the projection function p preserves the similarity between sentences or expressions in L as measured by the similarity metric d in $\mathcal{K}$. In other words, if $s_1, s_2 \in L$ are similar in meaning or information content, then $d(p(s_1), p(s_2))$ will be small.*

Definition 20 (Inverse Projection Function). *An inverse projection function $p^{-1} : \mathcal{K} \to L$ maps points in the knowledge space $\mathcal{K}$ back to points in the natural language space L, such that the information or meaning represented by a point in $\mathcal{K}$ is transformed into a corresponding sentence or expression in L.*

Assumption 7 (Existence of an Inverse Projection Function). *We assume that there exists an inverse projection function $p^{-1} : \mathcal{K} \to L$ that maps points in the knowledge space $\mathcal{K}$ back to points in the natural language space L, transforming the information or meaning represented by a point in $\mathcal{K}$ into a corresponding sentence or expression in L.*

Remark 7. *A human can be considered as an example of an inverse projection function $p^{-1} : \mathcal{K} \to L$. When a person is given an abstract representation of information or meaning from the knowledge space $\mathcal{K}$, they can generate a corresponding sentence or expression in the natural language space L. This process involves the cognitive ability to understand the meaning or information represented by a point in $\mathcal{K}$ and to transform it into a coherent and comprehensible sentence or expression in L. Thus, the human ability to communicate and express information can be viewed as an instantiation of the inverse projection function p^{-1}.*

Lemma 2 (Projection-Inverse Projection Composition). *Given a projection function $p : L \to \mathcal{K}$ and an inverse projection function $p^{-1} : \mathcal{K} \to L$, the composition of these functions, denoted by $p^{-1} \circ p : L \to L$, is an approximate identity mapping on the natural language space L.*

Proof. Let $s \in L$ be an arbitrary sentence or expression, and let $k = p(s) \in \mathcal{K}$ be the projection of s into the knowledge space. Since $p^{-1} : \mathcal{K} \to L$ is an inverse projection function, it maps k back to a sentence or expression $s' = p^{-1}(k) \in L$.

Now, consider the composition of the projection and inverse projection functions: $p^{-1} \circ p(s) = p^{-1}(k) = s'$. By Assumption 7, the information or meaning represented by k is transformed into the corresponding sentence or expression s'. Under Assumptions 4 and 5, we can deduce that s' is similar in meaning or information content to the original sentence s.

While s' might not be identical to s, their similarity in meaning or information content implies that the composition $p^{-1} \circ p$ is an approximate identity mapping on the natural language space L. This holds for any arbitrary $s \in L$. □

This lemma builds upon Lemma 1 and forms the underpinning of Theorem 2, which uses this approximate identity mapping for dimensionality reduction.

Theorem 2 (Dimensionality Reduction of Natural Language Space). *Given a natural language space L with dimensionality $\mathcal{D}_L$ and a knowledge space $\mathcal{K}$ with dimensionality $\mathcal{D}_\mathcal{K}$, where $\mathcal{D}_\mathcal{K} < \mathcal{D}_L$, there exists a projection function $p : L \to \mathcal{K}$ and an inverse projection function $p^{-1} : \mathcal{K} \to L$ that allows for dimensionality reduction while preserving the information or meaning conveyed by sentences or expressions in L.*

Proof. By Lemma 1, we have the existence of a projection function $p : L \to \mathcal{K}$ that maps points in the natural language space L to points in the knowledge space $\mathcal{K}$, preserving the information or meaning conveyed by the corresponding sentence or expression.

By Assumption 7, there exists an inverse projection function $p^{-1} : \mathcal{K} \to L$ that maps points in the knowledge space $\mathcal{K}$ back to points in the natural language space L, transforming the information or meaning represented by a point in $\mathcal{K}$ into a corresponding sentence or expression in L.

As shown in the proof of Lemma 2, the composition $p^{-1} \circ p$ is an approximate identity mapping on the natural language space L. Therefore, the information or meaning conveyed by sentences or expressions in L is approximately preserved through the projection to $\mathcal{K}$ and the inverse projection back to L. □

We now introduce a new assumption concerning the preservation of information or meaning when points are mapped between the natural language space and the knowledge space.

Assumption 8 (Preservation of Information). *We assume that for any sentence or expression $s \in L$ and its projection $k \in \mathcal{K}$, the inverse projection function p^{-1} preserves the information or meaning conveyed by s such that $p^{-1}(k) \approx s$.*

This assumption implies that the projection function p and the inverse projection function p^{-1} can be used to perform dimensionality reduction on the natural language space L while preserving the information or meaning conveyed by sentences or expressions in L.

We proceed to show that the composition of the projection function p and the inverse projection function p^{-1} can be used to approximately recover the original sentence or expression in L.

Proposition 4 (Approximate Recovery). *Given a sentence or expression $s \in L$, its projection $k \in \mathcal{K}$, and the inverse projection $p^{-1}(k)$, under Assumption 8, the composition $p^{-1} \circ p(s) \approx s$.*

Proof. By Assumption 8, the inverse projection function p^{-1} preserves the information or meaning conveyed by s such that $p^{-1}(k) \approx s$. Therefore, the composition $p^{-1} \circ p(s) = p^{-1}(p(s)) = p^{-1}(k) \approx s$. □

The above proposition demonstrates that the dimensionality reduction can be achieved while approximately preserving the information or meaning conveyed by sentences or expressions in the natural language space L. This result justifies the use of the projection function p and the inverse projection function p^{-1} for dimensionality reduction in the natural language space, allowing for a compact representation of human language in a lower-dimensional knowledge space $\mathcal{K}$.

4. Representation Space of GPT

Definition 21 (Representation Space of GPT). *The representation space of a GPT model, denoted by $\mathcal{R}$, is a high-dimensional space that contains vector representations of tokens or sequences typically obtained from an intermediate layer of the GPT model, such as the decoder output. Each point in the representation space can be represented as a vector in a high-dimensional space, typically $\mathbb{R}^{d_\mathcal{R}}$, with $d_\mathcal{R}$ being the dimensionality of the representation space.*

In the representation space of a GPT model, tokens and sequences from the natural language space L are mapped to high-dimensional vectors. This mapping allows for the manipulation and processing of language data in a continuous and differentiable space, which is particularly useful for training deep learning models. Importantly, the structure of the representation space should ideally capture the semantic and syntactic properties of the language so that similar meanings or structures are represented by nearby points in the space.

Definition 22 (GPT Vector Representation Function). *A GPT vector representation function $h : L \to \mathcal{R}$ maps sentences or expressions in the natural language space L to points in the representation space $\mathcal{R}$, where each point is represented as a unique vector. The function h ensures that each sentence or expression $s \in L$ has a corresponding vector $v_s \in \mathbb{R}^{d_\mathcal{R}}$ in the representation space $\mathcal{R}$.*

The GPT vector representation function h should be designed to preserve the semantic and syntactic properties of the language in the representation space. This often involves the use of continuous embeddings, which can be learned during the training process. As the GPT model is trained to optimize the autoregressive self-supervised learning objective, the model implicitly learns a mapping that captures the structure and relations between tokens and sequences in the natural language space. The resulting representation space should thus enable the GPT model to reason about and generate natural language text based on the learned representations.

Assumption 9 (Smoothness of Representation Space). *We assume that the representation space $\mathcal{R}$ is smooth, meaning that small changes in the coordinates of a point in the space correspond to small changes in the information or meaning conveyed by the corresponding token or sequence in the GPT model.*

The smoothness assumption on the representation space implies that the GPT model can generalize well to unseen examples, as the learned representations of similar tokens and sequences are expected to be close in the representation space. This smoothness property is crucial for the GPT model to perform well on a wide range of natural language understanding and generation tasks, as it allows the model to exploit the structure of the representation space and make meaningful predictions even for previously unseen combinations of tokens and sequences.

Definition 23 (GPT Inverse Projection Function). *A GPT inverse projection function $g : \mathcal{K} \to \mathcal{R}$ maps points in the knowledge space $\mathcal{K}$ to points in the representation space $\mathcal{R}$, such that the information or meaning represented by a point in $\mathcal{K}$ is transformed into a corresponding vector representation in $\mathcal{R}$, which can be decoded into a sentence or expression in the natural language space L by the GPT model.*

The GPT inverse projection function g serves as a bridge between the knowledge space $\mathcal{K}$ and the representation space $\mathcal{R}$. By mapping points in the knowledge space to corresponding vector representations in the representation space, the GPT model can leverage its learned representations to reason about and manipulate information in the knowledge space. The existence of such an inverse projection function is essential for establishing a connection between the GPT model's representation space and the underlying knowledge space, allowing the model to effectively access and generate knowledge in the form of natural language text.

Assumption 10 (Existence of a GPT Inverse Projection Function). *We assume that there exists a GPT inverse projection function $g : \mathcal{K} \to \mathcal{R}$ that maps points in the knowledge space $\mathcal{K}$ to points in the representation space $\mathcal{R}$, transforming the information or meaning represented by a point in $\mathcal{K}$ into a corresponding vector representation in $\mathcal{R}$, which can be decoded into a sentence or expression in the natural language space L by the GPT model.*

Lemma 3 (GPT as an Approximation of $p^{-1} \circ p$). *Under Assumptions 9 and 10, a GPT model trained using autoregressive self-supervised learning, as described in Definition 14, can be considered as an approximation of the function $p^{-1} \circ p : L \to L$.*

Proof. Let $x \in L$ be a sentence or expression in the natural language space. By Definition 18, we have $p(x) \in \mathcal{K}$, which is the corresponding point in the knowledge space.

Now, consider the GPT inverse projection function g as defined in Definition 23. We have $g(p(x)) \in \mathcal{R}$, which is a point in the representation space. Since GPT is trained using autoregressive self-supervised learning as described in Definition 14, it learns to approximate the function $p^{-1} \circ p : L \to L$ by minimizing the difference between its own output and the original input.

Let $\hat{x} \in L$ be the output of the GPT model for the input x. By the assumption of the existence of the GPT inverse projection function (Assumption 10), there exists a function $g : \mathcal{K} \to \mathcal{R}$ such that $g(p(x)) \in \mathcal{R}$.

Under the assumption of smoothness of the representation space (Assumption 9), small changes in the coordinates of a point in the space correspond to small changes in the information or meaning conveyed by the corresponding token or sequence in the GPT model. Since the GPT model is trained to minimize the difference between its output and the input, we have $\hat{x} \approx x$.

Therefore, the GPT model can be considered as an approximation of the function $p^{-1} \circ p : L \to L$. □

Lemma 3 suggests that a well-trained GPT model can approximate the composition of the projection function p and its inverse p^{-1}. This approximation enables the GPT model to effectively learn the structure and relations in the natural language space by transforming input sentences and expressions into a suitable representation space, processing them, and then transforming the resulting representations back into the natural language space. This capability allows the GPT model to perform a wide range of natural language understanding and generation tasks, as it can manipulate and reason about language data in a continuous and differentiable space.

Theorem 3 (GPT Representation Space as an Approximation of Knowledge Space). *Under Assumptions 9 and 10, the representation space $\mathcal{R}$ of a GPT model trained using autoregressive self-supervised learning can be considered as an approximation of the knowledge space $\mathcal{K}$, where the GPT model serves as an approximation of the function $p^{-1} \circ p$.*

Proof. Let $x \in L$ be a sentence or expression in the natural language space. By Lemma 3, the GPT model serves as an approximation of the function $p^{-1} \circ p : L \to L$, meaning that the GPT model learns to approximate the transformation from the natural language space to the knowledge space and back to the natural language space.

By Definition 18, we have $p(x) \in \mathcal{K}$, which is the corresponding point in the knowledge space. Now, consider the GPT inverse projection function g as defined in Definition 23. We have $g(p(x)) \in \mathcal{R}$, which is a point in the representation space.

As the GPT model is an approximation of $p^{-1} \circ p : L \to L$, it should also learn to approximate the inverse projection function g that maps points from the knowledge space to the representation space. Thus, the GPT model learns to approximate the transformation from the knowledge space to the representation space. Since the GPT model is trained to minimize the difference between its output and the input, we have $g(p(x)) \approx p(x)$.

Therefore, under Assumptions 9 and 10, the representation space $\mathcal{R}$ of a GPT model trained using autoregressive self-supervised learning can be considered as an approximation of the knowledge space $\mathcal{K}$. □

Theorem 3 serves as a crucial mathematical underpinning in our exploration of GPT-based models. It enables us to unravel the internal mathematical workings of these models by positing the GPT representation space $\mathcal{R}$ as an approximation of the knowledge space $\mathcal{K}$. This formalized definition brings a mathematical rigor to the understanding of the transformation process that the GPT model performs in mapping the natural language space L to the knowledge space $\mathcal{K}$ and vice versa through its layers of non-linear transformations and attention mechanisms. The proof of the theorem further buttresses this interpretation.

This assertion can be viewed as an encapsulation of the intuition prevalent among experts studying GPT-based models. The GPT model is essentially learning to transform natural language inputs into a dense representation space and vice versa. This dense representation is what we are referring to as the GPT representation space $\mathcal{R}$. Thus, the $\mathcal{R}$ serves as an approximation of $\mathcal{K}$, capturing the semantic essence of the sentences or expressions in the natural language space L.

5. Challenges and Limitations of GPT and Autoregressive Self-Supervised Learning

Definition 24 (Incomplete Inverse Projection Function). *An incomplete inverse projection function is an inverse projection function $p^{-1} : \mathcal{K} \to L$ that may not perfectly map all points in the knowledge space $\mathcal{K}$ to their corresponding points in the natural language space L. This implies that certain types of information or meaning may not be adequately represented in L using the inverse projection function p^{-1}.*

The projection function limitation refers to the inability of the projection function $p : L \to \mathcal{K}$ and its inverse $p^{-1} : \mathcal{K} \to L$ to accurately capture and represent specific knowledge or meaning within the natural language space L and knowledge space $\mathcal{K}$. This limitation could be attributed to the complexity of the relationship between these spaces or the insufficiency of the model's architecture in representing certain types of knowledge.

Assumption 11 (Incomplete Inverse Projection Function). *We assume that the inverse projection function $p^{-1} : \mathcal{K} \to L$, as described in Assumption 7, may be incomplete in the sense that it may not adequately map certain types of knowledge or meaning from $\mathcal{K}$ to L, as defined in Definition 24.*

Assumption 12 (Projection Function Limitation Impact). *We assume that the projection function limitation could adversely affect the performance of GPT-based models, such as ChatGPT, in tasks that require precise mapping between the knowledge space $\mathcal{K}$ and the natural language space L. This limitation could manifest as inaccuracies, ambiguities, or inconsistencies in the generated responses, particularly when dealing with complex or nuanced information.*

The impact of the projection function limitation on GPT-based models, as described in Assumption 12, not only influences the quality of the generated responses but can also affect the model's ability to make reliable inferences. In particular, when the projection function and its inverse fail to accurately map between the knowledge space and the natural language space, the model may encounter difficulties in synthesizing relevant information, comprehending contextual clues, and adapting to new or evolving concepts. This limitation may be exacerbated when handling specialized domains or interdisciplinary subjects where a precise understanding of terminology, relationships, and dependencies is paramount for generating coherent and contextually accurate responses.

Remark 8 (Calculation Limitation). *Assumption 11 implies that certain types of knowledge, such as calculation, may be difficult to represent in the natural language space L using the inverse projection function p^{-1}. Consequently, GPT-based models may face challenges in performing accurate calculations due to the limitations of their inverse projection function.*

Another potential challenge arising from the limitations of the inverse projection function in GPT-based models is the difficulty in processing and reasoning about abstract concepts, particularly when they involve logical, mathematical, or scientific principles. Due to the inherent complexity and often non-linear nature of these concepts, it can be difficult for the inverse projection function to effectively represent the associated knowledge within the natural language space. This may lead to suboptimal performance when attempting to generate responses that require reasoning about abstract or complex ideas, as the model may struggle to accurately represent and manipulate the relevant information within its internal representations.

Assumption 12 suggests that GPT-based models might face challenges in accurately understanding and interpreting certain types of information due to the limitations of the projection function and its inverse. This could result in a lack of understanding of the underlying meaning or context of the input data, leading to inappropriate or irrelevant responses.

Definition 25 (Model Complexity). *Model complexity refers to the number of parameters or the depth of a deep learning model. A model with a higher complexity generally has more parameters or deeper layers, enabling it to capture more intricate patterns and relationships within the input data.*

Corollary 1 (Complexity and Approximation). *Given Theorem 1, a deep learning model with a larger complexity, as defined in Definition 25, is more likely to satisfy the conditions of the Universal Approximation Theorem, allowing it to approximate a target function with higher accuracy.*

Corollary 2 (Complexity and Efficiency Trade-off). *Given Definition 25, there exists a trade-off between model complexity and model efficiency in deep learning models. Increasing the complexity of a model may improve its ability to approximate a target function, as stated in Corollary 1, but* it may also lead to increased computational costs and resource requirements, thereby reducing the model's efficiency.

Moreover, the trade-off between model complexity and efficiency, as described in Corollary 2, has implications for the practicality and accessibility of GPT-based models. As these models grow in size and complexity to better approximate target functions, their computational requirements can become increasingly demanding, making them more difficult to deploy and maintain in real-world applications. This can be particularly challenging for smaller organizations or individuals with limited resources who may struggle to harness the full potential of these large-scale models. Additionally, the increased computational demands can lead to higher energy consumption and environmental concerns, further highlighting the need to balance complexity and efficiency in the development of GPT-based models.

Corollary 3 (Model Complexity and Generalization). *While increasing model complexity, as defined in Definition 25, may improve the ability of a deep learning model to approximate a target function, as stated in Corollary 1, it may also lead to overfitting, resulting in reduced generalization capabilities. This trade-off between complexity and generalization is an important consideration when designing and training GPT-based models.*

Example 3 (Large Language Models and Universal Approximation). *Large language models, such as GPT-based models, have gained popularity due to their ability to satisfy the conditions of the Universal Approximation Theorem. The large number of parameters in these models enables them to capture intricate patterns and relationships within the input data, allowing them to perform tasks such as natural language understanding and generation with high accuracy. Consider a large language model such as GPT-3 being utilized for translation tasks. Given a complex sentence in English, the model, due to its extensive parameter space, is able to understand the intricate relationships between words and their context, translating it accurately to another language such as French. This capability demonstrates how the large number of parameters enables GPT-3 to approximate the intricacies of language translation.*

The advantages of large language models, such as GPT-based models, in terms of their ability to satisfy the conditions of the Universal Approximation Theorem, as described in Example 3, should not overshadow the potential pitfalls associated with their scale. As these models grow in size, they may become increasingly susceptible to overfitting, noise, or biases present in the training data. This can manifest as a heightened sensitivity to specific patterns, phrases, or concepts within the input data, potentially leading to the generation of responses that are less adaptable, less diverse, or less contextually appropriate. Consequently, it is important to carefully consider the impact of model size and complexity on both the benefits and potential drawbacks associated with GPT-based models.

Example 4 (Large Language Models and Generalization Challenges). *While large language models, such as GPT-based models, excel at capturing intricate patterns and relationships within input data, they may also face challenges related to generalization. As discussed in Corollary 3, the trade-off between complexity and generalization can result in overfitting, limiting the model's ability to generalize to new, unseen data or contexts. Despite the impressive capabilities of large language models, generalization remains a challenge. For instance, a GPT-3 model trained predominantly on English literature might struggle to accurately generate text in the style of an obscure, regional dialect or an emerging online slang despite its vast parameter space. This example illustrates the trade-off between complexity and generalization and the resultant risk of overfitting to familiar data at the expense of novel contexts.*

6. Conclusions

In this paper, we have explored the mathematical foundations of GPT-based models such as ChatGPT, delving into the intricate relationships between the natural language space L, knowledge space $\mathcal{K}$, and the representation space $\mathcal{R}$. We have formalized key concepts, definitions, assumptions, and theorems to provide a rigorous understanding of these models' underlying mechanisms.

Our investigation has revealed that GPT-based models, when trained using autoregressive self-supervised learning, can be considered as approximations of the composition of the projection function $p : \mathrm{L} \to \mathcal{K}$ and the inverse projection function $p^{-1} : \mathcal{K} \to \mathrm{L}$ (refer to the second research aspect in the introduction). Consequently, the GPT representation space $\mathcal{R}$ serves as an approximation of the knowledge space $\mathcal{K}$, capturing and preserving the information or meaning conveyed by sentences or expressions in L (pertaining to the first and third research aspects in the introduction).

Notwithstanding their remarkable capabilities, we have identified certain limitations of GPT-based models stemming from incomplete inverse projection functions, which may not adequately map all points in the knowledge space $\mathcal{K}$ to their corresponding points in the natural language space L (as outlined in the fourth research aspect in the introduction). This shortcoming results in challenges, such as difficulties in performing accurate calculations, which are inherently problematic for models such as ChatGPT (as illustrated in Examples 3 and 4).

In the pursuit of elucidating the complex mathematical foundations underpinning the GPT model, particularly its functional aspects denoted as $p^{-1} \circ p(s)$, we concede the inherent challenge of directly validating these findings through empirical experimentation due to their abstract nature. Nonetheless, our endeavor was not solely confined to the construction of mathematical arguments; instead, we endeavored to make these abstractions more comprehensible to the readers. To this end, we integrated illustrative examples within our discourse wherever feasible. These examples, coalesced with our theoretical discourse, are aimed at providing the readers with a more tangible grasp of the mathematical constructs that govern the GPT model. The objective of our study was twofold: firstly, to maintain the requisite mathematical rigor, and secondly, to enhance the accessibility of our exposition to a broad spectrum of readers. We trust that our efforts have been successful in striking a harmonious balance between these two critical aspects of academic writing.

This study has provided a mathematical characterization of GPT-based LLMs, establishing a framework that can serve as a launchpad for future investigations in this domain. Our findings, particularly the mathematical underpinnings of how GPT models capture and represent the semantic essence of natural language, present avenues for the optimization and expansion of these models. By unveiling the limitations of GPT-based models, we open doors for future research to focus on addressing these challenges, potentially advancing the development of LLMs that offer more accurate and comprehensive mappings between natural language and knowledge spaces. Our exploration of GPT as an approximation of the projection function and its inverse has potential implications for the development of more efficient, effective, and robust LLMs, thereby driving advancements in the field of language understanding and generation.

In the broader context, this work has several potential implications for future advancements in the field of GPT-based LLMs. Firstly, our formal definition of the natural language space L and the knowledge space $\mathcal{K}$, along with the associated projection functions, provides a strong mathematical foundation for understanding the complex mechanisms underlying these models. This understanding can guide future efforts to develop more efficient dimensionality reduction techniques, which could significantly improve the computational efficiency of these models.

Moreover, our theoretical analysis of the projection function p and its inverse p^{-1} may provide valuable insights for enhancing the language generation capabilities of GPT-based LLMs. Specifically, our observations regarding the limitations of the inverse projection function could spur research toward methods for improving these models' ability to generate accurate and contextually appropriate responses.

Funding: This work was supported by a research grant funded by Generative Artificial Intelligence System Inc. (GAIS).

Institutional Review Board Statement: Not applicable.

Informed Consent Statement: Not applicable.

Data Availability Statement: No new data were created or analyzed in this study.

Conflicts of Interest: The author declares no conflict of interest.

References

1. Radford, A.; Wu, J.; Child, R.; Luan, D.; Amodei, D.; Sutskever, I. Language models are unsupervised multitask learners. In *OpenAI Technical Report*; OpenAI Inc.: San Francisco, CA, USA, 2019.
2. OpenAI. GPT-4 Technical Report. In *OpenAI Technical Report*; OpenAI Inc.: San Francisco, CA, USA, 2023.
3. Brown, T.; Mann, B.; Ryder, N.; Subbiah, M.; Kaplan, J.D.; Dhariwal, P.; Neelakantan, A.; Shyam, P.; Sastry, G.; Askell, A.; et al. Language models are few-shot learners. *Adv. Neural Inf. Process. Syst.* **2020**, *33*, 1877–1901.
4. Radford, A.; Narasimhan, K.; Salimans, T.; Sutskever, I. Improving language understanding by generative pre-training. In *OpenAI Technical Report*; OpenAI Inc.: San Francisco, CA, USA, 2018.
5. Tirumala, K.; Markosyan, A.; Zettlemoyer, L.; Aghajanyan, A. Memorization without overfitting: Analyzing the training dynamics of large language models. *Adv. Neural Inf. Process. Syst.* **2022**, *35*, 38274–38290.
6. Wei, J.; Wang, X.; Schuurmans, D.; Bosma, M.; Xia, F.; Chi, E.H.; Le, Q.V.; Zhou, D. Chain-of-Thought Prompting Elicits Reasoning in Large Language Models. In Proceedings of the Advances in Neural Information Processing Systems, New Orleans, LA, USA, 29 November 2022.
7. Kung, T.H.; Cheatham, M.; Medenilla, A.; Sillos, C.; De Leon, L.; Elepaño, C.; Madriaga, M.; Aggabao, R.; Diaz-Candido, G.; Maningo, J.; et al. Performance of ChatGPT on USMLE: Potential for AI-assisted medical education using large language models. *PLoS Digit. Health* **2023**, *2*, e0000198. [CrossRef] [PubMed]
8. Shoeybi, M.; Patwary, M.; Puri, R.; LeGresley, P.; Casper, J.; Catanzaro, B. Megatron-lm: Training multi-billion parameter language models using model parallelism. *arXiv* **2019**, arXiv:1909.08053.
9. Lee, M. A Mathematical Investigation of Hallucination and Creativity in GPT Models. *Mathematics* **2023**, *11*, 2320. [CrossRef]
10. Carlini, N.; Tramer, F.; Wallace, E.; Jagielski, M.; Herbert-Voss, A.; Lee, K.; Roberts, A.; Brown, T.B.; Song, D.; Erlingsson, U.; et al. Extracting Training Data from Large Language Models. In Proceedings of the USENIX Security Symposium, Virtual, 11–13 August 2021; Volume 6.
11. Hu, E.J.; Shen, Y.; Wallis, P.; Allen-Zhu, Z.; Li, Y.; Wang, S.; Wang, L.; Chen, W. Lora: Low-rank adaptation of large language models. *arXiv* **2021**, arXiv:2106.09685
12. Ko, K.; Yeom, T.; Lee, M. Superstargan: Generative adversarial networks for image-to-image translation in large-scale domains. *Neural Netws.* **2023**, *162*, 330–339. [CrossRef]
13. Ku, H.; Lee, M. TextControlGAN: Text-to-Image Synthesis with Controllable Generative Adversarial Networks. *Appl. Sci.* **2023**, *13*, 5098. [CrossRef]
14. Kim, J.; Lee, M. Class-Continuous Conditional Generative Neural Radiance Field. *arXiv* **2023**, arXiv:2301.00950.
15. Kim, I.; Lee, M.; Seok, J. ICEGAN: Inverse covariance estimating generative adversarial network. *Mach. Learn. Sci. Technol.* **2023**, *4*, 025008. [CrossRef]
16. Luo, R.; Sun, L.; Xia, Y.; Qin, T.; Zhang, S.; Poon, H.; Liu, T.Y. BioGPT: Generative pre-trained transformer for biomedical text generation and mining. *Briefings Bioinform.* **2022**, *23*, bbac409. [CrossRef] [PubMed]
17. Zhu, Q.; Zhang, X.; Luo, J. Biologically Inspired Design Concept Generation Using Generative Pre-Trained Transformers. *J. Mech. Des.* **2023**, *145*, 041409. [CrossRef]
18. Albelwi, S. Survey on self-supervised learning: Auxiliary pretext tasks and contrastive learning methods in imaging. *Entropy* **2022**, *24*, 551. [CrossRef]
19. Liu, X.; Zhang, F.; Hou, Z.; Mian, L.; Wang, Z.; Zhang, J.; Tang, J. Self-supervised learning: Generative or contrastive. *IEEE Trans. Knowl. Data Eng.* **2021**, *35*, 857–876. [CrossRef]
20. Jaiswal, A.; Babu, A.R.; Zadeh, M.Z.; Banerjee, D.; Makedon, F. A survey on contrastive self-supervised learning. *Technologies* **2020**, *9*, 2. [CrossRef]
21. LeCun, Y.; Bengio, Y.; Hinton, G. Deep learning. *Nature* **2015**, *521*, 436–444. [CrossRef]
22. Lu, Y.; Lu, J. A universal approximation theorem of deep neural networks for expressing probability distributions. *Adv. Neural Inf. Process. Syst.* **2020**, *33*, 3094–3105.
23. Vaswani, A.; Shazeer, N.; Parmar, N.; Uszkoreit, J.; Jones, L.; Gomez, A.N.; Kaiser, Ł.; Polosukhin, I. Attention is all you need. *Adv. Neural Inf. Process. Syst.* **2017**, *30*, 6000–6010.
24. Xu, R.; Wang, X.; Chen, K.; Zhou, B.; Loy, C.C. Positional encoding as spatial inductive bias in gans. In Proceedings of the Proceedings of the IEEE/CVF Conference on Computer Vision and Pattern Recognition, Nashville, TN, USA, 20–25 June 2021; pp. 13569–13578.
25. Zheng, J.; Ramasinghe, S.; Lucey, S. Rethinking positional encoding. *arXiv* **2021**, arXiv:2107.02561
26. Ba, J.L.; Kiros, J.R.; Hinton, G.E. Layer normalization. *arXiv* **2016**, arXiv:1607.06450
27. Li, J.; Wang, X.; Tu, Z.; Lyu, M.R. On the diversity of multi-head attention. *Neurocomputing* **2021**, *454*, 14–24. [CrossRef]

28. Voita, E.; Talbot, D.; Moiseev, F.; Sennrich, R.; Titov, I. Analyzing multi-head self-attention: Specialized heads do the heavy lifting, the rest can be pruned. *arXiv* **2019**, arXiv:1905.09418.
29. Kaplan, J.; McCandlish, S.; Henighan, T.; Brown, T.B.; Chess, B.; Child, R.; Gray, S.; Radford, A.; Wu, J.; Amodei, D. Scaling laws for neural language models. *arXiv* **2020**, arXiv:2001.08361.
30. Orlitsky, A. Information Theory. In *Encyclopedia of Physical Science and Technology*, 3rd ed.; Meyers, R.A., Ed.; Academic Press: New York, NY, USA, 2003; pp. 751–769. [CrossRef]
31. Brown, P.F.; Della Pietra, S.A.; Della Pietra, V.J.; Lai, J.C.; Mercer, R.L. An estimate of an upper bound for the entropy of English. *Comput. Linguist.* **1992**, *18*, 31–40.
32. Santini, S.; Jain, R. Similarity measures. *IEEE Trans. Pattern Anal. Mach. Intell.* **1999**, *21*, 871–883. [CrossRef]

Disclaimer/Publisher's Note: The statements, opinions and data contained in all publications are solely those of the individual author(s) and contributor(s) and not of MDPI and/or the editor(s). MDPI and/or the editor(s) disclaim responsibility for any injury to people or property resulting from any ideas, methods, instructions or products referred to in the content.

Article

Reduction of Neural Machine Translation Failures by Incorporating Statistical Machine Translation

Jani Dugonik *, Mirjam Sepesy Maučec, Domen Verber and Janez Brest

Faculty of Electrical Engineering and Computer Science, University of Maribor, SI-2000 Maribor, Slovenia
* Correspondence: jani.dugonik@um.si; Tel.: +386-2-220-7432

Abstract: This paper proposes a hybrid machine translation (HMT) system that improves the quality of neural machine translation (NMT) by incorporating statistical machine translation (SMT). Therefore, two NMT systems and two SMT systems were built for the Slovenian–English language pair, each for translation in one direction. We used a multilingual language model to embed the source sentence and translations into the same vector space. From each vector, we extracted features based on the distances and similarities calculated between the source sentence and the NMT translation, and between the source sentence and the SMT translation. To select the best possible translation, we used several well-known classifiers to predict which translation system generated a better translation of the source sentence. The proposed method of combining SMT and NMT in the hybrid system is novel. Our framework is language-independent and can be applied to other languages supported by the multilingual language model. Our experiment involved empirical applications. We compared the performance of the classifiers, and the results demonstrate that our proposed HMT system achieved notable improvements in the BLEU score, with an increase of 1.5 points and 10.9 points for both translation directions, respectively.

Keywords: neural machine translation; statistical machine translation; sentence embedding; similarity; classification; hybrid machine translation

MSC: 68T50

Citation: Dugonik, J.; Sepesy Maučec, M.; Verber, D.; Brest, J. Reduction of Neural Machine Translation Failures by Incorporating Statistical Machine Translation. *Mathematics* **2023**, *11*, 2484. https://doi.org/10.3390/math11112484

Academic Editor: Florentina Hristea

Received: 21 April 2023
Revised: 24 May 2023
Accepted: 25 May 2023
Published: 28 May 2023

Copyright: © 2023 by the authors. Licensee MDPI, Basel, Switzerland. This article is an open access article distributed under the terms and conditions of the Creative Commons Attribution (CC BY) license (https://creativecommons.org/licenses/by/4.0/).

1. Introduction

The statistical machine translation (SMT) paradigm was the primary approach used in machine translation (MT) research for many years. About a decade ago, neural machine translation (NMT) emerged and produced remarkable results. As a result, SMT systems were largely replaced by NMT systems in practical applications. Today, SMT systems are rarely used, with NMT architectures dominating both research and practical applications of machine translation. While NMT generally outperforms SMT, there are certain cases where SMT remains superior. Research has shown that the errors made by NMT and SMT systems are complementary [1]. For instance, NMT outputs are more prone to accuracy-related errors, such as mistranslation and omission errors, while both systems tend to make word-form errors in morphologically rich languages, with NMT performing slightly better [2].

Languages that share similarities tend to be easier to translate due to the presence of equivalent linguistic structures. In machine translation, languages are often paired with English, due largely to the availability of bilingual corpora. The English language is an analytic language that employs helper words (such as particles and prepositions) and word order to express relationships between words. As such, the linguistic structures are relatively simple. Conversely, morphologically rich languages tend to have more complex linguistic structures, with inflectional languages using inflections to express relationships between words and having a more relaxed word order. While NMT approaches generally outperform SMT for the majority of language phenomena, there are still cases that are handled better by SMT. For instance, according to [2], SMT may, in some cases, be preferable for highly inflected languages.

In this paper, we examine the translation between English and the highly inflected Slovenian language in both directions. We propose a hybrid machine translation system that combines both approaches in order to capitalize on their respective strengths. The main contributions of this paper are to improve NMT translation quality by using SMT, and to represent the source sentence and both translations as the vectors in the same vector space, using a multilingual language model. The used multilingual language model, mBERT [3], supports more than 100 languages, making it versatile across multiple languages. The source and translation vectors are then utilized to extract features, which are subsequently fed into classifiers that predict which translation system produced a superior translation. The proposed method of combining SMT and NMT in the hybrid system is novel. Our framework is language-independent and can be applied to other languages supported by the multilingual language model.

The remainder of the paper is organized as follows. Section 2 presents the background of our research. It contains related work, preliminaries of NMT and SMT, the classification task, and our aims and research contributions. Section 3 presents the methodology of the proposed HMT. The experiments and results are described in Section 4. We discuss the obtained results in Section 5, and conclude the paper with Section 6.

2. Background

In this section, we present the related work and provide the necessary preliminaries for a better understanding of this paper.

2.1. Related Work

There is no doubt that NMT is currently the prevalent approach to MT. Before NMT, the most effective SMT systems were based on phrase-based models [4,5]. In these systems, different models (the translation model, reordering model, language model, etc.) were trained independently and combined in a log-linear scheme, in which each model was assigned a different weight by a tuning algorithm [6].

In NMT, there are no separate models; instead, a large network is trained as a whole [7,8]. This network is trained to transform the source sentence directly into the target sentence, and words are represented as continuous vectors called word embeddings. The learned word embeddings capture morphological, syntactic, and semantic similarity across words [9]. Methods for training word embeddings on raw text often consider the context in which the word frequently occurs. For MT, it is desirable to embed whole phrases or sentences instead of single words. To accomplish this, self-attention is used to find sentence representations [10].

Different NMT architectures have been developed over time, and they generally exhibit comparable performance. The first standalone architecture was Long Short-Term Memory (LSTM), which is a sequence-to-sequence encoder–decoder architecture that uses two Recurrent Neural Networks (RNNs) [7,8]. An encoder network produces a representation of the source sentence, and a decoder network generates the target sentence from that representation. LSTM is used as a gated activation function to address the vanishing gradient problem, which makes it difficult to train RNNs to capture long-range dependencies [8]. The first architectures represented the source sentence as a fixed-length vector and different word orders were examined in the source sentence. Bidirectional RNNs are able to capture both directions and are most commonly used [11]. The concept of attention was introduced in [11] to avoid a fixed-length source sentence representation. The attention decoder can place its attention on the parts of the source sentence that are useful for generating the next word in the translation using time-dependent context vectors. The attention mechanism is the interface between the encoder and decoder. Afterwards, convolutional architectures were introduced [12], which have several potential advantages over RNN models. They reduce sequential computation, and their hierarchical structure connects distant words via a shorter path. For the translation of long sentences, multiple convolutional layers are used, which increase the effective context size. Convolutional models are deeper and often more difficult to train. The attention mechanism called self-attention relates several positions in the source and target sentences without using sequence-aligned RNNs or convolutions [10]. The Transformer architecture uses multi-headed self-attention and is currently one of the most widely used NMT architectures [10].

The authors in [13,14] provide an overview of the literature and approaches to combining NMT and SMT paradigms. They highlight that, while NMT has become the dominant approach in recent years, NMT and SMT have complementary strengths. Two categories of hybrid approaches are discussed. The first category includes methods that incorporate key ideas or components from SMT into NMT, such as combining NMT scores with SMT features and incorporating symbolic SMT-style lexical translation tables into the NMT decoder. The second category involves system combination, where a fully trained SMT system is combined with an independently trained NMT system, often using rescoring and reranking methods or minimum Bayes risk (MBR)-based approaches. Various combinations and cascades of NMT and SMT are explored, demonstrating the flexibility and potential for improving translation quality through hybrid approaches. Ensembling different NMT models has been shown to outperform single ones. The number of different NMT models in ensemble architectures ranges from 2 to up to 72 translation models [8,15]. However, the decoding speed is significantly worse when using many translation models. The decoder needs to apply multiple models rather than only one. It makes sense if the models complement each other. Models are either trained independently [8] or they share some training iterations [16]. The ensemble decoder computes predictions for each model, which are then combined using the arithmetic or geometric average [8,17]. The authors in [18] proposed a hybrid MT system that combines NMT and rule-based MT (RBMT) to compensate for the inadequacy of NMT in rare-resource domains. They used a classifier to predict which translation from the two systems was more reliable, and to do so, they explored a set of features that reflected the reliability of the translation. They also made a comparison between feature- and text-based classification, and the results showed that the feature-based classification achieved better classification accuracy. In our paper, we combine NMT and SMT for translation in both directions. We also use different sets of feature vectors, where we first transform our source sentence and both translations into the same vector space. Then, we use similarity and distance measures to obtain feature vectors. The authors in [19] address the challenge of improving NMT systems in low-resource scenarios, where large-scale parallel corpora are not readily available. The proposed approach leverages an SMT system to extract parallel phrases from the original training data, augmenting the training data for the NMT system. The approach utilizes gated recurrent unit (GRU) and Transformer architecture, and is evaluated on Hindi–English and Hindi–Bengali datasets in the domains of Health, Tourism, and Judicial.

2.2. Preliminaries

This section describes the basics of two MT paradigms: NMT and SMT. Both approaches belong to supervised approaches to MT based on machine learning technology, where training is conducted using sentence-aligned (human) translations. Given a large number of source/target language sentence pairs, the MT system learns how to translate fully automatically. NMT is described first since it is the dominant approach today, followed by the description of SMT, as it is used as the complementary approach. In this paper, we propose the HMT architecture as a two-engine combination in which the selection between NMT and SMT is made by the classification algorithm. Therefore, a short description of the classification algorithms that we used is also given in this section.

2.2.1. Neural Machine Translation

NMT is an approach to MT that uses an artificial neural network. The state-of-the-art NMT systems use the Transformer architecture [10], which is shown in Figure 1, to produce high-quality translations. The Transformer architecture relies on the attention mechanism and remains the dominant architecture for several language pairs. Self-attention is an attention mechanism that connects different positions of a single sequence to compute a sequence representation. The self-attention mechanism is used successfully in various tasks, such as text summarization and textual integration. The self-attention layers of this architecture learn the dependencies between words in a sequence by studying the connections between all the words in the matching sequences and by directly modeling these relationships. This approach is simpler than the gating mechanism used by RNNs. The simplicity of this architecture has allowed for researchers to develop high-quality translation models with the Transformer architecture, even for languages with few resources. The Transformer architecture was the first to rely entirely on the self-attention mechanism to compute input and output representations, without using feed-forward or sequence-aligned convolutional neural networks. The encoder and decoder can be stacked N layers high, with each layer taking inputs from the encoder and the previous layers. By stacking layers, the model can learn to extract and focus on different combinations of attention from its attention heads, boosting prediction power.

During training, the model is optimized to minimize the difference between its predicted translations and the true translations in the training data. This is typically achieved using maximum likelihood estimation, where the model is trained to maximize the likelihood of generating the correct target sentence given the source sentence.

Overall, NMT with the Transformer architecture has shown great promise in producing high-quality translations across a wide range of language pairs [20]. It is now used widely in many real-world translation applications and continues to be an active area of research [21–24].

2.2.2. Statistical Machine Translation

Phrase-based SMT, shown in Figure 2, is a traditional approach to MT that has been used widely for many years. It is based on the idea of breaking down the input sentence into smaller phrases or sequences of words, translating them independently, and then recombining them to form the final translation. Phrase-based SMT systems learn dependencies between words, phrases, or sequences of words in both languages, as well as dependencies between words in the target language and local reorderings, among other things [4]. These learned dependencies are stored in the various models of the SMT system. M denotes a number of models used in SMT.

2.2.3. Classification

In a classification task [25,26], the goal is to assign a set of input instances to predefined categories or classes. A binary classification task [27] specifically involves dividing the instances into two distinct classes. The task aims to determine to which class a given instance belongs based on its features or attributes.

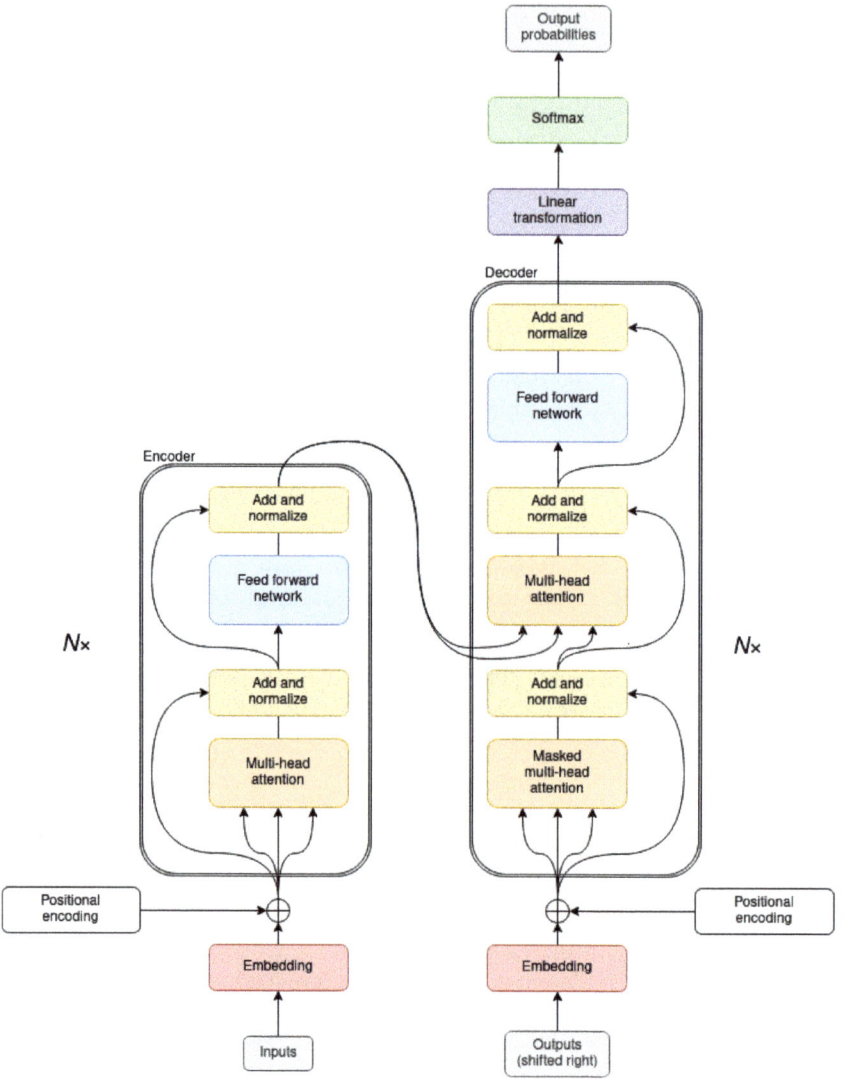

Figure 1. The Transformer architecture for training NMT systems.

In our framework, a vital part of the hybridization approach is the classification task that is used to choose either SMT or NMT translation as the final translation. Therefore, we used and compared some of the well-known algorithms for binary classification:

- Logistic Regression (LR) [28] is a simple and widely used algorithm for binary classification. It works by modeling the probability of the positive class using a logistic function.
- Decision Tree (DT) [29] is a simple algorithm for binary classification. It works by splitting the data recursively, based on the features that are most informative for the classification task.
- Gradient-Boosted Decision Tree (GBDT) [30] is an algorithm that sequentially builds decision trees to correct errors made by previous trees, making it effective for binary classification tasks. It combines the predictions of multiple trees to provide accurate

binary classification results, capturing complex patterns in the data while mitigating overfitting through regularization techniques.
- Random Forest (RF) [31] is an ensemble learning method that combines multiple decision trees to improve the accuracy and stability of the model. It works by selecting a subset of features randomly at each node in the decision tree.
- Naive Bayes (NB) [32] is a probabilistic algorithm that assumes independence between features and works by calculating the probability of the observation belonging to each class based on the likelihood and prior probabilities.
- K-Nearest Neighbors (kNN) [33] is a non-parametric algorithm that works by finding the k-nearest data points to a new observation and assigning the label based on the majority of the neighbors.
- Multilayer Perceptron (MLP) [28] is a type of neural network (NN) that can be used for binary classification problems. It works by building a network of interconnected nodes that process input data and produce an output.
- Convolutional Neural Network (CNN) [34] is a type of neural network that excels at analyzing and extracting features from structured data-like images. Layers of convolutional filters are used to automatically learn hierarchical representations, making them highly effective for binary classification tasks where they can capture intricate patterns and relationships in the data to make accurate predictions.
- Support Vector Machine (SVM) [28] is a powerful machine learning algorithm that is commonly used for binary classification problems. It works by finding a hyperplane that separates the two classes with the largest possible margin.

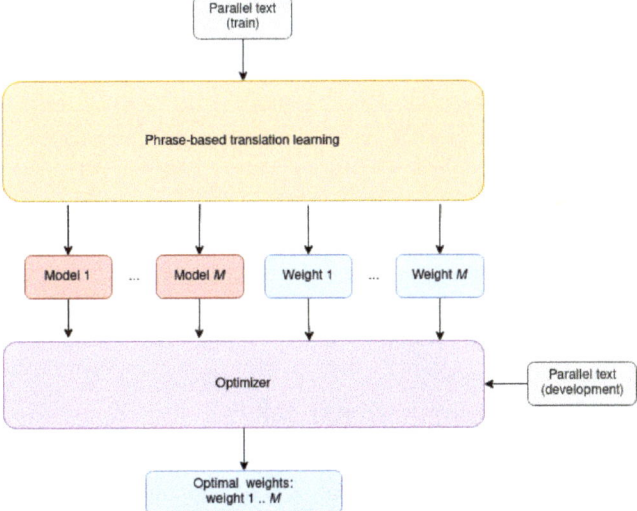

Figure 2. The SMT architecture for training SMT systems.

Equation (1) represents the obtaining of translations for a given source sentence s, where t_1 and t_2 are the translations generated by the NMT and SMT systems, respectively. The use of the trained models (obtained as shown in Figures 1 and 2) in the translation procedure is shown in Figure 3.

$$t_1 = NMT(s), \ t_2 = SMT(s) \tag{1}$$

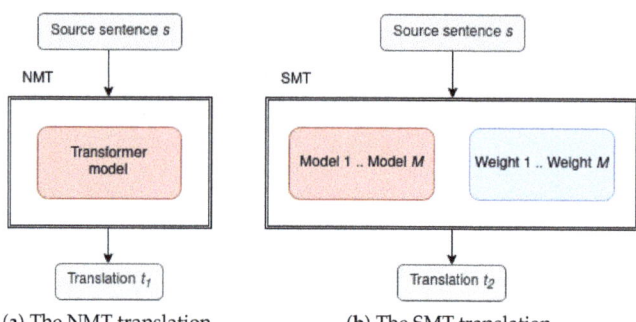

(a) The NMT translation. (b) The SMT translation.

Figure 3. NMT generates the translation t_1 using one large model, while SMT generates the translation t_2 using multiple models.

The classification task can be formalized as:

$$f: (x_{t_1}, x_{t_2}) \rightarrow \{0, 1\}, \quad f \in \{LR, DT, GBDT, RF, NB, kNN, MLP, CNN, SVM\}, \quad (2)$$

where x_{t_1} and x_{t_2} are the feature vectors of translations t_1 and t_2, respectively, and 0 denotes translation t_2 and 1 denotes translation t_1. The feature vectors fed into the classifier should reflect the adequacy of the translations. Therefore, they are constructed depending on the source sentence s. The construction of feature vectors is important for the accuracy of the classification task.

2.3. Aim and Research Contribution

The goal of this paper is to reduce translation failures in NMT by integrating SMT, and the source sentence and translations are represented as the vectors in the same vector space, using the multilingual language model. These source and translation vectors are then utilized to extract features, which are subsequently fed into classifiers that predict which translation system will produce a superior translation. Although NMT generally outperforms SMT, there are specific cases in which the SMT remains more competitive. HMT combines the strengths of both the SMT and NMT systems. By leveraging the best features of each system, HMT can offer improved translation quality compared to when either system is used independently.

3. Methodology

This section describes the proposed framework in detail, as shown in Figure 4. The core idea of our framework is to compare SMT and NMT translations and choose the better translation of the source sentence. All three sentences should be represented as vectors that can be compared in terms of semantic and syntactic similarities between the source and translation, and express the differences between the different translations. Sentence embedding is used to encode sentences into vectors. In the process of feature extraction, different measures are applied to determine the similarities and differences between vectors. Each measure provides the value of one feature in the vector. After obtaining informative feature vectors, various classifiers are trained to deduce which one has the better prediction power to select SMT or NMT translation. The following subsections will outline some of the relevant methods used in our framework.

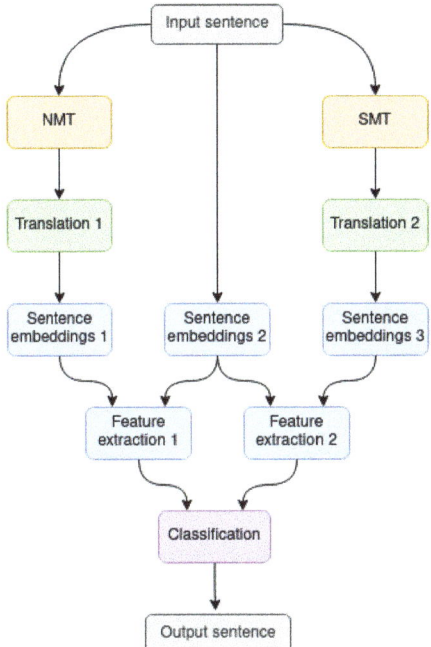

Figure 4. The HMT architecture.

3.1. Sentence Embeddings

Sentence embeddings in Natural Language Processing (NLP) refer to techniques that capture the semantic meaning of entire sentences by representing them as dense numerical vectors, enabling a wide range of downstream tasks such as sentence similarity, paraphrase detection, and text classification. BERT (Bidirectional Encoder Representations from Transformers) [35–37] embeddings capture rich contextual information and have revolutionized NLP tasks such as text classification, named entity recognition, and sentiment analysis. BOW and TF-IDF [38] embeddings are simpler but still useful for tasks such as document classification or information retrieval, where word frequency or presence is crucial. In our framework, three sentence embeddings were constructed for the source sentence and both translations. Because all three sentences could have different lengths, that makes them difficult to compare using similarity or distance measures. One of the most popular methods for generating sentence embeddings is to use pre-trained language models such as BERT. mBERT (Multilingual BERT) [3,39] is an extension of the original BERT model developed by Google, which was trained on a large corpus of text from more than 100 different languages. mBERT can learn to understand the meaning and context of words and sentences in multiple languages, and can be applied to a variety of NLP tasks, including text classification, question answering, and MT. One of the advantages of using mBERT is that it allows developers to build NLP applications that can work with multiple languages, without having to train separate models for each language. This can save time and resources, while also improving the overall accuracy and performance of the model. However, it is important to note that mBERT is not perfect and may not perform as well as language-specific models for certain languages. Additionally, it may not be able to capture all the nuances of each language, especially those with complex grammar or syntax.

3.2. Feature Extraction

Feature extraction is the process of transforming raw data into a set of meaningful features that are used as input to a machine learning algorithm. We are looking for informative features that would allow the learning algorithm to build a model that accurately predicts which translation is better, SMT or NMT. Feature extraction also helps to reduce the dimensionality of the input data, improve model performance, and increase the interpretability of the results. Features are extracted from sentence embeddings. To provide as accurate a classification as possible, we explore the following 11 features [18,40–43]: cosine similarity, Jensen–Shannon divergence, Euclidean distance, Cityblock distance, Squared Euclidean distance, Chebyshev distance, Canberra distance, Dice coefficient, Kulczynski distance, Russel–Rao similarity, and Sokal–Sneath similarity. Each feature has a value between 0 and 1. The full list of features and their positions in the feature vector can be seen in Table 1. We end up with two feature vectors: x_{t_1} represents the feature vector between the source sentence and the NMT translation, and x_{t_2} represents the feature vector between the source sentence and the SMT translation.

Table 1. The full list of features and their positions in the feature vector.

Feature	Name
x_1	Cosine similarity
x_2	Jensen–Shannon divergence
x_3	Euclidean distance
x_4	Cityblock distance
x_5	Squared Euclidean distance
x_6	Chebyshev distance
x_7	Canberra distance
x_8	Dice coefficient
x_9	Kulczynski distance
x_{10}	Russell–Rao similarity
x_{11}	Sokal–Sneath similarity

3.2.1. Cosine Similarity

The cosine similarity [44,45] is a measure of the similarity between two non-zero vectors of an inner product space that measures the cosine of the angle between them. In the context of comparing two real-valued vectors, cosine similarity is a popular feature similarity measure that is used commonly in machine learning and information retrieval. Cosine similarity is often used in text analysis applications, such as document similarity and clustering, but it can also be used in other domains where feature vectors are used to represent objects or entities.

3.2.2. Jensen–Shannon Divergence

The Jensen–Shannon divergence [46] is a measure of similarity or dissimilarity between two probability distributions. It is often used to compare two probability density functions or two sets of discrete probabilities. To use the Jensen–Shannon divergence to compare two real-valued vectors, we can first interpret them as probability distributions by normalizing them to sum to 1.

3.2.3. Euclidean Distance

The Euclidean distance [47] is a commonly used metric for comparing two real-valued vectors in machine learning and data analysis. It measures the straight-line distance between two points in the Euclidean space. The Euclidean distance can be used for a variety of tasks, such as clustering, classification, and anomaly detection. It is a useful metric for comparing vectors in many machine learning applications.

3.2.4. Cityblock Distance

The cityblock distance [48], also known as the Manhattan distance, is a way to measure the distance between two points in a two-dimensional space (or higher dimensions). In the context of comparing two real-valued vectors, the cityblock distance is a way to measure the similarity or dissimilarity between two vectors based on the sum of the absolute differences between their corresponding elements. The resulting distance is a non-negative value that represents the total distance between the two vectors. In other words, the larger the distance, the more dissimilar the vectors. The cityblock distance can be useful in many applications, such as image processing, clustering, and data analysis.

3.2.5. Squared Euclidean Distance

The squared Euclidean distance [49] metric is a way of measuring the distance between two real-valued vectors of equal length. This metric is sometimes preferred to the standard Euclidean distance, which calculates the square root of the sum of squared differences. The squared Euclidean distance can be useful in certain applications where the computation of square roots is computationally expensive or unnecessary, such as in some clustering or classification algorithms. It is worth noting that the squared Euclidean distance is always non-negative and symmetric, and satisfies the triangle inequality, which are all properties of a valid distance metric.

3.2.6. Chebyshev Distance

The Chebyshev distance [50] is a metric that can be used to compare two real-valued vectors. It is defined as the maximum absolute difference between the corresponding elements of the two vectors. The Chebyshev distance is a useful distance metric in many applications, such as image processing, pattern recognition, and clustering, where one wants to compare objects based on their maximum deviation in any one dimension.

3.2.7. Canberra Distance

The Canberra distance [51] is a measure of the distance between two points in a multi-dimensional space. It considers the magnitude of the differences between corresponding elements of two vectors, as well as their absolute values. The Canberra distance is a popular feature in data analysis and machine learning because it is robust to outliers and can handle sparse data. It is used commonly in clustering, classification, and regression problems.

3.2.8. Dice Coefficient

The Dice coefficient [52] is a similarity measure used to compare the similarity between two sets or vectors. The Dice coefficient ranges from 0 to 1, with 1 indicating that the two vectors are identical and 0 indicating that they are completely dissimilar. A higher Dice coefficient value indicates a higher degree of similarity between the two vectors. It is commonly used in clustering, classification, and information retrieval tasks where the similarity between two vectors needs to be computed.

3.2.9. Kulczynski Distance

The Kulczynski distance [53] is a statistical measure used to compare two real-valued vectors. It is a measure of similarity that considers the proportion of shared values between the two vectors. The Kulczynski distance has been used in a variety of applications, including information retrieval, data mining, and machine learning.

3.2.10. Russell-Rao Similarity

The Russell–Rao similarity [54] is a measure that can be used to compare two real-valued vectors. The Russell–Rao similarity is a simple and intuitive similarity measure that ranges from 0 to 1, where 0 indicates that the vectors have no coordinates in common, and 1 indicates that the vectors are identical. However, it does not consider the magnitude or direction of the vectors, and it can be sensitive to outliers.

3.2.11. Sokal–Sneath Distance

The Sokal–Sneath distance [55] is a measure of similarity between two real-valued vectors. It is used commonly in cluster analysis and classification problems. Intuitively, the Sokal–Sneath distance measures the proportion of non-matching values in the two vectors, considering the sparsity of the vectors. The Sokal–Sneath distance is useful when comparing sparse vectors, such as those that arise in text analysis or the analysis of high-dimensional data. It has the property of being symmetric and satisfying the triangle inequality, which makes it suitable for use in hierarchical clustering algorithms.

3.3. Classification

Before classification is applied, the feature vector $\mathbf{x}$ is constructed, in which each dimension $j = 1, \ldots, 11$ contains a value of a specific distance or similarity measure. Two feature vectors, $\mathbf{x}_{t_1}$ and $\mathbf{x}_{t_2}$, are constructed: one for the NMT translation and one for SMT translation. These feature vectors are used as input for a classification algorithm to determine which translation is more accurate or appropriate for a given input sentence. The construction of these feature vectors is crucial in determining the accuracy of the classification algorithm. Careful selection of the measures is required to ensure that they capture the relevant features of the input data.

As shown in Figure 4, a classification is adopted to select the best translations generated by NMT and SMT systems. Since the performance of SMT is lower than that of NMT in general cases, the classification accuracy becomes more important to prevent the hybridized results from being lower than the accuracy of NMT, which we consider as a baseline.

4. Experiments

In this section, we present experiments conducted on the Slovenian–English language pair. The Slovenian language is a Slavic language with rich inflectional morphology and a relaxed word order. English is an analytic language with very little inflection, where word order is very important for understanding the meaning. Considering this, we are translating between two structurally very different languages. The experiments were conducted in both translation directions, and we describe the corpora and tools used for data preprocessing and training the MT systems. The experimental settings are provided, and we present the results of the HMT systems, comparing them with the baseline NMT systems. Additionally, we show the results obtained with various well-known binary classification algorithms.

4.1. Corpora and Tools

The ParaCrawl corpus [56] is a valuable resource for researchers and developers working in the fields of MT and NLP, providing a large and diverse set of parallel texts that can be used to train and evaluate models in a variety of languages (more than 80). The corpus was created by crawling and scraping multilingual content from the web, using a combination of automated and manual methods to filter and clean the data.

The corpus used was tokenized and lowercased, and sentences longer than 80 words were removed. To obtain a representative sample, sentences were chosen from different parts of the corpus to create the training, development, and test sets. The training set consisted of 9,000,000 sentences, the development set had 90,000 sentences, and the test set also had 90,000 sentences. The training set was used to train both the SMT and NMT systems. The development set was split into two parts, with 45,000 sentences each. For the NMT systems, the first part was used during the training as a validation set, and for the SMT systems, we used 500 sentences for optimization. In Ref. [57], the authors recommend using a maximum of 1000 sentences for optimization, and in Refs. [58,59], 500–700 sentences were used for optimization. We used the second part of the development set to train the classifiers and augmented the data to obtain 90,000 sentences. To test the SMT, NMT, and HMT systems, we used 3000 sentences from the test set. The final corpus sizes of all the sets are shown in Table 2.

Table 2. The ParaCrawl corpus division for the training, development, and test sets.

	Training	Development			Test
		SMT	NMT	HMT	
Sentences	9,000,000	500	45,000	90,000	3000

To evaluate the MT systems, we used various evaluation metrics. Bilingual Evaluation Understudy (BLEU) [60] is a metric that operates on the principle of n-gram matching, which involves comparing sequences of words (or sometimes characters) between the machine translation and the reference translations. It considers both precision and brevity in its evaluation. The BLEU score is calculated by computing the precision of n-grams (usually up to a certain maximum length) in the translation and comparing this to the precision of the same n-grams in the reference translations. The precision values are then combined using a geometric mean. Additionally, BLEU incorporates a brevity penalty to discourage excessively short translations that may inflate the precision score. The resulting BLEU score ranges from 0 to 100, with a higher score indicating better translation quality. It is important to note that BLEU is a relatively simple metric that primarily measures lexical similarity and does not capture other aspects of translation quality, such as fluency, adequacy, or word order. Despite its limitations, BLEU remains widely used as a quick and automatic evaluation metric, especially when comparing different machine translation systems or evaluating improvements during system development. It provides a rough estimate of translation quality but should be used in conjunction with other evaluation metrics for a more comprehensive evaluation. Additional metrics have been included for more information about the quality. Character n-gram F-score (chrF) [61] is a metric that evaluates the translation quality based on character-level n-gram matches. It considers the precision and recall of character n-grams in both the machine translation and the reference translations. By considering character-level matches, chrF can capture the adequacy and fluency of the translation, even in cases where word order or word choice may differ. The resulting chrF score ranges from 0 to 100, with a higher score indicating better translation quality. Translation Edit Rate (TER) [62] is a metric that captures more global changes in the translation and is less sensitive to minor lexical variations. It aims to assess the overall fluency and adequacy of the translation by considering the broader context and number of changes needed to align it with the reference. The resulting TER score ranges from 0 to 100, with a lower score indicating better translation quality. For BLEU, chrF, and TER metrics, we utilized SacreBLEU [63], which provides a hassle-free computation of shareable, comparable, and reproducible scores. The Metric for Evaluation of Translation with Explicit ORdering (METEOR) [64] is a metric that primarily focuses on lexical similarity. METEOR incorporates more linguistic features and considers synonyms, stemming, and the reordering of words. It uses a combination of unigram matching, stemming, and WordNet synonym matching to compute an alignment score. Additionally, METEOR also incorporates a penalty for incorrect word order, rewarding translations that have a more similar word order to the references. The resulting METEOR score ranges from 0 to 100, with a higher score indicating better translation quality. The Consistent Translation Evaluation Metric (COMET) [65] is a metric that utilizes a pre-trained neural network model that is trained on a large parallel corpus of human translations. It compares the machine-generated translation against the human reference translations to compute a score that reflects the quality and similarity of the translation. The resulting COMET score ranges from 0 to 100, with a higher score indicating better translation quality.

In NMT, Byte Pair Encoding (BPE) [66] is used to address the out-of-vocabulary (OOV) words problem. Since NMT models learn from a fixed vocabulary, any word not present in the vocabulary is considered as an OOV word, and its translation cannot be learned. By applying BPE to the source and target language texts, we can split unknown words into subword units that are already present in the vocabulary. This helps the NMT model to translate sentences with OOV words accurately. For example, the rare word "petrichor" would be split into more common subwords, such as "pet", "rich", and "or".

4.2. Experimental Settings for Models' Training and Classification

To train NMT systems, we used Marian NMT [67], which is an efficient and free NMT framework written in pure C++ with minimal dependencies. Using toolkits such as Marian NMT, it is relatively straightforward to construct end-to-end NMT systems, which only require a little preprocessing of the training corpora and post-processing of the system output. We trained two NMT systems for both translation directions. The hyperparameters used for training are shown in Table 3.

Table 3. Marian NMT training parameters. For the description of parameters and their values, see [68].

Parameter	Value
type	transformer
workspace GPU memory	10 GB
max–length	100
mini–batch–fit	True
maxi–batch	1000
early–stopping	10
after–epochs	50
valid–metrics	cross–entropy and perplexity
valid–mini–batch	64
beam–size	6
normalize	0.6
enc–depth	6
dec–depth	6
transformer–heads	8
transformer–postprocess–emb	d
transformer–postprocess	dan
transformer–dropout	0.1
label–smoothing	0.1
learn–rate	0.0003
lr–warmup	16,000
lr–decay–inv–sqrt	16,000
optimizer–params	$0.9, 0.98, 1 \times 10^{-9}$
clip–norm	5
tied–embeddings–all	True
sync–sgd	True
exponential–smothing	True

To train the SMT systems, we used the Moses toolkit [69], which is an open-source toolkit with a wide variety of tools for the training and optimization of MT systems. We trained two independent phrase-based SMT systems for both translation directions. Each SMT system had six models and 14 parameters (model weights). To improve the SMT systems' translation quality, model weights were optimized by the DE algorithm. In our previous research [59], we showed the competitive performance of the DE algorithm in comparison with MERT, MIRA, and PRO optimizers, which are commonly used in SMT optimization. The hyperparameters used to train and optimize the SMT systems are shown in Table 4.

Table 4. Moses SMT training parameters [70]. The last three parameters are for DE optimization.

Parameter	Value
alignment	grow-diag-final-and
reordering	msd-bidirectional-fe
smoothing	improved-kneser-ney
evaluation metric	BLEU
n-gram language model order	5
number of generations	50
population size	25
dimension	14

4.3. Results

As NMT is the dominant approach, we used NMT as the baseline in our experiments. To evaluate the translation quality, the primary metric was the BLEU metric. We also included chrF, TER, METEOR, and COMET metrics for additional information. The ↑ and ↓ symbols in the tables indicate which values are better.

The results for the baseline (NMT) are shown in Table 5 for the BLEU, chrF, TER, METEOR, and COMET metrics. For translations from Slovenian to English, the baseline (NMT) achieved a BLEU score of 46.4, a chrF score of 65.5, a TER score of 40.1, a METEOR score of 70.5, and a COMET score of 83.3. For translations from English to Slovenian, the baseline (NMT) achieved a BLEU score of 32.0, a chrF score of 54.1, a TER score of 54.4, a METEOR score of 55.3, and a COMET score of 80.7.

Table 5. The results of baseline (NMT) for both translation directions.

	Baseline (NMT)				
	BLEU ↑	chrF ↑	TER ↓	METEOR ↑	COMET ↑
Slovenian ⇒ English	46.4	65.6	40.1	70.5	83.3
English ⇒ Slovenian	32.0	54.1	54.4	55.3	80.7

Note: The ↑ and ↓ symbols in the table indicate which values are better.

The results for HMT are presented in Tables 6 and 7 for the BLEU, chrF, TER, METEOR, and COMET metrics.

Table 6. The results of HMT for translation from Slovenian to English. The best results are in bold.

Classifiers in HMT	Slovenian ⇒ English				
	BLEU ↑	chrF ↑	TER ↓	METEOR ↑	COMET ↑
Logistic Regression (LR)	46.8	65.9	41.9	70.3	83.0
Decision Tree (DT)	47.1	65.9	42.4	69.9	82.2
Gradient-Boosted Decision Tree (GBDT)	47.8	66.4	40.2	70.5	83.8
Random Forest (RF)	47.7	66.4	40.4	70.5	83.5
Naive Bayes (NB)	47.7	66.3	40.1	70.5	83.8
K-Nearest Neighbor (kNN)	45.7	65.0	44.4	69.1	81.6
Multilayer Perceptron (MLP)	46.3	65.5	43.2	69.8	82.2
Convolutional Neural Network (CNN)	46.8	65.8	42.3	70.0	82.6
Support Vector Machine (SVM)	**47.9**	**66.6**	**39.9**	**70.9**	**83.9**

Note: The ↑ and ↓ symbols in the table indicate which values are better.

Table 7. The results of HMT for translation from English to Slovenian. The best results are in bold.

Classifiers in HMT	English ⇒ Slovenian				
	BLEU ↑	chrF ↑	TER ↓	METEOR ↑	COMET ↑
Logistic Regression (LR)	41.5	62.0	48.8	60.8	81.6
Decision Tree (DT)	40.4	60.8	50.6	59.2	80.1
Gradient-Boosted Decision Tree (GBDT)	42.4	62.5	47.5	61.4	82.4
Random Forest (RF)	41.5	62.0	48.6	60.8	81.8
Naive Bayes (NB)	42.4	62.6	**47.4**	**61.5**	**82.5**
K-Nearest Neighbor (kNN)	40.7	61.3	50.3	60.0	80.6
Multilayer Perceptron (MLP)	**42.9**	**63.1**	48.8	**61.5**	80.9
Convolutional Neural Network (CNN)	42.5	62.7	48.6	61.3	81.3
Support Vector Machine (SVM)	42.3	62.5	47.9	61.3	82.0

Note: The ↑ and ↓ symbols in the table indicate which values are better.

For the translation from Slovenian to English, seven classifiers achieved a better BLEU score than the baseline by a range of 0.4 to 1.5 points. The two classifiers achieved a worse or almost equal BLEU score compared to the baseline. Five classifiers achieved a better chrF score than the baseline by a range of 0.3 to 1.0 points. Four classifiers achieved a worse or almost equal chrF score compared to the baseline. One classifier achieved a better TER score than the baseline by 0.2 points. Eight classifiers achieved a worse or equal TER score compared to the baseline. One classifier achieved a better METEOR score than the baseline by 0.4 points. Eight classifiers achieved a worse or equal METEOR score compared to the baseline. Four classifiers achieved a better COMET score than the baseline by 0.2 to 0.6 points. Five classifiers achieved a worse or equal COMET score compared to the baseline.

For the translation from English to Slovenian, all nine classifiers achieved a better BLEU score than the baseline by a range of 8.4 to 10.9 points, a better chrF score than the baseline by a range of 6.7 to 9.0 points, a better TER score than the baseline by a range of 3.9 to 7.1 points, and a better METEOR score than the baseline by a range of 3.9 to 6.2 points. Seven classifiers achieved a better COMET score than the baseline by 0.3 to 1.8 points. Two classifiers achieved a worse COMET score compared to the baseline.

5. Discussion

We consider the NMT translation quality as our baseline. While NMT generally outperforms SMT, there are certain cases where SMT remains more competitive. As can be seen from the results, for translation from Slovenian to English, NMT achieved a better translation quality than SMT, while for the translation from English to Slovenian, SMT achieved a better translation quality. By using the best features of each system, HMT can offer an improved translation quality. HMT translates the source sentence using both systems and selects the more reliable translation depending on the features. In our experiment, the primary metric was the BLEU metric, while the other metrics were calculated as additional information. The results indicated similar conclusions to those obtained with the BLEU metric. For translation from Slovenian to English, SVM classifier achieved better scores according to all five metrics, with a BLEU score of 47.9, a chrF score of 66.6, a TER score of 39.9, a METEOR score of 70.9, and a COMET score of 83.9. For translation from English to Slovenian, two classifiers achieved the best scores. The MLP classifier achieved better scores according to BLEU and chrF metrics with a BLEU score of 42.9 and a chrF score of 63.1, while the NB classifier achieved better scores according to TER and COMET metrics, with a TER score of 47.4 and a COMET score of 82.5. Both MLP and NB classifiers achieved the same, better score according to the METEOR metric, with a METEOR score of 61.5. The results for the classifiers are shown in Tables 6 and 7 for the BLEU, chrF, TER, COMET, and METEOR metrics. The upper bound for the BLEU metric is presented so we can see the maximum potential improvement in the classification task.

It should be noted that the upper bound is only achievable if the classification is perfect, which is difficult to attain in reality.

To better understand the potential of HMT, Table 8 shows the maximum BLEU scores that can be achieved with perfect classification. For translation from Slovenian to English, this is 53.5, and for translation from English to Slovenian, this is 49.5. It also shows the percentage of translations where SMT or NMT is better based on their BLEU scores.

Table 8. The test set BLEU scores for SMT, NMT, and the maximum score of ideal classification (upper limit). The last three columns show the percentage of translations in the test set where SMT (NMT) is better and when they are equal.

	BLEU ↑			Distribution [%]		
	SMT	NMT	Upper	SMT	NMT	Equal
Slovenian ⇒ English	41.9	46.4	53.5	29.2	55.5	15.3
English ⇒ Slovenian	41.6	32.0	49.5	44.2	43.8	12.0

Note: The ↑ symbol in the table indicate which values are better.

The contribution of the proposed system to translation quality is evident in the case of English to Slovenian translation, where NMT achieved a BLEU score of 32.0, and HMT achieved a BLEU score of 42.9, showing an improvement of 10.9 points. On the other hand, in the case of Slovenian to English, NMT achieved a BLEU score of 46.4, and HMT achieved a BLEU score of 47.9, showing an improvement of 1.5 points. Improving translation quality by 0.5 points or more can be a challenging task, especially if the initial translation quality is already high. Even small improvements in the translation quality can require significant effort and experimentation. In general, as the quality of the baseline system improves, it becomes increasingly difficult to make further gains in translation quality. However, this also depends on the specific language pair, the quality of the training data, the complexity of the target language, and other factors. Many MT systems already exist, and instead of spending months training new ones, we should consider reusing and combining them with one or more systems.

The limitation of the proposed system is the multilingual language model. Although multilingual language model supports many languages, there are still languages that are not included in its support. Additionally, the coverage of supported languages might be sparse, depending on the data upon which it was built.

Translation Examples

In Tables 9 and 10, we present translation examples where SMT outperformed NMT. It is important to note that the ParaCrawl corpus used in our experiments was obtained through web crawling and filtering, resulting in a corpus that contains a significant amount of noise.

Table 9 shows some translation examples for translations from Slovenian to English. In the first example, we can see that the word order is different in the SMT and NMT translations. The NMT translation keeps the word order from the source sentence, while the SMT translation changes the word order and was closer to the reference translation. In the second example, we can see that the NMT translation literally translated the phrase as "golden wedding", while the SMT translation translated it as "50th wedding anniversary" and was closer to the reference translation. In the fourth example, we show that the SMT used the simple present tense, while the NMT used an expression with a modal verb. Additionally, all three translations used different units: SMT used feet, NMT used meters, and the reference used yards.

Table 10 shows some translation examples for translations from English to Slovenian. In the first example, we can see that the NMT translation uses the singular form instead of the plural form, probably because of the noun that follows, which is in the singular form. In the second example, we can see that the length of the NMT translation is much shorter than that of the reference, source, and even SMT translation. In the fourth example, we can see that although both translations look good, the SMT translation provides a more accurate translation.

Table 9. Translation examples generated by NMT and SMT systems from Slovenian to English, where SMT performed better than NMT.

		BLEU ↑	chrF ↑	TER ↓
REF	single market month: sharing ideas online to change europe			
SRC	mesec enotnega trga: spremenimo evropo z izmenjavo zamisli			
SMT	single market month: sharing ideas online to change europe	100.0	100.0	0.0
NMT	single market month: changing europe by sharing ideas	33.0	67.7	50.0
REF	that 's what they say when they need a card:) for some 50th wedding anniversary, or a special birthday.			
SRC	tako mi rečejo, ko želijo voščilnico:) za kakšno zlato poroko, pa okrogel rojstni dan.			
SMT	that 's what they say when they need a card:) for some 50th wedding anniversary, or a special birthday.	100.0	100.0	0.0
NMT	they tell me when they want a card:) for a golden wedding and a round birthday.	18.1	38.0	52.2
REF	a newly designed terrace lies in the comfortable shades of trees and shrubs, only a few meters from the sea, and offers an impressive view on the old part of the marina.			
SRC	na novo urejena terasa, le nekaj metrov oddaljena od morja, nudi v prijetnem hladu zelenja impresivni pogled na stari del marine.			
SMT	a newly designed terrace lies, only a few meters from the sea, and offers the comfortable shades of trees and shrubs in an impressive view on the old part of the marina.	83.1	94.2	5.7
NMT	the newly renovated terrace, only a few meters away from the sea, offers an impressive view of the old part of the marina in the pleasant shade of greenery.	39.6	60.0	45.7
REF	the old town of dubrovnik is easily reachable by a direct bus line departing 50 yards from the hotel.			
SRC	do starega mestnega jedra dubrovnika se lahko enostavno odpeljete z direktnim avtobusom, ki ustavlja 50 m stran.			
SMT	the old town of dubrovnik is easily reachable by a direct bus line departing 150 feet from the.	72.3	82.9	15.0
NMT	the old town of dubrovnik can be easily reached by direct bus, 50 m away.	23.1	48.6	50.0

Note: The ↑ and ↓ symbols in the table indicate which values are better.

Table 10. Translation examples generated by NMT and SMT systems from English to Slovenian, where SMT performed better than NMT.

		BLEU ↑	chrF ↑	TER ↓
REF	apartmaji mirko staničič, v lasti družine staničič, se nahajajo v mestu brela (splitsko-dalmatinska županija).			
SRC	apartments mirko stanicic, owned by the stanicic family, are located in brela (split-dalmatia county).			
SMT	apartmaji mirko staničič, v lasti družine staničič, se nahajajo v mestu brela (splitsko-dalmatinska županija).	100.0	100.0	0.0
NMT	apartma mirko staničič, v lasti družine staničič, se nahaja v mestu brela (splitsko-dalmatinska županija).	79.1	91.2	10.5

Table 10. Cont.

		BLEU ↑	chrF ↑	TER ↓
REF	da bi s svojo družino preživeli kvaliteten in nepozaben dopust, smo v našo ponudbo uvrstili počitniške hiše v tkon—otok pasman, ki so kompletno opremljene z vsem, kar vam je potrebno za popolne poletne počitnice.			
SRC	in order to spend quality and unforgettable holiday with your family, we have included in our accommodation offer the holiday houses in tkon—island pasman, which are fully equipped with everything you need for a perfect summer vacation.			
SMT	da bi preživeli kvaliteten in nepozaben dopust z družino, je v našo ponudbo uvrstili počitniške hiše v tkon—otok pasman, ki so kompletno opremljene z vsem, kar vam je potrebno za popolne poletne počitnice.	80.7	91.0	12.5
NMT	da bi s svojo družino našli kvaliteten in nepozaben dopust, smo v našo ponudbo uvrstili počitniške hiše v tkon—otok pasman.	43.6	59.1	42.5
REF	ko ste na opravilu, pritisnite tipko enter, da ga izberete in odprete v pogledu s podrobnostmi.			
SRC	use the down arrow key to browse through the results, press enter to select one.			
SMT	s tipko s puščico dol lahko brskate po rezultatih iskanja. pritisnite tipko enter, da izberete enega od njih.	19.1	44.5	89.5
NMT	če želite med rezultati brskati s puščičnimi tipkami dol, pritisnite enter.	4.9	25.5	89.5
REF	zaradi jasnosti bi bilo treba navedeno uredbo prenoviti.			
SRC	in the interests of clarity, that regulation should be recast.			
SMT	zaradi jasnosti bi bilo treba navedeno uredbo prenoviti.	100.0	100.0	0.0
NMT	zaradi jasnosti bi bilo treba to uredbo prenoviti.	59.7	81.5	11.1

Note: The ↑ and ↓ symbols in the table indicate which values are better.

6. Conclusions

The main contributions of this paper involve enhancing NMT translation quality through the integration of SMT and representing the source sentence and translations as vectors in a shared vector space using a multilingual language model. These features were utilized to capture and quantify the differences between the two translation approaches. To determine the best possible translation, the classification algorithm predicts which translation system produced a superior translation. Several classifiers were used to select the best possible translation, and the results showed that the proposed HMT system improved the BLEU score by 1.5 and 10.9 points for both translation directions, respectively. The proposed method of combining SMT and NMT in the hybrid system is novel. Our framework is language-independent and can be applied to other languages supported by the multilingual language model. As seen from the results, the proposed HMT system successfully combined the strengths of both NMT and SMT and, by using the best features of each system, can offer an improved translation quality.

For future work, researchers can explore novel approaches to integrate additional models or even incorporate domain-specific models for an improved translation performance. Another idea worth exploring is the development of an even larger multilingual language model, expanding its coverage and potentially enhancing translation quality.

Author Contributions: Conceptualization, J.D.; methodology, J.B. and M.S.M.; software, J.D. and D.V.; validation, J.B., M.S.M., and D.V.; formal analysis, J.D. and J.B.; investigation, J.D. and M.S.M.; resources, J.D. and M.S.M.; writing—original draft preparation, J.D., J.B., M.S.M., and D.V.; writing—review and editing, J.D., J.B., M.S.M., and D.V.; visualization, J.D.; supervision, J.B. All authors have read and agreed to the published version of the manuscript.

Funding: This work was supported by the Slovenian Research Agency (research core funding No. P2-0069— Advanced Methods of Interaction in Telecommunications, P2-0041—Computer Systems, Methodologies, and Intelligent Services, and P2-0057—Information systems).

Institutional Review Board Statement: Not applicable.

Informed Consent Statement: Not applicable.

Data Availability Statement: Publicly available datasets were analyzed in this study. The data can be found here: https://opus.nlpl.eu/ParaCrawl.php (accessed on 14 April 2023).

Acknowledgments: The authors thank the authors of the ParaCrawl parallel corpora, the authors of the Marian NMT and Moses SMT toolkits, and the authors of mBERT for making all of these publicly available.

Conflicts of Interest: The authors declare no conflict of interest.

Abbreviations

The following abbreviations are used in this manuscript:

MT	Machine Translation
NMT	Neural Machine Translation
SMT	Statistical Machine Translation
HMT	Hybrid Machine Translation
NLP	Natural Language Processing
LR	Logistic Regression
DT	Decision Tree
GBDT	Gradient-Boosted Decision Tree
RF	Random Forest
NB	Naive Bayes
kNN	K-Nearest Neighbors
MLP	Multilayer Perceptron
CNN	Convolutional Neural Network
SVM	Support Vector Machine
BLEU	BiLingual Evaluation Understudy
chrF	Character F-score
TER	Translation Edit Rate
BERT	Bidirectional Encoder Representations from Transformers
mBERT	Multilingual Bidirectional Encoder Representations from Transformers
DE	Differential Evolution
RNN	Recurrent Neural Networks
LSTM	Long Short-Term Memory
GRU	Gated Recurrent Unit
OOV	Out-of-vocabulary
WMT	Workshop on Machine Translation

References

1. Popović, M. Comparing Language Related Issues for NMT and PBMT between German and English. *Prague Bull. Math. Linguist.* **2017**, *108*, 209–220. [CrossRef]
2. Popović, M. Language-related issues for NMT and PBMT for English–German and English–Serbian. *Mach. Transl.* **2018**, *32*, 237–253. [CrossRef]
3. Pires, T.; Schlinger, E.; Garrette, D. How Multilingual is Multilingual BERT? In Proceedings of the 57th Annual Meeting of the Association for Computational Linguistics, Florence, Italy, 28 July–2 August 2019; Association for Computational Linguistics: Cedarville, OH, USA; pp. 4996–5001. [CrossRef]
4. Koehn, P.; Och, F.J.; Marcu, D. Statistical phrase-based translation. In Proceedings of the 2003 Human Language Technology Conference of the North American Chapter of the Association for Computational Linguistics, Edmonton, AB, Canada, 27 May–1 June 2003.
5. Koehn, P. *Statistical Machine Translation*; Cambridge University Press: Cambridge, UK, 2010.
6. Lopez, A. Statistical machine translation. *ACM Comput. Surv. (CSUR)* **2008**, *40*, 1–49. [CrossRef]

7. Cho, K.; Van Merriënboer, B.; Bahdanau, D.; Bengio, Y. On the properties of neural machine translation: Encoder-decoder approaches. *arXiv* **2014**, arXiv:1409.1259.
8. Sutskever, I.; Vinyals, O.; Le, Q.V. Sequence to sequence learning with neural networks. *Adv. Neural Inf. Process. Syst.* **2014**, *2*, 3104–3112.
9. Vashishth, S.; Bhandari, M.; Yadav, P.; Rai, P.; Bhattacharyya, C.; Talukdar, P. Incorporating syntactic and semantic information in word embeddings using graph convolutional networks. In Proceedings of the 57th Annual Meeting of the Association for Computational Linguistics, Florence, Italy, 28 July–2 August 2019; Association for Computational Linguistics: Cedarville, OH, USA, 2019; pp. 3308–3318.
10. Vaswani, A.; Shazeer, N.; Parmar, N.; Uszkoreit, J.; Jones, L.; Gomez, A.N.; Kaiser, Ł.; Polosukhin, I. Attention is all you need. *Adv. Neural Inf. Process. Syst.* **2017**, *30*. [CrossRef]
11. Bahdanau, D.; Cho, K.; Bengio, Y. Neural machine translation by jointly learning to align and translate. *arXiv* **2014**, arXiv:1409.0473.
12. Meng, F.; Lu, Z.; Wang, M.; Li, H.; Jiang, W.; Liu, Q. Encoding Source Language with Convolutional Neural Network for Machine Translation. *arXiv* **2015**, arXiv:1503.01838. [CrossRef]
13. Stahlberg, F.; Hasler, E.; Byrne, B. The edit distance transducer in action: The University of Cambridge English-German system at WMT16. *arXiv* **2016**, arXiv:1606.04963.
14. Stahlberg, F. Neural Machine Translation: A Review. *J. Artif. Intell. Res.* **2020**, *69*, 343–418. [CrossRef]
15. Wang, X.; Pham, H.; Dai, Z.; Neubig, G. SwitchOut: An efficient data augmentation algorithm for neural machine translation. *arXiv* **2018**, arXiv:1808.07512.
16. Sennrich, R.; Haddow, B.; Birch, A. Edinburgh neural machine translation systems for WMT 16. *arXiv* **2016**, arXiv:1606.02891.
17. Cromieres, F.; Chu, C.; Nakazawa, T.; Kurohashi, S. Kyoto university participation to WAT 2016. In Proceedings of the 3rd Workshop on Asian Translation (WAT2016), Osaka, Japan, 11–16 December 2016; pp. 166–174.
18. Huang, J.X.; Lee, K.S.; Kim, Y.K. Hybrid Translation with Classification: Revisiting Rule-Based and Neural Machine Translation. *Electronics* **2020**, *9*, 201. [CrossRef]
19. Sen, S.; Hasanuzzaman, M.; Ekbal, A.; Bhattacharyya, P.; Way, A. Neural machine translation of low-resource languages using SMT phrase pair injection. *Nat. Lang. Eng.* **2021**, *27*, 271–292. [CrossRef]
20. Yan, R.; Li, J.; Su, X.; Wang, X.; Gao, G. Boosting the Transformer with the BERT Supervision in Low-Resource Machine Translation. *Appl. Sci.* **2022**, *12*, 7195. [CrossRef]
21. Bacanin, N.; Zivkovic, M.; Stoean, C.; Antonijevic, M.; Janicijevic, S.; Sarac, M.; Strumberger, I. Application of Natural Language Processing and Machine Learning Boosted with Swarm Intelligence for Spam Email Filtering. *Mathematics* **2022**, *10*, 4173. [CrossRef]
22. Fuad, A.; Al-Yahya, M. Cross-Lingual Transfer Learning for Arabic Task-Oriented Dialogue Systems Using Multilingual Transformer Model mT5. *Mathematics* **2022**, *10*, 746. [CrossRef]
23. Baniata, L.H.; Kang, S.; Ampomah, I.K.E. A Reverse Positional Encoding Multi-Head Attention-Based Neural Machine Translation Model for Arabic Dialects. *Mathematics* **2022**, *10*, 3666. [CrossRef]
24. Alokla, A.; Gad, W.; Nazih, W.; Aref, M.; Salem, A.B. Retrieval-Based Transformer Pseudocode Generation. *Mathematics* **2022**, *10*, 604. [CrossRef]
25. Minaee, S.; Kalchbrenner, N.; Cambria, E.; Nikzad, N.; Chenaghlu, M.; Gao, J. Deep Learning–Based Text Classification: A Comprehensive Review. *ACM Comput. Surv.* **2021**, *54*, 62. [CrossRef]
26. Chen, L.C.; Chang, K.H.; Yang, S.C.; Chen, S.C. A Corpus-Based Word Classification Method for Detecting Difficulty Level of English Proficiency Tests. *Appl. Sci.* **2023**, *13*, 1699. [CrossRef]
27. Canbek, G.; Taskaya Temizel, T.; Sagiroglu, S. PToPI: A Comprehensive Review, Analysis, and Knowledge Representation of Binary Classification Performance Measures/Metrics. *SN Comput. Sci.* **2023**, *4*, 13. [CrossRef] [PubMed]
28. Hsu, B.M. Comparison of Supervised Classification Models on Textual Data. *Mathematics* **2020**, *8*, 851. [CrossRef]
29. Panigrahi, R.; Borah, S.; Bhoi, A.K.; Ijaz, M.F.; Pramanik, M.; Kumar, Y.; Jhaveri, R.H. A Consolidated Decision Tree-Based Intrusion Detection System for Binary and Multiclass Imbalanced Datasets. *Mathematics* **2021**, *9*, 751. [CrossRef]
30. Ding, W.; Chen, Q.; Dong, Y.; Shao, N. Fault Diagnosis Method of Intelligent Substation Protection System Based on Gradient Boosting Decision Tree. *Appl. Sci.* **2022**, *12*, 8989. [CrossRef]
31. Lučin, I.; Lučin, B.; Čarija, Z.; Sikirica, A. Data-Driven Leak Localization in Urban Water Distribution Networks Using Big Data for Random Forest Classifier. *Mathematics* **2021**, *9*, 672. [CrossRef]
32. Gan, S.; Shao, S.; Chen, L.; Yu, L.; Jiang, L. Adapting Hidden Naive Bayes for Text Classification. *Mathematics* **2021**, *9*, 2378. [CrossRef]
33. Kang, S. k-Nearest Neighbor Learning with Graph Neural Networks. *Mathematics* **2021**, *9*, 830. [CrossRef]
34. Nadeem, M.I.; Ahmed, K.; Li, D.; Zheng, Z.; Naheed, H.; Muaad, A.Y.; Alqarafi, A.; Abdel Hameed, H. SHO-CNN: A Metaheuristic Optimization of a Convolutional Neural Network for Multi-Label News Classification. *Electronics* **2023**, *12*, 113. [CrossRef]
35. Devlin, J.; Chang, M.W.; Lee, K.; Toutanova, K. BERT: Pre-training of Deep Bidirectional Transformers for Language Understanding. *arXiv* **2018**, arXiv:1810.04805. [CrossRef]
36. Savini, E.; Caragea, C. Intermediate-Task Transfer Learning with BERT for Sarcasm Detection. *Mathematics* **2022**, *10*, 844. [CrossRef]

37. Patil, R.; Boit, S.; Gudivada, V.; Nandigam, J. A Survey of Text Representation and Embedding Techniques in NLP. *IEEE Access* **2023**, *11*, 36120–36146. [CrossRef]
38. Dash, G.; Sharma, C.; Sharma, S. Sustainable Marketing and the Role of Social Media: An Experimental Study Using Natural Language Processing (NLP). *Sustainability* **2023**, *15*, 5443. [CrossRef]
39. de Lima, R.R.; Fernandes, A.M.R.; Bombasar, J.R.; da Silva, B.A.; Crocker, P.; Leithardt, V.R.Q. An Empirical Comparison of Portuguese and Multilingual BERT Models for Auto-Classification of NCM Codes in International Trade. *Big Data Cogn. Comput.* **2022**, *6*, 8. [CrossRef]
40. Gomaa, W.H.; Fahmy, A.A. A Survey of Text Similarity Approaches. *Int. J. Comput. Appl.* **2013**, *68*, 13–18.
41. Dzisevič, R.; Šešok, D. Text Classification using Different Feature Extraction Approaches. In Proceedings of the 2019 Open Conference of Electrical, Electronic and Information Sciences (eStream), Vilnius, Lithuania, 25 April 2019; pp. 1–4. [CrossRef]
42. Magalhães, D.; Pozo, A.; Santana, R. An empirical comparison of distance/similarity measures for Natural Language Processing. In Proceedings of the Anais do XVI Encontro Nacional de Inteligência Artificial e Computacional, SBC, Porto Alegre, Brasil, 15–18 October 2019; pp. 717–728. [CrossRef]
43. Wang, J.; Dong, Y. Measurement of Text Similarity: A Survey. *Information* **2020**, *11*, 421. [CrossRef]
44. Ristanti, P.Y.; Wibawa, A.P.; Pujianto, U. Cosine Similarity for Title and Abstract of Economic Journal Classification. In Proceedings of the 2019 5th International Conference on Science in Information Technology (ICSITech), Jogjakarta, Indonesia, 23–24 October 2019; pp. 123–127. [CrossRef]
45. Park, K.; Hong, J.S.; Kim, W. A Methodology Combining Cosine Similarity with Classifier for Text Classification. *Appl. Artif. Intell.* **2020**, *34*, 396–411. [CrossRef]
46. Eligüzel, N.; Çetinkaya, C.; Dereli, T. A novel approach for text categorization by applying hybrid genetic bat algorithm through feature extraction and feature selection methods. *Expert Syst. Appl.* **2022**, *202*, 117433. [CrossRef]
47. Kadhim, A.I. Survey on Supervised Machine Learning Techniques for Automatic Text Classification. *Artif. Intell. Rev.* **2019**, *52*, 273–292. [CrossRef]
48. Berciu, A.G.; Dulf, E.H.; Micu, D.D. Improving the Efficiency of Electricity Consumption by Applying Real-Time Fuzzy and Fractional Control. *Mathematics* **2022**, *10*, 3807. [CrossRef]
49. Inyang, U.; Akpan, E.; Akinyokun, O. A Hybrid Machine Learning Approach for Flood Risk Assessment and Classification. *Int. J. Comput. Intell. Appl.* **2020**, *19*, 2050012. [CrossRef]
50. Krivulin, N.; Prinkov, A.; Gladkikh, I. Using Pairwise Comparisons to Determine Consumer Preferences in Hotel Selection. *Mathematics* **2022**, *10*, 730. [CrossRef]
51. Machado, J.A.T.; Mendes Lopes, A. Fractional Jensen–Shannon analysis of the scientific output of researchers in fractional calculus. *Entropy* **2017**, *19*, 127. [CrossRef]
52. Shamir, R.R.; Duchin, Y.; Kim, J.; Sapiro, G.; Harel, N. Continuous dice coefficient: A method for evaluating probabilistic segmentations. *arXiv* **2019**, arXiv:1906.11031.
53. Cha, S.H. Comprehensive Survey on Distance/Similarity Measures between Probability Density Functions. *Int. J. Math. Model. Meth. Appl. Sci.* **2007**, *1*, 300–307.
54. Ibrahim, H.; El Kerdawy, A.M.; Abdo, A.; Eldin, A.S. Similarity-based machine learning framework for predicting safety signals of adverse drug–drug interactions. *Inform. Med. Unlocked* **2021**, *26*, 100699. [CrossRef]
55. Gutiérrez-Reina, D.; Sharma, V.; You, I.; Toral, S. Dissimilarity metric based on local neighboring information and genetic programming for data dissemination in vehicular ad hoc networks (VANETs). *Sensors* **2018**, *18*, 2320. [CrossRef] [PubMed]
56. Bañón, M.; Chen, P.; Haddow, B.; Heafield, K.; Hoang, H.; Esplà-Gomis, M.; Forcada, M.L.; Kamran, A.; Kirefu, F.; Koehn, P.; et al. ParaCrawl: Web-Scale Acquisition of Parallel Corpora. In Proceedings of the 58th Annual Meeting of the Association for Computational Linguistics, Online, 5–10 July 2020; pp. 4555–4567. [CrossRef]
57. Neubig, G.; Watanabe, T. Optimization for Statistical Machine Translation: A Survey. *Comput. Linguist.* **2016**, *42*, 1–54. [CrossRef]
58. Lü, Y.; Huang, J.; Liu, Q. Improving Statistical Machine Translation Performance by Training Data Selection and Optimization. In Proceedings of the 2007 Joint Conference on Empirical Methods in Natural Language Processing and Computational Natural Language Learning (EMNLP-CoNLL), Prague, Czech Republic, 28–30 June 2007; pp. 343–350.
59. Dugonik, J.; Bošković, B.; Brest, J.; Sepesy Maučec, M. Improving Statistical Machine Translation Quality Using Differential Evolution. *Informatica* **2019**, *30*, 629–645. [CrossRef]
60. Papineni, K.; Roukos, S.; Ward, T.; Zhu, W.J. Bleu: A Method for Automatic Evaluation of Machine Translation. In Proceedings of the 40th Annual Meeting of the Association for Computational Linguistics, Stroudsburg, PA, USA, 7–12 July 2002; pp. 311–318. [CrossRef]
61. Popović, M. chrF: Character n-gram F-score for automatic MT evaluation. In Proceedings of the Tenth Workshop on Statistical Machine Translation, Lisbon, Portugal, 17–18 September 2015; Association for Computational Linguistics: Cedarville, OH, USA, 2015; pp. 392–395. [CrossRef]
62. Snover, M.; Dorr, B.; Schwartz, R.; Micciulla, L.; Makhoul, J. A Study of Translation Edit Rate with Targeted Human Annotation. In Proceedings of the 7th Conference of the Association for Machine Translation in the Americas: Technical Papers, Cambridge, MA, USA, 8–12 August 2006; pp. 223–231.

63. Post, M. A Call for Clarity in Reporting BLEU Scores. In Proceedings of the Third Conference on Machine Translation: Research Papers, Belgium, Brussels, 31 October–1 November 2018; Association for Computational Linguistics: Cedarville, OH, USA, 2018; pp. 186–191.
64. Banerjee, S.; Lavie, A. METEOR: An Automatic Metric for MT Evaluation with Improved Correlation with Human Judgments. In Proceedings of the ACL Workshop on Intrinsic and Extrinsic Evaluation Measures for Machine Translation and/or Summarization, Ann Arbor, MI, USA, 29 June 2005; Association for Computational Linguistics: Cedarville, OH, USA, 2005; pp. 65–72.
65. Rei, R.; Stewart, C.; Farinha, A.C.; Lavie, A. COMET: A Neural Framework for MT Evaluation. In Proceedings of the 2020 Conference on Empirical Methods in Natural Language Processing (EMNLP), Online, 16–20 November 2020; Association for Computational Linguistics: Cedarville, OH, USA, 2020; pp. 2685–2702. [CrossRef]
66. Sennrich, R.; Haddow, B.; Birch, A. Neural Machine Translation of Rare Words with Subword Units. In Proceedings of the 54th Annual Meeting of the Association for Computational Linguistics (Volume 1: Long Papers), Berlin, Germany, 7–12 August 2016; pp. 1715–1725. [CrossRef]
67. Junczys-Dowmunt, M.; Grundkiewicz, R.; Dwojak, T.; Hoang, H.; Heafield, K.; Neckermann, T.; Seide, F.; Germann, U.; Fikri Aji, A.; Bogoychev, N.; et al. Marian: Fast Neural Machine Translation in C++. In Proceedings of the ACL 2018, System Demonstrations, Melbourne, Australia, 15–20 July 2018; pp. 116–121.
68. Marian NMT Documentation. Online. 2018. Available online: https://marian-nmt.github.io/docs/cmd/marian/ (accessed on 14 April 2023).
69. Koehn, P.; Hoang, H.; Birch, A.; Callison-Burch, C.; Federico, M.; Bertoldi, N.; Cowan, B.; Shen, W.; Moran, C.; Zens, R.; et al. Moses: Open Source Toolkit for Statistical Machine Translation. In Proceedings of the 45th Annual Meeting of the Association for Computational Linguistics Companion Volume Proceedings of the Demo and Poster Sessions, Prague, Czech Republic, 23–30 June 2007; pp. 177–180.
70. Moses SMT Documentation. Online. 2017. Available online: http://www2.statmt.org/moses/ (accessed on 14 April 2023).

Disclaimer/Publisher's Note: The statements, opinions and data contained in all publications are solely those of the individual author(s) and contributor(s) and not of MDPI and/or the editor(s). MDPI and/or the editor(s) disclaim responsibility for any injury to people or property resulting from any ideas, methods, instructions or products referred to in the content.

Article

Multilingual Multiword Expression Identification Using Lateral Inhibition and Domain Adaptation

Andrei-Marius Avram [1,*], Verginica Barbu Mititelu [2], Vasile Păiș [2], Dumitru-Clementin Cercel [1,*] and Ștefan Trăușan-Matu [1,2]

[1] Computer Science and Engineering Department, Faculty of Automatic Control and Computers, University Politehnica of Bucharest, 060042 Bucharest, Romania
[2] Research Institute for Artificial Intelligence "Mihai Drăgănescu", Romanian Academy, 050711 Bucharest, Romania
* Correspondence: andrei_marius.avram@stud.acs.upb.ro (A.-M.A.); dumitru.cercel@upb.ro (D.-C.C.)

Abstract: Correctly identifying multiword expressions (MWEs) is an important task for most natural language processing systems since their misidentification can result in ambiguity and misunderstanding of the underlying text. In this work, we evaluate the performance of the mBERT model for MWE identification in a multilingual context by training it on all 14 languages available in version 1.2 of the PARSEME corpus. We also incorporate lateral inhibition and language adversarial training into our methodology to create language-independent embeddings and improve its capabilities in identifying multiword expressions. The evaluation of our models shows that the approach employed in this work achieves better results compared to the best system of the PARSEME 1.2 competition, MTLB-STRUCT, on 11 out of 14 languages for global MWE identification and on 12 out of 14 languages for unseen MWE identification. Additionally, averaged across all languages, our best approach outperforms the MTLB-STRUCT system by 1.23% on global MWE identification and by 4.73% on unseen global MWE identification.

Keywords: multiword expression identification; multilingual; lateral inhibition; domain adaptation; PARSEME corpus

MSC: 68T50

1. Introduction

Natural language processing (NLP) is a significant domain of artificial intelligence, with applications ranging from language translation to text classification and information retrieval. NLP allows computers to interpret and process human language, enabling them to perform tasks such as understanding and responding to questions, summarizing texts, and detecting sentiments. Some phenomena present in language can preclude its correct understanding by machines (and even humans sometimes). Such a phenomenon is represented by multiword expressions (MWEs), which are groups of words that function as a unit and convey a specific meaning that is not the sum of the meanings of the component words (i.e., the expression lacks compositionality). Examples of MWEs include idioms (e.g., "break a leg" is used to wish someone good luck), collocations (e.g., "take an exam"), or compounds (e.g., "ice cream"), different authors assuming a more comprehensive or a narrower meaning of this term. The number of MWEs in a language is relatively high. The authors of [1] synthesized papers reporting the number or proportion of MWEs in different languages: English—with an almost equal number of MWEs and single words; French—with 3.3 times greater number of MWE adverbs than that of single adverbs and 1.7 times greater number of MWE verbs than that of single verbs; and Japanese—in which 44% of the verbs are MWEs. Despite being so numerous in the dictionary, MWEs' frequency in corpora is low [2].

Identifying and processing MWEs is crucial for various NLP tasks [3]. In machine translation, for instance, the correct translation of an MWE often depends on the specific context in which it appears. Suppose an MWE is translated rather than appropriately localized for the target language. In that case, the resulting translation may be difficult to understand for native speakers or may convey a wrong meaning [4]. In text classification tasks, MWEs are considered essential clues regarding the sentiment or topic of a text [5]. Additionally, to improve the accuracy of search engines in information retrieval, MWEs can help disambiguate the meaning of a query [6].

Acknowledged recent progress in the field has been made by the PARSEME community [7], which evolved from the COST action with the same name, where the topics of interest were parsing and MWEs (https://typo.uni-konstanz.de/parseme/ last accessed on 21 April 2023). There are two significant outcomes of their activity, (i) a multilingual corpus annotated for verbal MWEs (VMWEs) in 26 languages by more than 160 native annotators, with three versions so far (https://lindat.mff.cuni.cz/repository/xmlui/handle/11372/LRT-2282, https://lindat.mff.cuni.cz/repository/xmlui/handle/11372/LRT-2842, https://lindat.mff.cuni.cz/repository/xmlui/handle/11234/1-3367 last accessed on 21 April 2023) [8–10]; and (ii) a series of shared tasks (also three editions so far) dedicated to the automatic and semi-supervised identification of VMWEs in texts [11–13], in which the previously mentioned corpora were used for training and testing the participating systems.

Developing systems that can handle multiple languages is another important NLP area. In particular, the ability to accurately process and analyze text in various languages is becoming increasingly important as the world becomes more globalized and interconnected. For example, multilingual NLP systems can improve machine translation, allowing computers to translate text from one language to another accurately. This can be particularly useful in situations where there is a need to communicate with speakers of different languages, such as in global business or international relations. In addition to its practical applications, multilingual NLP is an important area of study from a theoretical perspective. Research in this field can help shed light on the underlying principles of language processing and how these principles differ across languages [14,15].

Multilingual Transformer models have become a popular choice for multilingual NLP tasks due to their ability to handle multiple languages and achieve strong performance on a wide range of tasks. Based on the Transformer architecture [16], these models are pre-trained on large amounts of multilingual data and can be fine-tuned for specific NLP tasks, such as language translation or text classification. Some models that have become influential in this area include the multilingual bidirectional encoder from transformers (mBERT) [17], cross-lingual language model (XLM) [18], XLM-RoBERTa (XLM-R) [19], and multilingual bidirectional auto-regressive transformers (mBART) [20]. One of the essential benefits of multilingual Transformer models is their ability to transfer knowledge between languages. These models can learn common representations of different languages, allowing them to perform well on tasks in languages that they have yet to be specifically trained on. Thus, multilingual Transformer models are a good choice for NLP tasks that involve multiple languages, such as machine translation or cross-lingual information retrieval [21].

In this work, we leverage the knowledge developed in the two research areas (i.e., MWEs and multilingual NLP) to improve the results obtained at the PARSEME 1.2 shared task [13]. We explore the benefits of combining them in a singular system by jointly fine-tuning the mBERT model on all languages simultaneously and evaluating it separately. In addition, we try to improve the performance of the overall system by employing two mechanisms, (i) the newly introduced lateral inhibition layer [22] on top of the language model and (ii) adversarial training [23] between languages. For the last mechanism, other researchers have experimented with this algorithm and have shown that it can provide better results with the right setting [24]; however, we are the first to experiment with and show the advantages of lateral inhibition in multilingual adversarial training.

Our results demonstrate that by employing lateral inhibition and multilingual adversarial training, we improve the results obtained by MTLB-STRUCT [25], the best system in edition 1.2 of the PARSEME competition, on 11 out of 14 languages for global MWE identification and 12 out of 14 languages for unseen MWE identification. Furthermore, averaged across all languages, our highest-performing methodology achieves F1-scores of 71.37% and 43.26% for global and unseen MWE identification, respectively. Thus, we obtain an improvement of 1.23% for the former category and a gain of 4.73% for the latter category compared to the MTLB-STRUCT system.

The rest of the paper is structured as follows. Section 2 summarises the contributions of the PARSEME 1.2 competition and the main multilingual Transformer models. The following section, Section 3, outlines the methodology employed in this work, including data representation, lateral inhibition, adversarial training, and how they were employed in our system. Section 4 describes the setup (i.e., dataset and training parameters) used to evaluate our models. Section 5 presents the results, and Section 6 details our interpretation of their significance. Finally, our work is concluded in Section 7 with potential future research directions.

2. Related Work
2.1. Multilingual Transformers

This subsection will present the most influential three multilingual language models (MLLMs): mBERT, XLM, and XLM-R. The mBERT model, similar to the original BERT model [17], is a Transformer model [16] with 12 hidden layers. However, while BERT was trained solely on monolingual English data with an English-specific vocabulary, mBERT is trained on the Wikipedia pages of 104 languages and uses a shared word-piece vocabulary. mBERT has no explicit markers indicating the input language and no mechanism specifically designed to encourage translation-equivalent pairs to have similar representations within the model. Although simple in its architecture, due to its multilingual representations, mBERT's robustness to generalize across languages is often surprising, despite needing to be explicitly trained for cross-lingual generalization. The central hypothesis is that using word pieces common to all languages, which must be mapped to a shared space, may lead to other co-occurring word pieces being mapped to this shared space [26].

XLM resulted from various investigations made by the authors in cross-lingual pre-training. They introduce the translation language modeling objective (TLM), which extends the masked language modeling (MLM) objective to pairs of parallel sentences. The reason for doing that is sound and straightforward. Suppose the model needs to predict a masked word within a sentence from a given language. In that case, it can consider that sentence and its translation into a different language. Thus, the model is motivated to align the representations of both languages in a shared space. Using this approach, XLM obtained state-of-the-art (SOTA) results on supervised and unsupervised machine translation using the WMT'16 German–English and WMT'16 Romanian–English datasets [27], respectively. In addition, the model also obtained SOTA results on the Cross-lingual Natural Language Inference (XNLI) corpus [28].

In contrast to XLM, XLM-R does not use the TLM objective and instead trains RoBERTa [29] on a large, multilingual dataset extracted from CommonCrawl (http://commoncrawl.org/ last accessed on 21 April 2023) datasets. In 100 languages, totaling 2.5 TB of text. It is trained using only the MLM objective, similar to RoBERTa, the main difference between the two being the vocabulary size, with XLM-R using 250,000 tokens compared to RoBERTa's 50,000 tokens. Therefore, XLM-R is significantly larger, with 550 million parameters, compared to RoBERTa's 355 million parameters. The main distinction between XLM and XLM-R is that XLM-R is fully self-supervised, whereas XLM requires parallel examples that may be difficult to obtain in large quantities. In addition, this work demonstrated for the first time that it is possible to develop multilingual models that do not compromise performance in individual languages. XLM-R obtained similar results to monolingual models on the GLUE [30] and XNLI benchmarks.

2.2. PARSEME 1.2 Competition

We present the results obtained by the systems participating in edition 1.2 of the PARSEME shared task [13] on discovering VMWEs that were not present (i.e., were not seen) in the training corpus. We will not focus on the previous editions of this shared task for two reasons, (i) the corpora were different, on the one hand, concerning the distribution of seen and unseen VMWEs in the train/dev/test sets, and, on the other hand, smaller for some languages; and (ii) the focus in the last edition, unlike the first two, was on the systems' ability to identify VMWEs unseen in the train and dev corpora, exploring alternative ways of discovering them. Thus, in a supervised machine learning approach, the systems were supposed to learn some characteristics of seen VMWEs and, based on those, find others in the test dataset.

The competing systems used recurrent neural networks [25,31–33], but also exploited the syntactic annotation of the corpus [34,35], or association measures [34,35]. The shared task was organized on two tracks, closed and open. The former allowed only for the use of the train and dev sets provided by the organizers, as well as of the raw corpora provided for each language, with sizes between 12 and 2474 million tokens. The latter track allowed for the use of any existing resource for training the system, and examples of such resources are as follows, VMWEs lexicons in the target language or another language (exploited due to their translation in the target language) or language models (monolingual or multilingual BERT [25,33], XLM-RoBERTa [32]). Only two systems participated in the closed track, while seven participated in the open one.

The best-performing system in the open track is MTLB-STRUCT [25]. It is a neural language model relying on pre-trained multilingual BERT and learning both MWEs and syntactic dependency parsing, using a tree CRF network [36]. The authors explain that the joint training of the tree CRF and a Transformer-based MWE detection system improves the results for many languages.

The second and third place in the same track is occupied by the model called TRAVIS [33] that came in two variants, TRAVISmulti (ranked second), which employs multilingual contextual embeddings, and TRAVISmono (ranked third), which employs monolingual ones. These systems rely solely on embeddings, and no other feature is used. The author claims that the monolingual contextual embeddings are much better at generalizations than the multilingual ones, especially concerning unseen MWEs.

3. Methodology

In this work, we perform two kinds of experiments, (i) train a model using only the data for a specific language (referred to as monolingual training) and (ii) put multiple corpora from different languages in one place, train the multilingual model on it and then evaluate the trained model on the test set of each language (referred to as multilingual training). For the latter, we also perform additional experiments to improve the results by employing lateral inhibition and adversarial training mechanisms, as depicted in Figure 1.

3.1. Data Representation

BERT has significantly impacted the field of NLP and has achieved SOTA performance on various tasks. Its success can be attributed to the training process, which involves learning from large amounts of textual data using a Transformer model and then fine-tuning it on a smaller amount of task-specific data. The masked language modeling objective used during pre-training allows the model to learn effective sentence representations, which can be fine-tuned for improved performance on downstream tasks with minimal task-specific training data. The success of BERT has led to the creation of language-specific versions of the model for various languages, such as CamemBERT (French) [37], AfriBERT (Afrikaans) [38], FinBERT (Finnish) [39], and RoBERT (Romanian) [40].

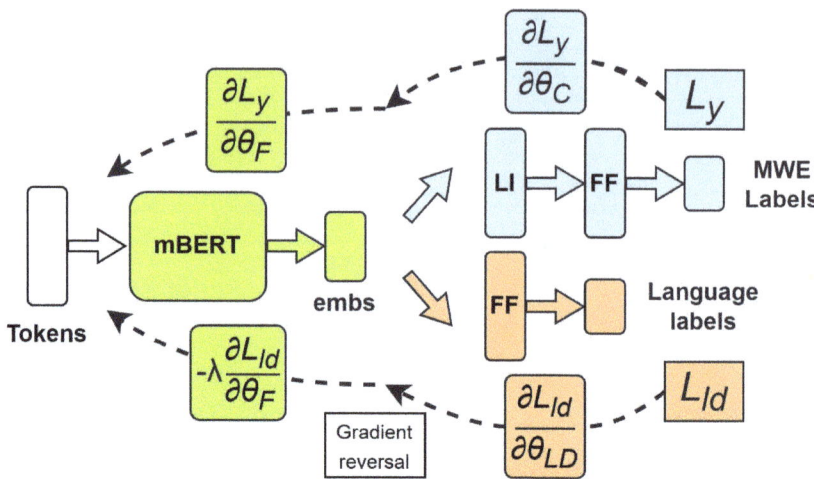

Figure 1. Domain adversarial training algorithm. We have the mBERT feature extractor F with green, whose role is to generate the token embeddings, the MWE label classifier C with blue, and the language classifier LD with orange, whose gradient is reversed and scaled by λ before it is fed into the feature extractor. Additionally, C has incorporated in its architecture the lateral inhibition mechanism.

The scarceness of data and resources has resulted in recent advances in NLP being limited to English and a few high-resource languages rather than being more widely applicable across languages. To address this issue, MLLMs have been developed and trained using large amounts of unlabeled textual data collected from multiple languages. These models are designed to benefit lower resource languages by leveraging their shared vocabulary, genetic relatedness, or contact relatedness with higher resource languages [41,42]. Many different MLLMs are available, which vary in terms of their architecture, training objective, data used for pre-training, and the number of languages covered. However, in our experiments, we employ only the mBERT model because it allows us to provide a cleaner comparison with the monolingual BERT models and thus emphasizes the strengths of our approach.

3.2. Lateral Inhibition

The biological process of lateral inhibition represents the capacity of excited neurons to reduce the activity of their neighbors [43]. In the visual cortex, this process is associated with an increased perception under challenging environments, such as low-lighting conditions. Previously, we proposed implementing the lateral inhibition mechanism in artificial neural networks (ANN) to improve the named entity recognition task [22,44]. The intuition behind introducing this mechanism is that it reduces noise associated with word representations in some instances, such as less frequent words or contexts.

The implementation uses an additional ANN layer that filters the values of a neuron from a previous layer (the word embedding representation) based on values from other adjacent neurons in the previous layer. Equation (1) describes the new layer's forward pass. Here, X is the layer's input vector (a token embedding representation), $Diag$ is a matrix with the diagonal set to the vector given as a parameter, $ZeroDiag$ produces a matrix with the value zero on the main diagonal, and W and B represent the weights and bias. Θ is the Heaviside function, described in Equation (2). The derivative of the Heaviside function in the backward pass is approximated with the sigmoid function using a scaling parameter k [45] (see Equation (3)), a method known as surrogate gradient learning [46].

$$F(X) = X * Diag(\Theta(X * ZeroDiag(W^T) + B)) \tag{1}$$

$$\Theta(x) = \begin{cases} 1, x > 0 \\ 0, x \leq 0 \end{cases} \tag{2}$$

$$\sigma(x) = \frac{1}{1 + e^{-kx}} \tag{3}$$

3.3. Adversarial Training

In recent years, adversarial training of neural networks had a significant influence, particularly in computer vision, where generative unsupervised models have demonstrated the ability to generate new images [47]. A crucial challenge in adversarial training is finding the proper balance between the generator and the adversarial discriminator. As a result, several methods have been proposed in recent times to stabilize the training process [48–50]. Therefore, Joty et al. [51] introduced cross-lingual adversarial neural networks designed to learn discriminative yet language-invariant representations. In this work, we use the same methodology to learn task-specific representations in a cross-lingual setting and improve the predictive capabilities of a multilingual BERT model.

Our approach is rooted in the Domain Adversarial Neural Network (DANN) algorithm, initially designed for domain adaptation [52]. DANN consists of a deep feature extractor F, responsible for extracting relevant features f from the input data, and a deep label classifier C, which uses those features to make predictions about the label of the input x. Together, these two components form a standard feed-forward architecture. In order to improve the performance of the model on a target domain where labeled data are scarce, an additional component is added to the architecture, called a domain classifier D, which is responsible for distinguishing between samples from the source and target domains d. This domain classifier is connected to the feature extractor via a gradient reversal layer, which multiplies the gradient by a negative constant during training. The gradient reversal layer helps ensure that the feature distributions over the two domains are as similar as possible, resulting in domain-invariant features that can better generalize to the target domain. The overall training process minimizes the label prediction loss on the source examples and the domain classification loss on all samples. Thus, we have the following equations that are used to update the parameters of each of the three components:

$$\begin{aligned} \theta_C &= \theta_C - \alpha \frac{\partial L_y}{\partial \theta_C} \\ \theta_D &= \theta_D - \alpha \frac{\partial L_d}{\partial \theta_D} \\ \theta_F &= \theta_F - \alpha (\frac{\partial L_y}{\partial \theta_F} - \lambda \frac{\partial L_d}{\partial \theta_F}) \end{aligned} \tag{4}$$

where θ_C are the parameters of the label classifier, L_y is the loss obtained by the label classifier when predicting the class labels y, θ_D are the parameters of the domain classifier, L_d is the loss obtained by the domain classifier when predicting the domain labels d, θ_F are the parameters of the feature extractor, λ is the hyperparameter used to scale the reverse gradients, and α is the learning rate.

3.4. Monolingual Training

In the monolingual training experiments, we treat the MWE task as sequence tagging, so we try to predict a label for each input token. To attain that, we employ a feed-forward layer that maps the embeddings produced by a BERT model into the specific MWE class logits and then apply the softmax activation function to obtain the probabilities. This mechanism is succinctly described in the following equation:

$$p_i = softmax(e_i W^T + b) \tag{5}$$

where p_i are the class MWE probabilities for the token i, e_i are the embeddings produced by the language model, W^T is the transpose of the feed-forward layer, and b is its bias. We use the same BERT models for each language as in [25]).

3.5. Multilingual Training

We fine-tune the mBERT model for multilingual training using the same methodology as in the monolingual case. However, we improve the predictions by first employing the lateral inhibition layer on top of the embeddings. The lateral inhibition layer has been shown to improve the performance of language models in named entity recognition tasks [22,44,53], and we believe that it would do the same for MWE identification since the methodology is similar for the two tasks. Therefore, the equation that describes the resulting system becomes:

$$p_i = softmax(LI(e_i)W^T + b) \qquad (6)$$

where LI is the lateral inhibition layer and the rest of the terms are the same as in Equation (5).

We also adapt the multilingual training by employing the DANN algorithm with a language discriminator instead of the domain discriminator. Thus, we create language-independent features out of the mBERT model by reversing the gradient that comes out of the language discriminator when backpropagating through the language model. The gradient reversal mechanism in our system is described using the following equations

$$\begin{aligned} \theta_C &= \theta_C - \alpha \frac{\partial L_y}{\partial \theta_C} \\ \theta_{LD} &= \theta_{LD} - \alpha \frac{\partial L_{ld}}{\partial \theta_{LD}} \\ \theta_F &= \theta_F - \alpha \left(\frac{\partial L_y}{\partial \theta_F} - \lambda \frac{\partial L_{ld}}{\partial \theta_F} \right) \end{aligned} \qquad (7)$$

where θ_C are the parameters of the MWE classifier, L_y is the loss obtained by the MWE classifier when predicting the MWE labels y, θ_{LD} are the parameters of the language discriminator, L_{ld} is the loss obtained by the language discriminator when predicting the language labels ld, θ_F are the parameters of the mBERT model (i.e., the feature extractor in DANN), λ is the hyperparameter used to scale the reversed gradients, and α is the learning rate.

Finally, we employ the lateral inhibition layer and the DANN methodology with a language discriminator on the mBERT model for multilingual training. The forward procedure of this approach, which is used to compute the loss between the predicted MWE probabilities for a given text and the corresponding ground truths, and the loss between the predicted language probabilities and the corresponding ground truths of the given text, is described in Algorithm 1 as follows:

- Tokenize the *text* using the mBERT tokenizer, obtaining the tokens tok_i (Line 1).
- Generate the multilingual embeddings emb_i for each of the above tokens tok_i using the mBERT model (Line 2).
- Apply the lateral inhibition layer on each of the embeddings emb_i (Line 3).
- Use the MWE classifier composed of lateral inhibition layer output to produce the probabilities $\hat{y}_i$ of a token to belong to a certain MWE class (Line 4).
- Use the language discriminator on the embedding $emb_{[CLS]}$ corresponding to the token [CLS] to produce the probabilities $\hat{ld}_i$ of the text to belong to a certain language (Line 5).
- Compute the loss L_y between the predicted MWE probabilities and the ground truth MWE labels (Line 6) and the loss L_{ld} between the predicted language probabilities and the ground truth language labels (Line 7).

In Algorithm 2, we outline the backward procedure used to update the parameters of our models as follows:

- Compute the gradients ∇_C for the MWE classifier using the MWE loss L_y (Line 1).
- Compute the gradients ∇_{LD} for the language discriminator using the language discriminator loss L_{ld} (Line 2).
- Compute the gradients ∇_F of the mBERT model using ∇_C and $-\nabla_{LD}$ multiplied by λ (Line 3).
- Update the model parameters (i.e., θ_C, θ_{LD}, and θ_F) using the gradient descent algorithm (Lines 4-6).

Algorithm 1: Algorithm describing the forward pass of the multilingual training with lateral inhibition and language adversarial training.

Input: text, ground truth MWE labels y_i, and ground truth language labels ld_i
Output: MWE identification loss L_y and language discrimination loss L_{ld}
$tok_i \leftarrow \text{tokenize}(text)$
$emb_i \leftarrow \text{mbert}(tok_i)$
$h_i \leftarrow \text{lateral\_inhibition}(emb_i)$
$\hat{y}_i \leftarrow \text{mwe\_classifier}(h_i)$
$\hat{ld}_i \leftarrow \text{language\_discriminator}(emb_{[CLS]})$
$L_y \leftarrow \text{cross\_entropy\_loss}(y_i, \hat{y}_i)$
$L_{ld} \leftarrow \text{cross\_entropy\_loss}(ld_i, \hat{ld}_i)$

Algorithm 2: Algorithm describing the backward pass of the multilingual training with lateral inhibition and language adversarial training.

Input: MWE identification loss L_y, language discrimination loss L_{ld}, and reversed gradient scaling factor λ
Output: Parameters θ_C, θ_{LD}, and θ_F
$\nabla_C \leftarrow \text{compute\_gradients}(L_y)$
$\nabla_{LD} \leftarrow \text{compute\_gradients}(L_{ld})$
$\nabla_F \leftarrow \text{compute\_gradients}(\nabla_C - \lambda \nabla_{LD})$
$\theta_C \leftarrow \text{update\_parameters}(\nabla_C)$
$\theta_{LD} \leftarrow \text{update\_parameters}(\nabla_{LD})$
$\theta_F \leftarrow \text{update\_parameters}(\nabla_F)$

---

4. Experimental Settings

4.1. Dataset

The corpus used to evaluate our models is the PARSEME dataset version 1.2. The corpus was manually annotated with VMWEs of several types. Some are universal because they exist and were annotated in all languages in the project. These universal types are verbal idioms (e.g., the Romanian "a face din țânțar armăsar"—eng. "to make a mountain out of a molehill") and light verb constructions (e.g., the Romanian "a face o vizită"—eng. "to pay a visit") in which their verb is light in the sense that its semantic contribution to the meaning of the whole expression is almost null, its role being rather only that of carrying the verb specific morphological information, such as tense, number, or person. There are also light verb constructions in which the verb carries a causative meaning (e.g., the Romanian "a da bătăi de cap"—eng. "to give a hard time"), and they are also annotated in all languages. The types of VMWEs that apply only to some of the languages in the project are called quasi-universal: inherently reflexive verbs (e.g., the Romanian "a-și imagina"—eng. "to imagine (oneself)"), verb-particle constructions (e.g., "to give up"), multi-verb constructions (e.g., "make do"), and inherently adpositional verbs (e.g., "to rely on"). For Italian, a language-specific type was defined, namely inherently clitic verbs (e.g., "prendersela"—eng. "to be angry").

The dataset used in the PARSEME shared task edition 1.2 contains 14 languages, including German (DE), Basque (EU), Greek (EL), French (FR), Irish (GA), Hebrew (HE),

Hindi (HI), Italian (IT), Polish (PL), Brazilian Portuguese (PT), Romanian (RO), Swedish (SV), Turkish (TR), and Chinese (ZH). The number of tokens ranges from 35 k tokens (HI) to 1015 k tokens (RO), while the number of annotated VMWEs ranges from 662 (GA) to 9164 (ZH). The dataset split was made to ensure a higher number of unseen VMWEs in the dev (100 unseen VMWEs with respect to the train set) and test (300 unseen VMWEs with respect to the train + dev files) sets. More statistics regarding the PARSEME 1.2 dataset are depicted in Table 1.

In addition to the annotation with VMWEs, the multilingual PARSEME corpus is also tokenized, morphologically, and syntactically annotated, mostly with UDPipe [54]. Thus, the syntactic analysis follows the principles of Universal Dependencies (https://universaldependencies.org/ last accessed on 21 April 2023) [55].

Table 1. The statistics of PARSEME 1.2: number of sentences (#Sent.), of tokens (#Tok.), and the sentence average length (Len.) on each of the three splits: training, validation, and test.

Lang.	Training			Validation			Test		
	#Sent.	#Tok.	Len.	#Sent.	#Tok.	Len.	#Sent.	#Tok.	Len.
DE	6.5 k	126.8 k	19.3	602	11.7 k	19.5	1.8 k	34.9 k	19.1
EL	17.7 k	479.6 k	27.0	909	23.9 k	26.3	2.8 k	75.4 k	26.7
EU	4.4 k	61.8 k	13.9	1.4 k	20.5 k	14.4	5.3 k	75.4 k	14.2
FR	14.3 k	360.0 k	25.0	1.5 k	39.5 k	25.1	5.0 k	126.4 k	25.2
GA	257	6.2 k	24.2	322	7.0 k	21.8	1.1 k	25.9 k	23.1
HE	14.1 k	286.2 k	20.2	1.2 k	25.3 k	20.2	3.7 k	76.8 k	20.2
HI	282	5.7 k	20.4	289	6.2 k	21.7	1.1 k	23.3 k	21.0
IT	10.6 k	282.0 k	27.4	1.2 k	32.6 k	27.1	3.8 k	106.0 k	27.3
PL	17.7 k	298.4 k	16.8	1.4 k	23.9 k	16.8	4.3 k	73.7 k	16.7
PT	23.9 k	542.4 k	22.6	1.9 k	43.6 k	22.1	6.2 k	142.3 k	22.8
RO	10.9 k	195.7 k	17.9	7.7 k	134.3 k	17.4	38.0 k	685.5 k	18.0
SV	1.6 k	24.9 k	15.5	596	8.8 k	14.9	2.1 k	31.6 k	15.0
TR	17.9 k	267.5 k	14.9	1.0 k	15.9 k	15.0	3.3 k	48.7 k	14.7
ZH	35.3 k	575.5 k	16.2	1.1 k	18.2 k	16.0	3.4 k	55.7 k	16.0
Total	175.7 k	3512.7 k	20.1	29.3 k	522.2 k	19.8 k	81.9 k	1581.6 k	20.0

4.2. Fine-Tuning

We followed the fine-tuning methodology employed by MTLB-STRUCT (the corresponding configuration files for each language are available at https://github.com/shivaat/MTLB-STRUCT/tree/master/code/configs last accessed on 21 April 2023) with the tree conditional random fields [56] disabled. Thus, we trained our models for 10 epochs using a batch size of 32 and the Adam optimizer [57] with a learning rate of 3×10^{-5}. We set the maximum input sequence length to 150, the scaling parameter k, used in the gradient approximation of the lateral inhibition Heaviside function, to 10, which was empirically shown to create a good enough surrogate gradient [22], and the hyperparameter λ to 0.01 in the DANN algorithm for scaling the reversed gradient. We did not employ k-fold cross-validation in our experiments, and we measured the model performance in terms of precision, recall, and F1-score at the token level using the following equations:

$$\text{Precision} = \frac{TP}{TP + FP} \tag{8}$$

$$\text{Recall} = \frac{TP}{TP + FN} \tag{9}$$

$$\text{F1-score} = \frac{2 \cdot Precision \cdot Recall}{Precision + Recall} \tag{10}$$

where TP is the number of true positives, FP is the number of false positives, and FN is the number of false negatives. As suggested by the PARSEME 1.2 competition evaluation methodology (https://www.davidsbatista.net/blog/2018/05/09/Named_Entity_Evaluation/ last accessed on 21 April 2023), we compute the strict variant of the F1-score. Thus, we consider the predicted label of a group of tokens as true positive only if it perfectly matches the ground truth [58].

5. Results

The results of our evaluation for both monolingual and multilingual training, with and without lateral inhibition and adversarial training, for all the 14 languages, are displayed in Table 2. We improved the performance of MTLB-STRUCT, the best overall system according to the competition benchmark (https://multiword.sourceforge.net/PHITE.php?sitesig=CONF&page=CONF_02_MWE-LEX_2020___lb__COLING__rb__&subpage=CONF_40_Shared_Task last accessed on 21 April 2023), on 11 out of 14 languages for global MWE prediction (the three remaining languages are German, Italian, and Romanian) and on 12 out of 14 languages for unseen MWE prediction (the two remaining languages are German and Greek). Out of all the cases where our methods underperformed, the only high difference was obtained in the German language, our best system being behind the MTLB-STRUCT system by approximately 3.43% on global MWE prediction and approximately 6.57% on unseen MWE prediction. We believe that this is due to the employment of the German BERT (https://huggingface.co/bert-base-german-cased last accessed on 21 April 2023) by the MTLB-STRUCT team, while we still used the mBERT model for this language.

For the global MWE prediction, we managed to improve the performance in 11 languages, the highest F1-score was obtained by the monolingual training once (i.e., Chinese), by the simple multilingual training three times (i.e., Greek, Irish, and Turkish), by the multilingual training with lateral inhibition three times (i.e., French, Hebrew, and Polish), by the multilingual adversarial training once (i.e., Basque), and by the multilingual adversarial training with the lateral inhibition three times (i.e., Hindi, Portuguese, and Swedish). On the other hand, for the unseen MWE prediction, we managed to achieve better results in 12 languages. The simple multilingual training obtained the highest F1-score only once (i.e., Swedish), the multilingual training with the lateral inhibition three times (i.e., French, Turkish, and Chinese), the multilingual adversarial training five times (i.e., Irish, Hebrew, Hindi, Polish, and Romanian), and the multilingual adversarial training with lateral inhibition three times (i.e., Basque, Italian, and Portuguese).

Table 2. The results obtained by the monolingual and multilingual training, together with the results obtained by the best system of the PARSEME 1.2 competition, MTLB-STRUCT. LI is the lateral inhibition component, while Adv is the domain adaptation technique for cross-lingual MWE identification. We measure the precision (P), recall (R), and F1-score (F1) for each global and unseen MWE identification experiment. The best results in each language are highlighted in bold.

Language	Method	Global MWE-Based			Unseen MWE-Based		
		P	R	F1	P	R	F1
DE	MTLB-STRUCT [25]	77.11	**75.24**	**76.17**	**49.17**	**49.50**	**49.34**
	Monolingual	74.26	72.82	73.53	40.35	41.79	41.06
	Multilingual	**77.26**	68.47	72.60	37.85	43.22	40.35
	Multilingual + LI	69.07	66.38	67.70	39.15	43.85	41.37
	Multilingual + Adv	69.00	68.33	68.66	39.18	45.11	41.94
	Multilingual + LI + Adv	71.37	68.08	69.69	41.47	43.85	42.77
EL	MTLB-STRUCT [25]	72.54	72.69	72.62	38.74	**47.00**	**42.47**
	Monolingual	72.33	**73.00**	72.66	38.30	46.75	42.11
	Multilingual	**74.60**	72.38	**73.48**	**38.92**	42.21	40.50
	Multilingual + LI	72.52	72.90	72.71	37.90	45.78	41.47
	Multilingual + Adv	73.23	72.18	72.70	38.81	44.48	41.45
	Multilingual + LI + Adv	73.42	72.59	73.00	38.64	44.16	41.21

Table 2. Cont.

Language	Method	Global MWE-Based			Unseen MWE-Based		
		P	R	F1	P	R	F1
EU	MTLB-STRUCT [25]	80.72	79.36	80.03	28.12	44.33	34.41
	Monolingual	81.61	**80.40**	81.00	34.94	**49.29**	40.89
	Multilingual	**86.49**	77.03	**81.49**	33.32	45.04	39.17
	Multilingual + LI	84.07	78.66	81.28	37.38	44.48	40.62
	Multilingual + Adv	82.77	78.71	80.69	36.46	48.44	41.61
	Multilingual + LI + Adv	84.80	78.42	81.48	**39.71**	46.46	**42.82**
FR	MTLB-STRUCT [25]	80.04	78.81	79.42	39.20	46.00	42.33
	Monolingual	79.84	**79.54**	79.69	38.89	44.87	41.67
	Multilingual	81.80	77.04	79.35	43.17	44.55	43.85
	Multilingual + LI	**81.85**	78.96	**80.37**	**45.48**	**48.40**	**46.89**
	Multilingual + Adv	80.12	78.59	79.35	41.60	**48.40**	44.74
	Multilingual + LI + Adv	80.47	78.22	79.33	40.87	45.19	42.92
GA	MTLB-STRUCT [25]	37.72	25.00	30.07	23.08	16.94	19.54
	Monolingual	33.67	23.17	27.45	24.02	17.28	20.10
	Multilingual	54.91	34.63	42.48	45.91	28.61	35.25
	Multilingual + LI	55.31	34.63	42.60	45.79	27.76	34.57
	Multilingual + Adv	**56.12**	**35.78**	**43.70**	**48.42**	**30.31**	**37.28**
	Multilingual + LI + Adv	55.72	34.63	42.72	45.79	27.76	34.57
HE	MTLB-STRUCT [25]	56.20	42.35	48.30	25.53	15.89	19.59
	Monolingual	54.09	40.76	46.49	26.02	15.94	19.77
	Multilingual	61.38	40.76	48.98	34.76	17.81	23.55
	Multilingual + LI	**61.63**	42.54	**50.23**	34.46	19.06	24.55
	Multilingual + Adv	58.40	42.15	48.96	**35.35**	**21.88**	**27.03**
	Multilingual + LI + Adv	59.89	**42.74**	49.88	34.92	20.62	25.93
HI	MTLB-STRUCT [25]	72.25	**75.04**	73.62	48.75	58.33	53.11
	Monolingual	66.53	70.28	68.35	49.35	61.35	54.70
	Multilingual	**77.78**	71.77	74.65	**62.72**	58.65	60.61
	Multilingual + LI	77.08	68.95	72.78	61.83	56.49	59.04
	Multilingual + Adv	75.46	73.11	74.26	60.95	**62.43**	**61.68**
	Multilingual + LI + Adv	75.53	73.85	**74.68**	60.31	**62.43**	61.35
IT	MTLB-STRUCT [25]	67.68	**60.27**	**63.76**	20.23	21.33	20.81
	Monolingual	64.53	59.59	61.96	20.81	**24.06**	22.32
	Multilingual	69.37	56.40	62.21	22.22	19.38	20.70
	Multilingual + LI	**71.27**	56.01	62.72	23.02	20.12	21.28
	Multilingual + Adv	65.65	58.33	61.78	20.83	21.88	21.43
	Multilingual + LI + Adv	69.18	57.85	63.01	**25.51**	23.44	**24.43**
PL	MTLB-STRUCT [25]	82.94	79.18	81.02	38.46	41.53	39.94
	Monolingual	81.89	79.33	80.85	38.30	41.99	40.06
	Multilingual	84.02	77.03	80.37	40.34	37.50	38.87
	Multilingual + LI	**85.14**	79.26	**82.09**	**44.48**	41.33	**42.84**
	Multilingual + Adv	82.55	**79.85**	81.18	40.75	**45.19**	42.86
	Multilingual + LI + Adv	83.19	78.74	80.90	41.01	41.67	41.34
PT	MTLB-STRUCT [25]	73.93	72.76	73.34	30.54	41.33	35.13
	Monolingual	74.81	70.94	73.01	33.81	39.05	35.98
	Multilingual	75.93	70.94	73.35	34.06	39.18	36.44
	Multilingual + LI	**77.15**	71.89	74.43	**35.61**	39.18	37.31
	Multilingual + Adv	73.36	73.48	73.42	30.33	40.13	34.55
	Multilingual + LI + Adv	75.51	**73.53**	**74.49**	33.76	**41.78**	**37.36**

Table 2. Cont.

Language	Method	Global MWE-Based			Unseen MWE-Based		
		P	R	F1	P	R	F1
RO	MTLB-STRUCT [25]	89.88	**91.05**	**90.46**	28.84	41.47	34.02
	Monolingual	90.39	90.11	90.25	46.82	51.09	48.86
	Multilingual	**91.34**	88.46	89.88	**49.90**	48.12	48.99
	Multilingual + LI	90.78	88.85	89.81	45.06	45.15	45.10
	Multilingual + Adv	89.14	90.13	89.63	46.27	**56.44**	**50.85**
	Multilingual + LI + Adv	89.95	88.78	89.36	45.44	50.30	47.74
SV	MTLB-STRUCT [25]	69.59	73.68	71.58	35.57	53.00	42.57
	Monolingual	73.01	73.68	73.34	44.32	**54.62**	48.93
	Multilingual	**78.92**	70.79	74.63	**50.78**	**54.62**	**52.63**
	Multilingual + LI	75.48	73.68	74.57	46.77	52.66	49.54
	Multilingual + Adv	75.42	**74.41**	74.91	46.70	53.50	49.87
	Multilingual + LI + Adv	77.62	74.10	**75.82**	49.47	51.82	50.62
TR	MTLB-STRUCT [25]	68.41	70.55	69.46	42.11	45.33	43.66
	Monolingual	69.11	72.89	70.95	43.75	47.88	45.72
	Multilingual	67.52	**73.27**	**71.18**	41.83	47.56	44.51
	Multilingual + LI	**69.92**	72.28	71.08	**47.94**	**49.19**	**48.55**
	Multilingual + Adv	68.41	70.37	69.38	43.54	47.23	45.31
	Multilingual + LI + Adv	68.22	69.77	68.99	43.04	44.30	43.66
ZH	MTLB-STRUCT [25]	68.56	70.74	69.63	58.97	53.67	56.20
	Monolingual	**72.33**	**72.88**	**72.60**	59.74	**58.03**	58.87
	Multilingual	72.03	71.32	71.67	62.30	55.87	58.91
	Multilingual + LI	69.82	70.36	70.09	62.50	57.31	**59.79**
	Multilingual + Adv	69.29	69.47	69.38	62.42	54.73	58.32
	Multilingual + LI + Adv	70.64	68.58	69.59	**65.41**	54.73	59.59

Also, the monolingual training has not achieved the highest F1-score for unseen MWE prediction for any language. These findings are summarized in Table 3).

Table 3. The number of times we managed to obtain the highest F1-score with each system developed in this work for both global MWE (#Highest Global MWE) and unseen MWE (#Highest Unseen MWE) predictions.

Method	#Highest Global MWE	#Highest Unseen MWE
MTLB-STRUCT [25]	3	2
Monolingual	1	0
Multilingual	3	1
Multilingual + LI	3	3
Multilingual + ADV	1	5
Multilingual + LI + ADV	3	3
Total (ours)	11	12

We further compared the average scores across all languages obtained by our systems. In Table 4, we compared our results with the ones obtained by each system at the latest edition of the PARSEME competition (https://multiword.sourceforge.net/PHITE.php?sitesig=CONF&page=CONF_02_MWE-LEX_2020___lb__COLING__rb__&subpage=CONF_50_Shared_task_results last accessed on 21 April 2023): MTLB-STRUCT [25], Travis-multi/mono [33], Seen2Unseen [34], FipsCo [10], HMSid [35], and MultiVitamin [32]. For the global MWE identification, we outperformed the MTLB-STRUCT results with all the multilingual training experiments, the highest average F1-score being obtained by the simple multilingual training without lateral inhibition or adversarial training. It achieved an average F1-score of 71.37%, an improvement of 1.23% compared to the MTLB-STRUCT F1-score (i.e., 70.14%).

For unseen MWE identification, we improved the average results obtained by MTLB-STRUCT using all the methodologies employed in this work. The highest average F1-score was obtained by the multilingual adversarial training with 43.26%, outperforming the MTLB-STRUCT system by 4.73%.

Table 4. The average precision (AP), recall (AR), and F1-scores (AF1) over all languages obtained by our systems are compared with the results obtained by each system at the PARSEME 1.2 competition on global and unseen MWE identification. We also depict the number of languages used to train each system (#Lang). The best results are highlighted in bold.

Method	#Lang.	Global MWE-Based			Unseen MWE-Based		
		AP	AR	AF1	AP	AR	AF1
MTLB-STRUCT [25]	14/14	71.26	**69.05**	70.14	36.24	41.12	38.53
TRAVIS-multi [33]	13/14	60.65	57.62	59.10	28.11	33.29	30.48
TRAVIS-mono [33]	10/14	49.50	43.48	46.34	24.33	28.01	26.04
Seen2Unseen [34]	14/14	63.36	62.69	63.02	16.14	11.95	13.73
FipsCo [10]	3/14	11.69	8.75	10.01	4.31	5.21	4.72
HMSid [35]	1/14	4.56	4.85	4.70	1.98	3.81	2.61
MultiVitaminBooster [32]	7/14	0.19	0.09	0.12	0.05	0.07	0.06
Monolingual	14/14	70.60	68.52	69.54	38.52	42.42	40.38
Multilingual	14/14	**75.23**	67.88	**71.37**	42.72	41.60	42.15
Multilingual + LI	14/14	74.36	68.24	71.17	**43.48**	42.20	42.78
Multilingual + Adv	14/14	72.78	68.92	70.80	42.26	**44.30**	**43.26**
Multilingual + LI + Adv	14/14	73.96	68.56	71.16	43.24	42.75	43.00

6. Discussion

According to our experiments, the average MWE identification performance can be improved by approaching this problem using a multilingual NLP system, as described in this work. An interesting perspective of our results on this task is how much improvement we brought compared to the PARSEME 1.2 competition's best system. These results are shown at the top of Figure 2 for global MWE prediction and at its bottom for unseen MWE prediction. In general, the most significant relative improvements were achieved in the Irish language by employing multilingual training that, combined with adversarial training, boosted the performance by 45.32% for the global MWE prediction and by 90.78% for the unseen MWE prediction. On the other hand, for the same language, by using the monolingual training, we decrease the system's performance on global MWE prediction by 8.71% and slightly increase it by 2.86% on unseen MWE prediction. We believe that these improvements in Irish were due to the benefits brought by the multilingual training since this language contained the least amount of training sentences (i.e., 257 sentences), and it has been shown in previous research that superior results are obtained when such fine-tuning mechanisms are employed [59]. However, the Hindi language also contains a small number of training samples (i.e., 282 sentences), but our multilingual training results are worse when compared to Irish. We assume that this is the outcome of the language inequalities that appeared in the mBERT pre-training data [60] and the linguistic isolation of Hindi since there are no other related languages in the fine-tuning data [61].

The second highest improvements for global MWE prediction were achieved in the Swedish language with 2.45% for the monolingual training, 4.26% for the multilingual training, 4.17% for the multilingual training with the lateral inhibition, 4.65% for the multilingual adversarial training, and 5.92% for the multilingual adversarial training with lateral inhibition. We observe a relatively high difference between the first and the second place, but we believe again that this is due to the small number of sentences for Irish compared to Swedish. On the other hand, the results for unseen MWE prediction outline that the second highest improvements were attained in Romanian with 43.62% for the monolingual training, 44.00% for the multilingual training, 32.56% for the multilingual training with lateral inhibition, 49.47% for the multilingual adversarial training, and 40.32% for the multilingual adversarial training with lateral inhibition. In addition, the improvements are more uniform on the unseen MWE prediction than the global one.

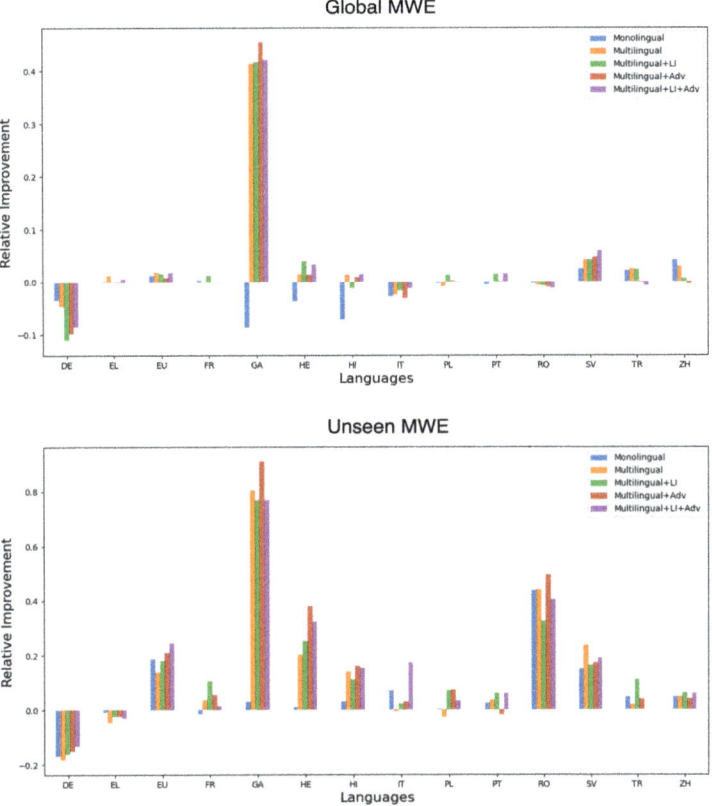

Figure 2. Improvements brought by our methodologies (i.e., Monolingual, Multilingual, Multilingual+LI, Multilingual+Adv, and Multilingual+LI+Adv) on global (**top**) and unseen (**bottom**) MWE prediction compared to the results of MTLB-STRUCT, the best system in the PARSEME shared task edition 1.2.

7. Conclusions and Future Work

Failure to identify MWEs can lead to misinterpretation of text and errors in NLP tasks, making this an important area of research. In this paper, we analyzed the performance of MWE identification in a multilingual setting, training the mBERT model on the combined PARSEME 1.2 corpus using all the 14 languages found in its composition. In addition, to boost the performance of our system, we employed lateral inhibition and language adversarial training in our methodology, intending to create embeddings that are as language-independent as possible. Our evaluation results highlighted that through this approach, we managed to improve the results obtained by MTLB-STRUCT, the best system of the PARSEME 1.2 competition, on 11 out of 14 languages for global MWE identification and 12 out of 14 for unseen MWE identification. Thus, with the highest average F1-scores of 71.37% for global MWE identification and 43.26% for unseen MWE identification, we class ourselves over MTLB-STRUCT by 1.23% for the former task and by 4.73% for the latter.

Possible future work directions involve analyzing how the language-independent features produced by mBERT are when lateral inhibition and adversarial training are involved, together with an analysis of more models that produce multilingual embeddings, such as XLM or XLM-R. In addition, we intend to analyze these two methodologies, with possible extensions, for multilingual training beyond MWE identification, targeting tasks, such as language generation or named entity recognition. Finally, since the languages in the PARSEME 1.2 dataset may share similar linguistic properties, we would like to explore how language groups improve each other's performance in the multilingual scenario.

Author Contributions: Conceptualization, A.-M.A., V.B.M., V.P. and D.-C.C.; methodology, A.-M.A. and V.P.; software, A.-M.A.; validation, A.-M.A., V.B.M., D.-C.C. and Ș.T.-M.; formal analysis, A.-M.A.; investigation, A.-M.A., V.B.M. and D.-C.C.; resources, A.-M.A. and V.B.M.; data curation, A.-M.A.; writing—original draft preparation, A.-M.A., V.B.M. and V.P.; writing—review and editing, A.-M.A., V.B.M., D.-C.C. and Ș.T.-M.; visualization, A.-M.A.; supervision, D.-C.C. and Ș.T.-M.; project administration, D.-C.C.; funding acquisition, D.-C.C. All authors have read and agreed to the published version of the manuscript.

Funding: This research has been funded by the University Politehnica of Bucharest through the PubArt program.

Data Availability Statement: The PARSEME 1.2 dataset used in this work has been open-sourced by the competition organizers and is available for public usage at https://lindat.mff.cuni.cz/repository/xmlui/handle/11234/1-3367 (last accessed on 21 April 2023).

Conflicts of Interest: The authors declare no conflict of interest.

References

1. Shudo, K.; Kurahone, A.; Tanabe, T. A comprehensive dictionary of multiword expressions. In Proceedings of the 49th Annual Meeting of the Association for Computational Linguistics: Human Language Technologies, Portland, OR, USA, 19–24 June 2011; pp. 161–170.
2. Savary, A. Computational inflection of multi-word units: A contrastive study of lexical approaches. *Linguist. Issues Lang. Technol.* **2008**, *1*, 1–53. [CrossRef]
3. Avram, A.; Mititelu, V.B.; Cercel, D.C. Romanian Multiword Expression Detection Using Multilingual Adversarial Training and Lateral Inhibition. In Proceedings of the 19th Workshop on Multiword Expressions (MWE 2023), Dubrovnik, Croatia, 2–6 May 2023; pp. 7–13.
4. Zaninello, A.; Birch, A. Multiword expression aware neural machine translation. In Proceedings of the 12th Language Resources and Evaluation Conference, Marseille, France, 11–16 May 2020; pp. 3816–3825.
5. Najar, D.; Mesfar, S.; Ghezela, H.B. Multi-Word Expressions Annotations Effect in Document Classification Task. In Proceedings of the International Conference on Applications of Natural Language to Information Systems, Paris, France, 13–15 June 2018; pp. 238–246.
6. Goyal, K.D.; Goyal, V. Development of Hybrid Algorithm for Automatic Extraction of Multiword Expressions from Monolingual and Parallel Corpus of English and Punjabi. In Proceedings of the 17th International Conference on Natural Language Processing (ICON): System Demonstrations, Patna, India, 18–21 December 2020; pp. 4–6.
7. Savary, A.; Candito, M.; Mititelu, V.B.; Bejček, E.; Cap, F.; Čéplö, S.; Cordeiro, S.R.; Eryiğit, G.; Giouli, V.; van Gompel, M.; et al. PARSEME multilingual corpus of verbal multiword expressions. In *Multiword Expressions at Length and in Depth: Extended Papers from the MWE 2017 Workshop*; Markantonatou, S., Ramisch, C., Savary, A., Vincze, V., Eds.; Language Science Press: Berlin, Germany, 2018; pp. 87–147. [CrossRef]
8. Savary, A.; Ramisch, C.; Cordeiro, S.R.; Sangati, F.; Vincze, V.; QasemiZadeh, B.; Candito, M.; Cap, F.; Giouli, V.; Stoyanova, I.; et al. *Annotated Corpora and Tools of the PARSEME Shared Task on Automatic Identification of Verbal Multiword Expressions*, 1.0 ed.; LINDAT/CLARIAH-CZ Digital Library at the Institute of Formal and Applied Linguistics (ÚFAL), Faculty of Mathematics and Physics, Charles University: Staré Město, Czech Republic, 2017.
9. Ramisch, C.; Cordeiro, S.R.; Savary, A.; Vincze, V.; Barbu Mititelu, V.; Bhatia, A.; Buljan, M.; Candito, M.; Gantar, P.; Giouli, V.; et al. *Annotated Corpora and Tools of the PARSEME Shared Task on Automatic Identification of Verbal Multiword Expressions*, 1.1 ed.; LINDAT/CLARIAH-CZ Digital Library at the Institute of Formal and Applied Linguistics (ÚFAL), Faculty of Mathematics and Physics, Charles University: Staré Město, Czech Republic, 2018.
10. Ramisch, C.; Guillaume, B.; Savary, A.; Waszczuk, J.; Candito, M.; Vaidya, A.; Barbu Mititelu, V.; Bhatia, A.; Iñurrieta, U.; Giouli, V.; et al. *Annotated Corpora and Tools of the PARSEME Shared Task on Semi-Supervised Identification of Verbal Multiword Expressions*, 1.2 ed.; LINDAT/CLARIAH-CZ Digital Library at the Institute of Formal and Applied Linguistics (ÚFAL), Faculty of Mathematics and Physics, Charles University: Staré Město, Czech Republic, 2020.
11. Savary, A.; Ramisch, C.; Cordeiro, S.; Sangati, F.; Vincze, V.; QasemiZadeh, B.; Candito, M.; Cap, F.; Giouli, V.; Stoyanova, I.; et al. The PARSEME Shared Task on Automatic Identification of Verbal Multiword Expressions. In Proceedings of the 13th Workshop on Multiword Expressions (MWE 2017), Valencia, Spain, 4 April 2017; pp. 31–47. [CrossRef]

12. Ramisch, C.; Cordeiro, S.R.; Savary, A.; Vincze, V.; Barbu Mititelu, V.; Bhatia, A.; Buljan, M.; Candito, M.; Gantar, P.; Giouli, V.; et al. Edition 1.1 of the PARSEME Shared Task on Automatic Identification of Verbal Multiword Expressions. In Proceedings of the Joint Workshop on Linguistic Annotation, Multiword Expressions and Constructions (LAW-MWE-CxG-2018), Santa Fe, NM, USA, 25–26 August 2018; pp. 222–240.
13. Ramisch, C.; Savary, A.; Guillaume, B.; Waszczuk, J.; Candito, M.; Vaidya, A.; Barbu Mititelu, V.; Bhatia, A.; Iñurrieta, U.; Giouli, V.; et al. Edition 1.2 of the PARSEME Shared Task on Semi-supervised Identification of Verbal Multiword Expressions. In Proceedings of the Joint Workshop on Multiword Expressions and Electronic Lexicons, Online, 13 December 2020; pp. 107–118.
14. Ponti, E.M.; O'horan, H.; Berzak, Y.; Vulić, I.; Reichart, R.; Poibeau, T.; Shutova, E.; Korhonen, A. Modeling language variation and universals: A survey on typological linguistics for natural language processing. *Comput. Linguist.* **2019**, *45*, 559–601. [CrossRef]
15. Arroyo González, R.; Fernández-Lancho, E.; Maldonado Jurado, J.A. Learning Effect in a Multilingual Web-Based Argumentative Writing Instruction Model, Called ECM, on Metacognition, Rhetorical Moves, and Self-Efficacy for Scientific Purposes. *Mathematics* **2021**, *9*, 2119. [CrossRef]
16. Vaswani, A.; Shazeer, N.; Parmar, N.; Uszkoreit, J.; Jones, L.; Gomez, A.N.; Kaiser, Ł.; Polosukhin, I. Attention is all you need. In Proceedings of the Advances in Neural Information Processing Systems, Long Beach, CA, USA, 4–9 December 2017; pp. 6000–6010.
17. Devlin, J.; Chang, M.W.; Lee, K.; Toutanova, K. BERT: Pre-training of Deep Bidirectional Transformers for Language Understanding. In Proceedings of the 2019 Conference of the North American Chapter of the Association for Computational Linguistics: Human Language Technologies, Volume 1 (Long and Short Papers), Minneapolis, MN, USA, 2–7 June 2019; pp. 4171–4186.
18. Conneau, A.; Lample, G. Cross-lingual language model pretraining. In Proceedings of the Advances in Neural Information Processing Systems, Vancouver, BC, Canada, 8–14 December 2019; pp. 7059–7069.
19. Conneau, A.; Khandelwal, K.; Goyal, N.; Chaudhary, V.; Wenzek, G.; Guzmán, F.; Grave, É.; Ott, M.; Zettlemoyer, L.; Stoyanov, V. Unsupervised Cross-lingual Representation Learning at Scale. In Proceedings of the 58th Annual Meeting of the Association for Computational Linguistics, Online, 5–10 July 2020; pp. 8440–8451.
20. Liu, Y.; Gu, J.; Goyal, N.; Li, X.; Edunov, S.; Ghazvininejad, M.; Lewis, M.; Zettlemoyer, L. Multilingual Denoising Pre-training for Neural Machine Translation. *Trans. Assoc. Comput. Linguist.* **2020**, *8*, 726–742. [CrossRef]
21. Kalyan, K.S.; Rajasekharan, A.; Sangeetha, S. Ammus: A survey of transformer-based pretrained models in natural language processing. *arXiv* **2021**, arXiv:2108.05542.
22. Pais, V. RACAI at SemEval-2022 Task 11: Complex named entity recognition using a lateral inhibition mechanism. In Proceedings of the 16th International Workshop on Semantic Evaluation (SemEval-2022), Seattle, WA, USA, 14–15 July 2022; pp. 1562–1569. [CrossRef]
23. Lowd, D.; Meek, C. Adversarial learning. In Proceedings of the Eleventh ACM SIGKDD International Conference on Knowledge Discovery in Data Mining, Chicago, IL, USA, 21–24 August 2005; pp. 641–647.
24. Dong, X.; Zhu, Y.; Zhang, Y.; Fu, Z.; Xu, D.; Yang, S.; De Melo, G. Leveraging adversarial training in self-learning for cross-lingual text classification. In Proceedings of the 43rd International ACM SIGIR Conference on Research and Development in Information Retrieval, Virtual, 25–30 July 2020; pp. 1541–1544.
25. Taslimipoor, S.; Bahaadini, S.; Kochmar, E. MTLB-STRUCT@ Parseme 2020: Capturing Unseen Multiword Expressions Using Multi-task Learning and Pre-trained Masked Language Models. In Proceedings of the Joint Workshop on Multiword Expressions and Electronic Lexicons, Online, 13 December 2020; pp. 142–148.
26. Pires, T.; Schlinger, E.; Garrette, D. How Multilingual is Multilingual BERT? In Proceedings of the 57th Annual Meeting of the Association for Computational Linguistics, Florence, Italy, 28 July–2 August 2019; pp. 4996–5001.
27. Bojar, O.; Graham, Y.; Kamran, A.; Stanojević, M. Results of the wmt16 metrics shared task. In *Proceedings of the First Conference on Machine Translation: Volume 2, Shared Task Papers*; Association for Computational Linguistics: Cedarville, OH, USA, 2016; pp. 199–231.
28. Conneau, A.; Rinott, R.; Lample, G.; Williams, A.; Bowman, S.; Schwenk, H.; Stoyanov, V. XNLI: Evaluating Cross-lingual Sentence Representations. In Proceedings of the 2018 Conference on Empirical Methods in Natural Language Processing, Brussels, Belgium, 31 October–4 November 2018; pp. 2475–2485.
29. Liu, Y.; Ott, M.; Goyal, N.; Du, J.; Joshi, M.; Chen, D.; Levy, O.; Lewis, M.; Zettlemoyer, L.; Stoyanov, V. Roberta: A robustly optimized bert pretraining approach. *arXiv* **2019**, arXiv:1907.11692.
30. Wang, A.; Singh, A.; Michael, J.; Hill, F.; Levy, O.; Bowman, S. GLUE: A Multi-Task Benchmark and Analysis Platform for Natural Language Understanding. In Proceedings of the 2018 EMNLP Workshop BlackboxNLP: Analyzing and Interpreting Neural Networks for NLP, Brussels, Belgium, 1 November 2018; pp. 353–355.
31. Yirmibeşoğlu, Z.; Güngör, T. ERMI at PARSEME Shared Task 2020: Embedding-Rich Multiword Expression Identification. In Proceedings of the Joint Workshop on Multiword Expressions and Electronic Lexicons, Online, 13 December 2020; pp. 130–135.
32. Gombert, S.; Bartsch, S. MultiVitaminBooster at PARSEME Shared Task 2020: Combining Window-and Dependency-Based Features with Multilingual Contextualised Word Embeddings for VMWE Detection. In Proceedings of the Joint Workshop on Multiword Expressions and Electronic Lexicons, Online, 13 December 2020; pp. 149–155.
33. Kurfalı, M. TRAVIS at PARSEME Shared Task 2020: How good is (m) BERT at seeing the unseen? In Proceedings of the Joint Workshop on Multiword Expressions and Electronic Lexicons, Online, 13 December 2020; pp. 136–141.

34. Pasquer, C.; Savary, A.; Ramisch, C.; Antoine, J.Y. Seen2Unseen at PARSEME Shared Task 2020: All Roads do not Lead to Unseen Verb-Noun VMWEs. In Proceedings of the Joint Workshop on Multiword Expressions and Electronic Lexicons, Online, 13 December 2020; pp. 124–129.
35. Colson, J.P. HMSid and HMSid2 at PARSEME Shared Task 2020: Computational Corpus Linguistics and unseen-in-training MWEs. In Proceedings of the Joint Workshop on Multiword Expressions and Electronic Lexicons, Online, 13 December 2020; pp. 119–123.
36. Rush, A. Torch-Struct: Deep structured prediction library. In Proceedings of the 58th Annual Meeting of the Association for Computational Linguistics: System Demonstrations, Online, 5–10 July 2020; pp. 335–342.
37. Martin, L.; Muller, B.; Suárez, P.J.O.; Dupont, Y.; Romary, L.; De La Clergerie, É.V.; Seddah, D.; Sagot, B. CamemBERT: A Tasty French Language Model. In Proceedings of the 58th Annual Meeting of the Association for Computational Linguistics, Seattle, WA, USA, 5–10 July 2020; pp. 7203–7219.
38. Ralethe, S. Adaptation of deep bidirectional transformers for Afrikaans language. In Proceedings of the 12th Language Resources and Evaluation Conference, Marseille, France, 11–16 May 2020; pp. 2475–2478.
39. Virtanen, A.; Kanerva, J.; Ilo, R.; Luoma, J.; Luotolahti, J.; Salakoski, T.; Ginter, F.; Pyysalo, S. Multilingual is not enough: BERT for Finnish. *arXiv* **2019**, arXiv:1912.07076.
40. Dumitrescu, S.; Avram, A.M.; Pyysalo, S. The birth of Romanian BERT. In Proceedings of the Findings of the Association for Computational Linguistics: EMNLP 2020, Online, 16–20 November 2020; pp. 4324–4328.
41. Doddapaneni, S.; Ramesh, G.; Kunchukuttan, A.; Kumar, P.; Khapra, M.M. A primer on pretrained multilingual language models. *arXiv* **2021**, arXiv:2107.00676.
42. Draskovic, D.; Zecevic, D.; Nikolic, B. Development of a Multilingual Model for Machine Sentiment Analysis in the Serbian Language. *Mathematics* **2022**, *10*, 3236. [CrossRef]
43. Cohen, R.A. Lateral inhibition. *Encyclopedia of Clinical Neuropsychology*; Springer: New York, NY, USA, 2011; pp. 1436–1437.
44. Mitrofan, M.; Pais, V. Improving Romanian BioNER Using a Biologically Inspired System. In Proceedings of the 21st Workshop on Biomedical Language Processing, Dublin, Ireland, 26 May 2022; pp. 316–322. [CrossRef]
45. Wunderlich, T.C.; Pehle, C. Event-based backpropagation can compute exact gradients for spiking neural networks. *Sci. Rep.* **2021**, *11*, 12829. [CrossRef] [PubMed]
46. Neftci, E.O.; Mostafa, H.; Zenke, F. Surrogate Gradient Learning in Spiking Neural Networks: Bringing the Power of Gradient-Based Optimization to Spiking Neural Networks. *IEEE Signal Process. Mag.* **2019**, *36*, 51–63. [CrossRef]
47. Gui, J.; Sun, Z.; Wen, Y.; Tao, D.; Ye, J. A review on generative adversarial networks: Algorithms, theory, and applications. *arXiv* **2020**, arXiv:2001.06937.
48. Wiatrak, M.; Albrecht, S.V.; Nystrom, A. Stabilizing generative adversarial networks: A survey. *arXiv* **2019**, arXiv:1910.00927.
49. Nam, S.H.; Kim, Y.H.; Choi, J.; Park, C.; Park, K.R. LCA-GAN: Low-Complexity Attention-Generative Adversarial Network for Age Estimation with Mask-Occluded Facial Images. *Mathematics* **2023**, *11*, 1925. [CrossRef]
50. Zhang, X.; Wang, J.; Cheng, N.; Xiao, J. Metasid: Singer identification with domain adaptation for metaverse. In Proceedings of the 2022 International Joint Conference on Neural Networks (IJCNN), Queensland, Australia, 18–23 June 2022; pp. 1–7.
51. Joty, S.; Nakov, P.; Màrquez, L.; Jaradat, I. Cross-language Learning with Adversarial Neural Networks. In Proceedings of the 21st Conference on Computational Natural Language Learning (CoNLL 2017), Vancouver, BC, Canada, 3–4 August 2017; pp. 226–237. [CrossRef]
52. Ganin, Y.; Ustinova, E.; Ajakan, H.; Germain, P.; Larochelle, H.; Laviolette, F.; Marchand, M.; Lempitsky, V. Domain-adversarial training of neural networks. *J. Mach. Learn. Res.* **2016**, *17*, 1–35.
53. Avram, A.M.; Păiș, V.; Mitrofan, M. Racai@ smm4h'22: Tweets disease mention detection using a neural lateral inhibitory mechanism. In Proceedings of the Seventh Workshop on Social Media Mining for Health Applications, Workshop & Shared Task, Gyeongju, Republic of Korea, 12–17 October 2022; pp. 1–3.
54. Straka, M.; Straková, J. Tokenizing, POS Tagging, Lemmatizing and Parsing UD 2.0 with UDPipe. In Proceedings of the CoNLL 2017 Shared Task: Multilingual Parsing from Raw Text to Universal Dependencies, Vancouver, BC, Canada, 3–4 August 2017; pp. 88–99.
55. de Marneffe, M.C.; Manning, C.D.; Nivre, J.; Zeman, D. Universal Dependencies. *Comput. Linguist.* **2021**, *47*, 255–308. [CrossRef]
56. Bradley, J.K.; Guestrin, C. Learning tree conditional random fields. In Proceedings of the 27th International Conference on Machine Learning (ICML-10), Haifa, Israel, 21–24 June 2010; pp. 127–134.
57. Kingma, D.P.; Ba, J. Adam: A method for stochastic optimization. *arXiv* **2014**, arXiv:1412.6980.
58. Sang, E.T.K.; De Meulder, F. Introduction to the CoNLL-2003 Shared Task: Language-Independent Named Entity Recognition. In Proceedings of the Seventh Conference on Natural Language Learning at HLT-NAACL 2003, Edmonton, AB, Canada, 31 May–1 June 2003; pp. 142–147.
59. Eisenschlos, J.; Ruder, S.; Czapla, P.; Kadras, M.; Gugger, S.; Howard, J. MultiFiT: Efficient Multi-lingual Language Model Fine-tuning. In Proceedings of the 2019 Conference on Empirical Methods in Natural Language Processing and the 9th International Joint Conference on Natural Language Processing (EMNLP-IJCNLP), Hong Kong, China, 3–7 November 2019; pp. 5702–5707.

60. Wu, S.; Dredze, M. Are All Languages Created Equal in Multilingual BERT? In Proceedings of the 5th Workshop on Representation Learning for NLP, Online, 9 July 2020; pp. 120–130.
61. Dhamecha, T.; Murthy, R.; Bharadwaj, S.; Sankaranarayanan, K.; Bhattacharyya, P. Role of Language Relatedness in Multilingual Fine-tuning of Language Models: A Case Study in Indo-Aryan Languages. In Proceedings of the 2021 Conference on Empirical Methods in Natural Language Processing, Punta Cana, Dominican Republic, 7–11 November 2021; pp. 8584–8595.

Disclaimer/Publisher's Note: The statements, opinions and data contained in all publications are solely those of the individual author(s) and contributor(s) and not of MDPI and/or the editor(s). MDPI and/or the editor(s) disclaim responsibility for any injury to people or property resulting from any ideas, methods, instructions or products referred to in the content.

Research on Relation Classification Tasks Based on Cybersecurity Text

Ze Shi [1], Hongyi Li [1,2], Di Zhao [1,2,*] and Chengwei Pan [3,4,*]

[1] School of Cyber Science and Technology, Beihang University, Beijing 100191, China; zb2039107@buaa.edu.cn (Z.S.); lihongyi@buaa.edu.cn (H.L.)
[2] School of Mathematical Sciences, Beihang University, Beijing 100191, China
[3] Institute of Artificial Intelligence, Beihang University, Beijing 100191, China
[4] Key Laboratory of Mathematics, Informatics and Behavioral Semantics, Ministry of Education, Beijing 100191, China
* Correspondence: zdzz@buaa.edu.cn (D.Z.); pancw@buaa.edu.cn (C.P.)

Abstract: Relation classification is a significant task within the field of natural language processing. Its objective is to extract and identify relations between two entities in a given text. Within the scope of this paper, we construct an artificial dataset (CS13K) for relation classification in the realm of cybersecurity and propose two models for processing such tasks. For any sentence containing two target entities, we first locate the entities and fine-tune the pre-trained BERT model. Next, we utilize graph attention networks to iteratively update word nodes and relation nodes. A new relation classification model is constructed by concatenating the updated vectors of word nodes and relation nodes. Our proposed model achieved exceptional performance on the SemEval-2010 task 8 dataset, surpassing previous approaches with a remarkable F1 value of 92.3%. Additionally, we propose the integration of a ranking-based voting mechanism into the existing model. Our best results are an F1 value of 92.5% on the SemEval-2010 task 8 dataset and a value 94.6% on the CS13K dataset. These findings highlight the effectiveness of our proposed models in tackling relation classification tasks.

Keywords: relation classification; graph neural network; cybersecurity; natural language processing

MSC: 68T50

1. Introduction

In light of the dynamic evolution of the cybersecurity field and the exponential expansion of cybersecurity data, traditional analysis methods became inadequate to fulfill the demands of the cybersecurity industry. Considering how to timely and accurately analyze and process massive amounts of data, extract key elements and relations, and mine potential valuable information emerged as pressing issues that require immediate resolution. The use of natural language processing technology can help cybersecurity experts quickly and accurately process and analyze large amounts of cybersecurity data and textual information, thereby better understanding and applying cybersecurity knowledge. Therefore, scholars attempted to leverage natural language processing techniques, including named entity recognition [1], relation extraction [2], and attribute extraction [3]; as well as mathematical representation methods, including quantization [4], dimensionality reduction [5], and interpolation [6,7]; as means of identifying, analyzing, defending against, and mitigating various cybersecurity attacks.

Relation classification is a classical problem within the domain of relation extraction and a crucial task in natural language processing (NLP). It primary objective is to identify the pre-defined relations between two target entities in a given sentence and represent these relations as triples with "subject, predicate, object" forms, which serve as foundational data sources for constructing knowledge graphs. BERT [8,9], which is a Transformer-based bidirectional language model, demonstrated impressive performance across diverse NLP tasks. Unlike conventional unidirectional language models, BERT stands out as it is trained in both left-to-right and right-to-left directions. This enables BERT to capture contextual information effectively, resulting in dynamic word vectors that adapt to the context, thereby capturing contextual semantics more effectively. The model attained state-of-the-art outcomes in various classification and sequence labeling tasks and was adopted and applied in various fields, including relation extraction, question answering, text representation, and natural language inference [8,10].

Graph Neural Networks (GNNs) are types of neural network specifically designed to handle graph-structured data. Due to their ability to handle data with arbitrary topology, GNNs found extensive applications in diverse fields, such as graph classification, node classification, relation prediction, object tracking, etc. [11]. Compared to traditional graph-based methods, GNNs can directly learn the representations of nodes and graphs from their topological structures. Meanwhile, Graph Attention Networks (GATs) integrate GNNs and attention mechanisms. In the GATs model, relationships between nodes are captured through attention weights, which are subsequently employed to perform weighted aggregation of the features of neighboring nodes. This process, in turn, updates the nodes' representations, enhancing the model's expressive power.

In this paper, we constructed a cybersecurity dataset named CS13K specifically for relation classification tasks using manual annotation. Given that the relation classification task requires high position information for the two entities, we inserted special markers before and after the target entities to identify their positions and transmit the information to the BERT model. Next, we located the positions of the two target entities within the output embeddings of the BERT model, allowing the model to capture the semantics of the sentence and the semantics of the entities in a simultaneous manner. Based on this method, we used GATs to iteratively update word nodes and relation nodes, and constructed a new GATs-based relation classification model (Bert-GAT). Furthermore, based on the work in the literature [12], we introduced a voting mechanism in the Bert–GAT and the R-Bert models, and constructed a new ensemble model called Bert–Vote, which was specifically tailored for relation classification tasks. In summary, the key contributions of this paper are:

(1) Based on our current understanding, the CS13K dataset we constructed is the first manually annotated text dataset for relation classification in the field of cybersecurity.
(2) To encode the entities and sentences, we inserted special marker symbols before and after the target entities to identify their positions, and utilized the BERT pre-training model. Additionally, we iteratively updated word nodes and relation nodes using GATs, resulting in the development of a novel relation classification model, named Bert–GAT. The proposed model attained a remarkable state-of-the-art performance, obtaining an F1 score of 92.3% on the SemEval-2010 task 8 dataset and a 94.1% score on the CS13K dataset.
(3) We employed an ensemble learning approach to construct a new relation classification model, known as Bert–Vote, which achieved a state-of-the-art performance of 92.5% in terms of F1 score on the SemEval-2010 task 8 dataset, as well as a 94.6% score on the CS13K dataset.

The remaining content of this paper is organized as follows: Section 2 discusses related work in terms of relation classification datasets, relation classification tasks, graph neural networks, and voting mechanisms; Section 3 provides a detailed introduction to the proposed cybersecurity relation classification dataset and relation classification model; in Section 4, the experiments and evaluation are presented and Section 5 provides the conclusions and future works of the article.

2. Related Work

In this section, we will conduct a comprehensive review of previous work on relation classification datasets, relation classification tasks, GNNs, voting mechanisms, and other related research, providing a comprehensive overview of these studies.

2.1. Relation Classification Datasets

Relation classification is a highly challenging problem in NLP. In recent years, significant progress was made in relation classification tasks in various fields. Common relation classification datasets include SemEval 2010 Task 8, DDRel, FewRel, TACRED, and MATRES [13–15]. SemEval 2010 Task 8 is a dataset for multi-dimensional relation classification in the general domain. DDRel is a dataset for interpersonal relation classification in binary dialogues. FewRel is a relation classification dataset containing 100 categories and 7836 sentences constructed from Wikipedia. The TACRED dataset contains approximately 90,000 sentences from news articles, each of which contains information about the relations between two entities. These relations are divided into 42 different types, such as "author", "organization member", "birthplace", etc. The MATRES dataset contains nearly 1000 news articles, with over 2000 events annotated with temporal relations to other events. This dataset has high annotation accuracy, and provides an important foundation for research on time relation recognition and event extraction. Although significant progress was made in relation classification in general domains, it has been slow in the field of cybersecurity. This issue is largely because the data in the field of cybersecurity are highly specialized, and there is a lack of open-source datasets for relation classification. Furthermore, existing publicly available datasets are of poor data quality, which has become one of the main obstacles in research on relation classification tasks in cybersecurity, particularly in the development of deep learning-based relation classification algorithms. Therefore, building a relation classification dataset that is as close to real-world situations as possible is crucial for promoting research in the field of cybersecurity.

2.2. Relation Classification

In current studies on relation classification, the main methods can be classified into three distinct categories: feature-, kernel-, and neural network-based approaches. Among them, feature-based methods excessively rely on expert knowledge, face difficulties in feature selection, and have poor transferability to new domains. In contrast, kernel-based methods have the advantage of automatically extracting a multitude of useful features, which can be obtained from syntax trees or strings, avoiding the trouble of manually constructing the feature space. Bunescu et al. [16] proposed a relation extraction kernel based on the shortest path between two entities by comparing the number of identical nodes in the paths. Culotta et al. [17] obtained a tree kernel by weighting and summing common subtrees, migrated the tree kernel to dependency trees, and then added syntactic parsing information, significantly improving the classification accuracy. The problem with these methods is that their recall rate is relatively low; therefore, many scholars subsequently focused on improving the recall rate.

Although neural network-based relation classification methods have constraints, such as high model complexity or the need for large-scale training corpus, they are still the most effective relation classification methods currently available, and scholars are still focusing on optimizing and improving the model's generalization ability. Liu et al. [18] were pioneers in utilizing neural networks to automatically extract features for relation classification, proposing a relation classification method based on convolutional neural networks (CNN). The network architecture consists of a single convolutional layer, followed by a fully connected layer, and a softmax layer, with a relatively simple structure. Based on this approach, scholars successively proposed many CNN-based improved methods [19,20]. Socher et al. [21] first attempted to use recursive neural networks to solve relation classification problems, and other scholars used recurrent neural networks to solve relation classification problems. Thang et al. [22] integrated CNN and RNN in their approach, utilizing both models to perform relation classification to identify connections between two entities, and then using a voting mechanism to filter out the final relation classification result, where the CNN and RNN voting weights can be adjusted. Recently, some scholars attempted to introduce the BERT model into relation classification tasks and combined it with information about target entities to handle relation classification problems, proposing the R-BERT model, which effectively integrates text features and semantic features of sentences, achieving an F1 value of 89.25% on the SemEval2010 task 8 relation classification dataset [12]. By constructing a heterogeneous graph to model entities and relations, the RIFRE model achieves outstanding performance in the joint extraction of entities and relations [23]. The CorefBERT model uses entity recognizers and coreference resolvers as two important components. The entity recognizer first identifies entities in the text and marks them, and then embeds their representations into the BERT model. The coreference resolver uses the output of the entity recognizer to determine to which entity each reference refers, and then embeds their representations into the BERT model. Finally, the model uses these embeddings to perform relation classification tasks, achieving an F1 value of 89.2% [24]. In the QA model, the input text is initially encoded using a bidirectional LSTM. Subsequently, an attention mechanism is employed to identify and select potential relation segments between the two entities of interest. Following that method, a span prediction layer is utilized to predict whether these segments contain a relation. During the prediction process, the model simultaneously predicts the label of each relation and the starting and ending positions of the relation text segment, enabling direct prediction of the relation text segment without the need for manual feature extraction [25]. The writing style and format of the translation should adhere to the conventions of academic papers written in English, and there should be no grammatical errors.

2.3. GNNs

In the research on GNNs, Xie et al. [26] proposed a method that uses sentence nodes and entity nodes as the basic units of the heterogeneous GNNs and captures the neighborhood information between relation nodes and sentence nodes. The advantage of this method is its ability to capture diverse data from various types of nodes and integrate them into a common node classification task. Sahu et al. [27] introduced a method for cross-sentence relation extraction, which utilizes document-level GNNs, considering the dependency relations between sentences as edges and capturing the interaction between sentences by constructing a document-level graph model, thus achieving accurate and effective cross-sentence relation extraction results. Mandya et al. [28] introduced a graph convolutional neural network model that incorporates multi-dependency subgraphs for relation extraction tasks in sentences. The model can capture semantic information from different parts of the sentence and fuse it to improve the efficiency and accuracy of relation extraction. Zhao et al. [29] proposed a new entity-pair-based graph neural network model called EPGNN. EPGNN uses GNNs to model the relations between entities and uses a combination of semantic features and graph topology features for relation classification. Compared to traditional feature-based methods, GNNs can handle complex relations between nodes and edges and use graph structural information to extract more accurate features.

2.4. Voting Mechanisms

The voting mechanism is a commonly used model ensemble method that combines the predictions of multiple models to improve the accuracy and robustness of the model. In classification problems, the voting mechanism is typically used to determine the ultimate classification outcome of each sample, with the basic idea of selecting the class with the most votes or highest scores as the sample's classification label. Mushtaq et al. [30] used a range of machine learning algorithms to train and optimize multiple biomedical features, and then integrated the output results of these algorithms using the voting mechanism to improve the accuracy of diabetes prediction. Bhati et al. [31] introduced a new voting-based ensemble method for intrusion detection systems (IDS). This method uses multiple separate IDS models, each of which is trained using different feature subsets and classifiers. Next, by voting on the results of each model, the outcomes of the conducted experiments showed that this method can significantly improve the performance of IDS. Khan et al. [32] constructed an IoT network intrusion detection method based on a voting classifier, which is composed of multiple classifiers to form a voting ensemble model, with each classifier using different feature sets and algorithms for training. When a new data sample is input into the system, each classifier generates a prediction result, which is then determined using the voting mechanism to achieve the final classification result. By employing this approach, different classifiers can be integrated to enhance the accuracy of intrusion detection. Maheshwari et al. [33] introduced a refined ensemble model that employs weighted voting for the purpose of detecting and mitigating DDoS attacks in SDN environments. The ensemble model consists of multiple base classifiers, each of which classifies data and then merges their classification results into a final classification result. The authors also introduced an optimized weighted voting strategy to enhance the accuracy and robustness of the model.

3. Methodology

In this section, we will offer a comprehensive introduction to the cybersecurity dataset that we constructed. Moreover, we will provide an in-depth elucidation of the architecture underlying our relation classification model.

3.1. Dataset

To advance research on relation classification tasks in the field of cybersecurity, we collected data from over 440 publicly available security reports and manually constructed a cybersecurity relation classification dataset, which is named CS13K. Each security report was published by internationally recognized security firms or government agencies, including cybersecurity blogs, research papers, and technical documents. The reports were analyzed, extracted, and annotated by multiple doctoral students from the Cybersecurity Institute, who possess good domain knowledge in the field of cybersecurity. The CS13K dataset comprises 12 relation types, namely belongTo, cause, exploits, hasAttackLocation, hasAttackTime, hasCharacteristics, hasVulnerability, indicates, mitigates, targets, use, and associate. The dataset contains 13,027 sentences, each of which includes two entities and the relation type between them.

The relations in the dataset exhibit directionality, meaning that relation(entity1, entity2) and relation(entity2, entity1) are distinct. Therefore, in this task, it is necessary not only to predict the relations between entities, but also to predict the direction of the relations. Hence, there are 24 relation types in the actual relation classification dataset. Table 1 shows examples of the exploits and hasVulnerability relation types. exploits(e1, e2) and exploits(e2, e1) represent two distinct relation types. For each sentence containing the target entities e1 and e2, we marked the entities with special symbols.

The statistical characteristics of the CS13K dataset are shown in Table 2. For training purposes, we utilized 11,500 samples, while 1527 samples were reserved for testing.

We validated the effectiveness of the relation classification model using the CS13K dataset and conducted comparative evaluations with the SemEval-2010 Task 8 dataset. The evaluation metric employed for these comparisons was the macro-averaged F1 score.

3.2. Relation Classification Models

In order to ensure that the model effectively incorporated the positional information of these two entities, for any sentence containing two target entities, we inserted special markers "\$" at the initial and final positions of the first entity, entity 1, and "#" at the initial and final positions of the second entity, entity 2. In addition, at the beginning of each sentence, we included the token "[CLS]", and at the end, we append the token "[SEP]". Based on the work in the literature [12], we used the BERT model to encode each word in the sentence. Assuming that entity 1 was embedded as a vector from V_j to V_k and entity 2 was embedded as a vector from V_p to V_q, we obtain the mean vector E_1 of entity 1 by averaging the vectors from V_j to V_k, and similarly, we obtained the mean vector E_2 of entity 2 by averaging the vectors from V_p to V_q, where $E_i \in \mathbb{R}^k$. Similarly, we embedded each pre-defined relation label as a high-dimensional vector r_i with the same dimension as the entity vectors using a relation encoder, where $r_i \in \mathbb{R}^k$.

$$E_1 = \frac{1}{k-j+1} \sum_{n=j}^{k} V_n \qquad (1)$$

$$E_2 = \frac{1}{q-p+1} \sum_{n=p}^{q} V_n \qquad (2)$$

Table 1. Examples of CS13K dataset.

Relation	Text
exploits(e1, e2)	In September, researchers alleged that \<e1\> APT27 \</e1\> was behind an attack campaign exploiting the vulnerability \<e2\> CVE-2021-40539 \</e2\> in Zoho's ManageEngine product.
exploits(e2, e1)	\<e1\> CVE-2013-2465 \</e1\>, which involves insufficient bounds checks in the storeImageArray function. This vulnerability is used by \<e2\> White Lotus \</e2\> and other exploit kits.
hasVulnerability(e1, e2)	APT28 exploited \<e1\> Microsoft Office \</e1\> vulnerability \<e2\> CVE-2017-0262 \</e2\> for execution.
hasVulnerability(e2, e1)	Apparently, the most dangerous vulnerability addressed in this update pack is \<e1\> CVE-2022-26925 \</e1\>, which is contained in the \<e2\> Windows Local Security Authority \</e2\>.

Table 2. Relation types in CS13K dataset and their statistical characteristics.

Relation	Proportion
belongTo	7.59%
cause	7.09%
exploits	6.08%
hasAttackLocation	15.88%
hasAttackTime	5.28%
hasCharacteristics	7.30%
hasVulnerability	7.75%
indicates	3.40%
mitigates	5.76%
targets	17.34%
use	11.43%
associate	5.10%
total	100.00%

Building on the work of [9,21], we denoted all entity nodes as $\{E_i\}_{i=1}^{N}$ and all relation nodes as $\{r_j\}_{j=1}^{M}$. We treated entity nodes and relation nodes as neighbors and updated their node representations through a message-passing mechanism. We incorporated a multi-head attention mechanism to augment the model's capability to attend and concentrate on node features. For each attention head $H \in [H_1, \ldots, H_j]$, we first constructed the query matrix Q, key matrix K, and value matrix V:

$$\begin{aligned} Q_{H_i} &= W_1 E_i \\ K_{H_j} &= W_2 r_j \\ V_{H_j} &= W_3 r_j \end{aligned} \qquad (3)$$

where W_1, W_2, and W_3 are trainable weight parameters.

Next, we calculated the attention weights.

$$x_{ij} = \frac{Q_{H_i}\left(K_{H_j}\right)^T}{\sqrt{d_k}} \tag{4}$$

$$\alpha_{ij} = \frac{\exp(x_{ij})}{\sum_{l \in N_i} \exp(x_{ij})} \tag{5}$$

where d_k is the dimension of the key matrix K.

Next, we utilized the attention weights to update the nodes and obtain the output of each attention head.

$$E'_{H_i} = E_i + \sum_{j \in N_i} \alpha_{ij} W_3 r_j \tag{6}$$

We concatenated the outputs of all attention heads, E'_{H_i}, together, and then multiplied the concatenated output vector by the weight matrix W_4 to obtain the final multi-head attention output.

$$E'_i = W_4 \left[\text{concat}(E'_{H_1}, E'_{H_2}, ..., E'_{H_j}) \right] \tag{7}$$

where W_4 is a trainable weight parameter, N_i, is a neighbor of node i, and α_{ij} is the attention weight between the entity node E_i and the relation node r_j.

A gating mechanism was used to calculate weight vectors for each node and edge, enabling the model to maintain its non-linear capacity.

$$y_i = sigmod\left(W_5 \left[\text{concat}(E_i, E'_i)\right]\right) \tag{8}$$

$$\tilde{E}_i = y_i \odot E'_i + (1 - y_i) \odot E_i \tag{9}$$

where W_5 is a trainable weight parameter and $\tilde{E}_i$ is the final output of node representation. We simplify the above node update process as follows:

$$\tilde{E}_i = \text{GAT}\left(E_i, \{r_j\}_{j \in N_i}\right) \tag{10}$$

where GAT refers to the mechanism employed to update the node E_i, $\{r_j\}_{j \in N_i}$ are all the neighboring nodes of the entity node E_i, and $\tilde{E}_i$ is the updated node representation of the node E_i.

The exchange in information between entity nodes and relation nodes can be illustrated as the message-passing process:

$$\tilde{E}_i^1 = \text{GAT}\left(E_i^0, \{r_j^0\}_{j \in N_i}\right) \tag{11}$$

$$E_i^1 = \tilde{E}_i^1 + E_i^0 \tag{12}$$

where E_i^0 is the node representation before the update, $\tilde{E}_i^1$ is the updated node representation of E_i^0, and E_i^1 is the final entity node representation.

Similarly, based on the update of entity nodes, the update process of relation nodes can be represented as:

$$\tilde{r}_j^1 = \text{GAT}\left(r_j^0, \{E_i^1\}_{i \in N_j}\right) \tag{13}$$

$$r_j^1 = \tilde{r}_j^1 + r_j^0 \tag{14}$$

where r_j^0 is the representation of the relation node before the update and r_j^1 is the updated representation of r_j^0. When the model contains multiple layers of GAT, the node update process of other layers is similar.

After obtaining the updated entity nodes and relation nodes, we applied a Dropout layer and introduce a fully connected layer in the model architecture to obtain output vectors V_1' and V_2' for entity nodes, as well as V_3' for relation nodes. Finally, we concatenated V_1', V_2', and V_3', and added a fully connected layer to obtain V. We then applied a Softmax classification layer for the final relation classification. This process is represented as follows:

$$V = W_6 [concat(V_1', V_2', V_3',)] + b \tag{15}$$

$$f = softmax(V) \tag{16}$$

where W_6 and b are trainable parameters. We denoted the relation classification model that used special marker symbols for entity tagging and iteratively updated the word nodes and relation nodes using graph neural networks as the Bert–GAT model. Figure 1 illustrates the model architecture.

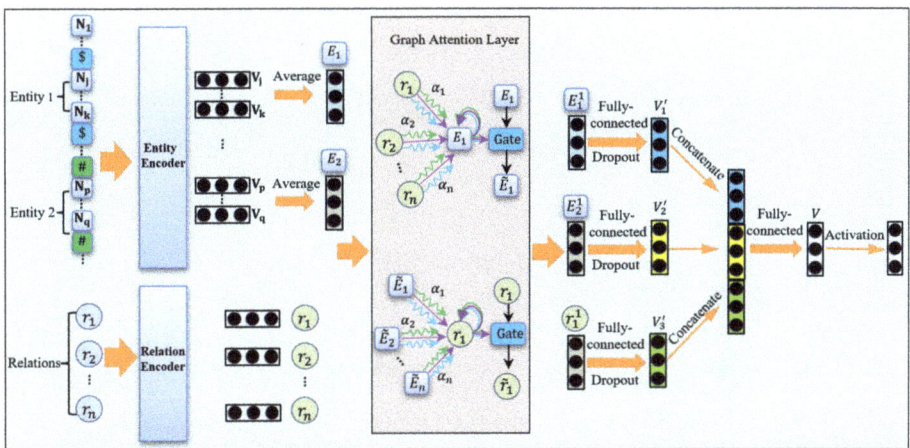

Figure 1. Bert–GAT model.

In addition, given that voting mechanisms can fully utilize the advantages of multiple models, thus enabling them to complement each other and enhance the robustness and generalization ability of the models, we introduced a new relation classification model called Bert–Vote. It was based on a ranking-based voting mechanism that combined the strengths of Bert–GAT and R-Bert models to determine the final classification result, aiming to achieve better performance in relation classification.

Specifically, for all sentences that comprise two target entities, the Bert–GAT and R-Bert models calculated the probability of the sentence belonging to any pre-defined relations. Firstly, we sorted the predicted results of the R-Bert and Bert–GAT models in descending order of probability and select the top three as candidate results, forming a candidate result list. We supposed that the anticipated candidate outcomes of the R-Bert and Bert–GAT models were A, B, C and B, D, E, respectively. Subsequently, the combined candidate result list was A, B, C, D, E. Secondly, we compared the candidate results of the R-Bert and Bert–GAT models. For each candidate result, we checked whether it existed in the candidate results of the other model. If it did exist, both models had the same prediction result; if it did not exist, the prediction outcomes of the two models were different. For the results predicted by both models, their probabilities were added to obtain the integrated result. For the results predicted by only one model, they were directly taken as the integrated result. Finally, we designated the type associated with the highest probability as the final classification result.

In the above process, we denoted the probabilities calculated via the Bert–GAT model as $p_{Bert-GAT}$, and similarly, we denoted the probabilities predicted using the R-Bert model as p_{R-Bert}. We integrated $p_{Bert-GAT}$ and p_{R-Bert} by allocating a voting weight to each model, which can be adjusted according to the classifier's performance.

$$p_{Bert-Vote} = \alpha p_{Bert-GAT} + (1-\alpha) p_{R-Bert} \tag{17}$$

where the probability of a sentence being classified as a certain type of relation by the Bert–Vote model is denoted as $p_{Bert-Vote}$. $\alpha > 0$ is an adjustable parameter. Figure 2 depicts the architecture of the Bert–Vote model.

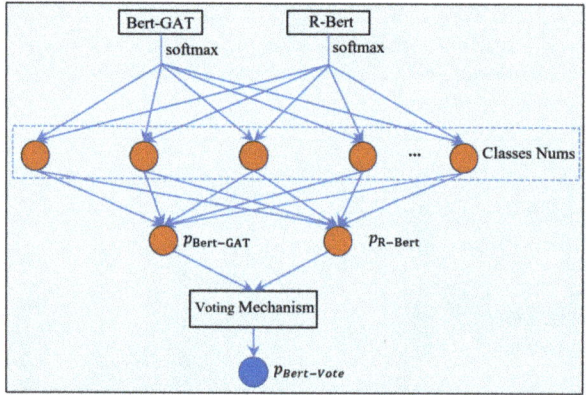

Figure 2. Schematic diagram of Bert–Vote model.

In addition, to compare them with the Bert–Vote model, we referred to the models that use a simple weighted voting mechanism as W-Vote and A-Vote. The W-Vote model selected the class with the maximum probability value among the predicted results of Bert–GAT and R-Bert as the final prediction result. In contrast, A-Vote performed weighted addition on the predicted results of Bert–GAT and R-Bert, before selecting the type with the maximum average probability value as the final prediction result.

4. Experiments and Evaluation

In this section, we will separately assess the effectiveness of the Bert–GAT and Bert–Vote models on the general dataset SemEval-2010 Task 8, and verify the performance of the two models on the cybersecurity dataset CS13K.

4.1. Experimental Settings and Evaluating Metrics

For the dataset of SemEval-2010 Task 8, we employ the Macro F1 value as the evaluation metric and the official scoring script to assess our model's performance on the relation classification task. The dataset includes nine pre-defined semantic relation types, along with one manually defined relation type called "Other". It contains a total of 10,717 sentences, which are further split into 8000 sentences for training purposes and 2717 sentences for testing purposes. The official scoring script calculates the Macro F1 score for the nine pre-defined actual relations and considers directionality. On the cybersecurity dataset CS13K, besides reporting the Macro F1 value, we also report the precision and recall values for a more comprehensive evaluation of the model's performance. Table 3 showcases the key parameter settings for the Bert–GAT model.

Table 3. Key parameter settings.

Batch size	6
Number of heads	8
Learning rate	0.1
Epochs	100
Dropout rate	0.1
Graph attention layers	2

4.2. Comparison with Other Models

On the dataset of SemEval-2010 Task 8, we conducted comparisons between our models and other baseline models, including RNN, CNN, Bi-LSTM, Att-Pooling-CNN, R-BERT, SPOT, and RIFRE. Macro F1 was used as the evaluation metric for all methods, and the results of these comparisons are presented in Table 4. It is noticeable that both the Bert–GAT model and Bert–Vote model exhibited superior performance compared to all baseline models, as indicated via the F1 score. Specifically, the Bert–GAT model achieved an F1 score of 92.3% on the dataset of SemEval-2010 Task 8, exhibiting a 3.0% increase compared to the R-BERT model. This finding suggests that by inserting special tokens before and after the target entities and using GATs to iteratively update the word nodes and relation nodes, the model excels at capturing intricate relationships within the text, leading to improved classification results.

Table 4. Results of relation classification tasks based on SemEval-2010 Task 8 dataset.

Method	Macro F1 (%)
RNN [34]	77.6
Bi-LSTM [35]	82.7
CNN [36]	82.7
FCM [37]	83.0
CR-CNN [38]	84.1
Entity Attention Bi-LSTM [39]	85.2
Attention CNN [2]	85.9
Att-Pooling-CNN [40]	88.0
KnowBert-W+W [41]	89.1
R-BERT [12]	89.3
BERTEM+MTB [42]	89.5
SPOT [24]	90.6
RIFRE [23]	91.3
W-Vote	91.6
A-Vote	92.1
Bert–GAT	92.3
Bert–Vote	92.5

On the dataset of SemEval-2010 Task 8, the F1 scores of the W-Vote and A-Vote models are 91.6% and 92.1%, respectively. This result may be due to the fact that the simple weighted voting mechanism cannot accurately capture the complex relationship between models, and cannot effectively combine the strengths of the Bert–GAT and R-Bert models. In contrast, the Bert–Vote model achieved an F1 score of 92.5%, surpassing the F1 score of the R-Bert model by 3.2% and the F1 score of the Bert–GAT model by 0.2%. This finding indicates that the ranking-based voting mechanism can increase the diversity of candidate results and enable models to complement each other, thereby improving the performance of relation classification.

4.3. Relation Classification in Cybersecurity

Furthermore, we performed relation classification experiments on the CS13K dataset utilizing the Bert–GAT and Bert–Vote models, and compared their performance to that of the baseline R-BERT model. The outcomes are presented in Table 5. Table 5 reveals that the

F1 scores of the Bert–GAT and Bert–Vote models on the CS13K dataset are 94.1% and 94.6%, respectively, which both outperform the R-BERT model. Compared to the outcomes on the SemEval-2010 Task 8, the classification accuracies of the two models slightly improved. This result may be due to the fact that the CS13K dataset was constructed by domain experts who have in-depth knowledge and experience in the field. Through careful data annotation, they were able to better control data quality, effectively reducing noise and redundant information in the dataset. As a result, the models' classification accuracy experienced notable improvement.

Table 5. Relation classification results on CS13K dataset.

Dataset	Method	Macro F1 (%)
CS13K	R-BERT	90.2
	Bert–GAT	94.1
	W-Vote	93.3
	A-Vote	93.9
	Bert–Vote	94.6

In addition, we reported the Precision, Recall, and F1 scores of the Bert–GAT model for each specific relation type, which are displayed in Table 6. By analyzing the Precision, Recall, and F1 scores for each distinct relation type, we can gain a deeper understanding of the model's classification performance under different relations. We found that the model exhibited different precision and recall rates in different relation types. For example, relations such as "cause(e2, e1)" and "hasCharacteristics(e2, e1)" had relatively high precision and recall rates, while the relation "associate(e2, e1)" had a relatively low one. This result suggests that the model's classification ability varies under different relation types, possibly due to differences in sample quality and features among different relations in the dataset.

4.4. Ablation Experiments

To examine the influence of individual components on the model's performance, we conducted a series of experiments to investigate the influence of various factors on the performance of our relation classification model. During the experiments, we set all parameters, except for the component being tested to their optimal values.

To verify the influence of GATs on the performance of the model, we conducted four groups of experiments with GATs layers set to 0, 1, 2, and 3, respectively. The 0 layer indicates the removal of the GATs layer in the model to verify the influence of adding GATs layers on the model's relation classification performance. The 1, 2, and 3 layers are used to assess the influence of the number of GATs layers on the performance of the model. We denote the settings with GATs layers set to 0, 1, 2, and 3 as Bert–GAT-layer-0, Bert–GAT-layer-1, Bert–GAT-layer-2, and Bert–GAT-layer-3, respectively.

The multi-head attention mechanism allows the capture of multiple interactions and dependencies among different neighboring nodes, thus enhancing the model's performance. However, the appropriate number of attention heads may vary depending on the dataset and task. Therefore, we investigated the influence of different numbers of attention heads on the model's effectiveness. In our experiments, we varied the number of attention heads used, specifically setting it to 0, 2, 4, 8, and 12, which we denote as Bert–GAT-head-0, Bert–GAT-head-2, Bert–GAT-head-4, Bert–GAT-head-8, and Bert–GAT-head-12, respectively. Here, Bert–GAT-head-0 refers to the configuration where the multi-head attention mechanism is removed.

In addition, we examined the impact of padding methods on the model's performance. One option is to process all sentences at a constant length, and we selected 512 as the length. If a sentence is shorter than 512, it is padded with zeros. We denote this method as Bert–GAT-padding-512. Another option is to use dynamic padding for each batch of sentences, where the padded length is equal to the maximum length of sentences in the batch. We denote this method as Bert–GAT-Dynamic-padding.

Table 6. Results for different relation types in CS13K dataset.

Relation	Precision (%)	Recall (%)	Macro F1 (%)
associate(e1, e2)	85.9	90.2	88.0
associate(e2, e1)	80.5	83.1	81.8
belongsTo(e1, e2)	95.0	73.1	82.6
belongsTo(e2, e1)	100.0	94.6	97.2
cause(e1, e2)	88.9	84.2	86.5
cause(e2, e1)	100.0	100.0	100.0
exploits(e1, e2)	95.0	96.2	95.6
exploits(e2, e1)	100.0	90.9	95.2
hasAttackLocation(e1, e2)	97.5	98.8	98.2
hasAttackLocation(e2, e1)	100.0	90.0	94.7
hasAttackTime(e1, e2)	93.8	95.8	94.8
hasAttackTime(e2, e1)	95.5	100.0	97.7
hasCharacteristics(e1, e2)	91.7	96.1	93.8
hasCharacteristics(e2, e1)	100.0	100.0	100.0
hasVulnerability(e1, e2)	100.0	94.9	97.4
hasVulnerability(e2, e1)	100.0	100.0	100.0
indicates(e1, e2)	100.0	95.7	97.8
indicates(e2, e1)	100.0	90.9	95.2
mitigates(e1, e2)	100.0	75.0	85.7
mitigates(e2, e1)	100.0	100.0	100.0
targets(e1, e2)	99.4	98.0	98.7
targets(e2, e1)	86.7	100.0	92.9
use(e1, e2)	97.2	97.9	97.5
use(e2, e1)	82.4	93.3	87.5
average	95.4	93.3	94.1

Meanwhile, we investigated the impact of the entity itself on the relation classification performance. We removed the special symbols '$' and '#' used to mark entities in the sentences and replaced both Entity1 and Entity2 with "[UNK]". We denote this method as Bert–GAT-UNK.

Finally, in order to further evaluate the performance of our proposed relation classification model under different BERT variants, we conducted comparative experiments with lightweight BERT models, such as DistillBERT, TinyBERT, and ALBERT. These lightweight BERT models reduce model complexity by reducing embedding dimensions, parameter sizes, or utilizing parameter-sharing schemes. We evaluated these models using the same experimental settings, and employed F1 score as the evaluation metric.

Table 7 presents the outcomes of the ablation experiments. Indeed, the number of layers in the GATs exhibits a substantial influence on the performance of the model, as evident from our observations. On the dataset of SemEval-2010 Task 8, when the number of layers in the GATs is 0, there is a 2.9% decrease in the F1 score compared to when the number of layers is 2, and a 3.8% decrease in the score for the CS13K dataset. As the number of layers in the GATs increases, we observe an improvement in the model's classification performance. When the number of layers is greater than 1, the model's performance tends to stabilize.

The inclusion of the multi-head attention mechanism also contributes to the improvement of the model's performance to some extent. Within a certain range, increasing the number of attention heads leads to improved model performance, and the best performance is achieved when the number of heads is 8. This trend is observed in both the SemEval-2010 Task 8 and CS13K datasets.

The padding method also has a certain impact on the model's performance. Using the dynamic padding method leads to slightly better results than using constant padding. This result may be due to the burden imposed on the model when the sentence length is too long. In addition, the meaning of the entities themselves has a significant impact on the model's performance. When Entity1 and Entity2 in the sentence are replaced with

"[UNK]", the model's classification performance decreases significantly compared to the optimal results.

Table 7. Influence of different components on the model performance.

Dataset	Method	Macro F1 (%)
SemEval-2010 Task 8	Bert–GAT-layer-0	89.4
	Bert–GAT-layer-1	91.4
	Bert–GAT-layer-2	92.3
	Bert–GAT-layer-3	92.2
	Bert–GAT-head-0	91.8
	Bert–GAT-head-2	92.0
	Bert–GAT-head-4	92.1
	Bert–GAT-head-8	92.3
	Bert–GAT-head-12	92.3
	Bert–GAT-Dynamic padding	92.3
	Bert–GAT-padding-512	91.7
	Bert–GAT-UNK	87.8
CS13K	Bert–GAT-layer-0	90.3
	Bert–GAT-layer-1	92.5
	Bert–GAT-layer-2	94.1
	Bert–GAT-layer-3	93.9
	Bert–GAT-head-0	93.1
	Bert–GAT-head-2	93.5
	Bert–GAT-head-4	94.0
	Bert–GAT-head-8	94.1
	Bert–GAT-head-12	94.0
	Bert–GAT-Dynamic padding	94.1
	Bert–GAT-padding-512	92.9
	Bert–GAT-UNK	89.5

As shown in Table 8, the performance and convergence time differences among DistillBERT, TinyBERT, and ALBERT can be attributed to their architectural variances and parameter settings. DistillBERT and TinyBERT achieve a balance between performance and model size reduction, while ALBERT sacrifices some performance for a more compact parameter configuration. In contrast, our Bert–GAT model combines the strengths of BERT, resulting in enhanced relational modeling capabilities.

Table 8. Performance of lighter BERT-based models.

Dataset	Method	Macro F1 (%)	Time
SemEval-2010 Task 8	DistillBERT	89.1	1.12 h
	TinyBERT	87.7	0.98 h
	ALBERT	85.9	0.95 h
	Bert-GAT	92.3	1.35 h

4.5. LIME Explanations for Relation Classification Results

We employed LIME to explain the relation classification results for both general text and cybersecurity text. Table 9 showcases examples of a general domain text and a cybersecurity domain text, along with their corresponding explanations obtained through as shown LIME in Figure 3. These explanations highlight the impact of different words on the classification results.

Table 9. Examples of Texts and Relations.

Type	Relation	Texts
General Text	Entity-Destination(e1, e2)	A <e1> woman </e1> has been placed into the <e2> house </e2> as well.
Cybersecurity Text	exploits(e1, e2)	<e1> Mustang Panda </e1> has exploited <e2> CVE-2017-0199 </e2> in Microsoft Word to execute code.

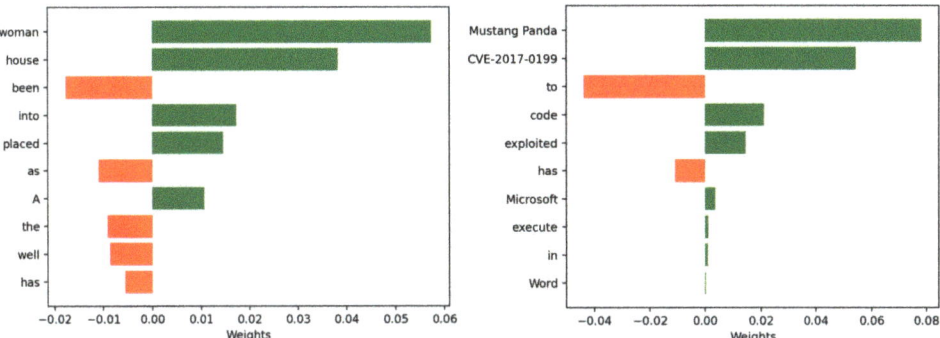

Figure 3. Weights Distribution of General Text (**left**) and Cybersecurity Text (**right**).

Specifically, LIME computes the weights of each word in the relation classification results, contributing to our understanding of the model's decision-making process. In Figure 3, we use green markers to indicate words that have a positive influence on the classification results, while red markers indicate words that have a negative influence. These visualizations provide an intuitive way of comprehending the model's decision-making process in relation classification to some extent.

5. Conclusions and Future Works

This paper focuses on investigating the task of relation classification in the field of cybersecurity, which involves discerning the relations between entities from texts. To address this issue, we first constructed a manually annotated cybersecurity dataset called CS13K, and proposed two new relation classification models: Bert-GAT and Bert-Vote. Experimental results showed that Bert-GAT attained an impressive F1 value of 92.3% on the SemEval-2010 task 8 dataset and a 94.1% value on the CS13K dataset, which verified the effectiveness of special entity position tags and the introduction of GATs in dealing with relation classification problems. We introduced a ranking-based voting mechanism in the Bert–Vote model, which achieved the best performance of 92.5% on the SemEval-2010 task 8 dataset and a 94.6% value on the CS13K dataset. This result demonstrates that the method based on the voting mechanism can integrate different classifier results to enhance the performance of the relation classification models. While our proposed models showed impressive performance, there is still room for further improvement. Future research can explore techniques to optimize these models, such as experimenting with different architectures or exploring diverse GNNs models to enhance the encoding of node representations.

Author Contributions: Conceptualization, Z.S. and H.L.; methodology, Z.S. and C.P.; software, Z.S.; validation, D.Z.; formal analysis, H.L. and C.P.; investigation, Z.S.; writing—original draft preparation, Z.S.; writing—review and editing, C.P. and D.Z.; visualization, Z.S.; supervision, H.L.; funding acquisition, H.L. All authors have read and agreed to the published version of the manuscript.

Funding: This research was funded by the National Natural Science Foundation of China (Grant no. 61771001).

Data Availability Statement: Publicly available datasets were analyzed in this research. The SemEval-2010 task 8 dataset can be found here (https://huggingface.co/datasets/sem_eval_2010_task_8; accessed on 1 January 2023). The CS13K dataset that supports the findings of this study is available from the corresponding author upon reasonable request.

Conflicts of Interest: The authors declare no conflict of interest.

References

1. Wang, X.; Liu, X.; Ao, S.; Li, N.; Jiang, Z.; Xu, Z.; Xiong, Z.; Xiong, M.; Zhang, X. Dnrti: A large-scale dataset for named entity recognition in threat intelligence. In Proceedings of the 2020 IEEE 19th International Conference on Trust, Security and Privacy in Computing and Communications (TrustCom), Guangzhou, China, 29 December 2020–1 January 2021; pp. 1842–1848.
2. Wang, Y.; Wang, Y.; Peng, Z.; Zhang, F.; Yang, F. A Concise Relation Extraction Method Based on the Fusion of Sequential and Structural Features Using ERNIE. *Mathematics* **2023**, *11*, 1439. [CrossRef]
3. Shen, G.; Qin, Y.; Wang, W.; Yu, M.; Guo, C. Distant Supervision for Relations Extraction via Deep Residual Learning and Multi-instance Attention in Cybersecurity. In Proceedings of the Security and Privacy in New Computing Environments: Third EAI International Conference, SPNCE 2020, Lyngby, Denmark, 6–7 August 2020; Proceedings 3. Springer: Berlin/Heidelberg, Germany, 2021; pp. 151–161.
4. Li, H.; Hu, K.; Zhao, D. The Golden Quantizer in Complex Dimension Two. *IEEE Commun. Lett.* **2021**, *25*, 3249–3252. [CrossRef]
5. Peng, Z.; Li, H.; Zhao, D.; Pan, C. Reducing the Dimensionality of SPD Matrices with Neural Networks in BCI. *Mathematics* **2023**, *11*, 1570. [CrossRef]
6. Li, H.; Qin, X.; Zhao, D. An improved empirical mode decomposition method based on the cubic trigonometric B-spline interpolation algorithm. *Appl. Math. Comput.* **2018**, *332*, 406–419. [CrossRef]
7. Li, H.; Gao, Z.; Zhao, D. Least squares solutions of the matrix equation AXB+ CYD= E with the least norm for symmetric arrowhead matrices. *Appl. Math. Comput.* **2014**, *226*, 719–724. [CrossRef]
8. Devlin, J.; Chang, M.W.; Lee, K.; Toutanova, K. Bert: Pre-training of deep bidirectional transformers for language understanding. *arXiv* **2018**, arXiv:1810.04805.
9. Xiong, H.; Yan, Z.; Zhao, H.; Huang, Z.; Xue, Y. Triplet Contrastive Learning for Aspect Level Sentiment Classification. *Mathematics* **2022**, *10*, 4099. [CrossRef]
10. Joshi, M.; Chen, D.; Liu, Y. Spanbert: Improving pre-training by representing and predicting spans. *Trans. Assoc. Comput. Linguist.* **2020**, *8*, 64–77. [CrossRef]
11. Velickovic, P.; Cucurull, G.; Casanova, A. Graph attention networks. *Stat* **2017**, *1050*, 10-48550.
12. Wu, S.; He, Y. Enriching pre-trained language model with entity information for relation classification. In Proceedings of the 28th ACM International Conference on Information and Knowledge Management, Beijing, China, 3–7 November 2019; pp. 2361–2364.
13. Jia, Q.; Huang, H.; Zhu, K.Q. Ddrel: A new dataset for interpersonal relation classification in dyadic dialogues. In Proceedings of the AAAI Conference on Artificial Intelligence, Virtually, 2–9 February 2021; pp. 13125–13133.
14. Hendrickx, I.; Kim, S.N.; Kozareva, Z.; Nakov, P. Semeval-2010 task 8: Multi-way classification of semantic relations between pairs of nominals. *arXiv* **2019**, arXiv:1911.10422.
15. Han, X.; Zhu, H.; Yu, P.; Wang, Z.; Yao, Y.; Liu, Z.; Sun, M. Fewrel: A large-scale supervised few-shot relation classification dataset with state-of-the-art evaluation. *arXiv* **2018**, arXiv:1810.10147.
16. Bunescu, R.; Mooney, R. A shortest path dependency kernel for relation extraction. In Proceedings of the Human Language Technology Conference and Conference on Empirical Methods in Natural Language Processing, Vancouver, BC, Canada, 6–8 October 2005; pp. 724–731.
17. Culotta, A.; Sorensen, J. Dependency tree kernels for relation extraction. In Proceedings of the 42nd Annual Meeting of the Association for Computational Linguistics, Barcelona, Spain, 21–26 July 2004; pp. 423–429.
18. Sekine, S. On-demand information extraction. In Proceedings of the COLING/ACL 2006 Main Conference Poster Sessions, Sydney, Australia, 17–18 July 2006; pp. 731–738.
19. Qin, P.; Xu, W.; Guo, J. An empirical convolutional neural network approach for semantic relation classification. *Neurocomputing* **2016**, *190*, 1–9. [CrossRef]
20. Liu, Y.; Wei, F.; Li, S.; Ji, H.; Zhou, M.; Wang, H. A dependency-based neural network for relation classification. *arXiv* **2015**, arXiv:1507.04646.
21. Zhang, D.; Wang, D. Relation classification via recurrent neural network. *arXiv* **2015**, arXiv:1508.01006.
22. Nguyen, T.H.; Grishman, R. Combining neural networks and log-linear models to improve relation extraction. *arXiv* **2015**, arXiv:1511.05926.
23. Zhao, K.; Xu, H.; Cheng, Y.; Li, X.; Gao, K. Representation iterative fusion based on heterogeneous graph neural network for joint entity and relation extraction. *Knowl.-Based Syst.* **2021**, *219*, 106888. [CrossRef]
24. Li, J.; Katsis, Y.; Baldwin, T.; Kim, H.C.; Bartko, A.; McAuley, J.; Hsu, C.N. SPOT: Knowledge-Enhanced Language Representations for Information Extraction. In Proceedings of the 31st ACM International Conference on Information & Knowledge Management, Atlanta, GA, USA, 17–21 October 2022; pp. 1124–1134.
25. Cohen, A.D.; Rosenman, S.; Goldberg, Y. Relation classification as two-way span-prediction. *arXiv* **2020**, arXiv:2010.04829.

26. Xie, Y.; Xu, H.; Li, J.; Yang, C.; Gao, K. Heterogeneous graph neural networks for noisy few-shot relation classification. *Knowl.-Based Syst.* **2020**, *194*, 105548. [CrossRef]
27. Sahu, S.K.; Christopoulou, F.; Miwa, M.; Ananiadou, S. Inter-sentence relation extraction with document-level graph convolutional neural network. *arXiv* **2019**, arXiv:1906.04684.
28. Mandya, A.; Bollegala, D.; Coenen, F. Graph Convolution over Multiple Dependency Sub-graphs for Relation Extraction. In Proceedings of the COLING, International Committee on Computational Linguistics, Barcelona, Spain, 8–13 December 2020; pp. 6424–6435.
29. Zhao, Y.; Wan, H.; Gao, J.; Lin, Y. Improving relation classification by entity pair graph. In Proceedings of the Asian Conference on Machine Learning, Nagoya, Japan, 17–19 November 2019; pp. 1156–1171.
30. Mushtaq, Z.; Ramzan, M.F.; Ali, S.; Baseer, S.; Samad, A.; Husnain, M. Voting classification-based diabetes mellitus prediction using hypertuned machine-learning techniques. *Mob. Inf. Syst.* **2022**, *2022*, 1–16. [CrossRef]
31. Bhati, N.S.; Khari, M. A new ensemble based approach for intrusion detection system using voting. *J. Intell. Fuzzy Syst.* **2022**, *42*, 969–979. [CrossRef]
32. Khan, M.A.; Khan Khattk, M.A. Voting classifier-based intrusion detection for iot networks. In *Advances on Smart and Soft Computing: Proceedings of the ICACIn 2021*; Springer: Singapore, 2022; pp. 313–328.
33. Maheshwari, A.; Mehraj, B.; Khan, M.S.; Idrisi, M.S. An optimized weighted voting based ensemble model for DDoS attack detection and mitigation in SDN environment. *Microprocess. Microsyst.* **2022**, *89*, 104412. [CrossRef]
34. Socher, R.; Huval, B.; Manning, C.D.; Ng, A.Y. Semantic compositionality through recursive matrix-vector spaces. In Proceedings of the 2012 Joint Conference on Empirical Methods in Natural Language Processing and Computational Natural Language Learning, Jeju, Republic of Korea, 12–14 July 2012; pp. 1201–1211.
35. Zhang, S.; Zheng, D.; Hu, X.; Yang, M. Bidirectional long short-term memory networks for relation classification. In Proceedings of the 29th Pacific Asia Conference on Language, Information and Computation, Shanghai, China, 30 October–1 November 2015; pp. 73–78.
36. Zeng, D.; Liu, K.; Lai, S.; Zhou, G.; Zhao, J. Relation classification via convolutional deep neural network. In Proceedings of the COLING 2014, the 25th International Conference on Computational Linguistics: Technical Papers, Dublin, Ireland, 23–29 August 2014; pp. 2335–2344.
37. Yu, M.; Gormley, M.; Dredze, M. Factor-based compositional embedding models. In Proceedings of the NIPS Workshop on Learning Semantics, Montreal, QC, Canada, 8–13 December 2014; pp. 95–101.
38. Santos CN, D.; Xiang, B.; Zhou, B. Classifying relations by ranking with convolutional neural networks. *arXiv* **2015**, arXiv:1504.06580.
39. Lee, J.; Seo, S.; Choi, Y.S. Semantic relation classification via bidirectional lstm networks with entity-aware attention using latent entity typing. *Symmetry* **2019**, *11*, 785. [CrossRef]
40. Wang, L.; Cao, Z.; De Melo, G.; Liu, Z. Relation classification via multi-level attention cnns. In Proceedings of the 54th Annual Meeting of the Association for Computational Linguistics, Berlin, Germany, 7–12 August 2016; pp. 1298–1307.
41. Peters, M.E.; Neumann, M.; Logan, R.L., IV; Schwartz, R.; Joshi, V.; Singh, S.; Smith, N.A. Knowledge enhanced contextual word representations. *arXiv* **2019**, arXiv:1909.04164.
42. Soares, L.B.; FitzGerald, N.; Ling, J.; Kwiatkowski, T. Matching the blanks: Distributional similarity for relation learning. *arXiv* **2019**, arXiv:1906.03158.

Disclaimer/Publisher's Note: The statements, opinions and data contained in all publications are solely those of the individual author(s) and contributor(s) and not of MDPI and/or the editor(s). MDPI and/or the editor(s) disclaim responsibility for any injury to people or property resulting from any ideas, methods, instructions or products referred to in the content.

Article

Parameter-Efficient Fine-Tuning Method for Task-Oriented Dialogue Systems

Yunho Mo, Joon Yoo * and Sangwoo Kang *

School of Computing, Gachon University, 1342, Seongnam-daero, Sujeong-gu, Seongnam-si 13120, Republic of Korea; ahdbsgh@gmail.com
* Correspondence: joon.yoo@gachon.ac.kr (J.Y.); swkang@gachon.ac.kr (S.K.)

Abstract: The use of Transformer-based pre-trained language models has become prevalent in enhancing the performance of task-oriented dialogue systems. These models, which are pre-trained on large text data to grasp the language syntax and semantics, fine-tune the entire parameter set according to a specific task. However, as the scale of the pre-trained language model increases, several challenges arise during the fine-tuning process. For example, the training time escalates as the model scale grows, since the complete parameter set needs to be trained. Furthermore, additional storage space is required to accommodate the larger model size. To address these challenges, we propose a new new task-oriented dialogue system called PEFTTOD. Our proposal leverages a method called the Parameter-Efficient Fine-Tuning method (PEFT), which incorporates an Adapter Layer and prefix tuning into the pre-trained language model. It significantly reduces the overall parameter count used during training and efficiently transfers the dialogue knowledge. We evaluated the performance of PEFTTOD on the Multi-WOZ 2.0 dataset, a benchmark dataset commonly used in task-oriented dialogue systems. Compared to the traditional method, PEFTTOD utilizes only about 4% of the parameters for training, resulting in a 4% improvement in the combined score compared to the existing T5-based baseline. Moreover, PEFTTOD achieved an efficiency gain by reducing the training time by 20% and saving up to 95% of the required storage space.

Keywords: natural language processing; task-oriented dialogue system; PEFT; fine-tuning; training efficiency

MSC: 68T50

Citation: Mo, Y.; Yoo, J.; Kang, S. Parameter-Efficient Fine-Tuning Method for Task-Oriented Dialogue Systems. *Mathematics* **2023**, *11*, 3048. https://doi.org/10.3390/math11143048

Academic Editor: Florentina Hristea

Received: 28 May 2023
Revised: 5 July 2023
Accepted: 7 July 2023
Published: 10 July 2023

Copyright: © 2023 by the authors. Licensee MDPI, Basel, Switzerland. This article is an open access article distributed under the terms and conditions of the Creative Commons Attribution (CC BY) license (https:// creativecommons.org/licenses/by/ 4.0/).

1. Introduction

In task-oriented dialogue systems, the primary objective is to enable user–system communication to accomplish specific tasks, such as a restaurant search, hotel reservation, or schedule management. These systems generally focus on understanding the user input, tracking dialogue states, and generating appropriate responses.

The conventional task-oriented dialogue system follows a pipelined structure, consisting of several interconnected modules: the Natural Language Understanding (NLU) module, the Dialogue State Tracking (DST) module, the Dialogue Policy Learning (POL) module, and the Natural-Language-Generation (NLG) module, as shown in Figure 1 [1]. First, the NLU module is responsible for extracting semantic information from user inputs. The DST module utilizes the previous conversation history to update the belief state at the time of the current utterance. The belief state is a structured expression method that represents the user's conversational goals and information gathered thus far. The system then searches the database for relevant information based on the belief state. The POL module determines the system action based on the knowledge retrieved from the database and the current belief state. Finally, the NLG module generates a system response based on the decision made by the POL module. In general, this pipelined architecture facilitates the flow of information in a task-oriented dialogue system, enabling efficient understanding of the user input, tracking dialogue states, determining system actions, and generating appropriate responses.

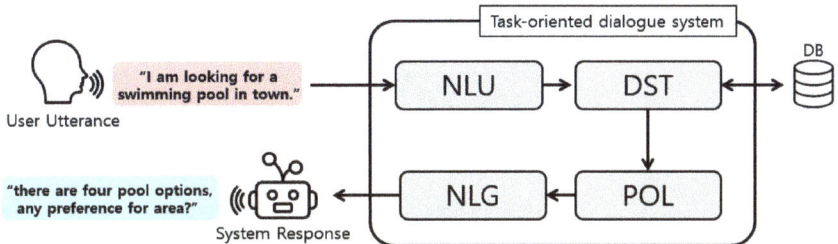

Figure 1. Conventional structure of the task-oriented dialogue system.

The conventional pipelined structure of task-oriented dialogue systems, however, suffers from error propagation between independent modules and limited adaptability to new domains. To address these problems, recent studies have proposed structures that integrate independent modules using pre-trained language models [2–4].

Recent language models have widely adopted the Transformer-based model [5] and have shown a dramatic increase in performance, in tasks such as object name recognition, natural language inference, and machine translation. Theses language models generally employ transfer learning [6], where knowledge is first learned from a source domain and then transferred to the target domain. The Transformer-based language model consists of a pre-training step, which first learns the syntax and semantics of the language from large text data, and a fine-tuning step, which adjusts the model's parameters for downstream tasks. Therefore, pre-trained language models that capture the syntax and semantics of a language render better performance compared to learning data from scratch. During fine-tuning, the entire parameter set of the pre-trained language model is adjusted to fit the downstream task.

A recent study [7] showed that larger pre-trained language models, with more parameters, tend to achieve better performance in downstream tasks. This trend also applies to task-oriented dialogue systems, where the parameter count of the pre-trained language models has reached tens of billions. However, fine-tuning such large-scale models poses challenges. First, the training time increases as the number of parameters grows since the entire parameter set is updated during fine-tuning. Second, fine-tuning a large-scale pre-trained language model requires significant storage space due to the increased model size.

In this paper, we propose PEFTTOD (the name PEFTTOD comes from integrating the PEFT method into TOD systems), a novel structure for solving task-oriented dialogue (TOD) systems using a large-scale pre-trained language model. PEFTTOD efficiently utilizes the parameters by employing the Adapter Layer [8] and prefix tuning [9] techniques from the Parameter-Efficient Fine-Tuning (PEFT) method [10]. The PEFT method incorporates a trainable layer into the pre-trained language model while freezing the parameters of the existing model and learning only the newly added layer. The PEFT method offers several advantages. First, although the PEFT method is trained with a much smaller parameter count than the pre-trained language model, it achieves performance comparable to fine-tuning. Second, by freezing the weight of the pre-trained language model and training only the added trainable layers, the original state of the pre-trained model is preserved. Third, whereas fine-tuning requires saving the entire model, the PEFT method only necessitates saving the parameters of the trainable layer, resulting in significantly reduced storage space. Lastly, since the parameters of the pre-trained language model remain frozen, the weight update process of the frozen layers is skipped, leading to faster training speeds.

PEFTTOD utilizes PPTOD [2] as its pre-trained language model, which integrates an extensive knowledge conversational domain based on T5 [11] and combines it with the PEFT method [10]. The performance of PEFTTOD was evaluated using the Multi-WOZ

2.0 benchmark dataset [12]. Compared to the conventional fine-tuning method, PEFTTOD uses only 4% of the parameters of the existing model during the training process. This leads to improvement in training time by 20% and storage space savings by up to 95%. Moreover, PEFTTOD demonstrated 4% improvement in the combined score compared to the baseline, despite using only 4% from the parameters of the previous model.

The main contribution of this paper is three-fold. Firstly, existing pre-trained language models typically employ billions of parameters, which leads to longer training times, as well as significant storage space due to the larger model size. In our proposed approach, PEFTTOD, we adopted the Adapter Layer and PEFT-based prefix tuning to decrease the number of parameters. Secondly, PEFTTOD was trained with a substantially smaller parameter count and, thus, requires less storage space. Consequently, as the parameters of the pre-trained language model remain frozen, the training speed is accelerated. Thirdly, we conducted extensive experiments using the Multi-WOZ 2.0 benchmark dataset to prove our advantages.

The remainder of the paper is organized as follows. In Section 2, we provide an overview of the related work. Section 3 presents the details and design of our proposed approach, and Section 4 presents the evaluation results. Finally, we conclude our paper in Section 5.

2. Related Work

This section describes technologies related to PEFTTOD: the pre-trained language model, the task-oriented dialogue system, and various PEFT methods.

2.1. Pre-Trained Language Models

In the field of natural language processing, since the advent of Transformer technology, the grammar and vocabulary of a language are first learned from a large corpus in order to apply transfer learning. This method of fine-tuning the pre-trained language model shows good performance in all tasks of natural language processing. Transformer's encoder-based models (BERT [13], RoBERTa [14], DeBERTa [15]) perform fine-tuning for natural-language-understanding tasks and show high performance. The parameters of the model are increased in the order of BERT (110 M)-RoBERTa (125 M)-DeBERTa (1.5 B). Transformer's decoder-based models (GPT-1 [16], GPT-2 [17], GPT-3 [7], LaMDA [18], OPT [19]) are fine-tuned for natural language generation and show high performance. The number of parameters for GPT-1 (117 M)-GPT-2 (1.5 B)-GPT-3 (175 B) are increasing, and the recently published LaMDA (137 B) and OPT (175 B) also have a very large number of parameters. Transformer's encoder–decoder-based models (BART [20], T5 [11]) are used after fine-tuning for the translation and summary tasks, which require natural language understanding and natural language generation. BART (400 M) and T5 (11 B) also have the problem of increasing parameters.

2.2. Task-Oriented Dialogue System

In the task-oriented dialogue system, the structure typically consists of three main components: Dialogue State Tracking (DST), Dialogue Policy Learning (POL), and Natural Language Generation (NLG). These components work together to understand user utterances, determine the dialogue objectives, and generate appropriate responses [1].

Before the emergence of pre-trained language models, several approaches were used in task-oriented dialogue systems. Some of these approaches included the following. First, the LSTM+CNN structure [21] combines Long Short-Term Memory (LSTM) networks with Convolutional Neural Networks (CNNs) for dialogue understanding. Second, the Sequence-to-Sequence (Seq2Seq) model [22–24] is used for generating responses in dialogue systems. Sequicity [22] is an example of Seq2Seq-based models applied to dialogue systems; DAMD [23] extended a single-domain dialogue system to multiple domains; LABES-S2S [24] attempted semi-supervised learning. Third, several studies have explored the application of reinforcement learning in dialogue systems, including models such as

JOUST [25], LAVA [26], DORA [27], SUMBT+LaRL [28], and CASPI [29]. With the advent of pre-trained language models, models such as DoTS [30] used Bidirectional Encoder Representations from Transformers (BERT) and Gated Recurrent Unit (GRU) for dialogue state tracking. Regarding the decoder structure, some models introduced specific methods. SimpleTOD [31] used special tokens and delexicalization [21] for domain adaptation, while SOLOIST [32] employed contrastive learning [33] and negative data samples. UBAR [34] uses the entire conversation history to generate an answer, as opposed to the traditional single-answer methods. The combination of encoder and decoder structure has also been explored. Models such as MinTL [3], PPTOD [2], and MTTOD [4] use pre-trained models such as BART and T5. In MTTOD, span prediction was applied as an auxiliary loss. GALAXY [35] used UNILM and unified reconciliation for multiple datasets as ISO norms.

2.3. Parameter-Efficient Fine-Tuning Method

Transformer-based pre-trained language models have become the foundation for natural language processing by learning the syntax and semantics in advance. It has become a common approach to fine-tune the entire model for transfer learning. However, recent studies have proposed more-efficient methods for utilizing pre-trained models: learning without adding parameters or learning by adding more parameters.

2.3.1. PEFT Method without Adding Parameters

One approach is to fine-tune only the top layer or prediction head of the pre-trained language model while keeping the remaining layers frozen. This partial fine-tuning method, as described by Lee et al. (2019) [36], achieves lower performance compared to fine-tuning all parameters. Another method called BitFit [37] trains only the bias term of the pre-trained language model, which has shown on-par performance with fine-tuning on certain resource-constrained tasks.

2.3.2. PEFT Method with Added Parameters

The PEFT method involves adding learnable parameters inside the pre-trained language model. During the learning process, the parameters of the pre-trained language model are frozen, and only the added parameters are trained. This method achieves performance similar to conventional fine-tuning.

Adapters have been introduced as an efficient way to incorporate additional parameters into pre-trained language models. Houlsby Adapter [8] was the pioneering work to apply the Adapter concept, featuring a bottleneck structure that can be added to the pre-trained model. It adds two Adapter Layers within one layer of the Transformer, one after the Attention Layer and another after the Feed-Forward layer.

AdapterFusion [38] proposed a structure called Pfeiffer Adapters and using the Adapters in parallel before merging. It adds an Adapter in one layer of the Transformer after the last Feed-Forward Network after the Add and Norm. Zhu et al. [39] proposed a parallel Adapter structure that uses the value before passing the input to the Attention Layer as the input in the existing Adapter structure.

Additionally, studies have explored Adapters for specific purposes. In the work in [40], a domain Adapter for domain adaptation in machine translation was proposed. MAD-X [41] proposed a language Adapter, a task Adapter, and an invertible Adapter, which are effective for learning the multilingual language models. LoRA [42] proposed a method to decompose the attention weight update process during fine-tuning in the pre-trained language model and applying it to the Adapter. He et al. [43] experimented with multiple adaptors on various downstream tasks to propose an effective Adapter structure. UniPELT [44] proposed an integration framework that integrates the PELT method into submodules and enables utilizing the best method for the current data or task setup through a gating mechanism.

Prefix tuning [9], inspired by the prompt methodology, aims to improve the performance of pre-trained language models. It involves modifying the input data format according to the learning method of the pre-trained language model. Prefix tuning adds a prefix vector, which can be trained within the pre-trained language model, allowing the treatment of prompts as if they were combined with a virtual token created by the learnable prefix vector, without directly modifying the input data.

3. Design

This paper proposes PEFTTOD, a Transformer-based task-oriented dialogue system that leverages a parameter-efficient language-model-tuning method. This system combines a Transformer-based language model with an efficient learning structure for conversational knowledge. PEFTTOD's pre-trained language model uses PPTOD [2], which is trained on a large amount of conversational domain knowledge, based on T5 [11]. In PPTOD, a prompt corresponding to the downstream task of the task-oriented dialogue system is combined with the input data. For example, prompts such as "translate dialogue to belief state:", "translate dialogue to dialogue action:", and "translate dialogue to system response:" are used. However, a prompt attached to the data may not be optimized for the model's performance [9]. To address this issue, the proposed PEFTTOD system incorporates a structure that enables the model to learn the prompt directly through prefix tuning.

3.1. End-to-End Dialogue Modeling

PEFTTOD incorporates a structured framework that effectively learns conversational knowledge by leveraging PPTOD [2], a T5-based language model trained on a substantial amount of information specific to the conversational domain.

The system architecture of PEFTTOD is based on a sequence-to-sequence architecture model, as shown in Figure 2. At each dialog turn, the encoder takes input consisting of the dialogue history and the user's utterance. On the basis of the encoded conversation information, the decoder generates a belief state, which represents the system's understanding of the user's intentions and requirements.

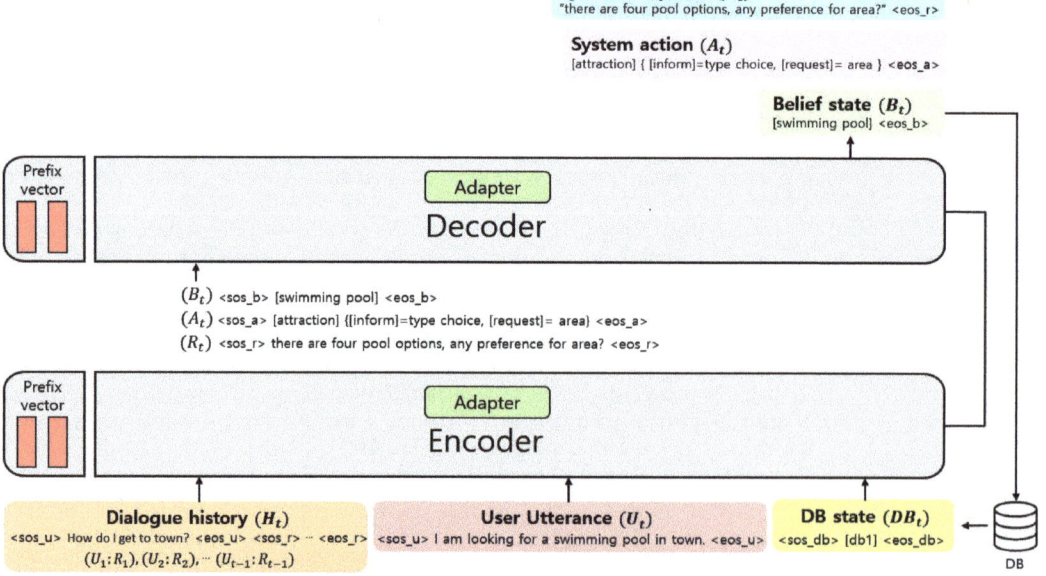

Figure 2. Structure of PEFTTOD.

The generated belief state is used for database search, enabling the system to obtain the corresponding DB state from the database. Additionally, based on the encoded dialog information and DB state, the decoder generates a system action and a system response. The system action determines the decision or action the dialogue system should take, while the system response represents the system's generated reply to the user.

PEFTTOD was trained on the Multi-WOZ 2.0 dataset, specifically on the task of the end-to-end dialogue modeling [45]. The proposed system was trained using the maximum likelihood method, a common approach in machine learning, which aims to optimize the model's parameters by maximizing the likelihood of generating the correct outputs given the inputs.

Say that $D = (x, y)$ (here, D is the data and $x = \{H_t, U_t\}, \{H_t, U_t, DB_t\}, y = B_t, A_t, R_t)$, then the loss ($L$) becomes:

$$L = -logP(y_t|x_t) \tag{1}$$

3.2. The Proposed Model

Figure 3 shows the encoder and decoder parts of Figure 2 in detail. PEFTTOD incorporates a PEFT method within a pre-trained language model. The left part of Figure 3 shows the structure of the existing system, while the right part represents the structure of PEFT-TOD. PEFTTOD effectively compresses the hidden state information as it passes through the Attention Layer and Feed-Forward Layer and then transfers it to the subsequent layers. It then adds an Adapter, i.e., a trainable bottleneck layer, to each layer. In addition, within the attention mechanism, prefix tuning is performed to learn P_K and P_V. This allows the model to directly learn the prompt information within the language model itself, making the structure task-independent. Unlike the existing system, which combines prompts with input data on a task-specific basis, PEFTTOD learns and utilizes prompt information within the language model itself. In the following subsection, we describe the parallel Adapter and prefix tuning in more detail.

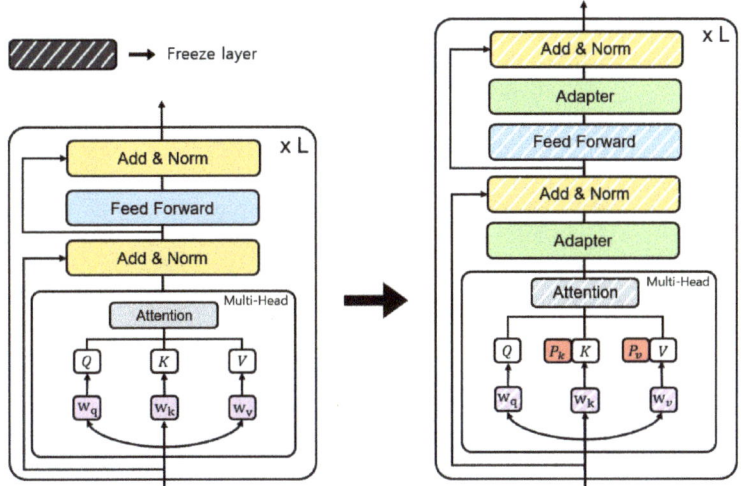

Figure 3. Combining the Transformer structure and PEFT method.

Figure 4 shows the structure with the parallel Adapter [39] applied in PEFTTOD. PEFTTOD is a Transformer-based architecture that incorporates two Adapter Layers within a single layer and input value x, replacing the input of the hidden state. The value x represents the value before passing through the Attention Layer.

$$h \leftarrow W_{up} \cdot f(W_{down} \cdot x) + h \tag{2}$$

In Equation (2), W_{down} down-projects the incoming hidden state h, f is a non-linear activation function, W_{up} up-projects the hidden state, and r is the residual network. Here, $W_{down} \in \mathbb{R}^{D_{hidden} \times D_{bottle}}$ and $W_{up} \in \mathbb{R}^{D_{bottle} \times D_{hidden}}$, where D_{hidden} is the hidden size and D_{bottle} is the bottleneck size. During training, the pre-trained language model combined with these Adapters freezes the parameters corresponding to the pre-trained language model, and only the Adapter is fine-tuned. Thus, the conversational knowledge can be efficiently forwarded within the pre-trained language model.

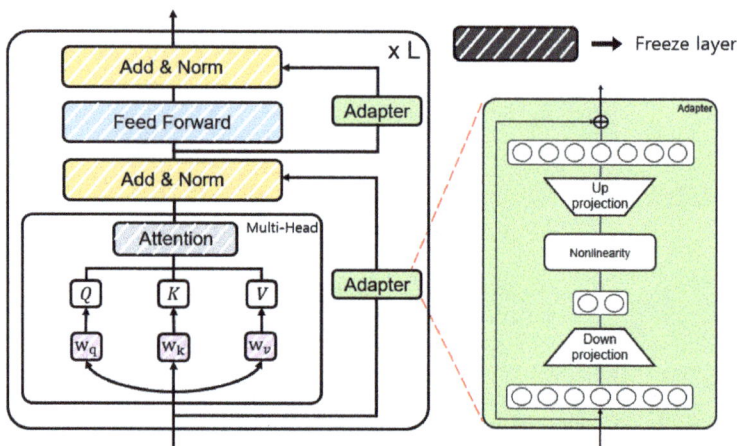

Figure 4. Structure of the parallel Adapter.

Figure 5 illustrates the structure of prefix tuning [9] in PEFTTOD. We combined the key (K) and value (V) of the Transformer's multi-head attention block with the prefix vectors P'_k and P'_v each of length l. P'_k and P'_v are defined as $P'_k, P'_v \in R^{l \times hidden}$. However, if we use the combined prefix vector as a direct parameter, then the performance will degrade. To solve this problem, we stabilized P by reparameterizing P' through a neural network identical to the structure of the Adapter, as shown in Equation (3) [46].

$$P = W_{up} \cdot f(W_{down} \cdot P') \qquad (3)$$

where $W_{down} \in \mathbb{R}^{D_{hidden} \times D_{bottle}}$, $W_{up} \in \mathbb{R}^{D_{bottle} \times D_{hidden}}$, f denotes the non-linear activation function, D_{hidden} is the hidden size, and D_{bottle} is the bottleneck size. This neural network only maintains the matrix corresponding to the reparameterized P and can be removed after training. In the training step, the query of the Transformer's attention block is defined as $Q \in R^{M \times hidden}$, the key is $K \in R^{M \times hidden}$, and the value is $V \in R^{M \times hidden}$. Here, M is the max sequence length. During training, as shown in Equation (4), we concatenate the prefix vectors P'_k and P'_v in K and V, respectively, where $P_k + K \in R^{(l+M) \times hidden}$ and $P_v + V R^{(l+M) \times hidden}$.

$$head_i = Attention(QW_q^i, concat(P_k^i, KW_k^i), concat(P_v^i, VW_v^i)) \qquad (4)$$

In PEFTTOD, the prefix tuning is trained by inserting a prefix vector into the attention mechanism of the pre-trained language model. This differs from the existing model where the prompt is combined with the input data in an arbitrary manner [2]. In contrast, the prefix vectors P_k and P_v inserted inside the model allow for the learning of the prompt that is optimized specifically for the entire conversation system.

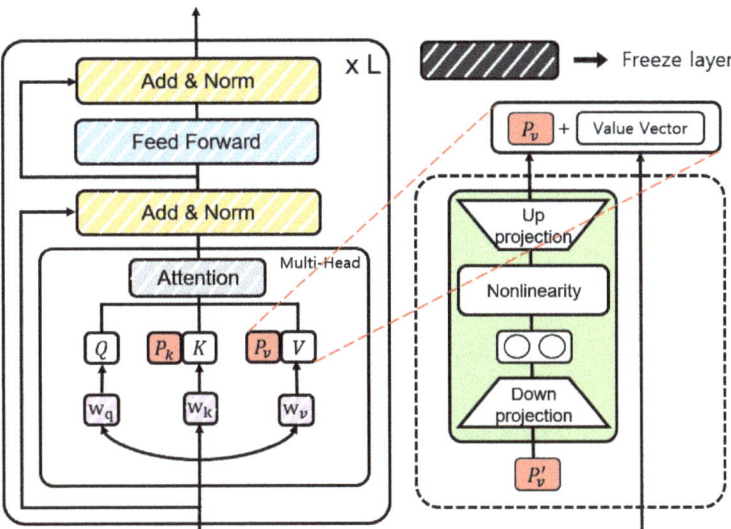

Figure 5. Structure of prefix tuning. (The parameters of the layer inside the dotted-line box can be removed after reparametrization).

3.3. Domain Adaptation

The proposed system uses two methods for domain adaptation. The first way is to use a special token. Special tokens are specifically designed to identify different components of the inputs corresponding to different subtasks. As demonstrated by SimpleTOD [31], the absence of special tokens can lead to the generation of much longer belief states, system actions, and system responses. Therefore, it is important to clearly distinguish between the user and the text of the system within the dialogue history of the system. To identify the user's utterance, the system's utterance, the dialogue state (belief state), the DB state, and the system action, the proposed system uses <sos_u>, <eos_u>, <sos_r>, <eos_r>, <sos_b>, <eos_b>, <sos_db>, <eos_db>, and <sos_a>, <eos_a>, respectively.

The second method employs delexicalization. The delexicalization method is a preprocessing method that groups specific slot values into categories [21]. For example, if there is a slot called "Food" with various food options, the corresponding slots related to food are pre-processed and categorized as "Food". During the generation process, the actual values are retrieved from the database and filled accordingly.

4. Evaluation

We evaluated the performance of PEFTTOD in the context of task-oriented dialogue systems for end-to-end dialogue modeling [45]. The evaluation was conducted using the benchmark dataset Multi-WOZ 2.0 [12]. The baseline model, PPTOD, which is described as a language model based on T5 [11], was trained to acquire a significant amount of knowledge about the conversation domain. We conducted a comparative experiment according to the structure of the system combined with the PEFT method.

PPTOD uses a smaller model, and it was trained directly to replicate the same experimental setup as the proposed system. In Tables 1–3, the baseline performance is indicated as "Fine-tuning", while the performance of direct training is indicated as "Fine-tuning (our run)". Additionally, "params" represents the trainable parameters of the language model with the PEFT method applied.

4.1. Dataset and Evaluation Metrics

The experiments used the Multi-Woz 2.0 dataset, which is widely used as a benchmark dataset for the task-oriented dialogue system. The dataset is a multi-domain dataset, which consists of 8438 conversations for seven domains: tourism, attractions, hospitals, police stations, hotels, restaurants, taxis, and trains. The experiment focused on five of these domains, excluding hospitals and police stations, due to the absence of dev and test data for these domains. Note that a single conversation can involve conversations from multiple domains and databases associated with the belief state are organized based on their respective domains. Therefore, the database state uses the dialogue state (belief state) generated through dialogue state tracking as a query to search from a predefined database and obtain the search result. The proposed system first predicts the dialogue state (belief state) through DST and searches the DB at the time of inference. Next, based on the DB state and dialogue history obtained as a search result, the system action and system response results are generated sequentially. To evaluate the performance of the model, an end-to-end dialogue modeling evaluation was conducted, which measured the quality of the generated belief state, system action, and system response when a user utterance is input. The model's evaluation metrics followed the automatic evaluation metrics [12]. The automatic evaluation metrics are widely used in dialogue system research utilizing the MultiWOZ 2.0 dataset. Inform measures whether the system has provided the correct entity, and success measures whether it has responded to all the requested information. Additionally, BLEU [47] was used to assess the quality of the generated response. The combined score was the performance evaluation index proposed in [48] and is shown as Equation (5).

$$Combined\ Score = (Inform + Success) \times 0.5 + BLEU \qquad (5)$$

4.2. Adapter Types

This experiment evaluated the performance of the Adapters with different structures, namely the Houlsby Adapter and Parallel Adapter. These Adapters were compared with PPTOD, a model that was pre-trained on the conversation knowledge. The results are presented in Table 1, indicating that the Parallel Adapter structure demonstrated the best performance among the evaluated options. Therefore, the paper leveraged this parallel Adapter structure for further experiments and analysis. Furthermore, we also explored the usage of prefix tuning on the dialogue system. When only prefix tuning was used, it resulted in a lack of communication knowledge within the language model. To address this limitation, the experiments in Section 4.5 combined the use of prefix tuning with the Adapter structure.

Table 1. Experimental results for Adapter types. In this and the following tables, the bold numbers indicate the highest performance for each criteria.

Method	Inform	Success	BLEU	Comb.	Params
Fine-tuning	87.8	75.3	19.89	101.44	100%
Fine-tuning (our run)	83.7	75.4	19.07	98.62	100%
Prefix tuning	58.5	42.7	12.28	62.88	0.30%
Houlsby Adapter	82.0	71.8	17.50	94.40	1.32%
Parallel Adapter	**83.4**	**74.0**	**19.14**	**97.84**	1.32%

4.3. Performance Comparison for the Number of Adapters

Generally, in a pre-trained language model, as more parameters are trained, the performance tends to improve [7]. Therefore, this experiment investigated the impact of increasing the number of Adapter Layers. Table 2 presents the results of this comparison for both the Houlsby Adapter and the Parallel Adapter. The numbers in the parentheses denote the number of Adapters connected in series. It was observed that, as the number of Adapter Layers increased, the performance of both Adapter structures improved. This suggested that incorporating more Adapter Layers enhanced the overall performance of the model. Notably, even when the parameters corresponding to the pre-trained language model were not trained, but the parameters related to the PEFT method increased, there was still a performance improvement. This indicated that the Adapter Layer played a crucial role. However, note that, when the Adapter number reached seven, we observed a performance degradation; thus, it is important to find the optimal number of Adapters to achieve the best performance.

Table 2. Experimental results for the number of Adapters.

Method	Inform	Success	BLEU	Comb.	Params
Fine-tuning	87.8	75.3	19.89	101.44	100%
Fine-tuning (our run)	83.7	75.4	19.07	98.62	100%
Houlsby Adapter	82.0	71.8	17.50	94.40	1.32%
Houlsby Adapter (3)	87.8	77.3	**17.73**	100.28	3.96%
Houlsby Adapter (5)	**89.4**	76.9	17.58	**100.73**	6.60%
Houlsby Adapter (7)	85.6	**77.7**	17.62	99.27	9.24%
Parallel Adapter	83.4	74.0	19.14	97.84	1.32%
Parallel Adapter (3)	**87.4**	76.1	17.58	99.33	3.96%
Parallel Adapter (5)	86.7	**76.9**	19.15	**100.95**	6.60%
Parallel Adapter (7)	87.0	75.4	**19.61**	100.81	9.24%

4.4. Prefix-Tuning Performance Comparison

In this experiment, we used the T5-based PPTOD-Small, which was trained to acquire conversation knowledge, in order to evaluate the performance of prefix tuning. PPTOD [2] is a trained model that incorporates a prompt with the input data. Therefore, for the models that use prefix tuning, we excluded the combination of prompts with the input data during training. Table 2 shows that the model with a combination of the Houlsby Adapters and Parallel Adapters in series for three and five times, respectively, achieved the highest performance. Hence, we incorporated prefix tuning into these Adapters in the experiments. In Table 3, we observe that the model combining prefix tuning after connecting the Parallel Adapter three times in series yielded the best performance. Consequently, we named this proposed model PEFTTOD. The inclusion of prefix tuning in the model's structure enhanced the performance by allowing the model to learn information related to specialized prompts within the conversation system, without explicitly combining prompts in the input data.

Table 3. Experimental results for prefix tuning.

Method	Inform	Success	BLEU	Comb.	Params
Fine-tuning	87.8	75.3	19.89	101.44	100%
Fine-tuning (our run)	83.7	75.4	19.07	98.62	100%
Houlsby Adapter (3)	87.8	77.3	17.73	100.28	3.96%
Houlsby Adapter (3) + prefix tuning	84.5	74.1	**18.38**	97.68	4.27%
Houlsby Adapter (5)	**89.4**	76.9	17.58	100.73	6.60%
Houlsby Adapter (5) + prefix tuning	88.3	**77.4**	18.01	**100.86**	6.90%
Parallel Adapter (3)	87.4	76.1	17.58	99.33	3.96%
Parallel Adapter (3) + prefix tuning	**88.3**	**78.4**	**19.38**	**102.73**	4.27%
Parallel Adapter (5)	86.7	76.9	19.15	100.95	6.60%
Parallel Adapter (5) + prefix tuning	86.5	75.2	18.92	99.77	6.90%

4.5. Low-Resource Conditions

This experiment examined how effectively PEFTTOD can transfer conversational knowledge under low-resource conditions. The MultiWOZ 2.0 dataset was used, with training conducted using 1%, 5%, 10%, and 20% of the available training data. As presented in the results in Table 4, when utilizing PEFTTOD with only 4.27% of the parameters compared to the baseline, the performance decreased at low-resource levels of 1% and 5%, but improved at higher-resource levels of 10% and 20%. This indicated that, even when PEFTTOD learns from a small number of parameters, if it exceeds the threshold of 10% on MultiWOZ 2.0, the performance begins to show improvement.

Table 4. Experimental results for low-resource conditions. MultiWOZ 2.0 was tested on 1%, 5%, 10%, and 20% of the training data (PEFTTOD is a proposed model that uses prefix tuning after connecting a parallel Adapter three times in series).

Model	Inform	Success	BLEU	Comb.
1% of training data				
Baseline	**66.5**	**51.1**	**12.05**	**70.85**
PEFTTOD	51.3	34.7	9.64	52.64
5% of training data				
Baseline	**80.0**	**63.1**	14.82	**86.37**
PEFTTOD	76.6	54.3	**17.03**	82.48
10% of training data				
Baseline	79.5	65.6	**16.73**	89.28
PEFTTOD	**84.5**	**69.7**	15.98	**93.08**
20% of training data				
Baseline	**85.4**	69.0	15.77	92.97
PEFTTOD	82.9	**70.9**	**17.17**	**94.07**

4.6. Prefix Length

In this experiment, we investigated the optimal length of the learnable vectors P_k and P_v, in the prefix tuning, as illustrated in Figure 5. We explored the range of lengths for P_k and P_v from 3 to 15 to determine the optimal value. The results revealed that the optimal prefix length for PEFTTOD was 10. The results indicated that the optimal prefix length for PEFTTOD was 10. Therefore, finding the optimal prefix length was crucial to achieving the best performance (Figure 6).

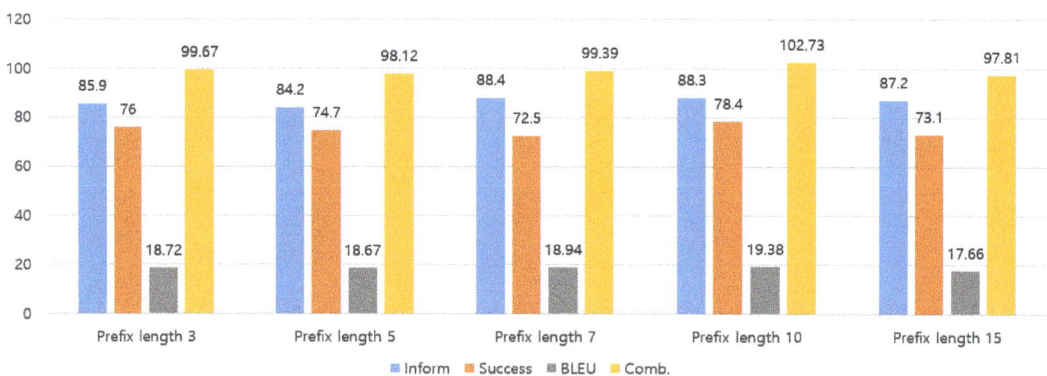

Figure 6. Experimental results for prefix length.

4.7. Efficiency

In order to evaluate the efficiency of PEFTTOD, we conducted experiments focusing on the training time and storage space. PEFTTOD takes advantage of the PEFT method by training only the Adapter Layers, without updating the baseline parameters. As a result, the training process is faster compared to traditional methods. Additionally, since only the parameters corresponding to the trained Adapter Layers are stored, significant storage space is saved.

The evaluation results in Table 5 show that PEFTTOD improved the training time by over 20%, while utilizing only 4% of the parameters compared to the baseline model. Additionally, it achieved a remarkable 96% savings in the storage space requirement. These findings highlight the efficiency gains achieved by adopting PEFTTOD in task-oriented dialogue systems.

Table 5. Experimental results for Efficiency (PEFTTOD uses prefix tuning after connecting a parallel Adapter three times in series).

Model	Training Time	Storage Space	Trainable Parameter
Baseline	1109 s (100%)	240 M (100%)	60.5 M (100%)
PEFTTOD	882 s (79.5%)	10 M (4.27%)	2.5 M (4.27%)

5. Conclusions and Future Work

This paper proposed a novel task-oriented dialogue system, called PEFTTOD, which incorporates the parameter-efficient language-model-tuning method. PEFTTOD leverages parallel Adapters and prefix tuning to efficiently train the conversation knowledge within a task-oriented dialogue system. Through experiments, we obtained the optimal Adapter structure and the number of stacks, and the effectiveness of combining the prefix tuning was demonstrated. The evaluation results revealed an improvement in the combined score, an evaluation metric of the Multi-Woz dataset, by 4% compared to the existing T5-based baseline model. Furthermore, despite utilizing only around 4% of the parameters compared to the baseline model, notable efficiency gains were achieved, including a 20% improvement in training speed and an approximately 96% reduction in storage space requirements.

As future work, we intend to extend our proposal to the open-domain dialogue systems rather than being limited to the task-oriented dialogue systems. Additionally, we plan to explore Adapters suitable for the ever-increasing large-scale pre-trained languages, in order to validate their effectiveness.

Author Contributions: Conceptualization, Y.M. and S.K.; methodology, Y.M.; validation, Y.M.; investigation, Y.M. and S.K.; resources, Y.M. and S.K.; data curation, Y.M.; writing—original draft preparation, Y.M. and J.Y.; writing—review and editing, Y.M. and J.Y.; visualization, Y.M. and J.Y.; supervision, S.K. and J.Y.; project administration, S.K.; funding acquisition, S.K. All authors have read and agreed to the published version of the manuscript.

Funding: This work was in part supported by the National Research Foundation of Korea (NRF) grant funded by the Korea government (MSIT) (2022R1A2C1005316 and 2021R1F1A1063640) and in part by the Gachon University research fund of 2021 (GCU-202106470001).

Data Availability Statement: Data sharing not applicable.

Conflicts of Interest: The authors declare no conflict of interest.

Abbreviations

The following abbreviations are used in this manuscript:

NLU	Natural Language Understanding
DST	Dialogue State Tracking
POL	Dialogue Policy Learning
NLG	Natural Language Generation
PEFT	Parameter-Efficient Fine-Tuning method
TOD	Task-Oriented Dialogue system

References

1. Young, S.J. Probabilistic methods in spoken–dialogue systems. *Philos. Trans. R. Soc. Lond. Ser. A Math. Phys. Eng. Sci.* **2000**, *358*, 1389–1402. [CrossRef]
2. Su, Y.; Shu, L.; Mansimov, E.; Gupta, A.; Cai, D.; Lai, Y.A.; Zhang, Y. Multi-task pre-training for plug-and-play task-oriented dialogue system. *arXiv* **2021**, arXiv:2109.14739.
3. Lin, Z.; Madotto, A.; Winata, G.I.; Fung, P. Mintl: Minimalist transfer learning for task-oriented dialogue systems. *arXiv* **2020**, arXiv:2009.12005.
4. Lee, Y. Improving end-to-end task-oriented dialog system with a simple auxiliary task. Findings of the Association for Computational Linguistics. In Proceedings of the EMNLP 2021, Punta Cana, Dominican Republic, 7 November 2021; pp. 1296–1303.
5. Vaswani, A.; Shazeer, N.; Parmar, N.; Uszkoreit, J.; Jones, L.; Gomez, A.; Kaiser, Ł.; Polosukhin, I. Attention is all you need. In *Advances in Neural Information Processing Systems 30, Proceedings of the NIPS, Long Beach, CA, USA, 4–9 December 2007*; MIT Press: Cambridge, MA, USA, 2007; pp. 5998–6008.
6. Pan, S.J.; Yang, Q. A survey on transfer learning. *IEEE Trans. Knowl. Data Eng.* **2010**, *22*, 1345–1359. [CrossRef]
7. Brown, T.; Mann, B.; Ryder, N.; Subbiah, M.; Kaplan, J.D.; Dhariwal, P.; Neelakantan, A.; Shyam, P.; Sastry, G.; Askell, A.; et al. Language models are few-shot learners. In *Advances in Neural Information Processing Systems 33, Proceedings of the NIPS 2020, Vancouver, BC, Canada, 6–12 December 2020*; MIT Press: Cambridge, MA, USA, 2020; pp. 1877–1901.
8. Houlsby, N.; Giurgiu, A.; Jastrzebski, S.; Morrone, B.; De Laroussilhe, Q.; Gesmundo, A.; Attariyan, M.; Gelly, S. Parameter-efficient transfer learning for NLP. In Proceedings of the International Conference on Machine Learning, PMLR, Long Beach, CA, USA, 9–15 June 2019; pp. 2790–2799.
9. Li, X.L.; Liang, P. Prefix tuning: Optimizing continuous prompts for generation. *arXiv* **2021**, arXiv:2101.00190.
10. Mangrulkar, S.; Gugger, S.; Debut, L.; Belkada, Y.; Paul, S. PEFT: State-of-the-Art Parameter-Efficient Fine-Tuning Methods. 2022 Available online: https://github.com/huggingface/peft (accessed on 6 July 2023).
11. Raffel, C.; Shazeer, N.; Roberts, A.; Lee, K.; Narang, S.; Matena, M.; Zhou, Y.; Li, W.; Liu, P.J. Exploring the limits of transfer learning with a unified text-to-text Transformer. *J. Mach. Learn. Res.* **2020**, *21*, 5485–5551.
12. Budzianowski, P.; Wen, T.H.; Tseng, B.H.; Casanueva, I.; Ultes, S.; Ramadan, O.; Gašić, M. MultiWOZ—A large-scale multi-domain wizard-of-oz dataset for task-oriented dialogue modeling. *arXiv* **2018**, arXiv:1810.00278.
13. Devlin, J.; Chang, M.W.; Lee, K.; Toutanova, K. Bert: Pre-training of deep bidirectional Transformers for language understanding. *arXiv* **2018**, arXiv:1810.04805.
14. Liu, Y.; Ott, M.; Goyal, N.; Du, J.; Joshi, M.; Chen, D.; Levy, O.; Lewis, M.; Zettlemoyer, L.; Stoyanov, V. Roberta: A robustly optimized bert pretraining approach. *arXiv* **2019**, arXiv:1907.11692.
15. He, P.; Liu, X.; Gao, J.; Chen, W. Deberta: Decoding-enhanced bert with disentangled attention. *arXiv* **2020**, arXiv:2006.03654.
16. Radford, A.; Narasimhan, K.; Salimans, T.; Sutskever, I. Improving Language Understanding by Generative Pre-Training. Technical Report. OpenAI. 2018. Available online: https://www.mikecaptain.com/resources/pdf/GPT-1.pdf (accessed on 6 July 2023).
17. Radford, A.; Wu, J.; Child, R.; Luan, D.; Amodei, D.; Sutskever, I. Language models are unsupervised multitask learners. *OpenAI Blog* **2019**, *1*, 9.
18. Thoppilan, R.; De Freitas, D.; Hall, J.; Shazeer, N.; Kulshreshtha, A.; Cheng, H.T.; Jin, A.; Bos, T.; Baker, L.; Du, Y.; et al. Lamda: Language models for dialog applications. *arXiv* **2022**, arXiv:2201.08239.
19. Zhang, S.; Roller, S.; Goyal, N.; Artetxe, M.; Chen, M.; Chen, S.; Dewan, C.; Diab, M.; Li, X.; Lin, X.V.; et al. Opt: Open pre-trained Transformer language models. *arXiv* **2022**, arXiv:2205.01068.
20. Lewis, M.; Liu, Y.; Goyal, N.; Ghazvininejad, M.; Mohamed, A.; Levy, O.; Stoyanov, V.; Zettlemoyer, L. Bart: Denoising sequence-to-sequence pre-training for natural language generation, translation, and comprehension. *arXiv* **2019** arXiv:1910.13461.
21. Wen, T.H.; Vandyke, D.; Mrksic, N.; Gasic, M.; Rojas-Barahona, L.M.; Su, P.H.; Ultes, S.; Young, S. A network-based end-to-end trainable task-oriented dialogue system. *arXiv* **2016**, arXiv:1604.04562.
22. Lei, W.; Jin, X.; Kan, M.Y.; Ren, Z.; He, X.; Yin, D. Sequicity: Simplifying task-oriented dialogue systems with single sequence-to-sequence architectures. In Proceedings of the 56th Annual Meeting of the Association for Computational Linguistics (Volume 1: Long Papers), Melbourne, Australia, 15–20 July 2018; pp. 1437–1447.
23. Zhang, Y.; Ou, Z.; Yu, Z. Task-oriented dialog systems that consider multiple appropriate responses under the same context. In Proceedings of the AAAI Conference on Artificial Intelligence, Hilton, NY, USA, 7–12 February 2020; Volume 34, pp. 9604–9611.
24. Zhang, Y.; Ou, Z.; Wang, H.; Feng, J. A probabilistic end-to-end task-oriented dialog model with latent belief states towards semi-supervised learning. *arXiv* **2020**, arXiv:2009.08115.
25. Tseng, B.H.; Dai, Y.; Kreyssig, F.; Byrne, B. Transferable dialogue systems and user simulators. *arXiv* **2021**, arXiv:2107.11904.
26. Lubis, N.; Geishauser, C.; Heck, M.; Lin, H.c.; Moresi, M.; van Niekerk, C.; Gašić, M. LAVA: Latent action spaces via variational auto-encoding for dialogue policy optimization. *arXiv* **2020**, arXiv:2011.09378.
27. Jeon, H.; Lee, G.G. DORA: Towards policy optimization for task-oriented dialogue system with efficient context. *Comput. Speech Lang.* **2022**, *72*, 101310. [CrossRef]
28. Lee, H.; Jo, S.; Kim, H.; Jung, S.; Kim, T.Y. Sumbt+ larl: Effective multi-domain end-to-end neural task-oriented dialog system. *IEEE Access* **2021**, *9*, 116133–116146. [CrossRef]

29. Ramachandran, G.S.; Hashimoto, K.; Xiong, C. Causal-aware safe policy improvement for task-oriented dialogue. *arXiv* **2021**, arXiv:2103.06370.
30. Jeon, H.; Lee, G.G. Domain state tracking for a simplified dialogue system. *arXiv* **2021**, arXiv:2103.06648.
31. Hosseini-Asl, E.; McCann, B.; Wu, C.S.; Yavuz, S.; Socher, R. A simple language model for task-oriented dialogue. In *Advances in Neural Information Processing Systems 33, Proceedings of the Annual Conference on Neural Information Processing Systems 2020, NeurIPS 2020, Virtual, 6–12 December 2020*; MIT Press: Cambridge, MA, USA, 2020; pp. 20179–20191.
32. Peng, B.; Li, C.; Li, J.; Shayandeh, S.; Liden, L.; Gao, J. Soloist: Building task bots at scale with transfer learning and machine teaching. *Trans. Assoc. Comput. Linguist.* **2021**, *9*, 807–824. [CrossRef]
33. Chopra, S.; Hadsell, R.; LeCun, Y. Learning a similarity metric discriminatively, with application to face verification. In Proceedings of the 2005 IEEE Computer Society Conference on Computer Vision and Pattern Recognition (CVPR'05), San Diego, CA, USA, 20–25 June 2005; Volume 1, pp. 539–546.
34. Yang, Y.; Li, Y.; Quan, X. Ubar: Towards fully end-to-end task-oriented dialog system with gpt-2. In Proceedings of the AAAI Conference on Artificial Intelligence, Virtual, 2–9 February 2021; Volume 35, pp. 14230–14238.
35. He, W.; Dai, Y.; Zheng, Y.; Wu, Y.; Cao, Z.; Liu, D.; Jiang, P.; Yang, M.; Huang, F.; Si, L.; et al. Galaxy: A generative pre-trained model for task-oriented dialog with semi-supervised learning and explicit policy injection. In Proceedings of the AAAI Conference on Artificial Intelligence, Virtual Event, 22 February–1 March 2022; Volume 36, pp. 10749–10757.
36. Lee, J.; Tang, R.; Lin, J. What would elsa do? freezing layers during Transformer fine-tuning. *arXiv* **2019**, arXiv:1911.03090.
37. Ravfogel, S.; Ben-Zaken, E.; Goldberg, Y. Bitfit: Simple parameter-efficient fine-tuning for Transformer-based masked language-models. *arXiv* **2021**, arXiv:2106.10199.
38. Pfeiffer, J.; Kamath, A.; Rücklé, A.; Cho, K.; Gurevych, I. AdapterFusion: Non-destructive task composition for transfer learning. *arXiv* **2020**, arXiv:2005.00247.
39. Zhu, Y.; Feng, J.; Zhao, C.; Wang, M.; Li, L. Counter-interference Adapter for multilingual machine translation. *arXiv* **2021**, arXiv:2104.08154.
40. Bapna, A.; Arivazhagan, N.; Firat, O. Simple, scalable adaptation for neural machine translation. *arXiv* **2019**, arXiv:1909.08478.
41. Pfeiffer, J.; Vulić, I.; Gurevych, I.; Ruder, S. Mad-x: An Adapter-based framework for multi-task cross-lingual transfer. *arXiv* **2020**, arXiv:2005.00052.
42. Hu, E.J.; Shen, Y.; Wallis, P.; Allen-Zhu, Z.; Li, Y.; Wang, S.; Wang, L.; Chen, W. Lora: Low-rank adaptation of large language models. *arXiv* **2021**, arXiv:2106.09685.
43. He, J.; Zhou, C.; Ma, X.; Berg-Kirkpatrick, T.; Neubig, G. Towards a unified view of parameter-efficient transfer learning. *arXiv* **2021**, arXiv:2110.04366.
44. Mao, Y.; Mathias, L.; Hou, R.; Almahairi, A.; Ma, H.; Han, J.; Yih, W.t.; Khabsa, M. Unipelt: A unified framework for parameter-efficient language model tuning. *arXiv* **2021**, arXiv:2110.07577.
45. Nekvinda, T.; Dušek, O. Shades of BLEU, flavours of success: The case of MultiWOZ. *arXiv* **2021**, arXiv:2106.05555.
46. Aghajanyan, A.; Zettlemoyer, L.; Gupta, S. Intrinsic dimensionality explains the effectiveness of language model fine-tuning. *arXiv* **2020**, arXiv:2012.13255.
47. Papineni, K.; Roukos, S.; Ward, T.; Zhu, W.J. Bleu: A method for automatic evaluation of machine translation. In Proceedings of the 40th Annual Meeting of the Association for Computational Linguistics, Philadelphia, PA, USA, 6–12 July 2002; pp. 311–318.
48. Mehri, S.; Srinivasan, T.; Eskenazi, M. Structured fusion networks for dialog. *arXiv* **2019**, arXiv:1907.10016.

Disclaimer/Publisher's Note: The statements, opinions and data contained in all publications are solely those of the individual author(s) and contributor(s) and not of MDPI and/or the editor(s). MDPI and/or the editor(s) disclaim responsibility for any injury to people or property resulting from any ideas, methods, instructions or products referred to in the content.

Article

A Study on Double-Headed Entities and Relations Prediction Framework for Joint Triple Extraction

Yanbing Xiao [1], Guorong Chen [1,*], Chongling Du [1], Lang Li [1], Yu Yuan [1], Jincheng Zou [1] and Jingcheng Liu [2]

[1] Department of Intelligent Technology and Engineering, Chongqing University of Science and Technology, Chongqing 401331, China; 2021208022@cqust.edu.cn (Y.X.); 2022208004@cqust.edu.cn (C.D.); 2021208019@cqust.edu.cn (L.L.); 2022208050@cqust.edu.cn (Y.Y.); 2023208002@cqust.edu.cn (J.Z.)

[2] China Academy of Liquor Industry, Luzhou Vocational and Technical College, Luzhou 646608, China; liujingcheng1980@126.com

* Correspondence: cgr@cqust.edu.cn

Abstract: Relational triple extraction, a fundamental procedure in natural language processing knowledge graph construction, assumes a crucial and irreplaceable role in the domain of academic research related to information extraction. In this paper, we propose a Double-Headed Entities and Relations Prediction (DERP) framework, which divides the entity recognition process into two stages: head entity recognition and tail entity recognition, using the obtained head and tail entities as inputs. By utilizing the corresponding relation and the corresponding entity, the DERP framework further incorporates a triple prediction module to improve the accuracy and completeness of the joint relation triple extraction. We conducted experiments on two English datasets, NYT and WebNLG, and two Chinese datasets, DuIE2.0 and CMeIE-V2, and compared the English dataset experimental results with those derived from ten baseline models. The experimental results demonstrate the effectiveness of our proposed DERP framework for triple extraction.

Keywords: triple extraction; entity recognition; relation extraction; joint extraction

MSC: 68T50 Natural language processing

1. Introduction

With the development of natural language processing and knowledge graphs, data storage and presentation methods for structured text have become more mature, but there are still many unsolved problems in the processing of unstructured and semi-structured text [1]. Extracting triple groups is crucial in natural language processing and knowledge graph construction. In constructing knowledge graphs, unstructured texts usually extract entities and form correspondences by forming a (head entity, relation, tail entity) triple.

Existing triple extraction methods mainly include two major kinds, pipeline extraction methods and joint extraction methods. Traditional pipeline extraction methods divide knowledge extraction into two subtasks [2]: named entity recognition and relation extraction. However, this approach ignores potential information interactions between entities and relations, leading to incorrect relation extractions or failure to recognize entity relations. Many previous experiments have demonstrated that a joint learning approach greatly improves the effectiveness of entity and relation extraction due to the consideration of the information interactions between the two subtasks, so most of the current research for the task of entity and relation extraction adopts the joint learning approach.

In recent scholarship, there has been a notable surge in research attention directed toward the intricacies of overlapping triples, as shown in Figure 1. This phenomenon is exemplified in sentences wherein there is the potential presence of both entity pair overlap (EPO) triples and single entity overlap (SEO) triples. This burgeoning area of inquiry underscores the escalating interest in dissecting and comprehending the complexities inherent to overlapping triples in textual data.

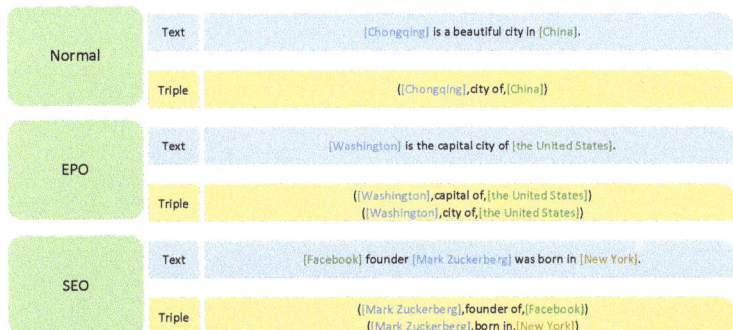

Figure 1. Normal, entity pair overlap (EPO) triple, and single entity overlap (SEO) triple cases. In each example, overlapping entities are marked with the same color.

Previous research has revealed several shortcomings in the extraction of multiple relationships (overlapping triples) within the same entity. For example, the NovelTagging method uses a joint decoding of sequence annotations to treat entity and relation extraction as a sequence annotation problem [3]; however, this method only assigns a single label to each token, rendering it incapable of handling overlapping triples in the data. In contrast, the CasRel framework models relations as functions that map subject to object [4], successfully overcoming the issue of poor handling of overlapping triples by previous models. Nevertheless, the CasRel framework suffers from the disadvantage of incorrectly identifying the head entity, leading to failure in identifying the relation and the tail entity. An overview of the CasRel framework structure is shown in Figure 2.

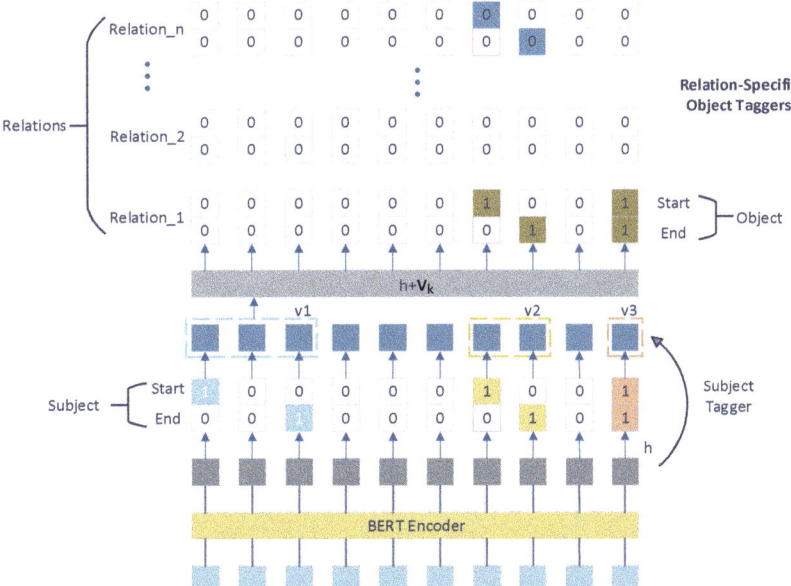

Figure 2. Overview of the CasRel framework structure.

In this study, a head entity recognition module is used to predict the triple related to the head entity and a tail entity recognition module is added to predict the triple related to the tail entity. Combining the information from the two modules results in a triple of higher accuracy. Experimental results show that the performance of the framework is improved by combining the BERT encoder. This work contributes as follows:

1. A double-headed entities and relations prediction framework for joint triple extraction based on the BERT encoder is proposed. The named entity recognition task is decomposed into head entity recognition and tail entity recognition.
2. To ensure recognition accuracy, a triple prediction module, which gives different weights to the triple derived from the head entity recognition and the triple extracted from the tail entity recognition, is set up to improve the accuracy of triple extraction.
3. To validate the method, experiments were conducted on two English public datasets, NYT and WebNLG, and two Chinese datasets, DuIE2.0 and CMeIE-V2, and the proposed framework was compared with ten baselines.

2. Related Work

In recent years, many methods have been proposed to accomplish knowledge extraction that can be categorized into pipeline extraction methods and joint learning methods based on the learning process.

2.1. Pipeline Extraction Methods

Usually, pipeline extraction methods consist of the entity recognition stage and the relation extraction stage, where the output of the previous stage becomes the input of the next stage. This approach has the advantage that a specific model can handle a responding task, but it may also lead to errors accumulating in each stage.

The primary objective of named entity recognition (NER) is to identify and classify named entities within textual content, such as people, places, time, purpose, etc., with specific meanings. It is mainly responsible for automatically extracting the basic element entities in the knowledge graph from the unstructured and semi-structured. In order to uphold the quality of the knowledge graph, it is imperative to ascertain the precision and comprehensiveness of the entities extracted therein. Li et al. proposed a meta-learning method, integrating distributed systems with a meta-learning approach to extract relations among Chinese entities [5]. Through the utilization of machine learning and neural network methodologies, particularly leveraging the attention mechanism within the domain of natural language processing, Li et al. proposed a combination of conditional random fields (CRF) and bidirectional long short-term memory (BILSTM) for extracting information in a mathematical language [6]. Luo et al. introduced a neural network model, known as the attention-based bidirectional long short-term memory with a conditional random field layer (Att-BiLSTM-CRF), for document-level chemical entity recognition [7]. Li et al. advocated the utilization of distinct layers, specifically long short-term memory (LSTM) for text feature extraction and conditional random field (CRF) for label prediction decoding [8]. Ren proposed a method to enhance entity recognition by transforming text into a vector representation combining contextual and global features through a pretrained model and a graph neural network GCN [9].

Relation extraction refers to extracting relations between connecting basic element entities from the unstructured and semi-structured. The mesh structure of the knowledge graph is similar to the structure of the brain for storing knowledge. Neurons represent entities and record basic information, and the process of extracting relations activates some of the neurons (entities) and adds them to the brain structure (knowledge graph), using relations to connect the entities to the whole knowledge graph. Zeng et al. conducted an analysis of the pivotal role played by the order of relation extraction and employed reinforcement learning techniques to ameliorate the efficiency of relation extraction [10]. Han et al. proposed a one pass model based on BERT, capable of predicting entity relations by processing the text in a single pass [11]. Chen et al. utilized a neutralized feature engineering approach for entity relation extraction, namely, enhancing neural networks with manually designed features [12]. Yuan et al. proposed a relation-aware attention network to construct relation-specific sentence representations [13]. Wan et al. proposed a span-based multi-modal attention network (SMAN) for joint entity and relation extraction [14].

2.2. Joint Learning Methods

In pipeline learning methods of relation extraction, the intrinsic connection between entities and relations is often overlooked, and the federated model is an excellent solution to this problem. Huang et al. suggested using soft label embedding as an effective means to facilitate information exchange between entity recognition and relation extraction [15]. Wei et al. proposed a novel cascade binary tagging framework (CASREL), which models relations as functions that map subjects to objects [4]. Liu et al. introduced an attention-driven integrated model, primarily comprising an entity extraction module and a relation detection module, as a means to effectively confront the prevailing challenges [16]. Yu et al. decomposed the comprehensive extraction task into two mutually interconnected subtasks: one subtask handles the head entities, and the other subtask deals with the tail entities related to the head entities and their respective relations [17]. Guo et al. introduced an integrated model for the extraction of entities and relations pertaining to concepts within the realm of cybersecurity (CyberRel) [18], and they adopted a perspective wherein the triple is conceived as a sequence of entity relations. Subsequently, Lv et al. constructed the joint extraction of entity mentions and relations model, which was based on the bidirectional long short-term memory and maximum entropy Markov model (Bi-MEMM) [19]. Zheng et al. introduced an integrated framework for extracting relational triples, underpinned by the principles of potential relation and global correspondence (PRGC) [20]. Li et al. proposed a relation-aware embedding mechanism (RA) for relation extraction, with attention mechanisms being used to merge relational tags into sentence embeddings, which are used to distinguish the importance of relational tags for each word [21]. Huang et al. proposed a novel translation-based unified framework, which is used to solve redundant predictions, overlapping triples, and relation connections problems [22]. Liu et al. presented a model referred to as the bidirectional encoder representation from transformers–multiple convolutional neural network (BERT–MCNN), which has demonstrated a high level of accuracy and stability [23].

3. CasRel Framework

The goal of triple extraction is to identify all possible triples (head entity, relation, tail entity) in a sentence, which may contain some overlapping and shared entities. The structure of the CasRel framework is shown in Figure 2. The CasRel framework presents a fresh perspective on the task of triple extraction. It introduces a novel cascade binary tagging framework, known as CasRel, that effectively addresses the complex challenge of managing overlapping relations by systematically establishing subject–object mappings within sentences [4]. This framework consists of a set of functions that identify entities and their related relations in an entity tagger and relation-specific object taggers. By employing the CasRel framework, the issue of sharing the same entity in multiple triples is addressed effectively, providing multiple related relations and corresponding entities for each entity. However, in the CasRel framework, if the subject tagger does not recognize an entity, the associated triad will be missed.

To solve the triple extraction omission that occurs in the CasRel framework, we propose an improved DERP framework based on the CasRel framework. Which improves the entity recognition accuracy by adding a tail entity recognition module in the entity tagger, and adding a triple prediction module after relation-specific object taggers. This framework will combine head entities, tail entities and relations to make predictions and comes up with a more accurate triple.

4. The DERP Framework

Entity recognition and relation extraction are the design priorities for triple extraction. The primary objective of this DERP framework is to ascertain the complete set of potential triples within a given sentence, acknowledging the potential existence of entities with overlapping attributes in some instances.

The ultimate prediction of the (head entity, relation, tail entity) triple is achieved through the recognition and forecasting of the acquired triples within the triple prediction layer. The DERP framework is shown in Figure 3.

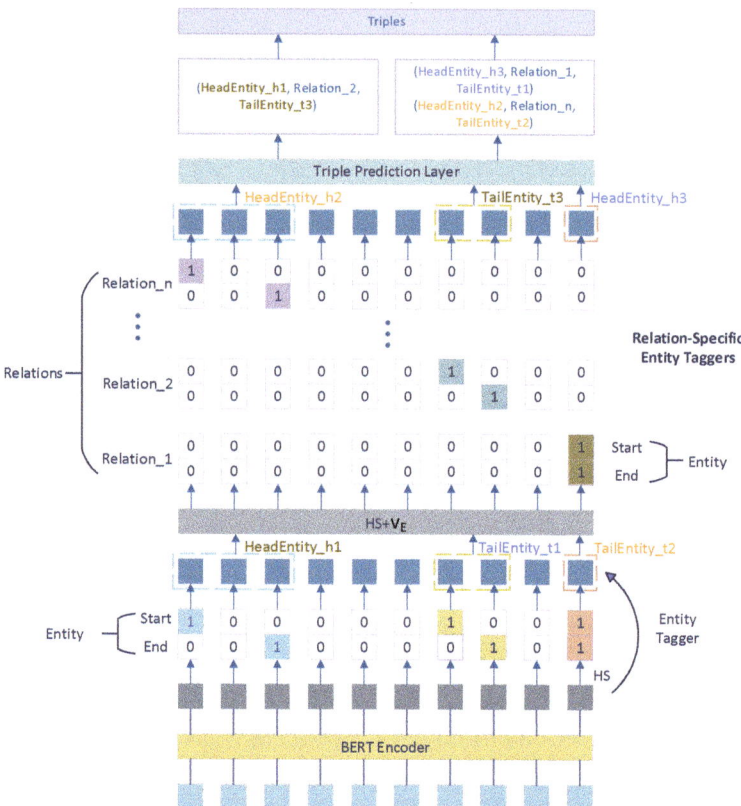

Figure 3. The architecture of the proposed DERP framework. In the framework, the start and end positions of predicted entities and relations are color-marked, with entities belonging to the same group marked with the same color.

In the DERP framework, we model relations as functions that map topics to objects. We optimize the previously commonly used learning relation classifiers $f(E_1, E_2) \rightarrow R$, to learning relation-specific taggers $f_R(E_1) \rightarrow E_2$. Each tagger will identify entities that may exist under a specific relationship, or entities that may not be returned. If the entity is not returned, it indicates that there is no triple in the current entity and relation.

When dealing with overlapping triples, the DERP framework uses an entity tagger for entity recognition and allows multiple relationship representations in relation-specific entity taggers. Within relation-specific entity taggers, multiple relationships and their corresponding entities can be obtained. By using the DERP framework, different types of data structures, including EPO triples and SEO triples, can be effectively handled.

We used an entity tagger to identify head entities at the very beginning of the research on framework development and used the identified head entities to find related relations and tail entities. During the experiments, it was found that if there is a head entity in the entity tagger that is missing, this triple will be missed in the final triple prediction, especially in the case of overlapping triples where a head entity corresponds to more than one related tail entity. There are also cases where some of the tail entities related to this head entity are missed when performing the triple extraction; in this case, we can better find these missing tail entities by adding a tail entity recognition module to the entity tagger. So, two matching entities and accurate relations between entities are achieved by adding a tail entity recognition module to the entity tagger, and by looking up the corresponding relation and another matching entity in the relation-specific entity taggers.

During the experiment, by learning and improving the previous model, we added the tail entity recognition module. If the probability of recognizing the correct triple by the head entity module only is $P(Head)$ and the probability of recognizing the correct triple by the tail entity module only is $P(Tail)$, we will increase the probability of finally recognizing the correct triple by combining the two entity modules with the following probability equation:

$$\begin{aligned} P(Triple) &= P(Head) \cup P(Tail) \\ &= P(Head) + P(Tail) - P(Head \cap Tail) \end{aligned} \quad (1)$$

where $P(Triple)$ is the probability of obtaining the correct triple, $P(Head)$ is the probability of obtaining the correct triple by only using a single head entity recognition module, $P(Tail)$ is the probability of obtaining the correct triple by only using a single tail entity recognition module, and $P(Head \cap Tail)$ is the probability of duplicate triples obtained by the head entity recognition module and tail entity recognition module.

4.1. BERT Encoder

BERT mainly consists of N layers of transformer block. A BERT encoder extracts sentence feature information from sentence S and inputs the feature information into the entity tagger.

$$h_0 = O_{hot} W_n + W_p \quad (2)$$

$$S_{ri} = BERT(ri) \quad (3)$$

where O_{hot} is the one-hot vector matrix indexed in the input sentence, W_n is the word embedding matrix, W_p is the positional embedding matrix, p in W_p denotes the positional index in the input sequence, and S_{ri} is the i-th relation type embedding.

4.2. Entity Tagger

Compared with the CasRel framework, the entity recognition is divided into head entity recognition and tail entity recognition in the entity tagger, which reduces the situation of missing triples due to the omission of the first stage of entity recognition, and also improves the accuracy of the extraction of overlapping triples [24].

The BERT encoded sentence is entered in the entity tagger to extract head and tail entities by the binary method.

Within the entity tagger, the identification of entity positions within sentences encoded by the BERT encoder is achieved. In this module, two binary classifiers are designed to check for the start and end positions of entity words. By setting specific thresholds, if the probability surpasses the designated threshold, the token is marked as 1; otherwise, it is marked as 0. The following is specific to the head entity recognizer and tail entity recognizer:

$$p_i^{HE\_start} = sigmoid\left(W_{start}^{HE} x_i^{HE} + b_{start}^{HE}\right) \quad (4)$$

$$p_i^{\text{HE\_end}} = sigmoid\left(W_{end}^{HE}x_i^{HE} + b_{end}^{HE}\right) \tag{5}$$

$$p_i^{\text{TE\_start}} = sigmoid\left(W_{start}^{TE}x_i^{TE} + b_{start}^{TE}\right) \tag{6}$$

$$p_i^{\text{TE\_end}} = sigmoid\left(W_{end}^{TE}x_i^{TE} + b_{end}^{TE}\right) \tag{7}$$

where $p_i^{\text{HE\_start}}$, $p_i^{\text{HE\_end}}$, $p_i^{\text{TE\_start}}$, and $p_i^{\text{TE\_end}}$ are the probability of the marker position being predicted to be the start and end positions of the head entity and the tail entity, x_i denotes the i-th marker in sentence S, W_{start}^{HE}, W_{end}^{HE}, W_{start}^{TE}, and W_{end}^{TE} denote the training weights of the head entities and tail entities, and b_{start}^{HE}, b_{end}^{HE}, b_{start}^{TE}, and b_{end}^{TE} denote the bias of the head entities and tail entities. In the use of the model, we need to keep the dimensions of the start binary classifier and the end binary classifier the same.

The entity recognition module uses the following likelihood function to recognize the range of sentences that have been encoded by the encoder:

$$p_\theta(E_{Head} \mid X_{HE}) = \prod_{t \in \{\text{HE\_start}, \text{HE\_end}\}} \prod_{i=1}^{L} \left(p_i^t\right)^{I\{y_i^t=1\}} \left(1 - p_i^t\right)^{I\{y_i^t=0\}} \tag{8}$$

$$p_\theta(E_{Tail} \mid X_{TE}) = \prod_{t \in \{\text{TE\_start}, \text{TE\_end}\}} \prod_{i=1}^{L} \left(p_i^t\right)^{I\{y_i^t=1\}} \left(1 - p_i^t\right)^{I\{y_i^t=0\}} \tag{9}$$

where L is the length of the sentence, $I\{z\} = 1$ if z is true and 0 otherwise, $y_i^{HE\_start}$, $y_i^{HE\_end}$, $y_i^{TE\_start}$, and $y_i^{TE\_end}$ are the i-th tag in the sequence that marks the start position and the end position.

4.3. Relation-Specific Entity Taggers

In the relation-specific entity taggers, an entity tagger is assigned to each relation word. The relation terms are used to correspond to the head entity or tail entity extracted in the previous layer to extract the entity in satisfying the relations. The calculations are shown below:

$$p_i^{\text{HR\_start}} = sigmoid\left(W_{start}^{HR}\left(x_i^{HE} + v_E^k\right) + b_{start}^{HR}\right) \tag{10}$$

$$p_i^{\text{HR\_end}} = sigmoid\left(W_{end}^{HR}\left(x_i^{HE} + v_E^k\right) + b_{end}^{HR}\right) \tag{11}$$

$$p_i^{\text{TR\_start}} = sigmoid\left(W_{start}^{TR}\left(x_i^{TE} + v_E^k\right) + b_{start}^{TR}\right) \tag{12}$$

$$p_i^{\text{TR\_end}} = sigmoid\left(W_{end}^{TR}\left(x_i^{TE} + v_E^k\right) + b_{end}^{TR}\right) \tag{13}$$

where $p_i^{\text{HR\_start}}$, $p_i^{\text{HR\_end}}$, $p_i^{\text{TR\_start}}$, and $p_i^{\text{TR\_end}}$ are the probabilities that the head entity and the tail entity at the labeled position are predicted to be the entity start position and end position, v_E^k is the relation-specific entity tagger's vector of coded representations of the kth subject detected in the module, W_{start}^{HE}, W_{end}^{HE}, W_{start}^{TE}, and W_{end}^{TE} denote the training weights of the head entities and tail entities, and b_{start}^{HE}, b_{end}^{HE}, b_{start}^{TE}, and b_{end}^{TE} indicate deviations of head entities and tail entities.

Relation-specific entity taggers use the following likelihood function to identify the range of sentences that the encoder has encoded:

$$p_\theta(E_{Tail} \mid E_{Head}, X_{HE}) = \prod_{t \in \{\text{HE\_start}, \text{HE\_end}\}} \prod_{i=1}^{L} \left(p_i^t\right)^{I\{y_i^t=1\}} \left(1 - p_i^t\right)^{I\{y_i^t=0\}} \tag{14}$$

$$p_\theta(E_{Head} \mid E_{Tail}, X_{TE}) = \prod_{t \in \{\text{TE\_start}, \text{TE\_end}\}} \prod_{i=1}^{L} \left(p_i^t\right)^{I\{y_i^t=1\}} \left(1 - p_i^t\right)^{I\{y_i^t=0\}} \tag{15}$$

where L is the length of the sentence, $I\{z\} = 1$ if z is true and 0 otherwise, and $y_i^{HE\_start}$, $y_i^{HE\_end}$, $y_i^{TE\_start}$, and $y_i^{TE\_end}$ are the i-th tags in the sequence that marks the start position and the end position.

4.4. Triple Prediction

The relation-specific entity taggers identify the head entity, tail entity, and the corresponding relations and use the method of entity relation prediction to match the head entities and tail entities identified in the entity tagger using the following method:

$$f_{HE\_start} = \begin{cases} 1, & p_i^{HR\_start} \geq \lambda_1 \\ 0, & p_i^{HR\_start} < \lambda_1 \end{cases} \tag{16}$$

$$f_{HE\_end} = \begin{cases} 1, & p_i^{HR\_end} \geq \lambda_2 \\ 0, & p_i^{HR\_end} < \lambda_2 \end{cases} \tag{17}$$

$$f_{TE\_start} = \begin{cases} 1, & p_i^{TR\_start} \geq \lambda_3 \\ 0, & p_i^{TR\_start} < \lambda_3 \end{cases} \tag{18}$$

$$f_{TE\_end} = \begin{cases} 1, & p_i^{TR\_end} \geq \lambda_4 \\ 0, & p_i^{TR\_end} < \lambda_4 \end{cases} \tag{19}$$

When f_{HE_start}, f_{HE_end}, f_{TE_start}, and f_{TE_end} equal to 1, the head entity or tail entity corresponding to the entity extracted in entity tagger and the corresponding relation is obtained, and if the value is equal to 0, the triple is excluded. λ_1, λ_2, λ_3, and λ_4 are the set thresholds.

$$g_{HE\_TE} = \{HeadEntity, Relation, TailEntity\} \tag{20}$$

$$g_{TE\_HE} = \{HeadEntity, Relation, TailEntity\} \tag{21}$$

$$g = g_{HE\_TE} \cup g_{TE\_HE} \tag{22}$$

where g_{HE_TE} represents the triplets of the tail entity and the relation between entities obtained based on the head entity, g_{TE_HE} represents the triplets of the head entity and the relation between entities obtained based on the tail entity, and g denotes the final predicted triplets.

4.5. Loss Function

The training loss is defined as below:

$$\mathcal{L} = \sum_{j=1}^{|D|} \Bigg[\sum_{E \in T_j} \log p_\theta \left(E_{Head} \Big| X_j^{HE} \right) + \sum_{E \in T_j} \log p_\theta \left(E_{Tail} \Big| X_j^{TE} \right) \\
+ \sum_{r \in T_j | E} \log p_{\phi_r} \left(E_{Tail} \mid E_{Head}, X_j^{HE} \right) \\
+ \sum_{r \in T_j | E} \log p_{\phi_r} \left(E_{Head} \mid E_{Tail}, X_j^{TE} \right) \\
+ \sum_{r \in R \setminus T_j | E} \log p_{\phi_r} \left(E_{Tail \varnothing} \mid E_{Head}, x_j \right) \\
+ \sum_{r \in R \setminus T_j | E} \log p_{\phi_r} \left(E_{Head \varnothing} \mid E_{Tail}, x_j \right) \Bigg] \tag{23}$$

where parameters $\theta = \{\theta, \{\varnothing_r\}_{r \in R}\}$, $p_\theta(E_{Head} \mid X_{HE})$, and $p_\theta(E_{Tail} \mid X_{TE})$ are defined in Equations (7) and (8), and $p_{\phi_r}(E_{Tail} \mid E_{Head}, X_{HE})$ and $p_{\phi_r}(E_{Head} \mid E_{Tail}, X_{TE})$ are defined in Equations (13) and (14).

5. Experiments

The effectiveness of the proposed framework is validated with experiments. The datasets and evaluation metrics are first introduced, and then the model names are compared with different baseline models.

5.1. Experiment Setup and Experiment Description

As most of the previous studies conducted experiments using English datasets, this study conducted experiments using two publicly English available datasets, NYT [25] and WebNLG [26], and compared the results of the experiments with 10 baseline models. Due to the specificity of the Chinese language, the complexity and difficulty of Chinese triple extraction is considerably greater than that of English relations [27]. We used two Chinese datasets, DuIE2.0 [28] and CMeIE-V2 [29]. DuIE2.0 is the most comprehensive Chinese relational extraction dataset in the industry [30]. CMeIE-V2 is a Chinese medical information extraction dataset, specifically designed for pediatrics and covering more than a hundred common diseases.

This model performs head entity recognition and tail entity recognition in the entity recognition part and performs the corresponding triple extraction based on the experimental results. In the experiments, the head entity recognition model and the tail entity recognition model are used individually for comparison experiments to verify the reliability and validity of the experiments. The schematic diagram of the head entity recognition module and the tail entity recognition module is shown in Figure 4.

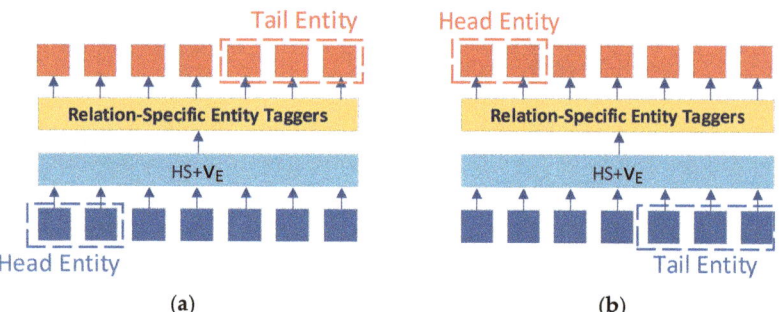

Figure 4. (**a**) Schematic diagram of the head entity recognition module. (**b**) Schematic diagram of the tail entity recognition module.

The DERP framework is implemented using TensorFlow. In the BERT encoder section, the framework is implemented on English datasets using the cased_L-12_H-768_A-12 model and on Chinese datasets using the RoBERTa model. Dropout is applied to word embeddings and hidden states with a rate of 0.1. Network weights are optimized with Adam. The learning rate is set as 1×10^{-5}. The max length of the input sentence is set to 100. The batch size is set as 6. We use 100 epochs and choose the model with the best performance on the validation set to output results on the test set.

In our experimental procedures, for the sake of maintaining consistency with prior research, an extracted triple is deemed accurate if the head entity, the relation, and the tail entity are each validated as correct. The study reports standard metrics, including micro-precision (Prec.), recall (Rec.), and F1 score (f1), in line with the established baselines.

5.2. Baseline

To evaluate the performance of the DERP Framework, it is compared with ten baseline models: NovelTagging [3], CopyRE [31], GraphRel [32], ETL-Span [17], CopyMTL [33], CasRel [4], TPLinker [34], RSAN [13], CGT [35], and RIFRE [36].

Unless otherwise noted, the results of these baseline models were taken from the original papers.

5.3. Results

Table 1 shows the results of our model relative to other baselines extracted from entities and relations on both datasets. On the WebNLG dataset, DERP outperformed all baselines in both recall and F1 score, and on the NYT dataset, DERP achieved the second highest F1 score. These results directly validate the utility of the proposed DERP framework.

Table 1. Precision (%), recall (%) and F1 score (%) of the compared models on the NYT and WebNLG databases. * marks results quoted directly from the original papers.

Model	NYT			WebNLG		
	Prec.	Rec.	f1	Prec.	Rec.	f1
NovelTagging* [3]	61.5	41.4	49.5	-	-	-
CopyRE* [31]	61.0	56.6	58.7	37.7	36.4	37.1
GraphRel* [32]	63.9	60.0	61.9	44.7	41.1	42.9
ETL-Span* [17]	53.8	65.1	59.0	84.3	82.9	83.1
CopyMTL* [33]	75.7	68.7	72.0	58.0	54.9	56.4
CasRel* [4]	89.7	89.5	89.6	93.4	90.1	91.8
TPLinker* [34]	91.3	92.5	91.9	91.8	92.0	91.9
RSAN* [13]	85.7	83.6	84.6	80.5	83.8	82.1
CGT* [35]	94.7	84.2	89.1	92.9	75.6	83.4
RIFRE* [36]	93.6	90.5	92.0	93.3	92.0	92.6
DERP	92.05	89.94	90.98	92.82	92.90	92.86
DERP_HeadEntity	91.12	90.47	90.80	92.10	92.18	92.28
DERP_TailEntity	92.03	72.49	81.10	93.42	86.70	90.35

Table 2 shows the experimental results of DERP on the DuIE2.0 and CMeIE-V2 datasets, which shows an improvement over CasRel in terms of F1 score results. The F1 score of DERP_HeadEntity is also higher than CasRel when experiments are conducted using DERP_HeadEntity.

Table 2. Precision (%), recall (%) and F1 score (%) of the compared models on the DuIE2.0 and CMeIE-V2 databases. * marks results of reproduced experiments.

Model	DuIE2.0			CMeIE-V2		
	Prec.	Rec.	f1	Prec.	Rec.	f1
CasRel*	69.56	65.54	67.49	47.56	42.56	44.91
DERP	71.06	65.35	68.09	47.51	46.11	46.80
DERP_HeadEntity	70.38	65.80	68.01	47.27	45.15	46.19
DERP_TailEntity	73.97	53.50	62.09	49.10	43.01	45.85

We conducted experiments on CasRel under the same experimental conditions as the DERP framework. On the NYT dataset, CasRel* scored precision 88.87%, recall 90.34%, and F1 score 89.60%; on the WebNLG dataset, CasRel* scored precision 91.92%, recall 91.39%, and F1 score 91.65%. Compared with the replicated CasRel* framework, DERP has 1.38 percent improvement in F1 score on the NYT dataset, 1.21 percent improvement in F1 score on the WebNLG dataset, 0.6 percent improvement in F1 score on the DuIE2.0 dataset, and 1.98 percent improvement in F1 score on the CMeIE-V2 dataset. On the four datasets of NYT, WebNLG, DuIE2.0, and CMeIE-V2, in the experiments using head entity recognition and tail entity recognition alone for triple prediction, DERP_HeadEntity has higher precision, recall and F1 score than the original CasRel model in the experiments. In the DERP tail entity experiment, the features of the tail entity are not as easy to recognize as the features of the head entity, resulting in weaker F1 experimental results than DERP_HeadEntity on the four datasets.

Table 1 also presents that in the experiments on the two English datasets, with the existing models compared, a significant gap in processing performance between the models is found, which proves that DERP performs better in dealing with redundant entities and overlapping triples. In the comparison experiments on four datasets, NYT, WebNLG, DuIE2.0, and CMeIE-V2, it is demonstrated that dividing entity recognition into head entity recognition and tail entity recognition, as in the DERP framework, can effectively improve the accuracy of entity recognition, and can produce more accurate results in relation extraction and triple prediction.

6. Conclusions

In this study, a double-headed entities and relations prediction framework for joint triple extraction is proposed. The entity recognition part is decomposed into head entity recognition and tail entity recognition. Specifically, relation prediction and tail entity recognition are executed for the head entities, and in parallel, relation prediction and head entity recognition are performed for the tail entities. In addition, a triple prediction module is designed to solve the entity overlapping problem in previous joint triple extractions. We systematically conducted experiments across four distinct datasets and compared them with ten baseline models. By proceeding with joint triple extraction, a good foundation is constructed for subsequent natural language processing or knowledge graph construction efforts. The results of these rigorous investigations substantiate that the conceptual framework introduced in this paper exhibits certain improvements when juxtaposed with prior models.

In the DERP framework, we have only improved the case of missing triple extraction, and in future work, we will conduct research on the case of error in triple extraction. We will also conduct research on Chinese text triple extraction to study the special characteristics of Chinese text triple extraction and improve the accuracy and effectiveness of Chinese text triple extraction.

Author Contributions: Conceptualization, Y.X. and G.C.; methodology, Y.X.; software, Y.X. and C.D.; validation, Y.Y., L.L. and J.Z.; formal analysis, J.L.; investigation, Y.X.; resources, Y.X.; data curation, L.L.; writing—original draft preparation, Y.X.; writing—review and editing, G.C.; visualization, C.D.; supervision, C.D.; project administration, Y.Y.; funding acquisition, G.C. All authors have read and agreed to the published version of the manuscript.

Funding: This research was funded by cooperative projects between universities in Chongqing and the Chinese Academy of Sciences, grant number Grant HZ2021015; the Chongqing Technology Innovation and Application Development Special Project, grant number cstc2019jscxmbdxX0016; the General Project of the Chongqing Municipal Science and Technology Commission, grant number cstc2021jcyjmsxm3332; the Sichuan Science and Technology Program 2023JDRC0033; the Young Project of Science and Technology Research Program of the Chongqing Education Commission of China, number KJQN202001513 and number KJQN202101501; the Luzhou Science and Technology Program 2021-JYJ-92; the Chongqing Postgraduate Scientific Research Innovation Project, grant number CYS23752; and the Chongqing University of Science and Technology Master and Doctoral Student Innovation Project, grant number YKJCX2120811.

Data Availability Statement: Not applicable.

Conflicts of Interest: The authors declare no conflict of interest.

References

1. Jiang, Z.; Chi, C.; Zhan, Y. Research on Medical Question Answering System Based on Knowledge Graph. *IEEE Access* **2021**, *9*, 21094–21101. [CrossRef]
2. Ma, L.; Ren, H.; Zhang, X. Effective Cascade Dual-Decoder Model for Joint Entity and Relation Extraction. *arXiv* **2021**. [CrossRef]
3. Zheng, S.; Wang, F.; Bao, H.; Hao, Y.; Zhou, P.; Xu, B. Joint Extraction of Entities and Relations Based on a Novel Tagging Scheme. In Proceedings of the 55th Annual Meeting of the Association for Computational Linguistics, Vancouver, BC, Canada, 30 July–4 August 2017; pp. 1227–1236.
4. Wei, Z.; Su, J.; Wang, Y.; Tian, Y.; Chang, Y. A Novel Cascade Binary Tagging Framework for Relational Triple Extraction. In Proceedings of the 58th Annual Meeting of the Association for Computational Linguistics, Online, 5–10 July 2020; pp. 1476–1488.
5. Li, L.; Zhang, J.; Jin, L.; Guo, R.; Huang, D. A Distributed Meta-Learning System for Chinese Entity Relation Extraction. *Neurocomputing* **2015**, *149*, 1135–1142. [CrossRef]

6. Li, H.; Xu, T.; Zhou, J. Mathematical Subject Information Entity Recognition Method Based on BiLSTM-CRF. In *Machine Learning for Cyber Security, Proceedings of the Third International Conference, ML4CS 2020, Guangzhou, China, 8–10 October 2020*; Proceedings, Part III 3; Springer International Publishing: Cham, Switzerland, 2020; pp. 259–268.
7. Luo, L.; Yang, Z.; Yang, P.; Zhang, Y.; Wang, L.; Lin, H.; Wang, J. An Attention-Based BiLSTM-CRF Approach to Document-Level Chemical Named Entity Recognition. *Bioinformatics* **2018**, *34*, 1381–1388. [CrossRef] [PubMed]
8. Li, X.; Zhang, H.; Zhou, X.-H. Chinese Clinical Named Entity Recognition with Variant Neural Structures Based on BERT Methods. *J. Biomed. Inform.* **2020**, *107*, 103422. [CrossRef] [PubMed]
9. Ren, Z. Joint Entity and Relation Extraction Based on Specific-Relation Attention Mechanism and Global Features. In Proceedings of the Second International Conference on Electronic Information Technology (EIT 2023), Wuhan, China, 31 March–2 April 2023; Volume 12719, pp. 685–691.
10. Zeng, X.; He, S.; Zeng, D.; Liu, K.; Liu, S.; Zhao, J. Learning the Extraction Order of Multiple Relational Facts in a Sentence with Reinforcement Learning. In Proceedings of the 2019 Conference on Empirical Methods in Natural Language Processing and the 9th International Joint Conference on Natural Language Processing (EMNLP-IJCNLP), Hong Kong, China, 3–7 November 2019; pp. 367–377.
11. Han, X.; Wang, L. A Novel Document-Level Relation Extraction Method Based on BERT and Entity Information. *IEEE Access* **2020**, *8*, 96912–96919. [CrossRef]
12. Chen, Y.; Yang, W.; Wang, K.; Qin, Y.; Huang, R.; Zheng, Q. A Neuralized Feature Engineering Method for Entity Relation Extraction. *Neural Netw.* **2021**, *141*, 249–260. [CrossRef] [PubMed]
13. Yuan, Y.; Zhou, X.; Pan, S.; Zhu, Q.; Song, Z.; Guo, L. A Relation-Specific Attention Network for Joint Entity and Relation Extraction. In Proceedings of the Twenty-Ninth International Joint Conference on Artificial Intelligence (IJCAI-20), Yokohama, Japan, 7–15 January 2021; ISBN 978-0-9992411-6-5.
14. Wan, Q.; Wei, L.; Zhao, S.; Liu, J. A Span-Based Multi-Modal Attention Network for Joint Entity-Relation Extraction. *Knowl.-Based Syst.* **2023**, *262*, 110228. [CrossRef]
15. Huang, W.; Cheng, X.; Wang, T.; Chu, W. BERT-Based Multi-Head Selection for Joint Entity-Relation Extraction. In *Natural Language Processing and Chinese Computing, Proceedings of the 8th CCF International Conference, NLPCC 2019, Dunhuang, China, 9–14 October 2019*; Proceedings, Part II; Springer: Cham, Switzerland, 2019; pp. 713–723.
16. Liu, J.; Chen, S.; Wang, B.; Zhang, J.; Li, N.; Xu, T. Attention as Relation: Learning Supervised Multi-Head Self-Attention for Relation Extraction. In Proceedings of the Twenty-Ninth International Joint Conference on Artificial Intelligence (IJCAI-20), Yokohama, Japan, 7–15 January 2021; pp. 3787–3793.
17. Yu, B.; Zhang, Z.; Shu, X.; Wang, Y.; Liu, T.; Wang, B.; Li, S. Joint Extraction of Entities and Relations Based on a Novel Decomposition Strategy. In Proceedings of the 24th European Conference on Artificial Intelligence—ECAI 2020, Santiago de Compostela, Spain, 29 August–8 September 2020.
18. Guo, Y.; Liu, Z.; Huang, C.; Liu, J.; Jing, W.; Wang, Z.; Wang, Y. CyberRel: Joint Entity and Relation Extraction for Cybersecurity Concepts. In *Information and Communications Security*; Gao, D., Li, Q., Guan, X., Liao, X., Eds.; Lecture Notes in Computer Science; Springer International Publishing: Cham, Switzerland, 2021; Volume 12918, pp. 447–463. ISBN 978-3-030-86889-5.
19. Lv, C.; Pan, D.; Li, Y.; Li, J.; Wang, Z. A Novel Chinese Entity Relationship Extraction Method Based on the Bidirectional Maximum Entropy Markov Model. *Complexity* **2021**, *2021*, e6610965. [CrossRef]
20. Zheng, H.; Wen, R.; Chen, X.; Yang, Y.; Zhang, Y.; Zhang, Z.; Zhang, N.; Qin, B.; Xu, M.; Zheng, Y. PRGC: Potential Relation and Global Correspondence Based Joint Relational Triple Extraction. In Proceedings of the 59th Annual Meeting of the Association for Computational Linguistics and the 11th International Joint Conference on Natural Language Processing, Online, 1–6 August 2021; pp. 6225–6235.
21. Li, X.; Li, Y.; Yang, J.; Liu, H.; Hu, P. A Relation Aware Embedding Mechanism for Relation Extraction. *Appl. Intell.* **2022**, *52*, 10022–10031. [CrossRef]
22. Huang, H.; Shang, Y.-M.; Sun, X.; Wei, W.; Mao, X. Three Birds, One Stone: A Novel Translation Based Framework for Joint Entity and Relation Extraction. *Knowl.-Based Syst.* **2022**, *236*, 107677. [CrossRef]
23. Liu, C.; Zhang, X.; Xu, Y.; Xiang, B.; Gan, L.; Shu, Y. Knowledge Graph for Maritime Pollution Regulations Based on Deep Learning Methods. *Ocean Coast. Manag.* **2023**, *242*, 106679. [CrossRef]
24. Zhuang, C.; Zhang, N.; Jin, X.; Li, Z.; Deng, S.; Chen, H. Joint Extraction of Triple Knowledge Based on Relation Priority. In Proceedings of the 2020 IEEE Intl Conf on Parallel & Distributed Processing with Applications, Big Data & Cloud Computing, Sustainable Computing & Communications, Social Computing & Networking (ISPA/BDCloud/SocialCom/SustainCom), Exeter, UK, 17–19 December 2020; pp. 562–569.
25. Riedel, S.; Yao, L.; McCallum, A. Modeling Relations and Their Mentions without Labeled Text. In *Machine Learning and Knowledge Discovery in Databases*; Balcázar, J.L., Bonchi, F., Gionis, A., Sebag, M., Eds.; Lecture Notes in Computer Science; Springer: Berlin/Heidelberg, Germany, 2010; Volume 6323, pp. 148–163. ISBN 978-3-642-15938-1.
26. Gardent, C.; Shimorina, A.; Narayan, S.; Perez-Beltrachini, L. Creating Training Corpora for Nlg Micro-Planning. In Proceedings of the 55th Annual Meeting of the Association for Computational Linguistics, Vancouver, BC, Canada, 30 July–4 August 2017.
27. Huang Xun, Y.H. A Review of Relation Extraction. *Data Anal. Knowl. Discov.* **2013**, *29*, 30–39. [CrossRef]

28. Li, S.; He, W.; Shi, Y.; Jiang, W.; Liang, H.; Jiang, Y.; Zhang, Y.; Lyu, Y.; Zhu, Y. DuIE: A Large-Scale Chinese Dataset for Information Extraction. In *Natural Language Processing and Chinese Computing*; Tang, J., Kan, M.-Y., Zhao, D., Li, S., Zan, H., Eds.; Lecture Notes in Computer Science; Springer International Publishing: Cham, Switzerland, 2019; Volume 11839, pp. 791–800, ISBN 978-3-030-32235-9.
29. Zhang, N.; Chen, M.; Bi, Z.; Liang, X.; Li, L.; Shang, X.; Yin, K.; Tan, C.; Xu, J.; Huang, F.; et al. CBLUE: A Chinese Biomedical Language Understanding Evaluation Benchmark. In Proceedings of the 60th Annual Meeting of the Association for Computational Linguistics (Volume 1: Long Papers), Dublin, Ireland, 22–27 May 2022; pp. 7888–7915.
30. Cheng, D.; Song, H.; He, X.; Xu, B. Joint Entity and Relation Extraction for Long Text. In *Knowledge Science, Engineering and Management*; Qiu, H., Zhang, C., Fei, Z., Qiu, M., Kung, S.-Y., Eds.; Lecture Notes in Computer Science; Springer International Publishing: Cham, Switzerland, 2021; Volume 12816, pp. 152–162. ISBN 978-3-030-82146-3.
31. Zeng, X.; Zeng, D.; He, S.; Liu, K.; Zhao, J. Extracting Relational Facts by an End-to-End Neural Model with Copy Mechanism. In Proceedings of the 56th Annual Meeting of the Association for Computational Linguistics (Volume 1: Long Papers), Melbourne, Australia, 15–20 July 2018; pp. 506–514.
32. Fu, T.-J.; Li, P.-H.; Ma, W.-Y. GraphRel: Modeling Text as Relational Graphs for Joint Entity and Relation Extraction. In Proceedings of the 57th Annual Meeting of the Association for Computational Linguistics, Florence, Italy, 28 July–2 August 2019; pp. 1409–1418.
33. Zeng, D.; Zhang, H.; Liu, Q. CopyMTL: Copy Mechanism for Joint Extraction of Entities and Relations with Multi-Task Learning. *Proc. AAAI Conf. Artif. Intell.* **2020**, *34*, 9507–9514. [CrossRef]
34. Wang, Y.; Yu, B.; Zhang, Y.; Liu, T.; Zhu, H.; Sun, L. TPLinker: Single-Stage Joint Extraction of Entities and Relations Through Token Pair Linking. In Proceedings of the 28th International Conference on Computational Linguistics, International Committee on Computational Linguistics, 2020, Online, 8–13 December 2020; pp. 1572–1582.
35. Ye, H.; Zhang, N.; Deng, S.; Chen, M.; Tan, C.; Huang, F.; Chen, H. Contrastive Triple Extraction with Generative Transformer. *Proc. AAAI Conf. Artif. Intell.* **2021**, *35*, 14257–14265. [CrossRef]
36. Zhao, K.; Xu, H.; Cheng, Y.; Li, X.; Gao, K. Representation Iterative Fusion Based on Heterogeneous Graph Neural Network for Joint Entity and Relation Extraction. *Knowl.-Based Syst.* **2021**, *219*, 106888. [CrossRef]

Disclaimer/Publisher's Note: The statements, opinions and data contained in all publications are solely those of the individual author(s) and contributor(s) and not of MDPI and/or the editor(s). MDPI and/or the editor(s) disclaim responsibility for any injury to people or property resulting from any ideas, methods, instructions or products referred to in the content.

Article

Sentiment Difficulty in Aspect-Based Sentiment Analysis

Adrian-Gabriel Chifu * and Sébastien Fournier

Aix-Marseille Université, Université de Toulon, CNRS, LIS, 13007 Marseille, France; sebastien.fournier@univ-amu.fr
* Correspondence: adrian.chifu@univ-amu.fr

Abstract: Subjectivity is a key aspect of natural language understanding, especially in the context of user-generated text and conversational systems based on large language models. Natural language sentences often contain subjective elements, such as opinions and emotions, that make them more nuanced and complex. The level of detail at which the study of the text is performed determines the possible applications of sentiment analysis. The analysis can be done at the document or paragraph level, or, even more granularly, at the aspect level. Many researchers have studied this topic extensively. The field of aspect-based sentiment analysis has numerous data sets and models. In this work, we initiate the discussion around the definition of sentence difficulty in this context of aspect-based sentiment analysis. To assess and quantify the difficulty of the aspect-based sentiment analysis, we conduct an experiment using three data sets: "Laptops", "Restaurants", and "MTSC" (Multi-Target-dependent Sentiment Classification), along with 21 learning models from scikit-learn. We also use two textual representations, TF-IDF (Terms frequency-inverse document frequency) and BERT (Bidirectional Encoder Representations from Transformers), to analyze the difficulty faced by these models in performing aspect-based sentiment analysis. Additionally, we compare the models with a fine-tuned version of BERT on the three data sets. We identify the most challenging sentences using a combination of classifiers in order to better understand them. We propose two strategies for defining sentence difficulty. The first strategy is binary and considers sentences as difficult when the classifiers are unable to correctly assign the sentiment polarity. The second strategy uses a six-level difficulty scale based on how many of the top five best-performing classifiers can correctly identify sentiment polarity. These sentences with assigned difficulty classes are then used to create predictive models for early difficulty detection. The purpose of estimating the difficulty of aspect-based sentiment analysis is to enhance performance while minimizing resource usage.

Keywords: sentiment analysis; aspect-based sentiment analysis; difficulty; sentiment polarity; text representation

MSC: 68T50; 68T07

Citation: Chifu, A.-G.; Fournier, S. Sentiment Difficulty in Aspect-Based Sentiment Analysis. *Mathematics* **2023**, *11*, 4647. https://doi.org/10.3390/math11224647

Academic Editor: Xiang Li

Received: 14 October 2023
Revised: 9 November 2023
Accepted: 10 November 2023
Published: 14 November 2023

Copyright: © 2023 by the authors. Licensee MDPI, Basel, Switzerland. This article is an open access article distributed under the terms and conditions of the Creative Commons Attribution (CC BY) license (https://creativecommons.org/licenses/by/4.0/).

1. Introduction

Sentiment analysis, also known as opinion mining, is a field of natural language processing that aims to automatically identify and extract subjective information from texts. Sentiment analysis has numerous applications, ranging from marketing to politics, and it has become an increasingly popular topic of research in the past decade [1,2]. Sentiment analysis can be used to identify the sentiments of customers towards a particular product, the opinions of voters towards a political candidate, or the emotions of patients towards their medical condition, among other applications.

Despite recent advancements in sentiment analysis, the detection and analysis of sentiments remain challenging due to several factors. One of the most significant challenges in sentiment analysis is the ambiguity of language [3–5]. For example, the word "hot" can refer to temperature, attractiveness, or anger, and it may be difficult for algorithms to determine which meaning is intended in a particular text. In the sentence "This new restaurant has some hot dishes", the sentiment may be positive because the dishes are delicious or negative because they are too spicy. Ambiguity in language is further complicated by the use of slang, idioms, and regional dialects, which can vary widely even within the same language. For instance, the phrase "cool beans" means "excellent" in American English, but it may be meaningless or confusing to non-native speakers.

Another challenge in sentiment analysis is the detection of tone and sarcasm [6–8]. Texts often contain tones that can be difficult for algorithms to detect, and sarcasm can be especially challenging. For example, a person might say "great" in a sarcastic tone to indicate the opposite of what the word usually means. In the sentence "I love spending hours in traffic every day", the sentiment may be negative despite the positive connotation of the word "love" because the text is sarcastic. Detecting the tone of a text is crucial in understanding the sentiment, as the same words can have different meanings depending on the tone in which they are expressed.

Cultural and contextual differences also pose a challenge to sentiment analysis [9]. Sentiments can vary based on culture and context, and what might be considered positive in one culture may not be the same in another. For example, in some cultures, being direct and blunt is considered a positive trait, while in others, it may be seen as negative. Let us analyze the sentence "The government imposed a strict lockdown to prevent the spread of COVID-19". This sentence expresses a positive sentiment towards the aspect of lockdown, as it implies that the government is taking proactive measures to protect the public health and safety. However, this sentiment may not be shared by people from cultures that value individual freedom and autonomy more than collective welfare and security. For them, the lockdown may be seen as a negative aspect that infringes on their personal rights and choices. Sentiment analysis algorithms must be trained on diverse data sets to overcome such differences.

Data quality and quantity are also crucial factors in the effectiveness of sentiment analysis algorithms. Sentiment analysis algorithms require large amounts of high-quality data to train effectively. However, it can be challenging to gather such data, especially for less common languages or topics. Additionally, data quality issues such as noise, missing data, or bias [10] can affect the accuracy of sentiment analysis. In the sentence "I bought a phone from XYZ company, and it's terrible", the sentiment may be negative towards the phone, but it could also be negative towards the company or the customer service. Without additional context or information, it may be difficult for algorithms to determine the sentiment accurately.

One way to perform sentiment analysis is to examine different levels of granularity: the whole document, a single paragraph, a sentence, or even a specific aspect. However, each level of analysis may encounter the challenges that are discussed previously in this introduction. In this work, we will focus on the most fine-grained level, the aspect level. Indeed, aspect-based is the level for which research is currently the most productive, and consequently also generates the production of corpora whose expressiveness of sentiment is more subtle and therefore potentially more difficult to analyze.

Finally, sentiment analysis algorithms may exhibit bias [10] and subjectivity due to the training data used or the biases of the developers. For example, if a sentiment analysis algorithm was trained on texts from a particular political perspective, it may not perform well on texts from other perspectives. Bias and subjectivity can also arise from the choice of sentiment lexicons, which are dictionaries of words and phrases that are labeled.

Recent years have seen advances in language models, particularly the emergence of BERT [11] and GPT [12]. These have enabled algorithms to better capture the semantics of texts, resulting in a marked improvement in performance. This raises the question of whether the challenges mentioned above still exist, and if so, how algorithms manage to overcome them. In this article, we explore how algorithms handle these difficulties and which subjective sentences pose the greatest challenge.

Contrary to the usual focus in current aspect-based sentiment analysis research, our aim does not involve achieving better results or introducing a new classification model.

Rather, it is to comprehend why existing models are not working in some cases and why some data sets are "simpler" than others. The aim is therefore to observe the behavior of classification models in the aspect-based sentiment analysis task and to estimate the degree of difficulty of the analyzed sentences. Thus, estimating the difficulty of sentiment analysis could enhance performance while minimizing resource usage.

In order to better understand the aspect-based sentiment analysis difficulty, we raise the following research questions:

- **RQ1**: How to define difficulty in aspect-based sentiment analysis?
- **RQ2**: Is difficulty data set-dependent?
- **RQ3**: What is the impact of text representation on performance?
- **RQ4**: What is the impact of classification models on performance?
- **RQ5**: Are we able to predict difficulty?
- **RQ6**: How to better understand difficult sentences (qualitative analysis on difficult sentences)?

To summarize, in order to answer these six research questions, we propose in our work to:

- Select 3 data sets whose purpose is to perform aspect-based classification. The data sets have been created at a 6–7 year time distance, and choosing three data sets that span over such a large period of time would reflect the evolution of the field;
- Select 21 models and two different text representations in order to analyze their respective behavior and performance when faced with aspect-based sentiment analysis;
- Conduct numerous experiments in order to better understand the challenges faced by the models;
- Investigate automatic sentence difficulty definition and estimation using learning-based models.

The remainder of this paper is organized as follows. Section 2 provides an overview of aspect-based sentiment analysis, text representation models and the concept of difficulty in Information Retrieval. Section 3 presents three different data sets used in the experiments. Then, Section 4 presents the 2 text representations that have been used and Section 5 presents the different used models and the employed implementations. Section 6 explains the experimental protocol and presents the aspect-based sentiment polarity classification results. Section 7 proposes difficulty definitions and tests if the difficulty may be predicted, while Section 8 discusses the results and answers the research questions. Finally, Section 9 concludes the paper and suggests directions for future work.

2. Related Work

We further divide our related work into themes that influence our analysis, including Sentiment Analysis, Aspect-based Sentiment Analysis, Text Representation, and Query Difficulty in Information Retrieval.

2.1. Sentiment Analysis and Aspect-Based Sentiment Analysis

The goal of sentiment analysis is to identify and categorize emotions and sentiments expressed in written text automatically. Sentiment analysis is a fairly broad area of research and can be defined at several levels—at a document level, paragraph level, or sentence level—but also at a much finer level, at an aspect level, which is the element on which subjectivity is focused. In the literature research works are often classified into three categories: machine learning, deeplearning, and ensemble learning. Among the most effective machine learning techniques for this task are naive Bayes [13–15] and SVM [16–18]. Algorithms based on deeplearning [19] include RNNs [20,21], LSTMs [22–24], and transformers [25,26]. Ensemble-based methods [27] combine multiple classifiers, which can fall into either of the previous categories. In response to the large amount of work on the subject of sentiment analysis, a number of surveys have been carried out recently [27–30]. However, for several years now, research has been more focused on multimodal, multilingual sentiment analysis and on the finest level of sentiment analysis: the aspect-based level.

The finesse of the analysis at the aspect level means that in the vast majority of cases we can be sure of having a uniqueness of subjectivity. In other words, there are not two opposite degrees of subjectivity for the same aspect. This aspect of sentiment analysis is often divided into two distinct tasks; the first consists of finding and extracting the aspects. The second is to estimate the subjectivity, generally reducing the problem of estimating the degree of subjectivity to a simpler problem of classification. This involves classifying the sentences or nominal phrases containing the aspects as neutral (no subjectivity), positive (the author speaks positively about the aspect), and negative (the author speaks negatively about the aspect). Sometimes the scale of values used is broader (often 5 classes) and sometimes there are other classes, as is the case for the data we are going to use (e.g., conflict). In this document, we will only deal with the second task, i.e., the classification of subjectivity by taking aspects into account. To carry out this task, the methods and models used are relatively similar to those used in sentiment analysis at a coarser level. This research was introduced by the seminal work of [31] and has been developed with the production of numerous models and data sets in various languages. As in the more general context of sentiment analysis, we found similar algorithms but adapted them to the task. Among these algorithms, we can cite the use of SVMs [32] and Naïve Bayes [33]. More recently, the advent of deeplearning has considerably improved model performance. For example, there are models using RNNs, LSTMs [34–36], and transformers [37,38]. For further reading, one can also refer to surveys on the subject [39–41]. As the most recent work has focused on aspect-based analysis, the recent corpora produced for this task seem to us to have a more subtle expressivity of sentiment. This is why, in order to have a more thorough study of the difficulty in sentiment analysis, we have focused in this work on the aspect-based sentiment analysis, although the conclusions and models we obtain can be applied to sentiment analysis in a general way.

2.2. Text Representation

Text representation for machine learning models has always been a major issue. Initially, the vector representation of documents was only done by taking into account the presence or absence of terms in the document. This representation was then improved by taking into account the frequency of terms in the documents and in the collection [42]. However, such representations take no account of the semantics expressed in the sentences. With the arrival of deeplearning and the emergence of less sparse representations, semantic aspects have been better taken into account. These representations were democratized thanks to the work of [43] and then improved through the work of [44]. The emergence of transformers has also made it possible to obtain new, more efficient representations [11].

2.3. Difficulty in Information Retrieval

As we have already noted, the various existing challenges in aspect-based sentiment analysis make it difficult to classify sentences. Therefore, it is important to detect such difficult sentences to choose a different strategy in order to extract the expressed sentiment. Having multiple strategies in order to classify sentiment based on the detected difficulty helps to reduce the use of resource-intensive algorithms. Thus, we reduce the economic and ecological costs of the models. Difficulty detection is a key area of research, especially in information retrieval. In the 2000s, research on query difficulty began and many predictors were defined based on distribution [45], ambiguity [46], and complexity [47]. In the field of information retrieval, models predicting difficulty are divided according to whether they use pre- or post-retrieval predictors. Models using pre-retrieval predictors include those presented in [48–50]. These models use statistics on the occurrence of query terms. Among the models using post-retrieval predictors we find the work of [51–55]. These models will use the results of the information retrieval models to make their predictions. With the advent of deep neural networks, recent work has used such models to predict difficulty.

These studies notably include [55,56]. Recently, [57,58] have raised the question of the effectiveness of evaluating the difficulty of Neural Information Retrieval based on PLM (Pre-trained Language Models).

Predicting the difficulty of a sentence in sentiment classification can not only improve the performance of the algorithms by selecting models according to the difficulty encountered, but can also make the systems more resource-efficient.

The notion of difficulty in aspect-based sentiment analysis has not yet been studied. Inspired by the work that has been conducted on information retrieval, particularly inspired by works on post-retrieval predictors, we are conducting experiments that will enable us to gain a better understanding of the notion of difficulty in this specific case. In addition, we have also sought to automate the estimation of difficulty for aspect-based sentiment analysis. In the remaining part of this paper we present the experiments that have been carried out in order to better understand where the difficulties lie in the sentiment classification task based on aspects.

3. Reference Data Sets Used for Corpus Building

In this section, we will introduce the reference data sets. These data sets have been essential because they provided the data for our corpus. Following that, we will explain the process of building the corpus. After that, we will move on to an exploratory analysis.

We used three data sets for our experiments: "Laptops", "Restaurants", and "MTSC". We provide details on the data sets below. In order to perceive the temporal evolution of the difficulty of the task, we selected three corpora, each spaced about 6–7 years apart. We also chose two different objects of study: reviews and political news. The first and second corpora concern Laptop and restaurant reviews, respectively. They were published in 2009 and 2014. The third concerns political news and was published in 2021.

On each of these corpora and two different representations (TF-IDF and BERT), we carried out experiments with 21 learning models in order to discover on which corpus the models had the most difficulty. We consider a model to have difficulty if its performance is below the median of model performance for a given corpus. We also consider difficulty at a more micro level, by looking at the sentences and paragraphs posing the most difficulty for the selected models.

3.1. Laptops

The SemEval Laptop Reviews data set [59] is often associated with the laptops data set for aspect-based sentiment analysis. It was first used in the SemEval-2014 Task 4: Aspect-Based Sentiment Analysis challenge. This data set is used for two subtasks: aspect identification (Subtask 1) and aspect-oriented sentiment polarity classification (Subtask 2).

It contains more than 3000 English sentences from customer reviews of laptops. It focuses on analyzing sentiments at a more granular level, targeting various aspects or attributes of laptops such as performance, battery life, design, and usability. Expert human annotators have labeled the aspect terms of the sentences and their sentiment. A part of this data set was kept as test data by the organizers of the SemEval-2014 competition.

This data set enables researchers to analyze sentiment polarities towards specific aspects of laptops. It provides insights into customers' preferences and satisfaction levels.

Each review may contain one or multiple aspects. Each aspect is assigned one of four possible labels: "positive", "negative", "neutral", or "conflict".

3.2. Restaurants

The restaurant data set for aspect-based sentiment analysis consists of more than 3000 English sentences from restaurant reviews initially proposed by Ganu et al. [60]. As it has already been pointed out, aspect-based sentiment analysis is different from traditional sentiment analysis which focuses on overall sentiment of reviews. The original data set includes annotations for coarse aspect categories and overall sentence polarities. It has been modified for SemEval-2014 [59] to include annotations for aspect terms occurring in the sentences (Subtask 1), aspect term polarities (Subtask 2), and aspect category-specific polarities (Subtask 4). Some errors in the original data set have been corrected. Human annotators identified the aspect terms of the sentences and their polarities (Subtasks 1 and 2). Additional restaurant reviews, not present in the original data set, have been annotated in the same manner and kept by the organisers of SemEval-2014 as test data.

This data set covers reviews related to various aspects of restaurants such as food quality, service, ambiance, price, and cleanliness. Each review is labeled with sentiment ratings for each aspect. The polarities that may be identified are "positive", "negative", "neutral", and "conflict".

3.3. MSTC

NewsMTSC is an aspect-based sentiment analysis data set proposed by the authors of [61]. It focuses on news articles about policy issues and contains over 11,000 labeled sentences sampled from online US news outlets.

Most of the sentences contain several aspects that are mentioned in the data set. The conflict class does not exist, so only three polarity levels may be encountered: "positive", "negative", and "neutral".

Next, we will describe how our corpus was constructed.

3.4. Corpus Preparation

There are several files formats across the considered data sets and each data set contains multiple files. The number of attributes per data set may also vary. We have unified the data into one file per corpus, in `csv` format.

We have kept one id generated by us, the id from the original data set (for tracing purposes), the sentences, the start position of the aspect, the end position of the aspect, the aspect, and the polarity class. We will make the data sets publicly available upon acceptance.

For the "Laptops" corpus, there are several files in the original data set. These files come in both `csv` and `xml` formats. We excluded the files `Laptops_Test_Data_PhaseA` and `Laptops_Test_Data_PhaseB` as they do not contain annotations. We used the annotated sentences from `Laptop_Train_v2` as training data and the annotated sentences from `laptops-trial` as test data. We merged all the data into one file named `laptops.csv`. It has 2407 rows in total.

The "Restaurants" corpus has the same structure as the Laptops corpus. We selected the same corresponding elements, which resulted in our `restaurants.csv` file with 3789 rows.

The MTSC data from the NewsMTSC corpus is in `json` format. The files containing the data are `train`, `devtest_mt`, and `devtest_rw`. We did not consider `devtest_mt` since it is designed to evaluate a model's classification performance only on sentences with at least two target mentions, which is out of the scope of our research. Thus, we used `train` as the train data and `devtest_rw` (w stands for "real-world") as the test data. The resulting data file, called `MTSC.csv`, contains 9885 rows in total.

This last data set contains polarity scores that we have encoded as classes. There are three possible scores: 2.0 = "negative", 4.0 = "neutral", and 6.0 = "positive". We have converted the scores to their corresponding strings. The "conflict" class is not present in this corpus. Sentences with multiple aspects have been duplicated the same number of times as the number of aspects. For example, a sentence with three aspects will appear three times in the data set, one time for each aspect.

The statistics of the data sets used for the experiments are shown in Table 1.

Table 1. Summary of the data set information.

Data Sets	Total	Train	Test	# of Classes
Laptops	2407	2358	49	4
Restaurants	3789	3693	96	4
MTSC	9885	8739	1146	3

3.5. Exploratory Analysis

In the following, we present our exploratory analysis conducted on the three data sets.

We analyzed the three data sets briefly to gain insight into their structure, detect any biases, and form hypotheses.

We first examined the polarity ratios in each data set. Figure 1 shows these ratios. The most balanced data set is "MTSC", with 37.9% of the data belonging to the negative class. The other two data sets are more unbalanced, with "Restaurants" being the most unbalanced, having 58.9% of the data in the positive class and only 2.4% in the conflict class. The conflict class is the rarest across all three data sets, with 1.9% in "Laptops" and none in "MTSC".

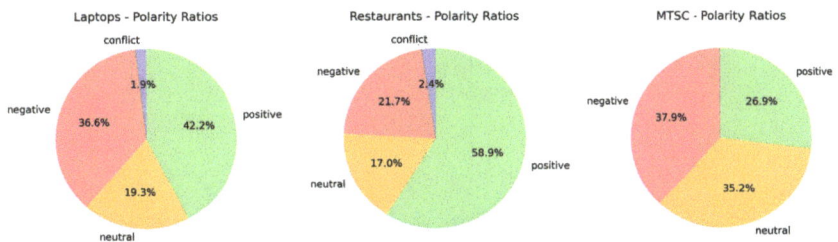

Figure 1. Polarity distributions for the three data sets.

First, we look at the polarity distributions for each data set, taking into account the train/test splits.

Figure 2 shows the class occurrences in the "Laptops" data set with respect to the train and test splits. Notably, the conflict class has no occurrences in the test set. Additionally, the data set relatively maintains the positive/negative/neutral ratios in the train set (41.0%, 36.0%, 19.1%) as compared to the test set (1.2%, 0.7%, 0.2%).

Figure 3 illustrates the "Restaurants" data set class occurrences. The remarks for "Laptops" are concurrent with this data set as well, and we underline once more that the positive class is significantly more represented than the others.

Figure 4 shows the class occurrences for the "MTSC" data set. This data set is balanced in both the train and test splits. The conflict class does not appear in this data set.

We have decided to keep the conflict class, even though it is not found in all data sets and there is no occurrence of it in any test data. This is to preserve the original data distributions for each data set as much as possible.

We now focus on analyzing the tokens and sentences from the data sets. The results are summarized in Table 2. It is common to find duplicate sentences in the data set, as one sentence may contain multiple aspects and thus may appear more than once, by design. However, the number of unique aspects is even lower than the number of unique sentences, meaning there may be multiple sentences for one aspect. Additionally, the maximum number of tokens per aspect ranges from 6 to 31 on the Laptops and MTSC data sets, respectively. This indicates that aspects may be lengthy and not necessarily composed of only one or two words.

Following this interesting observation, we continued analyzing the number of tokens from the aspects. Figure 5a depicts the frequency of the aspects by their length in terms of the number of tokens. One may notice that the vast majority of the tokens have one or two aspects. This holds for the three data sets. There is a long-tail distribution starting from aspects with four tokens per aspect and going up to 31 tokens per aspect in the case of MTSC. The maximum number of aspects for the Restaurants data set is 19. This long-tail distribution is illustrated in Figure 5b.

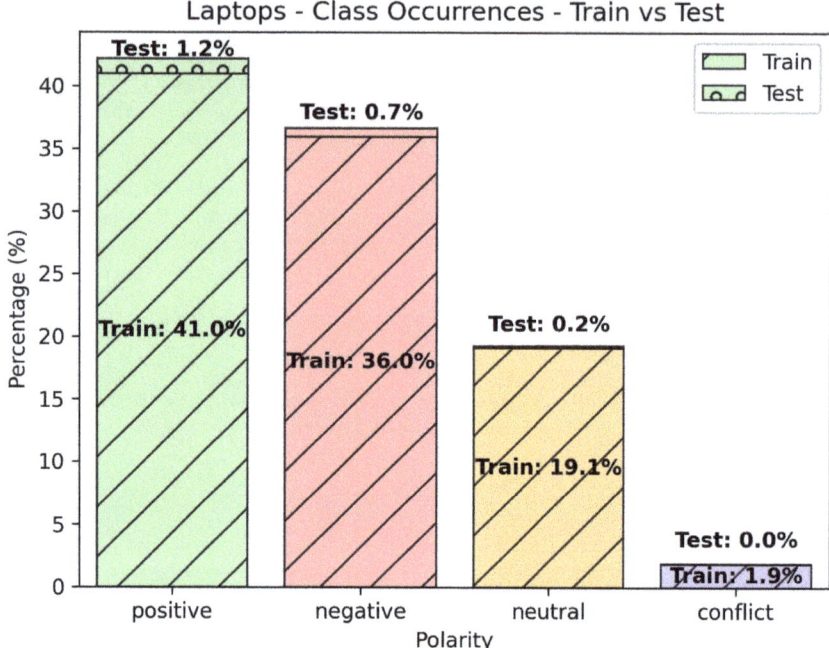

Figure 2. Class occurrences (Train vs. Test) for the "Laptops" data set.

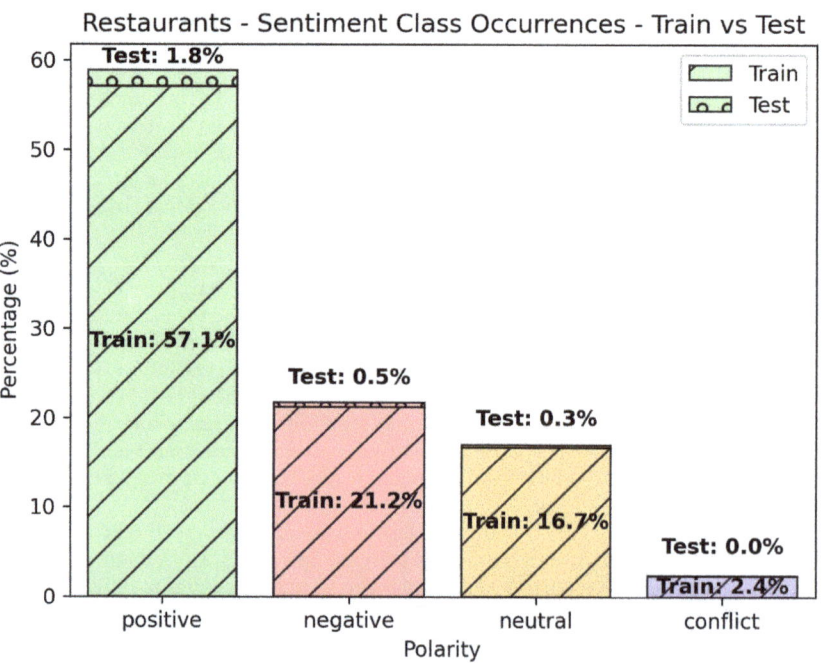

Figure 3. Class occurrences (Train vs. Test) for the "Restaurants" data set.

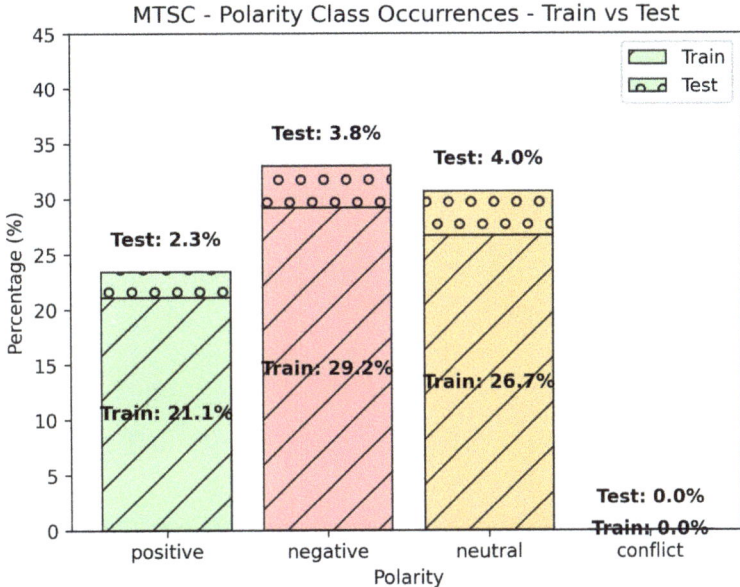

Figure 4. Class occurrences (Train vs. Test) for the MTSC data set.

Table 2. Token and sentence statistics for the data sets.

Data Set	# of Observations	# of Unique Aspects	# of Unique Sentences	Max # of Tokens per Aspect
Laptops	2407	1044	1484	6
Restaurants	3789	1289	2022	19
MTSC	9885	3525	8802	31

To gain a better understanding of the data sets, we conducted a linguistic analysis of sentiment polarity for each data set. We calculated the average number of tokens, nouns, verbs, named entities, and adjectives per instance. The results are shown in Table 3. One may notice that the sentences from MTSC are usually longer than the sentences from the other data set. However, it has been proven for query difficulty prediction that the query length is not correlated with the Average Precision performance measure [62]. Another interesting observation is that the average number of named entities in the MTSC corpus is significantly higher than for the other two data sets. This may add up to the difficulty of aspect-based polarity classification.

We wanted to investigate if the amount of nouns, verbs, or adjectives differs depending on the sentiment class. The statistics show that the positive classes have fewer nouns and verbs than the negative classes in the three data sets. However, if we normalize the number of tokens, the negative classes have the lowest values, except for "MTSC" where the ratio is almost the same. Moreover, these values are very close and the difference is not significant enough.

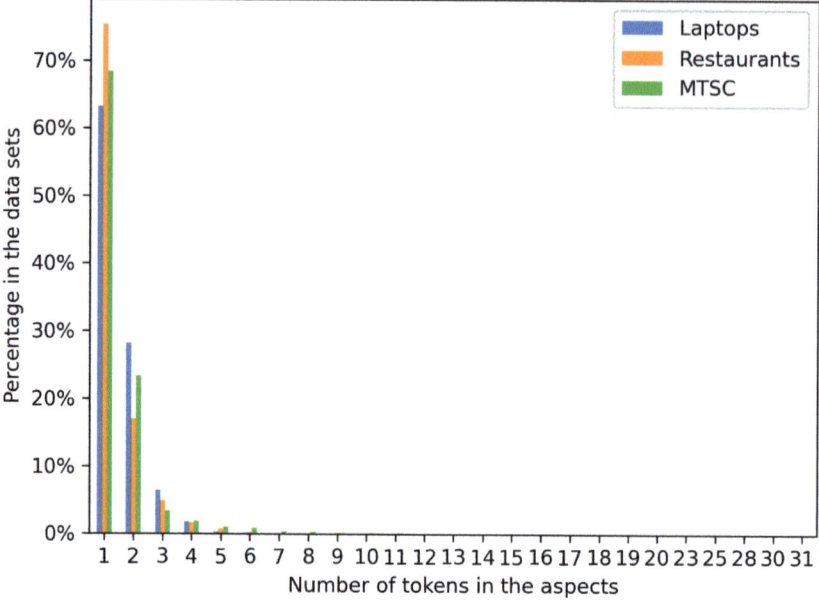

(a) The number of tokens per aspect, for the three data sets.

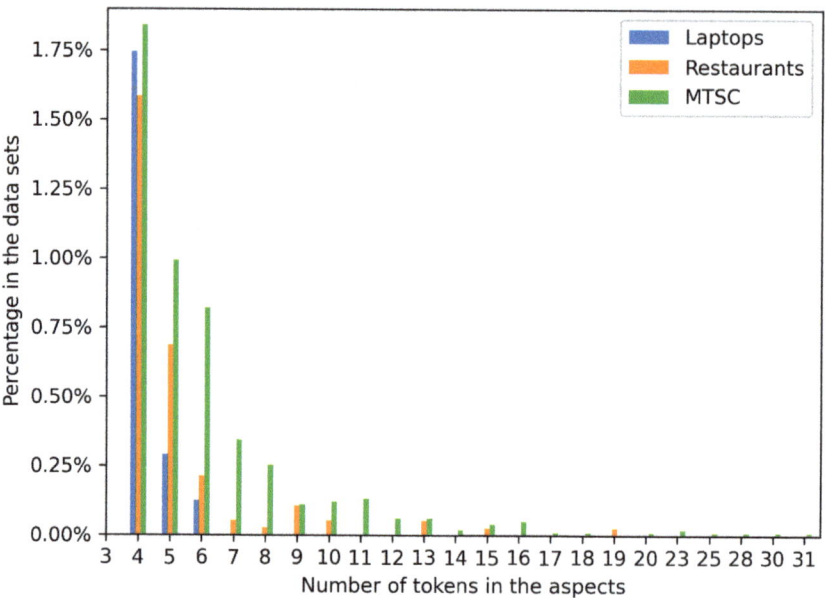

(b) Focus on the number of tokens per aspect (from 4 to 31 tokens), for the three data sets.

Figure 5. Number of tokens per aspect, for the three data sets.

Table 3. Average number of tokens, nouns, verbs, named entities, and adjectives per sentence.

Data Set/Class		Tokens	Nouns	Verbs	Named Entities	Adjectives
Laptops	Positive	20.04	3.72	1.98	0.64	1.94
	Negative	22.76	4.04	2.81	0.82	1.42
	Neutral	25.24	4.54	2.83	1.33	1.43
	Conflict	23.84	3.82	2.69	0.84	2.02
Restaurants	Positive	18.81	3.77	1.41	0.54	2.20
	Negative	22.50	4.10	2.18	0.50	1.99
	Neutral	21.62	4.14	2.26	0.74	1.48
	Conflict	22.31	3.60	1.76	0.48	2.67
MTSC	Positive	30.12	5.07	3.29	2.95	1.99
	Negative	31.58	5.31	3.55	3.27	1.94
	Neutral	27.63	4.13	3.03	3.30	1.40
	Conflict	0.00	0.00	0.00	0.00	0.00

4. Text Representations

To assess the effect of text representations on the accuracy of classification, we selected two different text representation models: TF-IDF and BERT.

4.1. TF-IDF

Term Frequency-Inverse Document Frequency (TF-IDF) [63] is a widely used technique in natural language processing. It assigns weights to words in a document based on their frequency in the document and their rarity across all documents in a corpus. TF-IDF captures the importance of words by emphasizing both their local and global significance. The term frequency component measures the occurrence of a word within a document, while the inverse document frequency factor highlights the rarity of a word across the corpus. By multiplying these values, TF-IDF assigns higher weights to terms that are both frequent within a document and unique across the entire corpus. This approach has been successful in various text mining tasks, such as information retrieval, text classification, and recommendation systems.

Thus, TF-IDF can be calculated following this formula: $TF-IDF_{i,j} = tf_{i,j} \cdot log(N/df_i)$, where $tf_{i,j}$ is the number of occurrences of the term i in the document j, df_i is the number of documents containing the term i, and N is the total number of documents in the data set.

We normalized the texts by removing HTML tags and non-alphabetic characters, transforming it into lowercase, tokenizing it with the nltk tokenizer (https://www.nltk.org/api/nltk.tokenize.html (accessed on 10 October 2023)), removing the stopwords with the nltk stopword list (https://www.nltk.org/api/nltk.corpus.html#module-nltk.corpus (accessed on 10 October 2023)), and stemming the tokens with Porter Stemmer (https://www.nltk.org/_modules/nltk/stem/porter.html (accessed on 10 October 2023)).

4.2. BERT

Bidirectional Encoder Representations from Transformers (BERT) [64] is a cutting-edge natural language processing technique. It uses transformer-based neural networks to generate contextualized word representations, instead of relying on fixed word embeddings. By pre-training on large amounts of text data and then fine-tuning on specific downstream tasks, BERT models can capture intricate semantic relationships between words and sentences. This leads to effective text vectorization, where each word or sentence is mapped to a dense representation in a high-dimensional vector space. BERT text vectorization has revolutionized many NLP tasks and opened up new possibilities in areas like sentiment analysis, question answering, and language translation.

We combined sentences and aspects into a list in the format [sentence, aspect], and then fed it to the tokenizer (https://huggingface.co/transformers/v3.0.2/model_doc/auto.html#autotokenizer (accessed on 10 October 2023)). We used the AutoModel from the transformers module (https://huggingface.co/transformers/v3.0.2/model_doc/auto.html#automodel (accessed on 10 October 2023)) to vectorize the tokens. Both the tokenizer and the model are based on distilbert-base-uncased, a pretrained model. A basic illustration of the sentence processing pipeline based on BERT is depicted in Figure 6. We tried marking the aspect inside the sentence at its corresponding position instead of adding it at the end, but the resulting representation was less effective.

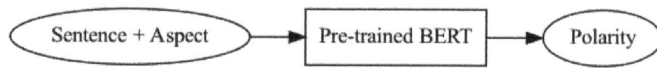

Figure 6. Sentence processing pipeline based on pretrained BERT.

5. Classification Models

This section presents the different models we used for our experiments. We have used the models proposed by the LazyText python module (https://github.com/jdvala/lazytext (accessed on 10 October 2023)) for text classification tasks. This module makes it easy to build and train text classification models. It provides a user-friendly interface and automates tedious tasks. With LazyText, users can preprocess their text data, apply feature extraction techniques such as TF-IDF or word embeddings, and train different classification models in a few lines of code. The module also offers functions to evaluate model performance and make predictions on new data. The LazyText model does not store details like the predicted class labels. To access elements such as class labels and confusion matrices, we created the models with Scikit-learn (https://scikit-learn.org/stable/supervised_learning.html (accessed on 10 October 2023)). Scikit-learn is also used internally by LazyText to train models and make predictions. The DummyClassifier is one of the classifiers. It makes predictions without considering the input features. This classifier serves as a baseline to compare with other complex classifiers. We applied the default strategy for this classifier, which always returns the most frequent class label in the data given to fit.

Next, we present the classification results using BERT and TF-IDF representations.

6. Experiments and Results

In this section, we present the results of our experiments on the three data sets presented while varying the textual representations and models used. Table 4 summarizes the hardware and software environments used for our experiments.

Table 4. Hardware and software specifications.

Hardware (*Computing Cluster Node*)	Specification
CPU	40 Intel(R) Xeon(R) Silver 4114 CPU @ 2.20 GHz
RAM	354 GB
GPU	8 (7 Nvidia A40 and 1 Nvidia GeForce RTX 3090)
Software (*Conda virtual environment*)	**Version**
python	3.11
Python modules	**Version**
huggingface_hub	0.14.1
lazy-text-predict	0.0.11
lazypredict	0.2.12
lazytext	0.0.2
matplotlib-base	3.7.1
nltk	3.7
numpy	1.24.3
pandas	1.3.5
scikit-learn	1.3.1
scipy	1.10.1
spacy	3.5.3
torch	2.0.1
transformers	4.29.2

6.1. Classification Results with TF-IDF Representations

We used the scikit-learn vectorizer (https://scikit-learn.org/stable/modules/generated/sklearn.feature_extraction.text.TfidfVectorizer.html (accessed on 10 October 2023)) with default parameters to vectorize the sentences and the aspects separately. Then, we combined the sentence and aspect vectorizations columnwise, by placing the sentence vector first, followed by the aspect vector.

We used 20 supervised classifiers from Scikit-learn and a `DummyClassifier` as described in Section 5. The `DummyClassifier` predicts the most frequent class. We report the macro-averaged metric and weighted-averaged metric results, for all the three data sets. The macro-averaged and weighted-averaged measure, respectively, are computed by the `classification\_report` function from the `scikit-learn` python module, as follows: "The reported averages include macro average (averaging the unweighted mean per label)" and "weighted average (averaging the support-weighted mean per label)" (https://scikit-learn.org/stable/modules/generated/sklearn.metrics.classification_report.html (accessed on 10 October 2023)).

Tables 5 and 6 show the classification results of macro and weighted metrics respectively, for the "Laptops" data set. These results are based on the TF-IDF text representations.

Analyzing Table 5, it is evident that `CalibratedClassifierCV` is the best classifier, achieving results higher than 90% in F1 measure. This is significantly better than `DummyClassifier`, indicating that the model was able to accurately distinguish between classes without any bias due to their distribution. Table 6 shows that six models achieved F1 scores of over 98%. This suggests that, even with a simple TF-IDF representation that does not capture advanced language semantics, the models can easily classify the corpus. Thus, we can conclude that this corpus is relatively easy to classify.

Table 5. Macro Metrics of Classification Models ("Laptops", TF-IDF representations).

Model	Precision (Macro)	Recall (Macro)	F1 (Macro)
AdaBoostClassifier	0.351852	0.356681	0.333003
BaggingClassifier	0.734375	0.725754	0.729989
BernoulliNB	0.888616	0.613506	0.663075
CalibratedClassifierCV	**0.968750**	**0.875000**	**0.913765**
DecisionTreeClassifier	0.750000	0.734375	0.741935
DummyClassifier	0.197279	0.333333	0.247863
ExtraTreeClassifier	0.750000	0.734375	0.741935
ExtraTreesClassifier	0.750000	0.734375	0.741935
GradientBoostingClassifier	0.648674	0.542026	0.567858
KNeighborsClassifier	0.604725	0.544540	0.560063
LinearSVC	0.725000	0.656250	0.685855
LogisticRegression	0.783127	0.801006	0.786207
LogisticRegressionCV	0.620202	0.571839	0.584436
MLPClassifier	0.750000	0.734375	0.741935
NearestCentroid	0.410417	0.382543	0.377963
PassiveAggressiveClassifier	0.750000	0.734375	0.741935
Perceptron	0.700000	0.718750	0.705556
RandomForestClassifier	0.750000	0.734375	0.741935
RidgeClassifier	0.671371	0.640625	0.653305
SGDClassifier	0.725000	0.656250	0.685855
SVC	0.740385	0.717672	0.725551

In Tables 7 and 8, we present the precision, recall, and F1-score results for the "Restaurants" data set. These results are based on the same text representation, TF-IDF, and are macro-averaged and weighted, respectively.

Table 7 shows that five models achieved an excellent score of 100% in F1 measure. Table 8 also reveals that the same models achieved a score of 100% when using TF-IDF. These results demonstrate that the models can easily distinguish between classes, even though the classes are imbalanced. Thus, the "Restaurants" data set is easier to classify than the "Laptops" data set.

Table 6. Weighted Metrics of Classification Models ("Laptops", TF-IDF representations).

Model	Precision (Weighted)	Recall (Weighted)	F1 (Weighted)
AdaBoostClassifier	0.695389	0.612245	0.615577
BaggingClassifier	0.979592	0.959184	0.969209
BernoulliNB	0.826355	0.795918	0.776692
CalibratedClassifierCV	0.944515	0.938776	0.937463
DecisionTreeClassifier	**1.000000**	**0.979592**	**0.989467**
DummyClassifier	0.350271	0.591837	0.440084
ExtraTreeClassifier	**1.000000**	**0.979592**	**0.989467**
ExtraTreesClassifier	**1.000000**	**0.979592**	**0.989467**
GradientBoostingClassifier	0.856602	0.795918	0.808693
KNeighborsClassifier	0.671202	0.673469	0.668267
LinearSVC	0.958503	0.938776	0.946707
LogisticRegression	0.859837	0.857143	0.854516
LogisticRegressionCV	0.738157	0.755102	0.734680
MLPClassifier	**1.000000**	**0.979592**	**0.989467**
NearestCentroid	0.684864	0.551020	0.602253
PassiveAggressiveClassifier	**1.000000**	**0.979592**	**0.989467**
Perceptron	0.983673	0.959184	0.969161
RandomForestClassifier	**1.000000**	**0.979592**	**0.989467**
RidgeClassifier	0.941409	0.918367	0.926085
SGDClassifier	0.958503	0.938776	0.946707
SVC	0.834969	0.836735	0.831855

Table 7. Macro Metrics of Classification Models ("Restaurants", TF-IDF representations).

Model	Precision (Macro)	Recall (Macro)	F1 (Macro)
AdaBoostClassifier	0.798309	0.413617	0.416818
BaggingClassifier	0.995169	0.981481	0.988043
BernoulliNB	0.828750	0.613617	0.672518
CalibratedClassifierCV	0.912913	0.791394	0.836613
DecisionTreeClassifier	**1.000000**	**1.000000**	**1.000000**
DummyClassifier	0.236111	0.333333	0.276423
ExtraTreeClassifier	**1.000000**	**1.000000**	**1.000000**
ExtraTreesClassifier	**1.000000**	**1.000000**	**1.000000**
GradientBoostingClassifier	0.936508	0.600000	0.674314
KNeighborsClassifier	0.724537	0.674292	0.696110
LinearSVC	0.924901	0.919826	0.920608
LogisticRegression	0.866234	0.702505	0.756657
LogisticRegressionCV	0.873585	0.819826	0.843531
MLPClassifier	**1.000000**	**1.000000**	**1.000000**
NearestCentroid	0.482186	0.450817	0.445678
PassiveAggressiveClassifier	0.930936	0.839542	0.879074
Perceptron	0.688576	0.700980	0.689108
RandomForestClassifier	**1.000000**	**1.000000**	**1.000000**
RidgeClassifier	0.924984	0.824728	0.865804
SGDClassifier	0.924901	0.919826	0.920608
SVC	0.933455	0.707407	0.771812

Finally, we summarize the classification results of the "MTSC" data set using TF-IDF text representations in Tables 9 and 10. Both macro-averaged and weighted results are presented.

Table 9 shows different results from the previous two data sets. BernoulliNB has the highest F1 measure of 61%. Table 10 also reveals that BernoulliNB is the best model with an F1 measure of 62.6%. This indicates that it is more challenging to differentiate classes in the "MTSC" data set than in the "Restaurants" and "Laptops" corpora. Table 1 reveals that sentences in this data set are longer and the text is from newspapers instead of reviews. The sentiment vocabulary is likely to be more subtle and less direct than in the case of the other two data sets. This raises the question of how to incorporate semantics into the models. In this experiment, we used TF-IDF, which does not capture the semantics intrinsically. Therefore, using BERT to represent the text may be a solution or may at least improve the results. This is what we will explore in the next section.

Table 8. Weighted Metrics of Classification Models ("Restaurants", TF-IDF representations).

Model	Precision (Weighted)	Recall (Weighted)	F1 (Weighted)
AdaBoostClassifier	0.772796	0.729167	0.645017
BaggingClassifier	0.989734	0.989583	0.989473
BernoulliNB	0.834485	0.833333	0.810978
CalibratedClassifierCV	0.915634	0.916667	0.910002
DecisionTreeClassifier	**1.000000**	**1.000000**	**1.000000**
DummyClassifier	0.501736	0.708333	0.587398
ExtraTreeClassifier	**1.000000**	**1.000000**	**1.000000**
ExtraTreesClassifier	**1.000000**	**1.000000**	**1.000000**
GradientBoostingClassifier	0.865079	0.833333	0.806849
KNeighborsClassifier	0.803964	0.812500	0.806575
LinearSVC	0.950264	0.947917	0.948238
LogisticRegression	0.873782	0.875000	0.862497
LogisticRegressionCV	0.913046	0.916667	0.913535
MLPClassifier	**1.000000**	**1.000000**	**1.000000**
NearestCentroid	0.824674	0.562500	0.650863
PassiveAggressiveClassifier	0.928760	0.927083	0.924641
Perceptron	0.965389	0.947917	0.953627
RandomForestClassifier	**1.000000**	**1.000000**	**1.000000**
RidgeClassifier	0.926900	0.927083	0.923168
SGDClassifier	0.950264	0.947917	0.948238
SVC	0.895795	0.885417	0.871685

Table 9. Macro Metrics of Classification Models ("MTSC", TF-IDF representations).

Model	Precision (Macro)	Recall (Macro)	F1 (Macro)
AdaBoostClassifier	0.536569	0.511031	0.511124
BaggingClassifier	0.546274	0.539847	0.542036
BernoulliNB	**0.620338**	**0.609301**	**0.613077**
CalibratedClassifierCV	0.598696	0.590106	0.591621
DecisionTreeClassifier	0.483979	0.483880	0.482779
DummyClassifier	0.124782	0.333333	0.181587
ExtraTreeClassifier	0.449816	0.446374	0.446124
ExtraTreesClassifier	0.610337	0.597893	0.601791
GradientBoostingClassifier	0.584919	0.547793	0.550139
KNeighborsClassifier	0.483402	0.473172	0.474578
LinearSVC	0.589215	0.584575	0.586015
LogisticRegression	0.605643	0.594484	0.597691
LogisticRegressionCV	0.609529	0.602939	0.605218
MLPClassifier	0.539425	0.537760	0.538246
NearestCentroid	0.480083	0.437883	0.416298
PassiveAggressiveClassifier	0.562594	0.558242	0.559689
Perceptron	0.569177	0.551341	0.554123
RandomForestClassifier	0.582065	0.564524	0.567516
RidgeClassifier	0.602595	0.597642	0.599191
SGDClassifier	0.599942	0.602576	0.600953
SVC	0.578846	0.562540	0.565638

Table 10. Weighted Metrics of Classification Models ("MTSC", TF-IDF representations).

Model	Precision (Weighted)	Recall (Weighted)	F1 (Weighted)
AdaBoostClassifier	0.544459	0.537522	0.527558
BaggingClassifier	0.556988	0.560209	0.557818
BernoulliNB	**0.626705**	**0.629145**	**0.626609**
CalibratedClassifierCV	0.610622	0.615183	0.610546
DecisionTreeClassifier	0.497215	0.496510	0.495555
DummyClassifier	0.140135	0.374346	0.203929
ExtraTreeClassifier	0.463308	0.465969	0.462460
ExtraTreesClassifier	0.617598	0.620419	0.617156
GradientBoostingClassifier	0.586393	0.586387	0.573521
KNeighborsClassifier	0.494559	0.500000	0.494082
LinearSVC	0.602032	0.605585	0.603095

Table 10. *Cont.*

Model	Precision (Weighted)	Recall (Weighted)	F1 (Weighted)
LogisticRegression	0.614704	0.618674	0.614889
LogisticRegressionCV	0.621267	0.624782	0.622249
MLPClassifier	0.554007	0.556719	0.555062
NearestCentroid	0.500953	0.457243	0.430506
PassiveAggressiveClassifier	0.575761	0.579407	0.577021
Perceptron	0.578566	0.583770	0.576333
RandomForestClassifier	0.590895	0.595986	0.588793
RidgeClassifier	0.615804	0.619546	0.616933
SGDClassifier	0.617770	0.615183	0.616206
SVC	0.587705	0.592496	0.586000

6.2. Classification Results with BERT Representations

As in Section 6.1, we present here the classification results, macro-averaged and weighted, for the three data sets. The difference is that the text representations are based on BERT instead of TF-IDF.

Tables 11 and 12 present the classification results for the "Laptops" data set, with BERT text representations.

Eleven out of twenty-one models showed an increase (and even a great increase for some) in results when using BERT, compared to TF-IDF. Four models stayed the same, while six models (`BernoulliNB`, `CalibratedClassifierCV`, `BaggingClassifier`, `DecisionTreeClassifier`, `Perceptron`, and `PassiveAgressiveClassifier`) experienced a decrease. These models did not take into account the new representation or the semantic dimension. The best model was `MLPClassifier`, with an F1 measure of 98%. This result was 7 points higher than the best result previously observed. On the other hand, results presented in Table 12 showed the same maximum as with TF-IDF, but for different models and only for four of them.

Next, Tables 13 and 14 summarize the classification results with BERT text representations for the "Restaurants" data set.

TF-IDF already gave excellent results. Four of the models that achieved the best score with TF-IDF kept this score when using BERT-based representation. `BaggingClassifier` improved and got the highest score, while `MLPClassifier` decreased slightly. Surprisingly, most models saw a decrease in F1 measures. Twelve models dropped, four increased, and five stayed the same. The models that stayed the same were the decision tree-based models and the `DummyClassifier`, whose performance was unaffected by the textual representation. The high performance of TF-IDF compared to a more complex representation of the text using BERT may explain this drop. The relative simplicity of the sentences in the corpus means a complex representation of the text is not necessary for classification. This experiment suggests a hypothesis that can be tested further: a sentence can be considered difficult if it requires a complex representation incorporating semantics. Can we then construct an indicator of difficulty on this basis? We believe that a selective model can be trained to determine sentence difficulty. When a sentence is deemed difficult, its text can be represented using a complex model such as BERT instead of TF-IDF. This increases the likelihood of accurately classifying the polarity. The benefit of this approach is improved efficiency. Simple sentences can be processed quickly, while complex, time-, and resource-consuming text representation is reserved for difficult sentences.

Finally, the classification results on the "MTSC" data set, based on BERT text representation, are shown in Tables 15 and 16, macro-averaged, and weighted, respectively.

Table 11. Macro Metrics of Classification Models ("Laptops", BERT representations).

Model	Precision (Macro)	Recall (Macro)	F1 (Macro)
AdaBoostClassifier	0.811111	0.597701	0.628514
BaggingClassifier	0.750000	0.734375	0.741935
BernoulliNB	0.579808	0.550647	0.563304
CalibratedClassifierCV	0.956944	0.884339	0.914598
DecisionTreeClassifier	0.741667	0.718750	0.729096
DummyClassifier	0.197279	0.333333	0.247863
ExtraTreeClassifier	0.750000	0.734375	0.741935
ExtraTreesClassifier	0.750000	0.734375	0.741935
GradientBoostingClassifier	0.741667	0.671875	0.701984
KNeighborsClassifier	0.707283	0.713362	0.709995
LinearSVC	0.967672	0.967672	0.967672
LogisticRegression	0.915535	0.738506	0.794381
LogisticRegressionCV	0.866071	0.778017	0.814312
MLPClassifier	**0.988889**	**0.979167**	**0.983598**
NearestCentroid	0.443548	0.394397	0.414286
PassiveAggressiveClassifier	0.752381	0.729167	0.686800
Perceptron	0.703680	0.808190	0.705096
RandomForestClassifier	0.750000	0.734375	0.741935
RidgeClassifier	0.915323	0.768678	0.813889
SGDClassifier	0.700893	0.692888	0.696820
SVC	0.840404	0.611351	0.649462

Table 12. Weighted Metrics of Classification Models ("Laptops", BERT representations).

Model	Precision (Weighted)	Recall (Weighted)	F1 (Weighted)
AdaBoostClassifier	0.753061	0.734694	0.724577
BaggingClassifier	**1.000000**	**0.979592**	**0.989467**
BernoulliNB	0.785871	0.755102	0.767912
CalibratedClassifierCV	0.940136	0.938776	0.937837
DecisionTreeClassifier	0.980272	0.959184	0.968200
DummyClassifier	0.350271	0.591837	0.440084
ExtraTreeClassifier	**1.000000**	**0.979592**	**0.989467**
ExtraTreesClassifier	**1.000000**	**0.979592**	**0.989467**
GradientBoostingClassifier	0.980272	0.959184	0.967774
KNeighborsClassifier	0.797805	0.795918	0.796472
LinearSVC	0.959184	0.959184	0.959184
LogisticRegression	0.870440	0.857143	0.850731
LogisticRegressionCV	0.819060	0.816327	0.813943
MLPClassifier	0.980272	**0.979592**	0.979436
NearestCentroid	0.703094	0.673469	0.683382
PassiveAggressiveClassifier	0.851895	0.795918	0.779637
Perceptron	0.828240	0.775510	0.783489
RandomForestClassifier	**1.000000**	**0.979592**	**0.989467**
RidgeClassifier	0.882818	0.877551	0.872789
SGDClassifier	0.916910	0.897959	0.907268
SVC	0.787384	0.775510	0.760764

We can observe from Table 15 that, in the case of "MTSC", only `BernouilliNB` and `ExtraTreeClassifier` have lower performances when using BERT representations compared to TF-IDF. This indicates that the semantics in the textual representation significantly enhance the model's performance. The longer sentences and more subtle expressions of sentiment in the data set require additional knowledge to better comprehend the sentences to classify. This confirms our earlier hypothesis, namely that in order to better classify sentiment polarity in the case of difficult sentences, a more complex text representation would be better suited. The same trends can be seen in Table 16. The best-performing model is `LogisticegressionCV`, with an F1 measure of 70.8%.

Table 13. Macro Metrics of Classification Models ("Restaurants", BERT representations).

Model	Precision (Macro)	Recall (Macro)	F1 (Macro)
AdaBoostClassifier	0.537594	0.456618	0.486397
BaggingClassifier	**1.000000**	**1.000000**	**1.000000**
BernoulliNB	0.512220	0.512418	0.508235
CalibratedClassifierCV	0.909456	0.585185	0.641217
DecisionTreeClassifier	**1.000000**	**1.000000**	**1.000000**
DummyClassifier	0.236111	0.333333	0.276423
ExtraTreeClassifier	**1.000000**	**1.000000**	**1.000000**
ExtraTreesClassifier	**1.000000**	**1.000000**	**1.000000**
GradientBoostingClassifier	0.968889	0.811111	0.870047
KNeighborsClassifier	0.718704	0.645861	0.674860
LinearSVC	0.926190	0.640741	0.688251
LogisticRegression	0.891105	0.598802	0.647447
LogisticRegressionCV	0.903175	0.566667	0.623642
MLPClassifier	0.923077	0.985294	0.949003
NearestCentroid	0.512138	0.395915	0.425557
PassiveAggressiveClassifier	0.879584	0.511111	0.563584
Perceptron	0.727431	0.720153	0.716450
RandomForestClassifier	**1.000000**	**1.000000**	**1.000000**
RidgeClassifier	0.918724	0.637037	0.702541
SGDClassifier	0.780556	0.529630	0.578348
SVC	0.900000	0.533333	0.571188

Table 14. Weighted Metrics of Classification Models ("Restaurants", BERT representations).

Model	Precision (Weighted)	Recall (Weighted)	F1 (Weighted)
AdaBoostClassifier	0.787320	0.791667	0.781311
BaggingClassifier	**1.000000**	**1.000000**	**1.000000**
BernoulliNB	0.778746	0.739583	0.756588
CalibratedClassifierCV	0.854942	0.833333	0.802002
DecisionTreeClassifier	**1.000000**	**1.000000**	**1.000000**
DummyClassifier	0.501736	0.708333	0.587398
ExtraTreeClassifier	**1.000000**	**1.000000**	**1.000000**
ExtraTreesClassifier	**1.000000**	**1.000000**	**1.000000**
GradientBoostingClassifier	0.933889	0.927083	0.922239
KNeighborsClassifier	0.800064	0.812500	0.802541
LinearSVC	0.880357	0.864583	0.837967
LogisticRegression	0.848726	0.833333	0.804811
LogisticRegressionCV	0.846329	0.822917	0.789030
MLPClassifier	0.975962	0.968750	0.970436
NearestCentroid	0.800187	0.614583	0.682193
PassiveAggressiveClassifier	0.818521	0.791667	0.746228
Perceptron	0.810547	0.791667	0.797258
RandomForestClassifier	**1.000000**	**1.000000**	**1.000000**
RidgeClassifier	0.870692	0.854167	0.832109
SGDClassifier	0.800174	0.802083	0.762642
SVC	0.839583	0.812500	0.769105

Table 15. Macro Metrics of Classification Models ("MTSC", BERT representations).

Model	Precision (Macro)	Recall (Macro)	F1 (Macro)
AdaBoostClassifier	0.617579	0.607600	0.611387
BaggingClassifier	0.583002	0.570900	0.574723
BernoulliNB	0.594007	0.599098	0.594284
CalibratedClassifierCV	0.717618	0.697904	0.704669
DecisionTreeClassifier	0.502683	0.506414	0.503590
DummyClassifier	0.124782	0.333333	0.181587
ExtraTreeClassifier	0.420560	0.422548	0.420626
ExtraTreesClassifier	0.652450	0.637024	0.641867
GradientBoostingClassifier	0.674504	0.659606	0.664726
KNeighborsClassifier	0.575093	0.552326	0.554446

Table 15. *Cont.*

Model	Precision (Macro)	Recall (Macro)	F1 (Macro)
LinearSVC	0.706773	0.694961	0.699503
LogisticRegression	0.719955	**0.700226**	0.707067
LogisticRegressionCV	**0.726826**	0.700067	**0.708159**
MLPClassifier	0.692743	0.686242	0.688107
NearestCentroid	0.574224	0.574224	0.574224
PassiveAggressiveClassifier	0.657355	0.629713	0.582214
Perceptron	0.630884	0.547369	0.446289
RandomForestClassifier	0.670888	0.659953	0.663928
RidgeClassifier	0.710743	0.692509	0.698889
SGDClassifier	0.687735	0.672053	0.659408
SVC	0.720193	0.690442	0.698967

Table 16. Weighted Metrics of Classification Models ("MTSC", BERT representations).

Model	Precision (Weighted)	Recall (Weighted)	F1 (Weighted)
AdaBoostClassifier	0.619690	0.620419	0.619124
BaggingClassifier	0.587681	0.589878	0.587083
BernoulliNB	0.607692	0.602094	0.602517
CalibratedClassifierCV	0.718311	0.718150	0.715857
DecisionTreeClassifier	0.518598	0.513089	0.515090
DummyClassifier	0.140135	0.374346	0.203929
ExtraTreeClassifier	0.437334	0.431065	0.433455
ExtraTreesClassifier	0.654367	0.655323	0.652600
GradientBoostingClassifier	0.678232	0.679756	0.677239
KNeighborsClassifier	0.578520	0.575916	0.568944
LinearSVC	0.710757	0.710297	0.709302
LogisticRegression	0.720905	0.719895	0.717951
LogisticRegressionCV	**0.726504**	**0.724258**	**0.721086**
MLPClassifier	0.696425	0.696335	0.694988
NearestCentroid	0.579407	0.579407	0.579407
PassiveAggressiveClassifier	0.674502	0.608202	0.570665
Perceptron	0.648515	0.521815	0.417314
RandomForestClassifier	0.676899	0.678883	0.676761
RidgeClassifier	0.712000	0.712042	0.709899
SGDClassifier	0.698238	0.672775	0.661620
SVC	0.717385	0.715532	0.711701

6.3. Fine-Tuned BERT

Fine-tuned BERT models have become popular in natural language processing for their capacity to improve performance on various text classification tasks. BERT, which is pre-trained on a large corpus of unlabeled text data, provides a strong base for language comprehension. The fine-tuning process involves training the model on domain-specific labeled data to make it suitable for the target task. A basic illustration of the sentence processing pipeline based on fine-tuned BERT is depicted in Figure 7. By changing the model's parameters, it learns task-specific patterns and increases its predictive accuracy. This fine-tuning approach has been successful in achieving the best results in sentiment analysis [65], named entity recognition [66], and other classification tasks.

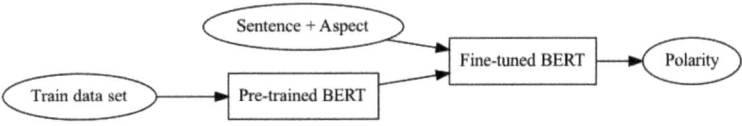

Figure 7. Sentence processing pipeline based on fine-tuned BERT.

We fine-tuned three BERT models, one for each data set, using `BertTokenizer` and `BertForSequenceClassification` (https://huggingface.co/docs/transformers/model_d

oc/bert (accessed on 10 October 2023)) from the `transformers` python module (https://github.com/huggingface/transformers (accessed on 10 October 2023)), starting from the `bert-base-uncased` pre-trained model. We tried the distilled model as well, but the results were very low. We trained the models for three epochs with a batch size of 8, using the default parameters (Adam optimizer, padding, truncation, and a learning rate of 10^{-5}).

We emphasize that we used the default parameter settings for all models and representations. Our goal is to gain a better understanding of the difficulty in aspect-based sentiment analysis, not to introduce a new model or enhance existing results.

Tables 17–19 show the classification report results of the fine-tuned BERT on the "Laptops", "Restaurants", and "MTSC" data sets, respectively.

Comparing with previous experiments, fine-tuned BERT is better than TF-IDF for any model in the "Laptops" data set for the same reasons mentioned in the comparison between BERT and TF-IDF. We observe the same behavior in the "Restaurants" data set, where the use of BERT does not improve the results. However, the improvement is greater in the "MTSC" data set. Here, using the fine-tuned BERT model is even better than just using BERT as a textual representation. This improvement shows that the model takes advantage of the semantics embedded in the BERT model and also benefits from the adaptation of BERT to the "MTSC" data set, particularly the adaptation to the numerous named entities present in the "MTSC" data set.

Table 17. Classification report for fine-tuned BERT ("Laptops").

Model	Precision	Recall	F1-Score	Support
negative	0.97	0.97	0.97	29
neutral	1.00	0.88	0.93	16
positive	0.67	1.00	0.80	4
conflict	0.00	0.00	0.00	0
Accuracy	-	-	0.94	49
Weighted Avg	0.88	0.95	0.90	49
Macro Avg	0.95	0.94	0.94	49

Table 18. Classification report for fine-tuned BERT ("Restaurants").

Model	Precision	Recall	F1-Score	Support
negative	0.89	0.99	0.94	68
neutral	1.00	0.50	0.67	18
positive	0.64	0.70	0.67	10
conflict	0.00	0.00	0.00	0
Accuracy	-	-	0.86	96
Weighted Avg	0.63	0.55	0.57	96
Macro Avg	0.89	0.86	0.86	96

Table 19. Classification report for fine-tuned BERT ("MTSC").

Model	Precision	Recall	F1-Score	Support
negative	0.57	0.79	0.66	262
neutral	0.93	0.68	0.79	429
positive	0.72	0.75	0.73	455
Accuracy	-	-	0.73	1146
Weighted Avg	0.74	0.74	0.73	1146
Macro Avg	0.77	0.73	0.74	1146

6.4. Ensemble Learning to Improve Performance

Ensemble learning is a machine learning technique that boosts prediction accuracy and robustness. It combines the outputs of multiple models to make collective predictions, leading to a more reliable result. Bagging, boosting, and stacking are popular ensemble methods. This approach leverages the diversity of models, reducing biases and variances, and improving overall model performance. It has been effective in various domains, such as classification, regression, and anomaly detection, resulting in significant advancements [67–69].

We used ensemble learning (majority vote) for the three collections with both TF-IDF and BERT text representations. We employed two strategies: one that included all the classification models, and the other that only included the top 5 models with the highest accuracy.

6.4.1. Majority Vote for TF-IDF

Table 20 shows the majority vote classification report for the "Laptops" data set. Table 21 lists the top 5 models based on accuracy. Table 22 displays the classification report for these 5 models. In this scenario, we do not see any advantage in using a combination of classifiers. The top classifiers have a very low error rate, and the error stays the same for all classifiers. Because the outcomes are not diverse enough, the ensemble of classifiers has the same error as the individual classifiers.

Table 20. Classification Report for Majority Vote ("Laptops", TF-IDF representations, all models).

Model	Precision	Recall	F1-Score	Support
conflict	0.00	0.00	0.00	0
negative	1.00	0.88	0.93	16
neutral	1.00	1.00	1.00	4
positive	0.97	1.00	0.98	29
Accuracy	-	-	0.96	49
Weighted Avg	0.98	0.96	0.97	49
Macro Avg	0.74	0.72	0.73	49

Table 21. Top five models with respect to accuracy ("Laptops", TF-IDF representations).

Model	Accuracy
DecisionTreeClassifier	0.9796
ExtraTreeClassifier	0.9796
ExtraTreesClassifier	0.9796
MLPClassifier	0.9796
PassiveAggressiveClassifier	0.9796

Table 22. Classification report for majority vote ("Laptops", TF-IDF representations, top five models).

Model	Precision	Recall	F1-Score	Support
conflict	0.00	0.00	0.00	0
negative	1.00	0.94	0.97	16
neutral	1.00	1.00	1.00	4
positive	1.00	1.00	1.00	29
Accuracy	-	-	0.98	49
Weighted Avg	1.00	0.98	0.99	49
Macro Avg	0.75	0.73	0.74	49

Similarly, Tables 23–25, referring to the "Restaurants" data set, present the classification report for all the models, the top 5 models, and the classification report for the top 5 models, respectively.

A perfect score is achieved by the top classifiers on the restaurant corpus. The overall accuracy drops when all the classifiers are combined by majority vote, as the best ones are outnumbered by the rest. However, when only the five best classifiers are chosen, the resulting classifiers are flawless.

Table 23. Classification Report for Majority Vote ("Restaurants", TF-IDF representations, all models).

Model	Precision	Recall	F1-Score	Support
negative	1.00	0.89	0.94	18
neutral	1.00	0.90	0.95	10
positive	0.96	1.00	0.98	68
Accuracy	-	-	0.97	96
Weighted Avg	0.97	0.97	0.97	96
Macro Avg	0.99	0.93	0.96	96

Table 24. Top five models with respect to accuracy ("Restaurants", TF-IDF representations).

Model	Accuracy
DecisionTreeClassifier	1.0000
ExtraTreeClassifier	1.0000
ExtraTreesClassifier	1.0000
MLPClassifier	1.0000
RandomForestClassifier	1.0000

Table 25. Classification report for majority vote ("Restaurants", TF-IDF representations, top 5 models).

Model	Precision	Recall	F1-Score	Support
negative	1.00	1.00	1.00	18
neutral	1.00	1.00	1.00	10
positive	1.00	1.00	1.00	68
Accuracy	-	-	1.00	96
Weighted Avg	1.00	1.00	1.00	96
Macro Avg	1.00	1.00	1.00	96

Finally, Tables 26–28 present the classification report for all the models, the top five models, and the classification report for the top five models, respectively, for the "MTSC" data set.

The "MTSC" data set presents more challenges, resulting in diverse outcomes for the models. Therefore, using an ensemble of classifiers is more appropriate compared to the "Restaurants" and "Laptops" data sets. However, using all 21 classifiers leads to a small decrease in results (around 1 point in F1 measure). On the other hand, using the top five models as an ensemble improves accuracy and maintains the F1 measure. The results from these five classifiers do not differ significantly to make a notable impact on the overall outcome.

Table 26. Classification Report for Majority Vote ("MTSC", TF-IDF representations, all models).

Model	Precision	Recall	F1-Score	Support
negative	0.64	0.67	0.66	429
neutral	0.62	0.69	0.65	455
positive	0.59	0.43	0.50	262
Accuracy	-	-	0.62	1146
Weighted Avg	0.62	0.62	0.62	1146
Macro Avg	0.62	0.60	0.60	1146

Table 27. Top five models with respect to accuracy ("MTSC", TF-IDF representations).

Model	Accuracy
BernoulliNB	0.6291
LogisticRegressionCV	0.6248
ExtraTreesClassifier	0.6204
RidgeClassifier	0.6195
LogisticRegression	0.6187

Table 28. Classification Report for Majority Vote ("MTSC", TF-IDF representations, top 5 models).

Model	Precision	Recall	F1-Score	Support
negative	0.65	0.70	0.67	429
neutral	0.64	0.66	0.65	455
positive	0.56	0.45	0.50	262
Accuracy	-	-	0.63	1146
Weighted Avg	0.62	0.63	0.62	1146
Macro Avg	0.61	0.60	0.61	1146

6.4.2. Majority Vote for BERT

Similarly to the TF-IDF text representations, Tables 29–31 display the results for the "Laptops" data set. Tables 32–34 show the results for the "Restaurants" data set. Lastly, Tables 35–37 present the results for the "MTSC" data set. These results include the classification report for all the models, the top 5 models based on accuracy, and the classification report for the majority vote of the top 5 models corresponding to each data set.

Table 29. Classification Report for Majority Vote ("Laptops", BERT representations, all models).

Model	Precision	Recall	F1-Score	Support
conflict	0.00	0.00	0.00	0
negative	1.00	0.81	0.90	16
neutral	1.00	0.75	0.86	4
positive	0.91	1.00	0.95	29
Accuracy	-	-	0.92	49
Weighted Avg	0.94	0.92	0.93	49
Macro Avg	0.73	0.64	0.68	49

Table 30. Top five models with respect to accuracy ("Laptops", BERT representations).

Model	Accuracy
ExtraTreesClassifier	0.9796
RandomForestClassifier	0.9796
DecisionTreeClassifier	0.9592
ExtraTreeClassifier	0.9592
GradientBoostingClassifier	0.9592

Table 31. Classification Report for Majority Vote ("Laptops", BERT representations, top five models).

Model	Precision	Recall	F1-Score	Support
conflict	0.00	0.00	0.00	0
negative	1.00	0.94	0.97	16
neutral	1.00	1.00	1.00	4
positive	1.00	1.00	1.00	29
Accuracy	-	-	0.98	49
Weighted Avg	1.00	0.98	0.99	49
Macro Avg	0.75	0.73	0.74	49

The sentiment analysis task for the "Laptops" data set is relatively simple. This task produces similar results across different models. Therefore, using majority voting with TF-IDF does not improve performance. It does not matter if all the models are used or if only the top five are used.

The majority vote method, using either all the models or the top five models, did not improve the performance of the BERT-based text representation models on the "Restaurants" data set, as it did not on the "Laptops" data set.

Table 32. Classification Report for Majority Vote ("Restaurants", BERT representations, all models).

Model	Precision	Recall	F1-Score	Support
negative	0.92	0.61	0.73	18
neutral	1.00	0.30	0.46	10
positive	0.84	1.00	0.91	68
Accuracy	-	-	0.85	96
Weighted Avg	0.87	0.85	0.83	96
Macro Avg	0.92	0.64	0.70	96

Table 33. Top five models with respect to accuracy ("Restaurants", BERT representations).

Model	Accuracy
BaggingClassifier	1.0000
DecisionTreeClassifier	1.0000
ExtraTreeClassifier	1.0000
ExtraTreesClassifier	1.0000
RandomForestClassifier	1.0000

Table 34. Classification Report for Majority Vote ("Restaurants", BERT representations, top five models).

Model	Precision	Recall	F1-Score	Support
negative	1.00	1.00	1.00	18
neutral	1.00	1.00	1.00	10
positive	1.00	1.00	1.00	68
Accuracy	-	-	1.00	96
Weighted Avg	1.00	1.00	1.00	96
Macro Avg	1.00	1.00	1.00	96

Table 35. Classification Report for Majority Vote ("MTSC", BERT representations, all models).

Model	Precision	Recall	F1-Score	Support
negative	0.71	0.84	0.77	429
neutral	0.75	0.70	0.73	455
positive	0.71	0.58	0.64	262
Accuracy	-	-	0.73	1146
Weighted Avg	0.73	0.73	0.72	1146
Macro Avg	0.72	0.71	0.71	1146

Table 36. Top five models with respect to accuracy ("MTSC", BERT representations).

Model	Accuracy
LogisticRegressionCV	0.7243
LogisticRegression	0.7199
CalibratedClassifierCV	0.7182
SVC	0.7155
RidgeClassifier	0.7120

Table 37. Classification Report for Majority Vote ("MTSC", BERT representations, top five models).

Model	Precision	Recall	F1-Score	Support
negative	0.76	0.77	0.76	429
neutral	0.70	0.79	0.75	455
positive	0.73	0.57	0.64	262
Accuracy	-	-	0.73	1146
Weighted Avg	0.73	0.73	0.73	1146
Macro Avg	0.73	0.71	0.72	1146

When we apply the majority vote to the models on the "MTSC" data set, we can improve performance. This is true whether we use all models or just the top five. It shows that using text representations that are aware of meaning and having diverse model outputs can lead to better results. We can make the task easier by using representations that have semantic information and by combining multiple classifiers.

7. Sentence Difficulty Definition and Prediction

In this section, we first define the difficulty using two strategies. Following that, we attempt to predict difficult sentences automatically using our data sets. We also present two sampling strategies for the classification models. Additionally, we analyze difficult sentences qualitatively and evaluate the outcomes of our difficulty predictions.

7.1. Defining Difficulty

Correctly predicting difficult sentences in the context of aspect-based sentiment analysis can lead to effective selective approaches. We can leave the easy sentences for light models that do not require much computation, and submit the difficult sentences to heavy, complex models. This way, we can achieve a balance between efficiency and effectiveness.

We propose two strategies to define the difficulty classes:

- **Binary classification.** For this strategy, we conducted an analysis of the incorrect predictions across all data sets. To do this, we investigated the majority votes produced by the top five classifiers using both TF-IDF and BERT text representations for each data set. We identified the sentences that were incorrectly classified by both text representations as 'difficult'. For instance, a sentence is assigned to the difficult class if it is wrongly classified by the majority votes of both the BERT and TF-IDF models; otherwise, it is assigned to the easy class. In terms of exact numbers, on the test sets, we found one such difficult sentence in the "Laptops" data set, none in the "Restaurants" data set, and 197 in the "MTSC" data set.
- **Fine-grained (multi-class) classification.** For this strategy, we established several levels of difficulty, taking into account the number of correct classifications made by each of the top 5 performing models, while considering both text representations. For instance, the most difficult sentences are those of level 0, since no top 5 classifier was able to correctly classify it. On the other hand, the easiest sentences are those of level 5, for which all the top 5 classifiers had the correct polarity. Since "MTSC" was the most difficult data set, we focused this strategy only on this data set. The most represented classes for BERT are level 5, with 693 and level 0, with 217 sentences, respectively. The remaining 236 sentences are relatively evenly distributed among the four remaining classes.

One can easily notice that both strategies yield unbalanced test data, in terms of class membership. Figure 8 depicts this lack of balance. This leads us to consider two types of sampling, the default one, without any class balancing, and the SMOTE sampling [70], an oversampling technique where the synthetic samples are generated for the minority class.

To begin our analysis, we first focus on qualitative aspects, and then we analyse the difficulty prediction performance.

7.2. Qualitative Analysis of Difficult Sentences in the Chosen Data Sets

We examined the sentences that were incorrectly classified, with respect to the binary strategy. In the "Laptops" data set, there is only one such sentence. This sentences is: "But see the macbook pro is different because it may have a huge price tag but it comes with the full software that you would actually need and most of it has free future updates", its aspect is "price tag", and the polarity is "negative". We have tried ChatGPT to predict the polarity of this sentence and it yielded "positive". The term "huge" usually has a positive connotation. However, when it is used with "price tag", it becomes negative. This is because "huge" is a specialized vocabulary used to describe prices, and thus has a negative connotation. This example demonstrates that when specialized terms are the same as everyday language, it can make understanding more challenging.

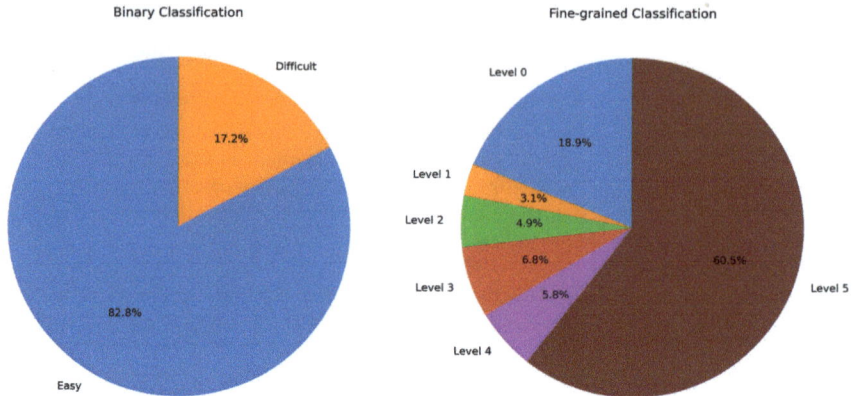

Figure 8. Class repartition for the binary strategy and for the BERT fine-grained strategy, respectively.

The "Restaurants" data set contains no difficult sentences. However, the "MTSC" data set has 197 difficult sentences. In order to observe the behavior of very large language models on the most difficult sentences, we chose six of them to analyze and predict their sentiment using ChatGPT. The sentences and predictions are summarized in Table 38.

We can observe that two of the six ChatGPT predictions are incorrect. The sentence "His persona is generally adult" is difficult to classify as "positive" even for a human annotator, due to the implicit reference "his". Similarly, the last sentence about "President Muhamadu Buhari" appears to be quite neutral.

7.3. Difficulty Prediction Results for MTSC

For both binary and fine-grained classification strategies, with or without SMOTE sampling, we used the test data from MTSC and applied 10-fold cross-validation (https://scikit-learn.org/stable/modules/generated/sklearn.model_selection.cross_val_score.html (accessed on 10 October 2023)) to make sure every observation passed as test data. We employed the same 21 classifiers as we did for the previous experiments. As well, both BERT and TF-IDF text representations are considered. To summarize, there are 21 classifiers, two class definition strategies, two text representations, and two sampling strategies. The mean cross-validation scores are depicted in Figures 9 and 10, by the binary classification strategy and by the fine-grained strategy, respectively.

We noticed that the best performing model in all the cases was the DummyClassifier and we first hypothesized that this occurs because it predicts everything towards the majority class. However, even with SMOTE oversampling, the situation does not change in terms of the best performing models.

For the fine-grained strategy, the performance is significantly lower than for the binary strategy, in general. This is justifiable, since it is more difficult to classify with 6 classes than with 2 classes. BERT is better performing with the fine-grained strategy, while the performances with respect to the text representations are close in the case of the binary classification.

The SMOTE oversampling method allows a better evaluation of the quality of the classifiers for the proposed tasks. For instance, we noticed that the KNeighborsClassifier constantly drops in performance when SMOTE is applied.

Table 38. Selected sentences from the "MTSC" data set that were wrongly classified by the majority vote, with ChatGPT predicted polarities. The wrong predictions are in bold.

Sentence	Aspect	True Polarity	ChatGPT Polarity
In an atmosphere where some delegates remain anti-Trump and party leaders like Paul Ryan are barely mentioning Trump in their speeches, Hillary Clinton is a unifying force.	Hillary Clinton	positive	positive
A new presidential cabinet will be formed as well as a national reconciliation committee, which will include youth movements that have been behind anti-Morsi demonstrations.	Morsi	negative	negative
His persona is generally adult.	His	positive	**neutral**
The more left wing candidate for deputy leader—Julie Morgan, widow of former first minister of Wales, Rhodri—was defeated by Carolyn Harris at the party's spring conference.	Carolyn Harris	positive	positive
In a statement Saturday, London Moore, the president of the Theta Gamma chapter of Delta Delta Delta, condemned the "racist, offensive and disgraceful" behavior seen in the video.	London Moore, the president of the Theta Gamma chapter of Delta Delta Delta	positive	positive
President Muhammadu Buhari was poised to win a second term despite falling short on promises to recharge the economy and defeat the Boko Haram insurgents.	President Muhammadu Buhari	negative	**neutral**

Decision tree-based models, logistic regressions, and SVC are generally the best-performing models.

Even though the mean accuracy is high across the models for the binary classification strategy, we cannot conclude that this is a good approach for difficulty prediction, mainly due to the score of the `DummyClassifier`. This suggests that the models are hardly learning to classify difficulty. However, this launches the discussion about the task of predicting difficulty.

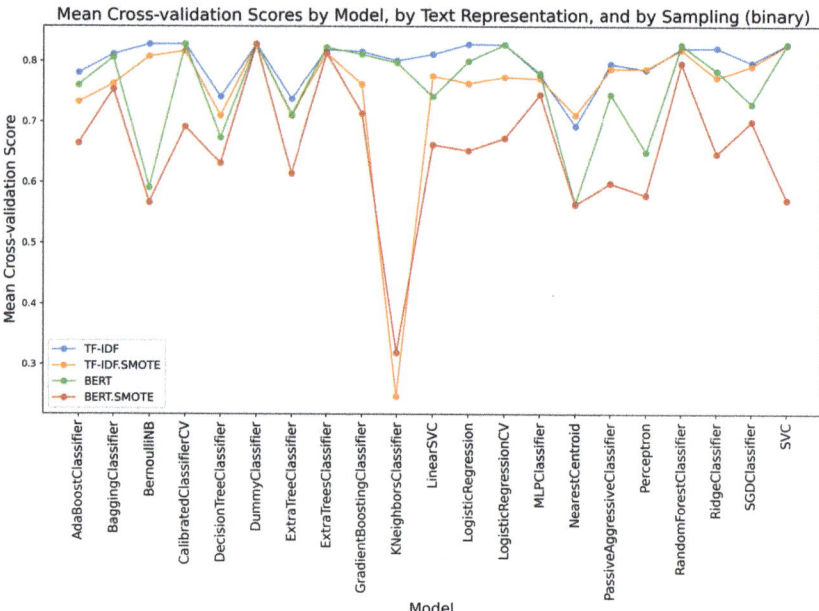

Figure 9. Mean cross-validation scores by model, by text representation, and by sampling, for difficulty prediction as binary classification.

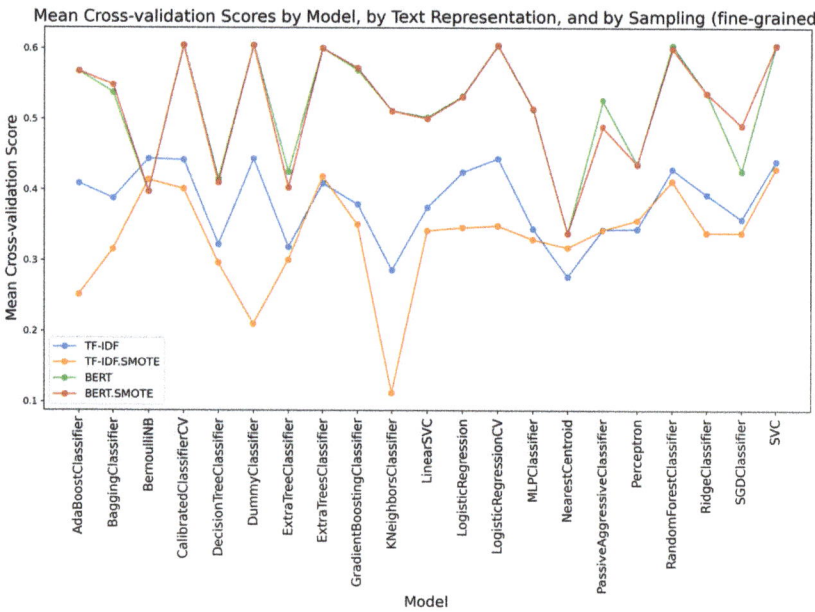

Figure 10. Mean cross-validation scores by model, by text representation, and by sampling, for difficulty prediction as multi-class, fine-grained classification.

8. Discussion

In this section, we address the research questions outlined in the introduction. We do this by examining the results of our experiments and analysis.

- **RQ1**: *How to define difficulty in aspect-based sentiment analysis?* This is not a straightforward question. If we extrapolate to the field of Information Retrieval, many studies on difficulty prediction focus on the correlation between the predicted and actual effectiveness, without requiring an exact definition of query difficulty [71]. We may struggle to assign the right sentiment to a sentence, regardless of the text format, the type of classifier, and so on. We suggest that the definition of "difficulty" could be context dependent and inherently, the quality of an eventual difficulty prediction depends on the criteria of the definition.
- **RQ2**: *Is difficulty data set dependent?* It appears to be. We have observed that on the "Laptops" and "Restaurants" data sets, there are few or no test sentences for which we fail to predict the polarity. However, this is not the case for the third data set, "MTSC". We believe that this takes place because the first two data sets are more specific to their domain than the third, which is from the wider news domain. We have noticed that the "MTSC" data set contains more named entities and implicit references, which may contribute to the difficulty level. Expressing subjectivity is less overt and more nuanced. We also note that some sentences from "MTSC" are challenging, even for human annotators. Moreover, "MTSC", the most recent data set is the most challenging. We hypothesize that this may correlate with the advances in terms of performance of aspect-based sentiment analysis models that require more challenging data sets to accurately quantify effectiveness.
- **RQ3**: *What is the impact of text representation on performance?* When we look at the classification results from Section 6, we can see that BERT, the most advanced text representation, usually performs better than TF-IDF. BERT captures more complex semantics than TF-IDF. Fine-tuning also appears to be beneficial. But we must be careful not to overfit and the fine-tuning process can be time-consuming. In conclusion, the choice of text representation method can affect performance. Choosing the right representation for a task depends on its difficulty. If the task is simple, selecting a complex representation may lead to a decrease in performance and an increase in IT costs.
- **RQ4**: *What is the impact of classification models on performance?* We observed a similar pattern for the classification models as for the text representation in **RQ3**. The selection of the classifier has a significant impact on the classification performance. Thus, we proposed ensemble learning and a variety of classification methods of different types. For instance, in the "MTSC" data set, we found the fine-tuned BERT model more effective than just BERT, indicating its advantage in leveraging embedded semantics, especially with the data set's numerous named entities. Moreover, BERT is generally better performing than TF-IDF, and the majority vote yields encouraging results.
- **RQ5**: *Are we able to predict difficulty?* We are far from being able to predict sentence difficulty, as indicated by the results in Section 7.3. Nevertheless, we have several ideas to enhance the prediction accuracy. Our initial attempts have started the discussion on this topic, but we do not claim to propose the best models for predicting sentence difficulty. We hope this work will stimulate the research community to pay more attention to this topic.
- **RQ6**: *How to better understand difficult sentences (qualitative analysis on difficult sentences)?* After looking at the difficult sentences that we identified, we noticed that the difficulty may be raised by several aspects, such as ambiguity, subjectivity, implicit references, and the presence of named entities. Some of the difficult sentences may be considered challenging even for human annotators, and the annotation process may be subject to subjectivity. For some difficult sentences, even advanced LLMs are not able to correctly identify the sentiment polarity.

9. Conclusions and Future Work

The goal of this paper is to better understand sentence difficulty in aspect-based sentiment analysis, and not to introduce new models or enhance current results. To our knowledge, this topic has never been formally discussed before. We conducted thorough experiments on three well-known aspect-based sentiment analysis data sets—"Laptops", "Restaurants" and "MTSC"—testing more than 20 classification models on two different textual representations: TF-IDF and BERT. In studying performance enhancement, we considered fine-tuned BERT representations and also applied ensemble learning (majority vote).

On the "MTSC" data set, using the fine-tuned BERT model is more effective than just using BERT as a textual representation. This shows that the model utilizes the semantics embedded in the BERT model and benefits from adapting BERT to the "MTSC" data set, particularly to the many named entities present in it. The "MTSC" data set presents further challenges, resulting in diverse outcomes for the models. Using an ensemble of classifiers is more suitable compared to the "Restaurants" and "Laptops" data sets. However, using all 21 classifiers results in a small decrease (around 1 point in F1 measure). However, utilizing the top five models as an ensemble improves accuracy and maintains the F1 measure. The performance results from these top five classifiers do not differ significantly, therefore their collective contribution does not notably influence the overall result.

By applying majority vote to the models on the "MTSC" data set, we can improve performance. This holds whether we use all models or just the top five best performing classifiers. It is clear that using text representations that have a sense of meaning combined with diverse model outputs can produce better results. We can simplify the task by using representations with semantic information and combining multiple classifiers.

Regarding the difficulty of aspect-based sentiment analysis, we identified the sentences as difficult which the classifiers did not judge correctly, implying a binary classification strategy. From this viewpoint, only one sentence was considered difficult in the "Laptops" corpus compared to 197 in the recent "MTSC" corpus, indicating that "MTSC" sentences are more challenging. A different strategy for defining difficulty would be more nuanced, considering six levels of difficulty regarding how many of the top five best performing classifiers can correctly identify sentiment polarity. For instance, level 0 means all five classifiers are wrong, while level 5 means all five were correct. In analyzing sentences identified as difficult, we conclude that defining difficulty in this aspect-based sentiment analysis context is not a straightforward task.

The classification difficulty seems to be reliant on the data set. The text representation and the classification model also influence performance. Implicit references, intricate semantics, ambiguity, and other factors make polarity classification difficult. For example, of the six sentences we analyzed qualitatively, two were very difficult, even for a human. The first contained an implicit reference and the second could have been classified as neutral by a human being. Lastly, we assert that predicting difficulty is not an easy task, but there are signs that it is feasible, at least partially.

As future work, we plan to extend our experiments to other data sets, perform domain adaptation to validate model robustness and verify data set biases, and aim to propose difficulty predictors that are correlated to classification performance, inspired by the works of Query Performance Prediction (QPP) in Information Retrieval. We also intend to propose and analyze various definitions of difficulty classes by adjusting the scale levels differently than our binary proposal, or finer than the 6 level scale, based on the top five majority vote.

Author Contributions: Conceptualization, A.-G.C. and S.F.; methodology, A.-G.C. and S.F.; investigation, S.F.; data curation, A.-G.C.; writing—original draft, A.-G.C. and S.F.; writing—review & editing, A.-G.C. and S.F.; visualization, A.-G.C.; funding acquisition, S.F. All authors have read and agreed to the published version of the manuscript.

Funding: This research received no external funding.

Data Availability Statement: Data will available at https://github.com/adrianchifu/sentimentdifficultyABSA, accessed on 10 October 2023.

Conflicts of Interest: The authors declare no conflict of interest.

References

1. van Atteveldt, W.; van der Velden, M.A.C.G.; Boukes, M. The Validity of Sentiment Analysis: Comparing Manual Annotation, Crowd-Coding, Dictionary Approaches, and Machine Learning Algorithms. *Commun. Methods Meas.* **2021**, *15*, 121–140. [CrossRef]
2. Wankhade, M.; Rao, A.C.S.; Kulkarni, C. A survey on sentiment analysis methods, applications, and challenges. *Artif. Intell. Rev.* **2022**, *55*, 5731–5780. [CrossRef]
3. Cambria, E.; Schuller, B.; Liu, B.; Wang, H.; Havasi, C. Knowledge-based approaches to concept-level sentiment analysis. *IEEE Intell. Syst.* **2013**, *28*, 12–14. [CrossRef]
4. Deng, S.; Sinha, A.P.; Zhao, H. Resolving Ambiguity in Sentiment Classification: The Role of Dependency Features. *ACM Trans. Manage. Inf. Syst.* **2017**, *8*, 1–13. [CrossRef]
5. Gref, M.; Matthiesen, N.; Hikkal Venugopala, S.; Satheesh, S.; Vijayananth, A.; Ha, D.B.; Behnke, S.; Köhler, J. A Study on the Ambiguity in Human Annotation of German Oral History Interviews for Perceived Emotion Recognition and Sentiment Analysis; Thirteenth Language Resources and Evaluation Conference; European Language Resources Association: Marseille, France, 2022; pp. 2022–2031.
6. Maynard, D.G.; Greenwood, M.A. Who cares about sarcastic tweets? investigating the impact of sarcasm on sentiment analysis. In Proceedings of the Ninth International Conference on Language Resources and Evaluation (LREC 2014), Reykjavik, Iceland, 26–31 May 2014.
7. Farias, D.H.; Rosso, P. Irony, sarcasm, and sentiment analysis. In *Sentiment Analysis in Social Networks*; Elsevier: Amsterdam, The Netherlands, 2017; pp. 113–128.
8. Li, Q.; Zhang, K.; Sun, L.; Xia, R. Detecting Negative Sentiment on Sarcastic Tweets for Sentiment Analysis. In *Artificial Neural Networks and Machine Learning: Proceedings of the 2nd International Conference on Artificial Neural Networks, Heraklion, Crete, Greece, 26–29 Septembe 2023*; Iliadis, L., Papaleonidas, A., Angelov, P., Jayne, C., Eds.; Springer: Cham, Switzerland, 2023; Volume 14263.
9. Kong, J.; Lou, C. Do cultural orientations moderate the effect of online review features on review helpfulness? A case study of online movie reviews. *J. Retail. Consum. Serv.* **2023**, *73*, 103374. [CrossRef]
10. Asyrofi, M.H.; Yang, Z.; Yusuf, I.N.B.; Kang, H.J.; Thung, F.; Lo, D. Biasfinder: Metamorphic test generation to uncover bias for sentiment analysis systems. *IEEE Trans. Softw. Eng.* **2021**, *48*, 5087–5101. [CrossRef]
11. Devlin, J.; Chang, M.; Lee, K.; Toutanova, K. BERT: Pre-training of Deep Bidirectional Transformers for Language Understanding. In Proceedings of the 2019 Conference of the North American Chapter of the Association for Computational Linguistics: Human Language Technologies, NAACL-HLT 2019, Minneapolis, MN, USA, 2–7 June 2019; Burstein, J., Doran, C., Solorio, T., Eds.; Association for Computational Linguistics: : Toronto, ON, Canada, 2019; Volume 1 (Long and Short Papers), pp. 4171–4186. [CrossRef]
12. Brown, T.; Mann, B.; Ryder, N.; Subbiah, M.; Kaplan, J.D.; Dhariwal, P.; Neelakantan, A.; Shyam, P.; Sastry, G.; Askell, A.; et al. Language Models are Few-Shot Learners. In *Advances in Neural Information Processing Systems*; Larochelle, H., Ranzato, M., Hadsell, R., Balcan, M., Lin, H., Eds.; Curran Associates, Inc.: Red Hook, NY, USA 2020; Volume 33, pp. 1877–1901.
13. Villavicencio, C.; Macrohon, J.J.; Inbaraj, X.A.; Jeng, J.H.; Hsieh, J.G. Twitter sentiment analysis towards COVID-19 vaccines in the Philippines using naïve bayes. *Information* **2021**, *12*, 204. [CrossRef]
14. Mubarok, M.S.; Adiwijaya.; Aldhi, M.D. Aspect-based sentiment analysis to review products using Naïve Bayes. *AIP Conf. Proc.* **2017**, *1867*, 020060. [CrossRef]
15. Goel, A.; Gautam, J.; Kumar, S. Real time sentiment analysis of tweets using Naive Bayes. In Proceedings of the 2016 2nd International Conference on Next Generation Computing Technologies (NGCT), Dehradun, India, 14–16 October 2016; pp. 257–261. [CrossRef]
16. Mittal, P.; Tiwari, K.; Malik, K.; Tyagi, M. Feedback Analysis of Online Teaching Using SVM. In *International Conference on Recent Trends in Computing*; Mahapatra, R.P., Peddoju, S.K., Roy, S., Parwekar, P., Eds.; Springer Nature Singapore: Singapore, 2023; pp. 119–128.
17. Ahmad, M.; Aftab, S.; Bashir, M.S.; Hameed, N. Sentiment analysis using SVM: A systematic literature review. *Int. J. Adv. Comput. Sci. Appl.* **2018**, *9*, 182–188. [CrossRef]
18. Fikri, M.; Sarno, R. A comparative study of sentiment analysis using SVM and SentiWordNet. *Indones. J. Electr. Eng. Comput. Sci.* **2019**, *13*, 902–909. [CrossRef]
19. Li, D.; Rzepka, R.; Ptaszynski, M.; Araki, K. HEMOS: A novel deep learning-based fine-grained humor detecting method for sentiment analysis of social media. *Inf. Process. Manag.* **2020**, *57*, 102290. [CrossRef]
20. Wang, X.; Jiang, W.; Luo, Z. Combination of convolutional and recurrent neural network for sentiment analysis of short texts. In Proceedings of the COLING 2016, the 26th International Conference on Computational Linguistics: Technical Papers, Osaka, Japan, 11–16 December 2016; pp. 2428–2437.
21. Basiri, M.E.; Nemati, S.; Abdar, M.; Cambria, E.; Acharya, U.R. ABCDM: An attention-based bidirectional CNN-RNN deep model for sentiment analysis. *Future Gener. Comput. Syst.* **2021**, *115*, 279–294. [CrossRef]
22. Ma, Y.; Peng, H.; Khan, T.; Cambria, E.; Hussain, A. Sentic LSTM: A hybrid network for targeted aspect-based sentiment analysis. *Cogn. Comput.* **2018**, *10*, 639–650. [CrossRef]
23. Rehman, A.U.; Malik, A.K.; Raza, B.; Ali, W. A hybrid CNN-LSTM model for improving accuracy of movie reviews sentiment analysis. *Multimed. Tools Appl.* **2019**, *78*, 26597–26613. [CrossRef]

24. Ahmed, A.; Yousuf, M.A. Sentiment Analysis on Bangla Text Using Long Short-Term Memory (LSTM) Recurrent Neural Network. In *International Conference on Trends in Computational and Cognitive Engineering*; Kaiser, M.S., Bandyopadhyay, A., Mahmud, M., Ray, K., Eds.; Springer: Singapore, 2021; pp. 181–192.
25. Hoang, M.; Bihorac, O.A.; Rouces, J. Aspect-based sentiment analysis using bert. In Proceedings of the 22nd Nordic Conference on Computational Linguistics, (NoDaLiDa), Turku, Finland, 30 September–2 October 2019; pp. 187–196.
26. Gao, Z.; Feng, A.; Song, X.; Wu, X. Target-dependent sentiment classification with BERT. *IEEE Access* **2019**, *7*, 154290–154299. [CrossRef]
27. Tiwari, D.; Nagpal, B.; Bhati, B.S.; Mishra, A.; Kumar, M. A systematic review of social network sentiment analysis with comparative study of ensemble-based techniques. *Artif. Intell. Rev.* **2023**, *56*, 13407–13461. [CrossRef] [PubMed]
28. Liu, R.; Shi, Y.; Ji, C.; Jia, M. A Survey of Sentiment Analysis Based on Transfer Learning. *IEEE Access* **2019**, *7*, 85401–85412. [CrossRef]
29. Bordoloi, M.; Biswas, S.K. Sentiment analysis: A survey on design framework, applications and future scopes. *Artif. Intell. Rev.* **2023**, *56*, 12505–12560. [CrossRef]
30. Cui, J.; Wang, Z.; Ho, S.B.; Cambria, E. Survey on sentiment analysis: evolution of research methods and topics. *Artif. Intell. Rev.* **2023**, *56*, 8469–8510. [CrossRef]
31. Hu, M.; Liu, B. Mining and Summarizing Customer Reviews. In *Tenth ACM SIGKDD International Conference on Knowledge Discovery and Data Mining*; Association for Computing Machinery: New York, NY, USA, 2004; KDD '04, pp. 168–177. [CrossRef]
32. Varghese, R.; Jayasree, M. Aspect based Sentiment Analysis using support vector machine classifier. In Proceedings of the 2013 International Conference on Advances in Computing, Communications and Informatics (ICACCI), Mysore, India, 22–25 August 2013; pp. 1581–1586.
33. Mubarok, M.S.; Adiwijaya, A.; Aldhi, M.D. Aspect-based sentiment analysis to review products using Naïve Bayes. In Proceedings of the International Conference on Mathematics: Pure, Applied and Computation: Empowering Engineering using Mathematics, Surabaya, Indonesia, 1 November 2016.
34. Ma, Y.; Peng, H.; Cambria, E. Targeted aspect-based sentiment analysis via embedding commonsense knowledge into an attentive LSTM. In Proceedings of the Thirty-Second AAAI Conference on Artificial Intelligence (AAAI-18), New Orleans, LA, USA, 2–7 February 2018.
35. Do, H.H.; Prasad, P.W.; Maag, A.; Alsadoon, A. Deep learning for aspect-based sentiment analysis: A comparative review. *Expert Syst. Appl.* **2019**, *118*, 272–299. [CrossRef]
36. Liu, H.; Chatterjee, I.; Zhou, M.; Lu, X.S.; Abusorrah, A. Aspect-based sentiment analysis: A survey of deep learning methods. *IEEE Trans. Comput. Soc. Syst.* **2020**, *7*, 1358–1375. [CrossRef]
37. Karimi, A.; Rossi, L.; Prati, A. Improving BERT Performance for Aspect-Based Sentiment Analysis. In Proceedings of the International Conference on Natural Language and Speech Processing, Copenhagen, Denmark, 25–26 April 2020.
38. Mutlu, M.M.; Özgür, A. A Dataset and BERT-based Models for Targeted Sentiment Analysis on Turkish Texts. In Proceedings of the 60th Annual Meeting of the Association for Computational Linguistics: Student Research Workshop, Dublin, Ireland, 22–27 May 2022; Association for Computational Linguistics: Dublin, Ireland, 2022; pp. 467–472. [CrossRef]
39. Zhang, W.; Li, X.; Deng, Y.; Bing, L.; Lam, W. A Survey on Aspect-Based Sentiment Analysis: Tasks, Methods, and Challenges. *IEEE Trans. Knowl. Data Eng.* **2023**, *35*, 11019–11038. [CrossRef]
40. Brauwers, G.; Frasincar, F. A Survey on Aspect-Based Sentiment Classification. *ACM Comput. Surv.* **2022**, *55*, 1–37. [CrossRef]
41. Chauhan, G.S.; Nahta, R.; Meena, Y.K.; Gopalani, D. Aspect based sentiment analysis using deep learning approaches: A survey. *Comput. Sci. Rev.* **2023**, *49*, 100576. [CrossRef]
42. Joachims, T. *A Probabilistic Analysis of the Rocchio Algorithm with TFIDF for Text Categorization*; Technical Report; Carnegie-Mellon Univ Pittsburgh Pa Dept of Computer Science: Pittsburgh, PA, USA, 1996.
43. Mikolov, T.; Sutskever, I.; Chen, K.; Corrado, G.S.; Dean, J. Distributed representations of words and phrases and their compositionality. *Adv. Neural Inf. Process. Syst.* **2013**, *26*, 3111–3119.
44. Pennington, J.; Socher, R.; Manning, C.D. Glove: Global vectors for word representation. In Proceedings of the 2014 Conference on Empirical Methods in Natural Language Processing (EMNLP), Doha, Qatar, 25–29 October 2014; pp. 1532–1543.
45. de Loupy, C.; Bellot, P. Evaluation of Document Retrieval Systems and Query Difficulty. In Proceedings of the Second International Conference on Language Resources and Evaluation (LREC 2000) Workshop, Athens, Greece, 31 May–2 June 2000; pp. 32–39.
46. Mothe, J.; Tanguy, L. Linguistic features to predict query difficulty. In Proceedings of the 28th Annual International ACM SIGIR Conference on Research and Development in Information Retrieval (SIGIR 2005), Salvador de Bahia, Brazil, 15–19 August 2005; pp. 7–10.
47. Goeuriot, L.; Kelly, L.; Leveling, J. An Analysis of Query Difficulty for Information Retrieval in the Medical Domain. In Proceedings of the 37th International ACM SIGIR Conference on Research & Development in Information Retrieval, Gold Coast, Australia, 6–11 July 2014; Association for Computing Machinery: New York, NY, USA, 2014; SIGIR '14, pp. 1007–1010. [CrossRef]
48. Zhao, Y.; Scholer, F.; Tsegay, Y. Effective Pre-retrieval Query Performance Prediction Using Similarity and Variability Evidence. In *Advances in Information Retrieval*; Macdonald, C., Ounis, I., Plachouras, V., Ruthven, I., White, R.W., Eds.; Springer: Berlin/Heidelberg, Germany, 2008; pp. 52–64.

49. Cronen-Townsend, S.; Zhou, Y.; Croft, W.B. *A Language Modeling Framework for Selective Query Expansion*; Technical Report, Technical Report IR-338; Center for Intelligent Information Retrieval, University of Massachusetts Amherst: Amherst, MA, USA, 2004.
50. Scholer, F.; Williams, H.E.; Turpin, A. Query association surrogates for Web search. *J. Am. Soc. Inf. Sci. Technol.* **2004**, *55*, 637–650. [CrossRef]
51. Carmel, D.; Yom-Tov, E. Estimating the Query Difficulty for Information Retrieval. In Proceedings of the 33rd International ACM SIGIR Conference on Research and Development in Information Retrieval, Geneva, Switzerland, 19–23 July 2010; Association for Computing Machinery: New York, NY, USA, 2010; SIGIR '10, p. 911. [CrossRef]
52. Cronen-Townsend, S.; Zhou, Y.; Croft, W.B. Predicting Query Performance. In Proceedings of the 25th Annual International ACM SIGIR Conference on Research and Development in Information Retrieval, Tampere, Finland, 11–15 August 2002; Association for Computing Machinery: New York, NY, USA, 2002; SIGIR '02, pp. 299–306. [CrossRef]
53. Shtok, A.; Kurland, O.; Carmel, D.; Raiber, F.; Markovits, G. Predicting Query Performance by Query-Drift Estimation. *ACM Trans. Inf. Syst.* **2012**, *30*, 1–15. [CrossRef]
54. Zhou, Y.; Croft, W.B. Query Performance Prediction in Web Search Environments. In Proceedings of the 30th Annual International ACM SIGIR Conference on Research and Development in Information Retrieval, Amsterdam, The Netherlands, 23–27 July 2007; Association for Computing Machinery: New York, NY, USA, 2007; SIGIR '07, pp. 543–550. [CrossRef]
55. Tao, Y.; Wu, S. Query Performance Prediction By Considering Score Magnitude and Variance Together. In Proceedings of the 23rd ACM International Conference on Conference on Information and Knowledge Management, Shanghai, China, 3–7 November 2014; Association for Computing Machinery: New York, NY, USA, 2014; CIKM '14, pp. 1891–1894. [CrossRef]
56. Hashemi, H.; Zamani, H.; Croft, W.B. Performance Prediction for Non-Factoid Question Answering. In Proceedings of the 2019 ACM SIGIR International Conference on Theory of Information Retrieval, Santa Clara, CA, USA, 2–5 October 2019; Association for Computing Machinery: New York, NY, USA, 2019; ICTIR '19, pp. 55–58. [CrossRef]
57. Faggioli, G.; Formal, T.; Marchesin, S.; Clinchant, S.; Ferro, N.; Piwowarski, B. Query Performance Prediction For Neural IR: Are We There Yet? In Proceedings of the Advances in Information Retrieval: 45th European Conference on Information Retrieval, ECIR 2023, Dublin, Ireland, 2–6 April 2023; Proceedings, Part I; Springer: Berlin/Heidelberg, Germany, 2023; pp. 232–248. [CrossRef]
58. Faggioli, G.; Formal, T.; Lupart, S.; Marchesin, S.; Clinchant, S.; Ferro, N.; Piwowarski, B. Towards Query Performance Prediction for Neural Information Retrieval: Challenges and Opportunities. In Proceedings of the 2023 ACM SIGIR International Conference on Theory of Information Retrieval, Taipei, Taiwan, 23–27 July 2023; Association for Computing Machinery: New York, NY, USA, 2023; ICTIR '23, pp. 51–63. [CrossRef]
59. Pontiki, M.; Galanis, D.; Pavlopoulos, J.; Papageorgiou, H.; Androutsopoulos, I.; Manandhar, S. SemEval-2014 task 4: Aspect Based Sentiment Analysis. In Proceedings of the 8th International Workshop on Semantic Evaluation (SemEval 2014), Dublin, Ireland, 23–24 August 2014; pp. 27–35.
60. Ganu, G.; Elhadad, N.; Marian, A. Beyond the stars: Improving rating predictions using review text content. *WebDB* **2009**, *9*, 1–6.
61. Hamborg, F.; Donnay, K. NewsMTSC: (Multi-)Target-dependent Sentiment Classification in News Articles. In Proceedings of the 16th Conference of the European Chapter of the Association for Computational Linguistics (EACL 2021), Online, 19–23 April 2021.
62. He, B.; Ounis, I. Inferring query performance using pre-retrieval predictors. In Proceedings of the String Processing and Information Retrieval: 11th International Conference, SPIRE 2004, Padova, Italy, 5–8 October 2004; Proceedings 11; Springer: Berlin/Heidelberg, Germany, 2004; pp. 43–54.
63. Salton, G.; Wong, A.; Yang, C.S. A vector space model for automatic indexing. *Commun. ACM* **1975**, *18*, 613–620. [CrossRef]
64. Devlin, J.; Chang, M.W.; Lee, K.; Toutanova, K. Bert: Pre-training of deep bidirectional transformers for language understanding. *arXiv* **2018**, arXiv:1810.04805.
65. Geetha, M.; Renuka, D.K. Improving the performance of aspect based sentiment analysis using fine-tuned Bert Base Uncased model. *Int. J. Intell. Netw.* **2021**, *2*, 64–69. [CrossRef]
66. Zhao, X.; Greenberg, J.; An, Y.; Hu, X.T. Fine-Tuning BERT Model for Materials Named Entity Recognition. In Proceedings of the 2021 IEEE International Conference on Big Data (Big Data), Orlando, FL, USA, 15–18 December 2021; pp. 3717–3720.
67. Sagi, O.; Rokach, L. Ensemble learning: A survey. *Wiley Interdiscip. Rev. Data Min. Knowl. Discov.* **2018**, *8*, e1249. [CrossRef]
68. Wang, G.; Sun, J.; Ma, J.; Xu, K.; Gu, J. Sentiment classification: The contribution of ensemble learning. *Decis. Support Syst.* **2014**, *57*, 77–93. [CrossRef]
69. Zhang, J.; Li, Z.; Nai, K.; Gu, Y.; Sallam, A. DELR: A double-level ensemble learning method for unsupervised anomaly detection. *Knowl.-Based Syst.* **2019**, *181*, 104783. [CrossRef]
70. Chawla, N.V.; Bowyer, K.W.; Hall, L.O.; Kegelmeyer, W.P. SMOTE: Synthetic minority over-sampling technique. *J. Artif. Intell. Res.* **2002**, *16*, 321–357. [CrossRef]
71. Mothe, J.; Laporte, L.; Chifu, A.G. Predicting query difficulty in IR: Impact of difficulty definition. In Proceedings of the 2019 11th International Conference on Knowledge and Systems Engineering (KSE), Da Nang, Vietnam, 24–26 October 2019; pp. 1–6.

Disclaimer/Publisher's Note: The statements, opinions and data contained in all publications are solely those of the individual author(s) and contributor(s) and not of MDPI and/or the editor(s). MDPI and/or the editor(s) disclaim responsibility for any injury to people or property resulting from any ideas, methods, instructions or products referred to in the content.

Article

Transformer-Based Composite Language Models for Text Evaluation and Classification

Mihailo Škorić [1], Miloš Utvić [2] and Ranka Stanković [1,*]

[1] Faculty of Mining and Geology, University of Belgrade, Djusina 7, 11120 Belgrade, Serbia; mihailo.skoric@rgf.bg.ac.rs
[2] Faculty of Philology, University of Belgrade, Studentski Trg 3, 11000 Belgrade, Serbia; milos.utvic@fil.bg.ac.rs
[*] Correspondence: ranka.stankovic@rgf.bg.ac.rs

Abstract: Parallel natural language processing systems were previously successfully tested on the tasks of part-of-speech tagging and authorship attribution through mini-language modeling, for which they achieved significantly better results than independent methods in the cases of seven European languages. The aim of this paper is to present the advantages of using composite language models in the processing and evaluation of texts written in arbitrary highly inflective and morphology-rich natural language, particularly Serbian. A perplexity-based dataset, the main asset for the methodology assessment, was created using a series of generative pre-trained transformers trained on different representations of the Serbian language corpus and a set of sentences classified into three groups (expert translations, corrupted translations, and machine translations). The paper describes a comparative analysis of calculated perplexities in order to measure the classification capability of different models on two binary classification tasks. In the course of the experiment, we tested three standalone language models (baseline) and two composite language models (which are based on perplexities outputted by all three standalone models). The presented results single out a complex stacked classifier using a multitude of features extracted from perplexity vectors as the optimal architecture of composite language models for both tasks.

Keywords: language modeling; language models; composite structures; machine learning; Serbian language; text classification

MSC: 68T50

Citation: Škorić, M.; Utvić, M.; Stanković, R. Transformer-Based Composite Language Models for Text Evaluation and Classification. *Mathematics* **2023**, *11*, 4660. https://doi.org/10.3390/math11224660

Academic Editor: Florentina Hristea

Received: 20 October 2023
Revised: 10 November 2023
Accepted: 13 November 2023
Published: 16 November 2023

Copyright: © 2023 by the authors. Licensee MDPI, Basel, Switzerland. This article is an open access article distributed under the terms and conditions of the Creative Commons Attribution (CC BY) license (https://creativecommons.org/licenses/by/4.0/).

1. Introduction

Nearing the end of the twentieth century, the accelerated development of artificial intelligence (especially machine learning methods) rekindled the idea that good results are obtainable in a much faster way and in many engineering spheres, including language modeling. In practice, it was established that one of the biggest disadvantages of formal grammar (language modeling state-of-the-art at the time) was the high cost of their creation. The extraction of grammatical rules from the corpus of texts can, of course, be carried out simply by making a list, but this leads to the problem of over-fitting the model, where individual rules are taken for general ones and the broader picture is lost. On the other hand, the derivation of general rules from individuals must be carried out carefully and requires an enormous amount of time. With new technological developments, however, the researchers began to investigate the creation of completely new probability-based models, which emulate automata and rule-based grammars. Instead of assigning a Boolean response to input strings, these new systems, called language models, assign probabilities based on a previously observed textual (training) corpus (Figure 1).

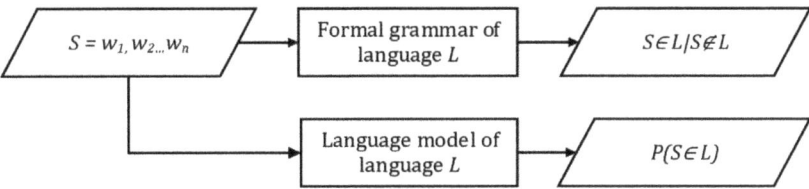

Figure 1. A rough comparison of the functionality of a formal grammar (**top**) and a language model (**bottom**) for some language L, where S represents a string, and $P(S \in L)$ represents the probability that S belongs to L.

Language models are thus defined as systems that assign probabilities to strings (based on the context in which they occur), and the models are based on the previously collected corpus. Input strings refer to sequences of tokens $(w_1, w_2 \ldots w_n)$, usually representing n-grams of words or characters.

In the previous couple of decades, language modeling was developed primarily using artificial neural networks (ANNs), according to the inspiring idea of Elman [1,2], who, while experimenting with time series as input data for machine learning (ML) models, constructed an artificial neural network whose goal was to predict the next element in a sequence. Although the potential of using ANNs for language modeling was recognized early on, the limitations imposed by this approach caused a stagger in development. A large amount of training data necessary for the correct generalization of grammatical rules, as well as satisfactory computing resources (especially working memory and processing power), were not available (at least not to the general public) at the time of the methodology's development. In addition, the problem of the vanishing gradient, a consequence of backpropagation when training multi-layer and recurrent ANNs, was observed often in practice [3], especially on the task of natural language modeling.

Nevertheless, the exponential growth in the PC computing power that followed, as well as the exponential increase in the amount of data available (via the Big Data phenomenon), enabled the theory to finally be technologically supported, triggering a new wave of fresh research, based on the idea of deep learning [4], which is currently the most represented sub-field of machine learning research, and artificial intelligence in general. The use of the long short-term memory method (LSTM) [5] in language modeling solved the problem of the vanishing gradient at first glance, while also providing previously unattainable results.

1.1. State-of-the-Art

Only with the emergence of the Transformer architecture by Google [6], as an adequate alternative to LSTM models, a new step forward was made in the field of natural language modeling. The main difference between transformers and LSTM models is that transformers do not rely on recurrent structures, but have an improved model for *attention*, a special parameter propagated during learning, which serves to separate relevant from irrelevant information. Today, the most significant and widespread language models are built using this architecture, i.e., an encoder-decoder structure for model training, supported by pre-trained word vectorizations (word embeddings) for preprocessing.

The first outstandingly influential of the type models were BERT (*bidirectional encoder representations from transformers*) by Google [7] and GPT (*generative pre-trained transformer*) by OpenAI [8,9]. The former is an encoder-based model used primarily for text annotation and classification and the latter is a decoder-based model used primarily for language generation (prediction of the next token for some given left context). Fast forward to today, decoder-based language models are most prominent in the field, with the OpenAI GPT models (now in the fourth generation) being especially popular for instruction tuning [10]. However, their last model published in open code (and also the latest one available for

Serbian) is still GPT-2 [11], with the efforts still being focused mainly on the development of encoder-based models both for Serbian [12] and similar Slavic languages [13–16].

1.2. Text Quality Evaluation and Perplexity

With the beginning of the twenty-first century and the emergence of the Big Data phenomenon, the necessity to separate significant, quality data from unusable or non-quality data became even more apparent. Machine-based classification methods that rely on automatically collected attributes such as user ratings or predefined expressions (e.g., [17]) are widely used today and represent the basis for web-originated data analysis.

Classical assessment methods such as evaluation by users or experts tend to be subjective, but an adequate alternative still does not exist. Evaluating the quality of a stimulus (irrelevant of its nature) must be subjective because different people perceive it differently. The evaluation metrics vary depending on the natural language processing (NLP) task, the phase (the model building, deployment, production phase), the focus (intrinsic and extrinsic, ML and business), etc. [18]. The extrinsic metric focuses on evaluating performance on the final objective of the concrete NLP task, while the intrinsic focuses on intermediary objectives.

Intrinsic evaluation metrics have the advantage of not relying on specific tasks or reference texts, but rather on the (language) models previously trained on reference texts, which are taken as the gold standard. A typical application of intrinsic metrics is to compare two models and analyze how likely they are to generate the same text. The most common intrinsic metric used in computational linguistics is *perplexity*, a measure of how much the model is surprised by seeing new input text. Another way to think about perplexity is to treat it as the *weighted average branching factor of a language, i.e., the average number of possible next words that can follow any word* [19].

Definition 1. *Let $\mathcal{LM}$ be a language model. Perplexity (PP) of a language model $\mathcal{LM}$ on a string of tokens $W = w_1 w_2 \ldots w_n$ (sentence, text) is defined as the inverse probability that a model $\mathcal{LM}$ will generate W, normalized by the number of tokens n. Accordingly, perplexity is calculated as follows:*

$$PP_{\mathcal{LM}}(W) = P_{\mathcal{LM}}(w_1 w_2 \ldots w_n)^{-\frac{1}{n}} \quad (1)$$

where $P_{\mathcal{LM}}(w_1 w_2 \ldots w_n)$ is the probability that a model $\mathcal{LM}$ will generate W. If $L_{\mathcal{LM}}$ represents language generated by model $\mathcal{LM}$ and P is a probability function, then

$$P_{\mathcal{LM}}(w_1 w_2 \ldots w_n) = P(w_1 w_2 \ldots w_n \in L_{\mathcal{LM}}) \quad (2)$$

This implies that the higher the value of perplexity, the poorer the fit of the tested input string and the model. If we have text that is taken as a gold standard, we can use perplexity as a measure of the quality of a model, or we can measure the quality of the generated text if we take a model as the gold standard. In both cases, we want the measure of perplexity to be as low as possible. In the worst case, if the model is completely unprepared and the probability for each token is the same, then the perplexity is equal to the size of the lexicon of tokens.

The aforementioned properties allow for perplexity to be used for automatically distinguishing between the high- and low-quality data [20], with one of the motives being the selection of data used to train new language models [21]. Perplexity can also be used for text classification based on language [22], the detection of harmful content [23], and fact checking [24].

1.3. Research Questions, Aims, Means, and Novelty

Recent developments in NLP (primarily statistically based language models) have brought us numerous new methods and technologies of language modeling [25], with new and arguably better language models appearing every so often. This paper constitutes an expansion of prior scholarly investigations dedicated to processing and evaluating texts written in arbitrary highly inflective and morphology-rich natural language, particularly Serbian. Two prior investigations considering (Serbian) language processing tasks are revisited, specifically, part-of-speech tagging [26] and literature authorship attribution [27] in order to inspect advantages of using composite language models. In these papers, several feature combination techniques were tested (e.g., voting, weighted voting, bidding), but it was concluded that the trained stacked classifier is the optimal method of feature combination, with the main advantage of distinguishing between quality and noise-inducing features. Additionally, if the trained stacked classifier's complexity is kept low, their explicitness is reasonable and the risk of overfitting them is minimal. The specific aim of this research is to further develop the methodology for the creation of composite intelligent systems to aid in solving the task of language modeling, particularly focusing on the tasks of perplexity-based text evaluation and classification [20]. The main motivation of the experiment was to support the distinction between high-quality and low-quality text, particularly that acquired from the web, in order to secure the integrity of automatically constructed corpora.

In order to achieve this goal, a group of *standalone* transformer-based language models (GPT-2), previously trained on a corpus of texts in Serbian [28], were used to develop several different *composite* language models. The expediency of the models will be illustrated in the example of solving two binary classification tasks:

C_1 Detection of *low-quality* sentences;
C_2 Machine translation detection.

The first classification task was chosen because of its direct alignment with the goal of the research (distinguishing between high-quality and low-quality text), while the second task was chosen as an alternative, which is more difficult benchmark, especially with the recent advances in the field of machine translation [29]. The ability of the standalone models to classify the sentences will be tested using only the sentence perplexity value outputted by the model. The obtained results will be used as a baseline for the evaluation of the composite models. The first of the two envisioned composite models, CM_1, will use sentence perplexities outputted by each of the three standalone models (M_1, M_2, and M_3, Section 2.1) as classification features. Besides the CM_1 features, the second composite model, CM_2, will use additional features extracted from standalone models M_1, M_2, and M_3.

This paper will address three research questions:

RQ1 Are semantic and syntactic models justified tools to use for sentence classification tasks, e.g., low-quality sentence or machine translation detection?
RQ2 Can composite language models based on outputted perplexities and *the wisdom of crowds*-based compositions improve on the accuracy of standalone models on classification tasks?
RQ3 Can features extracted from perplexity vectors be used to further improve the classification accuracy of composite models?

The main contributions of this research are:

1. Development of a perplexity-based dataset for testing and validation of composite and standalone language models using existing models and parallel language corpora;
2. Development of a detailed model of the composite systems for parallel unification of created models (which can be applied to both future models and other languages);
3. Creation of composite Serbian language models that can be used in natural language processing tasks, including document classification and text evaluation;
4. Evaluation of created models on two well-known binary classification problems.

The developed composite model architectures are to enable a more precise calculation of fitness between models and texts (i.e., a more precise calculation of perplexity) which could also induce performance improvement for generative language models. Additionally, the knowledge gathered through the inspection of the results should enable researchers to further develop the methodology of composite intelligent systems creation.

Section 2 of this paper will present the creation of the main evaluation dataset and its merits, and Section 3 will describe the process of feature extraction and model compositions. Section 4 will present the evaluation process and the results obtained, which will be followed by the discussion and concluding remarks, together with plans for future research in Section 5.

2. Dataset

The dataset used to evaluate the proposed methodology approach for this experiment is envisioned as a series of matrices containing perplexity values obtained through standalone language model evaluation. In order to prepare the dataset, several standalone language models (M_1, M_2, and M_3) that output different perplexity values for the same text were needed, and also several series of textual sentences (T_1, T_2, and T_3) not previously used for the training or fine-tuning of M_1, M_2, and M_3. The final dataset is obtained by evaluation of M_1, M_2, and M_3 using T_1, T_2, and T_3 as the test sets.

The textual dataset T was envisioned as a list of three separate sets:

T_1 High-quality sentences in Serbian, obtained from the expert translation of appraised novels written in other languages;

T_2 List of low-quality sentences, i.e., a list of sentences from the dataset T_1 corrupted using several different methods in order to make them semantically or syntactically incorrect;

T_3 List of machine translations of the original literary sentences, as opposed to the expert translations from the dataset (T_1).

The final dataset D was generated by recording the perplexity values of prepared language models against the prepared sets of sentences, and it was used to evaluate the methodology on both envisioned classification tasks. The detection of low-quality sentences (C_1) is summed up as the classification between datasets T_1 and T_2, and the detection of machine translations (C_2) as the classification between datasets T_1 and T_3. The complete process of the dataset generation can be summed up in three steps:

1. Preparation of pre-trained language models for Serbian that tend to output different perplexity measures for textual input (M_1, M_2, and M_3);
2. Preparation of textual data T_1, T_2, and T_3 (based on text not used for the training or fine-tuning of aforementioned language models), which will be used for the creation of evaluation dataset for both classification tasks (C_1 and C_2);
3. Generation of the final dataset, based on perplexity outputs obtained via evaluation of the prepared sentences from the previous step (T_1, T_2, and T_3) using prepared language models from the first step (M_1, M_2, and M_3).

2.1. Language Models

A total of three standalone language models that were previously trained [28] on a collected corpus of Serbian texts and based on a second-generation generative pre-trained transformers architecture (GPT2, 137 million parameters) were used for this research:

M_1 Control model trained using a standard corpus of contemporary Serbian texts (1 billion tokens), and standard training configuration for GPT2-based models;

M_2 Experimental semantic model, trained on a specially prepared corpus representation, i.e., a corpus processed using latent semantic analysis methods [30], namely removal of stop words and lemmatization;

M_3 Experimental syntactic model, trained on a different corpus representation that was processed using morphological dictionaries in such a way that the content words [31] were replaced with their grammatical category.

The two experimental models were supposed to model two complementary aspects of the text in natural language (semantics and syntax) and therefore produce potentially different perplexities when faced with the same piece of input text. It should be noted that when calculating perplexity using these models, input text must be preprocessed using the same transformation that was used for the generation of the training corpus data for the respective model in order to obtain correct readings. All three of these models are available in open access on the *Huggingface* platform and linked in the Data Availability Statement at the end of the paper. See Appendix A for the implementation details.

2.2. Textual Data

Textual data used to build the evaluation dataset for this research is based on a parallel corpus of literary texts (novels originally written in German and Italian and their expert translations into the Serbian language). The bigger share of the texts was pooled from parallel Serbian–German corpus, *SrpNemKor* [32], where only the novels originally written in German were used. The rest of the textual data represent the parallel translation of the third part of the *Naples stories* series [33,34], prepared as the part of the parallel Serbian–Italian corpus within the It-Sr-Ner project (supported by CLARIN ERIC "Bridging Gaps Call 2022") [35]. A total of seven novel translations were used (Table 1).

Table 1. A list of novels from which evaluation sentences were extracted.

Author	Translator	Title	Sentences #
Tomas Bernhard	B. Denić	Meine Preise	1009
Elfride Jelinek	T. Tropin	Die Klavierspielerin	6679
Milo Dor	T. Bekić	Wien, Juli 1999	1249
Günter Grass	A. G. Rajić	Im Krebsgang	2868
Günter de Bruyn	A. Bajazetov-Vučen	Buridans Esel	2890
Christof Ransmayr	Z. Krasni	Die letzte Welt	3107
Elena Ferrante	J. Brborić	Storia di chi fugge e di chi resta	8316

The first envisioned set of 26,118 sentences (a set of expert translations, T_1) was created by simply extracting sentences from the translations listed in novels. The set contains 536,639 tokens (about 20.55 per sentence) and has a type-token ratio of 0.1124.

The second set (low-quality sentences, T_2) was created by taking each sentence from the first set and applying one of the following transformations at random:

- **Lemmatization:** Each word in the sentence is replaced with its lemma based on Serbian Morphological Dictionaries, to make the sentences prone to morphosyntactic incorrectness. Although it is possible that the lemmatized sentence is equal to the original one (in case all words in the original sentence were already lemmas), a simple equality comparison between them calculated that this happens less than 0.8% of the time;
- **Random mixing of word order within a sentence:** A sentence was transformed into a list of words and punctuation marks, which was then randomly shuffled and put back together into text. This was also conducted to make the sentences prone to syntactical incorrectness, especially regarding the position of prepositions and adjectives. As in the previous case, this does not necessarily mean that the sentences are incorrect, but a manual evaluation of a set of 400 sentences found that this happens in less than 0.6% of the cases;
- **Random replacement of words in the sentence:** namely, each word in the sentence is replaced by another, random word of the same grammatical category from the Serbian Morphological dictionaries, in order to make it prone to semantic incorrectness.

The application of these transformations does not affect sentence lengths, but the type-token ratio is decreased to 0.0902 (due to the lemmatization of one part of the sentences).

The third set of sentences (machine translations, T_3) was obtained by running the original sentences (in German and Italian) through the *Google Translate* service and translating them into Serbian. Another simple equality comparison revealed that they differ from expert translations about 98% of the time. These sentences are somewhat shorter (average of 19.03 tokens per sentence and 496,989 total), but the type-token ratio of 0.1106 is quite similar to the one of the first set.

The complete textual dataset $T = \bigcup_{j=1}^{3} T_j$ is a sequence comprising 78,354 sentences divided into three subsequences T_j of equal size $|T_j| = 26{,}118$.

2.3. Sentence Perplexities and Perplexity Vectors

Definition 2. *Let $i, j \in \mathbb{Z}$. Integer interval $[i \mathinner{..} j]$ is defined as $\{k \in \mathbb{Z} \mid i \leq k \leq j\}$.*

Definition 3. *Let $x = (x_i)_{i=1}^{n} \in \mathbb{R}^n$ and $\prod_{i=1}^{n} x_i \neq 0$. The vector $x^{\circ -1} = (\frac{1}{x_i})_{i=1}^{n}$ is the element-wise inverse (also called Hadamard inverse) of vector x.*

Definition 4. *Perplexity vector (PPV) [36] of a language model $\mathcal{LM}$ on a sentence $s = w_1 w_2 \ldots w_n$ is calculated applying the Equation (1) to each N-gram of tokens within a sentence (N fixed, $N \in [1 \mathinner{..} n]$):*

$$PPV_{\mathcal{LM}}(s) = PPV_{\mathcal{LM}}(w_1 w_2 \ldots w_n) = \begin{bmatrix} P_{\mathcal{LM}}(w_1 w_2 \ldots w_N)^{-\frac{1}{N}} \\ P_{\mathcal{LM}}(w_2 w_3 \ldots w_{N+1})^{-\frac{1}{N}} \\ \vdots \\ P_{\mathcal{LM}}(w_{n-N+1} w_{n-N+2} \ldots w_n)^{-\frac{1}{N}} \end{bmatrix} \quad (3)$$

Size $N = 5$ is used during this experiment. The size of PPV for a given sentence s is $n - N + 1$ and therefore varies depending on the number of tokens n in s.

Let $i, j, k \in \mathbb{N}, i, j \in [1 \mathinner{..} 3], k \in [1 \mathinner{..} m]$. The final dataset D consists of:

D_1 Subset containing three sequences of inverse perplexity triples, one for each dataset T_j, i.e.,

$$(\frac{1}{pp^{(jk)}[1]}, \frac{1}{pp^{(jk)}[2]}, \frac{1}{pp^{(jk)}[3]})_k \quad (4)$$

where $pp^{(jk)}[i]$ represents perplexity of the model M_i on the kth sentence in the dataset T_j, calculated using (1). See Appendix A for the implementation details.

D_2 The subset comprised three sequences, one for each dataset T_j, where every sequence element is a triple containing the Hadamard inverse of perplexity vectors, i.e.,

$$((ppv^{(jk)}[1])^{\circ -1}, (ppv^{(jk)}[2])^{\circ -1}, (ppv^{(jk)}[3])^{\circ -1})_k \quad (5)$$

and $ppv^{(jk)}[i]$ represents the perplexity vector of the model M_i on the kth sentence in the dataset T_j, calculated using (3).

Values stored in sets $D1$ and $D2$ were used to measure the classification performance of (both standalone and composite) language models on the tasks of detecting low-quality sentences and machine translations (see Section 4).

Definition 5. *Let $(x_i)_{i=1}^{n}$ and $(y_i)_{i=1}^{n}$ be two sequences of length n. The Pearson linear correlation coefficient r is defined as*

$$r = \frac{\sum_{i=1}^{n}(x_i - \bar{x})(y_i - \bar{y})}{\sqrt{\sum_{i=1}^{n}(x_i - \bar{x})^2 \sum_{i=1}^{n}(y_i - \bar{y})^2}}, \quad (6)$$

where $\bar{x} = \frac{1}{n} \sum_{i=1}^{n} x_i$ represents the mean of x and analogously for $\bar{y}$.

Let $i, j, k, l \in [1 \mathinner{..} 3]$ and $M_i T_j$ be a sequence $(pp^{(jk)}[i])_k$ such that $|M_i T_j| = |T_j| = m$, i.e., a sequence of perplexity values obtained for sentences of dataset T_j using model M_i. In order to ensure that the perplexity values differ between both different models and different textual datasets, the Pearson coefficients r_{ijkl} were calculated using (6), as the primary measure of linear correlation between every two pairs M_iT_j and M_kT_l, where pairs share either a model ($i = k$) or a dataset ($j = l$).

Tables 2 and 3 contain the resulting r_{ij} coefficients between M_iT_j pairs, where pairs share the same dataset in Table 2, while pairs in Table 3 share the same model.

Table 2. Pearson correlation coefficients between sequences of perplexities obtained using two different pairs (model, dataset) M_iT_j with the mutual dataset.

Model	M_1T_1	M_2T_1	M_3T_1
M_1T_1		0.265	0.044
M_2T_1	0.265		−0.019
M_3T_1	0.044	−0.019	
	M_1T_2	M_2T_2	M_3T_2
M_1T_2		0.166	0.174
M_2T_2	0.166		−0.116
M_3T_2	0.174	−0.116	
	M_1T_3	M_2T_3	M_3T_3
M_1T_3		0.225	0.065
M_2T_3	0.225		−0.060
M_3T_3	0.065	−0.060	

Table 3. Pearson correlation coefficients between sequences of perplexities obtained using different pairs (model, dataset) M_iT_j with the mutual model.

	M_1T_1	M_1T_2	M_1T_3
M_1T_1		0.515	0.645
M_1T_2	0.515		0.369
M_1T_3	0.645	0.369	
	M_2T_1	M_2T_2	M_2T_3
M_2T_1		0.803	0.512
M_2T_2	0.803		0.419
M_2T_3	0.512	0.419	
	M_3T_1	M_3T_2	M_3T_3
M_3T_1		0.790	0.676
M_3T_2	0.790		0.544
M_3T_3	0.676	0.544	

The results presented in Table 2 confirm the uniqueness of perplexities outputted using the prepared models, with the highest correlation coefficient being 0.265 between the models M_1 (control) and M_2 (semantic) and all of the other correlation coefficients being less than 0.05. On the other hand, the much higher correlation was apparent in Table 3, averaging at about 0.56, indicating that the models have trouble differing between the datasets, especially model M_2 between the datasets T_1 and T_2 (inability to distinguish the control set from the artificially-defected, low-quality sentences), with a correlation coefficient of over 0.8. In Section 3, we introduce composite models as a form of overcoming this insufficiency.

Once the data were confirmed to be of value, all of the perplexity values in sets D_1 and D_2 were converted to their inverse value, which concluded the creation of the dataset D according to Equations (4) and (5). This was carried out for the sake of their easier input into the machine learning algorithms afterwards in the experiment.

3. Features and Compositions

As mentioned in Section 1.3, two composite models, CM_1 and CM_2, built on the resulting perplexities were envisioned for this experiment. The first, simpler model (Section 3.1) is based on a stacked classifier architecture which is directly derived from the previous research on the subject [26,27]. The second, more complex model (Section 3.2) was designed specially for this experiment and relies on features extracted using several different scenarios.

3.1. Simple Neural Network Classifier (CM_1)

The stacked sentence classifier used in the first composition (CM_1) is based on a simple neural network architecture consisting of one fully connected layer—two perceptrons, one for each class, sharing a triple of input values $p = (P_1, P_2, P_3)$, an element of dataset D_1. The triple p corresponds to a sentence being classified and each P_i is an inverse of the perplexity value of model M_i, $i, j \in [1..3]$ (Figure 2).

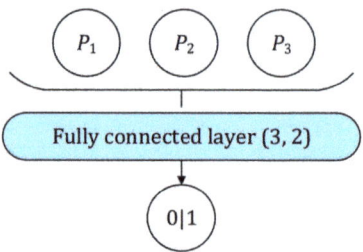

Figure 2. A simple neural network for binary sentence classification, consisting of one fully connected layer with input values $(P_i)_{i=1}^{3}$ (perplexities of the models M_i on an input sentence, $i \in [1..3]$).

The CM_1 output y is the predicted class of the sentence. The value of y can be either 0, meaning expert translation, or 1, meaning an alternative class the network was trained to recognize, depending on the classification task. The calculation of y can be described in the following manner:

$$y = f(pW^T + b) = pW^T + b \qquad (7)$$

where:

- $p = (P_1, P_2, P_3) \in \mathbb{R}^3$ is a triple containing inverse of perplexities corresponding to the input sentence;
- $W = (w_{ij}) \in \mathbb{R}^{2 \times 3}$ is a weight matrix. For a fixed $i \in [1..2]$, $(w_{ij})_j \in \mathbb{R}^3$ are learnable weights of the ith perceptron in CM_1, $j \in [1..3]$;
- $b \in \mathbb{R}^2$ components are learnable biases of the corresponding perceptrons in CM_1;
- f is an activation function defined as identity $f(z) = z$, i.e., linear activation is used.

See Appendix A for the implementation details and Section 4 for training details.

The goal of this model was to confirm the advantages of using a stacked classifier on the perplexity outputs of transformer-based language models, as was already confirmed for using it on probabilistic outputs of part-of-speech taggers [26] and cosine similarities of documents before that [27], in order to give an answer to **RQ2**.

3.2. Complex Multi-Featured Neural Network (CM_2)

In contrast to CM_1 (Section 3.1), the second composite model (CM_2) was designed to maximize the volume of inputted features at the expense of simplicity. The goal of the feature extraction for this experiment was to create a large, determined, and finite list of inputs for a binary classifier; hence, all of the features are represented as numerical values in the range -1 to 1. In addition to the three features used by CM_1, a multitude of additional features are extracted from subset D_2 (Section 2.3), using three separate neural network components:

NN_1 The time-and-frequency-domain-based component represents a small, single-layer neural network used to extract eight features from a multitude of properties calculated using a set of prepared formulas over each vector from D_2 (see Section 3.2.1);

NN_2 The recurrent neural network (RNN) [37] component represents a small neural network with a recurrent layer with four hidden states. Vector triples from dataset D_2 are inputted into this layer in order to extract four additional features for each triple (see Section 3.2.2);

NN_3 The convolutional neural network (CNN) [38] component represents a small neural network with a convolutional and a pooling layer instead of a recurrent one, which is used to extract eight more features from each vector triple of dataset D_2 (see Section 3.2.3).

For the purpose of training components NN_2 and NN_3, the length of the vector inputs (extracted from the D_2 set) for these two components was resized to the length $\ell = 64$, employing either truncation (if the vector was longer) or zero-padding (if the vector was shorter). This was conducted for the purpose of easier batching of vector inputs during the training procedure for recurrent and convolutional layers. The NN_1 component uses the original vectors. All of the mentioned components are connected to one final component:

NN_4 The classifying component represents a neural network with two fully connected layers that takes all of the aforementioned features as input and then outputs the class of the inspected sentence.

The four components are trained together as one binary classification system (for each of two envisioned classification tasks) in order to give a definite answer to **RQ3**.

3.2.1. Time-and-Frequency-Domain-Based Component (NN_1)

The first CM_2 component is used to extract features from different time-domain and frequency-domain properties of the vectors from dataset D_2, while treating them as either time-series (by using tokens as a unit of time and inspecting the perplexity value at each point) or signals. In the case of time-domain (TD), the twelve properties TD_1–TD_{12} were examined using each vector as an input for twelve different formulas. Some of them are reused to examine six frequency-domain (FD) properties FD_1–FD_6, but the input is changed to be a *power spectrum* calculated using a *fast Fourier transform* of each vector.

The following time-domain properties were determined for vector $x = (x_i)_{i=1}^n$:

TD_1 Minimum value found in the inspected vector:

$$Min(x) = \min_{i \in [1..n]} x_i; \tag{8}$$

TD_2 Maximum value found in the inspected vector:

$$Max(x) = \max_{i \in [1..n]} x_i; \tag{9}$$

TD_3 Peak-to-peak, calculated as the difference between the maximum and minimum value:

$$P_k(x) = Max(x) - Min(x); \tag{10}$$

TD_4 The arithmetic mean of the values in the inspected vector:

$$\bar{x} = \frac{1}{n} \sum_{i=1}^n x_i; \tag{11}$$

TD_5 Root mean square:

$$RMS(x) = \sqrt{\frac{1}{n} \sum_{i=1}^n x_i^2}; \tag{12}$$

TD_6 Variance, i.e., the spread of data around the mean:

$$\sigma^2 = \frac{1}{n}\sum_{i=1}^{n}(x_i - \bar{x})^2;\tag{13}$$

TD_7 The standard deviation of the inspected vector:

$$\sigma = \sqrt{\frac{\sum_{i=1}^{n}(x_i - \bar{x})^2}{n-1}};\tag{14}$$

TD_8 Crest factor, i.e the quotient of the maximum value and the root mean square:

$$CF(x) = \frac{Max(x)}{RMS(x)};\tag{15}$$

TD_9 Form factor, i.e., the quotient of the root mean square and mean:

$$FF(x) = \frac{RMS(x)}{\bar{x}};\tag{16}$$

TD_{10} Pulse indicator, i.e., the quotient of the maximum value and the mean of the vector:

$$PI(x) = \frac{Max(x)}{\bar{x}};\tag{17}$$

TD_{11} Vector (Pearson) kurtosis, i.e., the measure of the outlier presence in the inspected vector:

$$\beta_2 = \mathbb{E}\left[\left(\frac{x-\bar{x}}{\sigma}\right)^4\right],\tag{18}$$

where $\mathbb{E}$ is the expectation operator;

TD_{12} Vector skewness, i.e., the measure of the data symmetry around the mean:

$$\gamma_1 = \mathbb{E}\left[\left(\frac{x-\bar{x}}{\sigma}\right)^3\right],\tag{19}$$

where $\mathbb{E}$ is the expectation operator.

As the second set of properties is based in the frequency domain, each vector was first subjected to the fast discrete Fourier transform, calculating a new vector $(\mathcal{F}_k)_{k\in[0..n-1]} \in \mathbb{C}^n$:

$$\mathcal{F}_k = \sum_{j=1}^{n} x_j e^{-\frac{2i\pi}{n}k(j-1)}, \quad k \in [0..n-1],\tag{20}$$

where n is the length of the vector x that is being transformed and $i \in \mathbb{C}$ is the imaginary unit, $i^2 = -1$.

Afterwards, the *power spectrum vector* $y = (y_k)_{k\in[0..n-1]}$ is calculated:

$$y_k = \frac{|\mathcal{F}_k^2|}{n}, \quad k \in [0..n-1].\tag{21}$$

With the calculated power spectrum of the vector, the following frequency-domain properties were extracted:

FD_1 Power spectrum maximum, calculated using Equation (9), where x is the power spectrum of the inspected vector;

FD_2 Power spectrum peak, calculated as the absolute maximum value found in the power spectrum:

$$P_m = \max_{i \in [1..n]} |x_i|, \qquad (22)$$

where x is the power spectrum of the inspected vector;

FD_3 Power spectrum mean, calculated as an arithmetic mean of the values in the power spectrum using Equation (11), where n is the length of the power spectrum x;

FD_4 Power spectrum variance, calculated using Equation (13), where n is the length of the power spectrum x and $\bar{x}$ is its sample mean;

FD_5 Power spectrum kurtosis, calculated using Equation (18), where $\bar{x}$ is the mean of the power spectrum vector x, σ its standard deviation, and $\mathbb{E}$ is the expectation operator;

FD_6 Power spectrum skewness, calculated using Equation (19), where $\bar{x}$ is the mean of the inspected vector x, σ its standard deviation, and $\mathbb{E}$ is the expectation operator.

These 54 properties (18 for each vector in a D_2 dataset triple) are used as an input for a simple fully connected layer in order to extract eight final features $(F_j)_{j=1}^{8}$ as depicted in Figure 3. This was conducted in order to reduce the total number of features, as well as to extract only their most important aspects. The rectified linear unit function (ReLU) is applied to the output in order to prepare it for passing through the adjacent linear layer in NN_4. The neural network component is visualized in Figure 3. The calculation of the features can thus be described as follows:

$$(F_j)_{j=1}^{8} = ReLU(gW^T + b) \qquad (23)$$

where:

- $g \in \mathbb{R}^{54}$ is a series of time-domain and frequency domain properties extracted from the triple containing the Hadamard inverse of perplexity vectors using TD_1–TD_{12} and FD_1–FD_6, corresponding to the input sentence;
- $W = (w_{ij}) \in \mathbb{R}^{8 \times 54}$ is a weight matrix; $(w_{ij})_j \in \mathbb{R}^{54}$ are learnable weights of the ith perceptron of NN_1, $i \in [1..8]$, $j \in [1..54]$;
- Components of $b \in \mathbb{R}^8$ are learnable biases of the corresponding perceptrons of NN_1;
- If $z = (z_i)_{i=1}^{8} \in \mathbb{R}^8$, $ReLU$ is a rectified linear unit function defined as $ReLU(z) = (ReLU(z_i))_{i=1}^{8} = (\max(0, z_i))_{i=1}^{8}$.

See Appendix A for the implementation details.

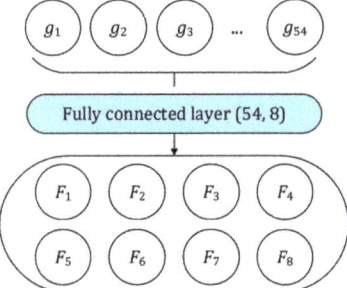

Figure 3. Fully connected layer with an input size of 54 (for 18 vector properties extracted from each of three input vectors) that is used to extract a total of eight time and frequency-domain features $F = (F_j)_{j=1}^{8}$.

3.2.2. RNN Component (NN_2)

A second set of features $(F_j)_{j=9}^{12}$ was extracted using a recurrent neural network component (Figure 4). One recurrent layer with four hidden states $h = (h^{(j)})_{j=1}^{4}$ was used to process each D_2 dataset triple of vectors $x = (x^{(1)}, x^{(2)}, x^{(3)})$, where $x^{(i)} \in \mathbb{R}^\ell$, $i \in [1..3]$, and ℓ is the resized length of input vector, introduced at the beginning of Section 3.2. For each $t \in [1..\ell]$, a triple $x_t = (x_t^{(1)}, x_t^{(2)}, x_t^{(3)}) \in \mathbb{R}^3$ is processed with hidden states $h_{t-1} = (h_{t-1}^{(1)}, h_{t-1}^{(2)}, h_{t-1}^{(3)}, h_{t-1}^{(4)}) \in \mathbb{R}^4$ from the previous loop pass-through (if any) with the goal to extract a number of recurrent features.

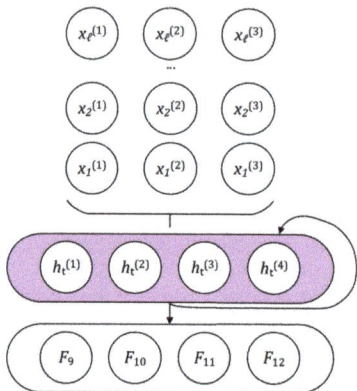

Figure 4. Visualization of neural network component based on a recurrent layer with four hidden states h used to process input values $x_t = (x_t^{(1)}, x_t^{(2)}, x_t^{(3)}) \in \mathbb{R}^3$, where $x_t^{(i)}$ corresponds to time point $t \in [1..\ell]$ and language model M_i, $i \in [1..3]$.

The calculation of the hidden state values is performed as follows:

$$h_t = \tanh(x_t W_{ih}^T + b_{ih} + h_{t-1} W_{hh}^T + b_{hh}), \quad t \in [1..\ell], \tag{24}$$

where:

- $h_t \in \mathbb{R}^4$ is the hidden state at time t. The initial hidden state at time 0 is $h_0 = \mathbf{0} \in \mathbb{R}^4$;
- $x_t \in \mathbb{R}^3$ is the input at time t;
- $W_{ih} \in \mathbb{R}^{4 \times 3}$ are the learnable input-hidden weights of the (only) layer (4 hidden states, 3 input values) of NN_2;
- $b_{ih} \in \mathbb{R}^4$ is the learnable input-hidden bias of the (only) layer of NN_2;
- $W_{hh} \in \mathbb{R}^{4 \times 4}$ are the learnable hidden-hidden weights of the (only) layer of NN_2;
- $b_{hh} \in \mathbb{R}^4$ is the learnable hidden-hidden bias of the (only) layer of NN_2;
- tanh is the hyperbolic tangent activation function.

See Appendix A for the implementation details.

The recurrent layer outputs (from four hidden states after the final pass-through) are taken as four extracted features $(F_j)_{j=9}^{12} = h_\ell$. The visualization of the component is depicted in Figure 4.

3.2.3. CNN Component (NN_3)

Definition 6. *For finite discrete functions $f, g \in \mathbb{C}^N$, $N \in \mathbb{N}$, the (circular) cross-correlation [39] is defined as:*

$$(f \star g)[n] = \sum_{m=0}^{N-1} \overline{f[m]} g[(m+n)_{\bmod N}] \tag{25}$$

A somewhat more complicated process was the extraction of the final eight features from the triples using the convolutional architecture, comprising three layers:

1. A one-dimensional convolutional layer with three input channels ($C_{in} = 3$), eight output channels ($C_{out} = 8$), a size-five kernel ($K_c = 5$), and a stride of two ($S_c = 2$);

2. A one-dimensional max pooling layer [40] with a size-five kernel ($K_p = 5$) and stride of two ($S_p = 2$);
3. A fully connected linear layer with an input layer with a size corresponding to the number of features extracted using the previous (pooling) layer and the output size of eight. Just like for NN_1, a ReLU activation function was applied in order to prepare features for passing through the first layer of the NN_4 component.

During the processing of input $x = (x^{(1)}, x^{(2)}, x^{(3)})$ using the first layer, the kernel is sliding simultaneously across the values in all three vectors $x^{(j)} \in \mathbb{R}^\ell$, $j \in [1..3]$, extracting eight features for each inspection. The total number of inspections performed, m, is calculated as follows:

$$m = \left\lfloor \frac{\ell - K_c}{S_c} \right\rfloor + 1 \tag{26}$$

where ℓ is the resized and fixed length of the inputted sequences ($\ell = 64$), K_c the size of the kernel ($K_c = 5$), and S_c stride length ($S_c = 2$). Features outputted for each inspection $co = (co_{ij}) \in \mathbb{R}^{m \times C_{out}}$ are calculated in the following manner:

$$co_{ij} = b_j + \sum_{k=1}^{C_{in}} W_{jk} \star \text{input}_{ik}, \tag{27}$$

where:
- $i \in [1..m]$ is the inspection index;
- $j \in [1..C_{out}] = [1..8]$ is the outputted feature index;
- $k \in [1..C_{in}] = [1..3]$ is the input channel index;
- Components of $b \in \mathbb{R}^8$ are learnable biases of the corresponding output channels for the convolutional layer;
- $W = (w_{jk}) \in \mathbb{R}^{8 \times 3}$ is a weight matrix; $(w_{jk})_k \in \mathbb{R}^3$ are learnable weights of the jth output channel and kth input channel, $j \in [1..8], k \in [1..3]$;
- Input $= (\text{input}_{ik}) \in \mathbb{R}^5$ represents the inspected values for the ith inspection and for kth input channel, with inspection being defined via the kernel size ($K_c = 5$) and stride ($S_c = 2$).

Outputted values co are then processed using a max pooling layer, where a second kernel of the same size is sliding across the values in each channel, performing the inspections and extracting the maximum value for each one. This step results in M number of new features, where M is calculated as:

$$M = \left(\left\lfloor \frac{m - K_p}{S_p} \right\rfloor + 1 \right) * C_{out}, \tag{28}$$

where m is the number of inspection of the convolutional layer (26), K_p the size of the kernel ($K_p = 5$), S_p stride length ($S_p = 2$), and C_{out} the number of convolutional layer output channels.

Values compiled using the max pooling layer $po = (po_i)_{i=1}^M$ are calculated as follows:

$$po_i = \max_{j \in [1..K_p]} \text{input}_{ij}, \tag{29}$$

where:
- $i \in [1..M]$ is the inspection index;
- $j \in [1..K_p]$ is the index of values within inspections;
- K_p is the size of the kernel of the max pooling layer;
- Input $= (\text{input}_i) \in \mathbb{R}^M$ represents the inspected values of the ith inspection, with inspection being defined via the kernel size ($K_p = 5$), stride ($S_p = 2$) and output channel of the convolutional being inspected.

Lastly, values compiled using the max pooling layer $po = (po_i)_{i=1}^{M}$ are used as an input for a fully connected linear layer with input size M and output size of eight, which is used to produce a final tally of eight features extracted by this specific method $(F_j)_{j=13}^{20}$, where the feature values are calculated in the following manner:

$$(F_j)_{j=13}^{20} = ReLU(po \cdot W^T + b) \tag{30}$$

where:

- po is an array of features outputted from the max pooling layer, $po = (po_j)_{j=1}^{M} \in \mathbb{R}^M$;
- $W = (w_{ij}) \in \mathbb{R}^{8 \times M}$ is a weight matrix; $(w_{ij})_j \in \mathbb{R}^M$ are learnable weights of the ith perceptron in the sole linear layer in NN_3, $i \in [1..8]$, $j \in [1..M]$;
- Components of $b \in \mathbb{R}^8$ are learnable biases of the corresponding perceptrons of the sole linear layer in NN_3;
- If $z = (z_i)_{i=1}^{8} \in \mathbb{R}^8$, ReLU is a rectified linear unit function defined as $ReLU(z) = (ReLU(z_i))_{i=1}^{8} = (\max(0, z_i))_{i=1}^{8}$.

See Appendix A for the implementation details.

A complete neural network component used to extract them is visualized in Figure 5.

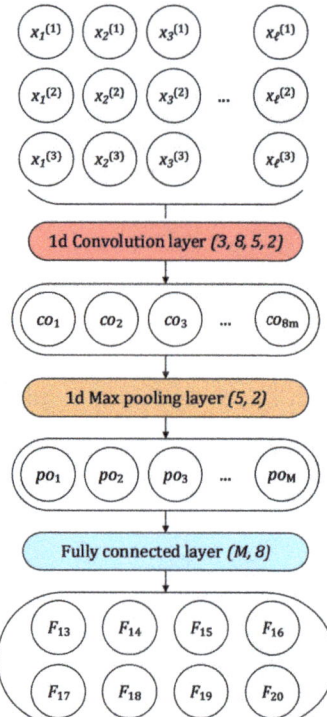

Figure 5. A neural network component featuring a single one-dimensional convolutional layer (with three input channels, a size-five kernel, and a stride of two) used to process input values $x = (x_j^{(1)}, x_j^{(2)}, x_j^{(3)}) \in \mathbb{R}^3$, where $x_j^{(i)}$ corresponds to time point $j \in [1..\ell]$ and language model M_i, $i \in [1..3]$. Outputs of this step $(co = (co_j)_{j=1}^{8m})$ are inputted into a single one-dimensional max pooling layer (with a size-five kernel and a stride of two), and the outputs of the max pooling layer $(po = (po_j)_{j=1}^{M})$ are used as inputs for a fully connected layer, which is used to extract the final features $(F_j)_{j=13}^{20}$.

3.2.4. Classifying Component (NN_4)

Eight features were extracted using the first component (NN_1, Section 3.2.1), four features were extracted using the second component (NN_2, Section 3.2.2), and eight features were extracted using the third component (NN_3, Section 3.2.3) together with three values that were used by the first composition (CM_1, Section 3.1), which were used as an input for one final fully connected neural network component for binary classification. This final component consists of one input layer with input size 23 (20 for extracted features $F = (F_j)_{j=1}^{20}$ and 3 for a triple of inverse perplexity values $p = (P_1, P_2, P_3)$), connected to the output layer via one hidden layer with eight neurons (Figure 6).

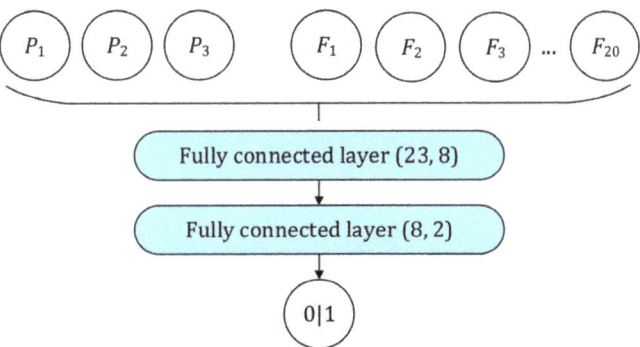

Figure 6. A neural network component consisting of one fully connected linear size-23 input layer (20 for extracted features $F = (F_j)_{j=1}^{20}$ and 3 for a triple of inverse perplexity values $p = (P_1, P_2, P_3)$), and one fully connected linear size-8 hidden layer used to perform binary classification based on the inputted features.

As is the same for CM_1, the output y of CM_2 is the predicted class of the sentence. The value of y can be either 0 (expert translation) or 1 (alternative class the network was trained to recognize, depending on the classification task). Calculation of the y for CM_2 can be described in the following manner:

$$y = ReLU((p\frown F)W^{(1)^T} + b_1)W^{(2)^T} + b_2 \qquad (31)$$

where:

- $p\frown F \in \mathbb{R}^{23}$ is a concatenation of $p = (P_1, P_2, P_3) \in \mathbb{R}^3$, a triple containing inverse of perplexities corresponding to the input sentence, and $F = (F_j)_{j=1}^{20} \in \mathbb{R}^{20}$, a triple containing the inverse of perplexities corresponding to the input sentence;
- $W^{(1)} = (w_{ij}^{(1)}) \in \mathbb{R}^{8 \times 23}$ is a weight matrix; $(w_{ij}^{(1)})_j \in \mathbb{R}^{23}$ are learnable weights of the ith perceptron in the input layer, $i \in [1..8], j \in [1..23]$;
- $W^{(2)} = (w_{ij}^{(2)}) \in \mathbb{R}^{2 \times 8}$ is a weight matrix; $(w_{ij}^{(2)})_j \in \mathbb{R}^8$ are learnable weights of the ith perceptron in the hidden layer, $i \in [1..2], j \in [1..8]$;
- Components of $b_1 \in \mathbb{R}^8$ and $b_2 \in \mathbb{R}^2$ are learnable biases of the corresponding perceptrons in the first (b_1) and second (b_2) fully connected layer;
- If $z = (z_i)_{i=1}^8 \in \mathbb{R}^8$, $ReLU$ is a rectified linear unit function defined as $ReLU(z) = (ReLU(z_i))_{i=1}^8 = (\max(0, z_i))_{i=1}^8$.

A complete stacked classifier that uses transformer outputs as inputs is composed of all of the described components and is depicted in Figure 7. See Appendix A for the implementation details and Section 4 for training details.

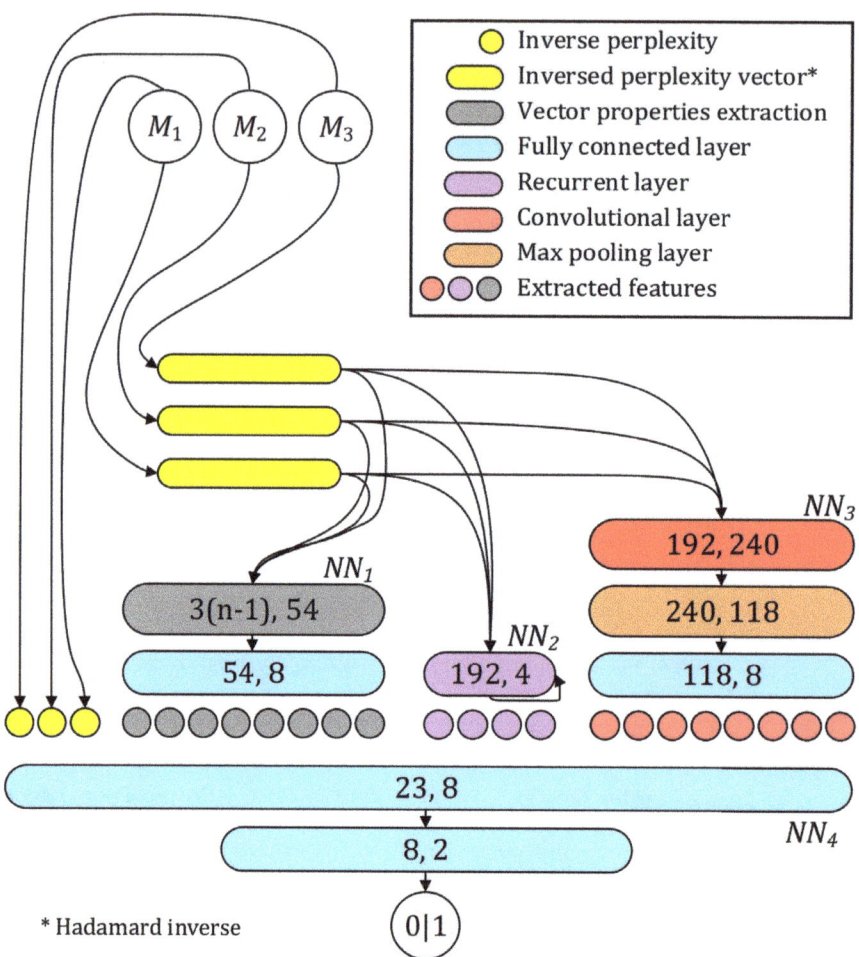

Figure 7. A visualization of the complete architecture of composite model CM_2 where Hadamard inverse perplexity vectors (depicted as yellow stadiums) are generated using standalone language models (M_1–M_3) and are being used as input for NN_1–NN_3. All layers are denoted with a number of input and output parameters, and stadiums of different colors: violet for the recurrent, red for the convolutional, orange for the max pooling layer, and blue for fully connected linear ones. The gray stadium represents vector properties extraction (not a trainable layer), where n is a variable sentence length. The colored circles mark different features used for NN_4 (yellow: inverse perplexities calculated using M_1–M_3; gray: time-and-frequency-based features calculated using NN_1; violet: recurrent features calculated using NN_2; red: convolutional features calculated using NN_3).

4. Results

For the evaluation, we used five-fold cross-validation over dataset D, for which both subsets were split into five (nearly) equal, class-balanced chunks. For each of the five folds, a different chunk was used for testing, while the other four were used to train ten classifiers, including five for each classification task (C_1, C_2). Three *simple classifiers* were based directly on standalone models (M_1, M_2, and M_3), while two *composite classifiers* (CM_1 and CM_2) were trained on top of all three standalone models. Different training procedures were deployed depending on the classifier being trained, where different levels of input data complexity influenced the complexity of the models (Table 4).

Table 4. Five classifiers used for each classification task, input data they are using (middle) (cf. Section 2), and the description of their architecture (right).

Model	Input Data	Stacked Classifier Type
M_1	Values from D_1 dataset originated from model M_1	An extension of the model in the form of a single input perceptron for binary classification, which uses that model's (inversed) perplexity output as input
M_2	Values from D_1 dataset originated from model M_2	
M_3	Values from D_1 dataset originated from model M_3	
CM_1	Value triples from D_1 dataset, i.e., values originated from all three standalone models (M_1, M_2 and M_3)	A simple neural network with two perceptrons and three shared inputs (cf. Section 3.1)
CM_2	All of the triples from both D_1 and D_2 sets	A complex neural network comprising four different components (cf. Section 3.2)

For each training session, the Adam optimizer [41] with a learning rate of 0.01 and a batch size of 64 was used, and the number of training epochs was limited to 50. In order to measure the improvements achieved using the proposed composite models, the results achieved using the standalone models (M_1, M_2, and M_3) were marked as the baseline. More precisely, the baseline was defined as the best result achieved by any of these M_i, $i \in [1..3]$ for each classification task C_1 and C_2. The experiment was conducted to explore whether the composite models would achieve a statistically significant improvement.

As already mentioned, during the preparation of the five data chunks for each of the two binary classification tests, an equal number of samples for both classes (T_1 and T_2 for task C_1 or T_1 and T_3 for task C_2) was prepared by stratifying the already balanced data according to the output class. This resulted not only in the effective training but also in the accuracy always being equal to the F_1 score. For that reason, we will focus on the classification accuracy metric when presenting the results of the cross-validation, or relative accuracy increase when depicting the improvements the composite models achieved over the baseline. The results of the evaluation will be presented in Section 4.1.

4.1. Quantitative Results

The cross-validation accuracy of all of the five inspected models (M_1, M_2, M_3, CM_1 and CM_2) on the task of low-quality sentence detection (C_1), as well as the highest achieved accuracy and mean accuracy, are presented in Table 5. The accuracy results of the same models, but on the task of machine translation detection (C_2), are presented in the same manner in Table 6.

Table 5. Cross-validation accuracy results achieved by three simple (left) and two composite models (right) on the low-quality sentence detection task (C_1). The upper part of the table depicts the results for each of the five folds, while the lower part of the table depicts maximum (Max) and mean (μ) accuracy. The highest accuracy among standalone models (baseline) and the best overall scores are marked in bold.

	M_1	M_2	M_3	CM_1	CM_2
fold 1	0.8468	0.5599	0.6117	0.8528	0.8631
fold 2	0.8456	0.5559	0.6187	0.8548	0.8648
fold 3	0.8506	0.5617	0.6198	0.8564	0.8716
fold 4	0.8486	0.5576	0.6181	0.8592	0.8628
fold 5	0.8522	0.5572	0.6194	0.8616	0.8690
Max	**0.8522**	0.5617	0.6198	0.8616	**0.8716**
μ	**0.8488**	0.5584	0.6175	0.8569	**0.8663**

Table 6. Cross-validation accuracy results achieved by three simple (left) and two composite models (right) on the machine translation detection task (C_2). The upper part of the table depicts the results for each of the five folds, while the lower part of the table depicts maximum (Max) and mean (μ) accuracy. The highest accuracy among standalone models (baseline) and the best overall scores are marked in bold.

	M_1	M_2	M_3	CM_1	CM_2
fold 1	0.5000	0.5000	0.5086	0.5077	0.5334
fold 2	0.5000	0.5000	0.5075	0.5157	0.5497
fold 3	0.5000	0.5000	0.5069	0.5242	0.5389
fold 4	0.5000	0.5000	0.5091	0.5205	0.5381
fold 5	0.5000	0.5000	0.5131	0.5176	0.5600
Max	0.5000	0.5000	**0.5131**	0.5242	**0.5600**
μ	0.5000	0.5000	**0.5090**	0.5171	**0.5440**

The average relative accuracy increase (RAI) and average error rate reduction (ERR) compared to the baseline are calculated for both composite models (CM_1 and CM_2) on both classification tasks (C_1 and C_2) using the equations:

$$RAI = \frac{a' - a}{a} \qquad (32)$$

and

$$ERR = \frac{a' - a}{1 - a}, \qquad (33)$$

where a is the baseline accuracy and a' is the alleged improved accuracy.

These results, aiming to give a definite answer to the research questions **RQ1–RQ3**, are presented in Table 7.

Table 7. Relative accuracy increase (RAI) and error rate reduction (ERR) achieved by each composite model (CM_1 and CM_2) for each classification task (C_1 and C_2), relative to the baseline results (highest achieved accuracy among the standalone models: M_1, M_2, and M_3). The highest relative accuracy increase and error rate reduction for each task are marked in bold.

	Relative Accuracy Increase (RAI)		Error Rate Reduction (ERR)	
	C_1	C_2	C_1	C_2
CM_1	0.0095	0.0159	0.0536	0.0165
CM_2	**0.0206**	**0.0688**	**0.1157**	**0.0713**

4.2. Qualitative Results

The improvement achieved by the composite model CM_2 over the baseline (2.06% relative accuracy increase on C_1 and 6.88% relative accuracy increase on C_2) is probably not due to mere chance, but despite that, we cannot ascertain the statistical significance via simple comparison. In order to check the integrity of the results, we used the *corrected repeated k-fold cross-validation test* [42] to determine the actual statistical significance of the achieved improvements. The *t-score* was calculated as:

$$t = \frac{\frac{1}{k}\sum_{i=1}^{k}(a'_i - a_i)}{\sqrt{(\frac{1}{k} + r)\sigma^2}}, \qquad (34)$$

where k is the number of cross-validation folds ($k = 5$), a_i the baseline accuracy at fold i, a'_i the improved accuracy at fold i, r the size ratio of test and training sets ($r = 0.25$), and σ^2 the variance of the difference of a and $a\prime$ across folds.

For each composite model (CM_1, CM_2) and for each classification task (C_1, C_2), we calculate the t-score using Equation (34) and from it the p-value using Student's Cumulative distribution function [43]. These results are presented in Table 8. Here, we observe a high statistical significance of the accuracy increase in three out of four cases with the p-values being below 0.05, in accordance with the standard confidence level of 0.95. The only outlier represents what the improvements classifier CM_1 achieved over the baseline for task C_1 (machine translation detection), $p = 0.5224$, in which case the *null hypothesis* (stating that no statistical significance exists) cannot be rejected.

Table 8. Calculated t-score and p-value, indicating statistical significance of accuracy improvements the composite classifiers (CM_1 and CM_2) achieved over the determined baseline for each classification task (C_1 and C_2).

	t-Score		p-Value	
	C_1	C_2	C_1	C_2
CM_1	2.0674	0.6397	0.0387	0.5224
CM_2	3.5974	2.0536	0.0003	0.0400

5. Discussion

In this paper, we experiment with two separate classification tasks: low-quality sentence detection (C_1) and machine translation detection (C_2). On both tasks, we test the improvements achieved using composite language models (built upon perplexity outputs of several language models) over the accuracy of standalone models, which is taken as a baseline.

From the results presented in previous section, precisely Table 5 (cross-validation results on task C_1), the following observations are made:

Q_1 Model M_1 is the best standalone model for low-quality sentence detection (average accuracy of 84.88%), and should thus be taken as the baseline for C_1;

Q_2 Composite model CM_1 outperforms this baseline on each cross-validation fold (with an average accuracy of 85.69%;

Q_3 Composite model CM_2 outperforms the composite model CM_1 across all cross-validation folds with an average accuracy of 86.63%.

Additionally, from the results presented in Table 6 (cross-validation on task C_2), we note the following observations:

Q_4 Model M_3 (syntactic) is the best-performing standalone model for machine-translation detection and should thus be taken as the baseline for C_2, although with an accuracy of only 50.9%;

Q_5 None of the other standalone models managed to surpass the 50% accuracy score (on any fold), indicating that perplexities outputted by the control (M_1) and semantic model (M_2) are not indicators for machine translation detection;

Q_6 Composite model CM_1 slightly outperforms the baseline on four out of five cross-validation folds, and also on average (accuracy of 51.71%);

Q_7 Composite model CM_2 outperforms the baseline, as well as composite model CM_1 across all cross-validation folds, with an average accuracy of 54.4%.

Lastly, from the results presented in Table 7 (average relative accuracy increase and error rate reduction per composite model and per task) and Table 8 (statistical significance of achieved accuracy improvements per composite model and per task), the following is observed:

Q_8 Composite model CM_1 achieved the average RAI of 0.95% for classification task C_1 and 1.59% for classification task C_2. The former is deemed statistically significant for a confidence level of 95% ($p = 0.0387$), while the latter is deemed statistically insignificant ($p = 0.5224$);

Q_9 Composite model CM_2 achieved the average RAI of 2.06% for C_1, 6.88% for C_2, error rate reduction of 11.57% for C_1, and 7.13% for C_2. Both improvements are deemed statistically significant for a confidence level of 95% ($p = 0.0003$ and $p = 0.4$, respectively);

Q_{10} The results achieved by all tested models, and especially M_1, CM_1, and CM_2, are comparable to the state-of-the-art results achieved for low-quality sentence detection for the English language [20].

Based on the collected cues, primarily Q_4 and Q_5, we conclude that there is indeed a use for semantic and syntactic models in sentence classification. While the positive results achieved using composite classifiers that incorporate these models indicate their importance for refinement of the classification, the fact that syntactic model M_3 outperformed the control model M_1 for classification task C_2 indicates a positive answer to the research question **RQ1**:

RQ1: *Are semantic and syntactic models justified tools to use for sentence classification tasks, e.g., low-quality sentence or machine translation detection?*

This notion that models M_2 and M_3 provide additional information despite being trained on the same text (just different representation) is additionally apparent through results achieved by composite model CM_1 (Q_2, Q_6, Q_8). While there is not definite statistical significance in its improvements over the baseline for the CM_2 task ($p > 0.05$), it definitely improved over the baseline on the CM_1 task ($p = 0.0387$) as evident in Q_8, confirming a positive answer to the first research question and imploring a positive answer to the research question **RQ2**:

RQ2: *Can composite language models based on outputted perplexities and the wisdom of crowds-based compositions improve on the accuracy of standalone models on classification tasks?*

Finally, the improvements the composite model CM_2 achieved over both the standalone models (M_1, M_2, and M_3) and the composite model CM_1 (Q_3, Q_7, Q_9) undoubtedly provide a positive answer to the final research question **RQ3**:

RQ3: *Can features extracted from perplexity vectors be used to further improve the classification accuracy of composite models?*

This also furthers the indication of the value of semantic and syntactic models, but most of all, it affirms the value of perplexity vectors [36] in perplexity-based sentence classification.

If we revisit the results for low-quality sentence detection task C_1 (Q_1, Q_2, Q_3), we conclude that for the task, while partially solvable using a standard language model, with an accuracy of nearly 85%, a significant improvement can be made via incorporating other language models and perplexity vectors. No statistically significant improvements over the baseline were found using the model CM_1 for this task, which is probably caused by the poor performance of the semantic and syntactic model (average accuracy of 55.84% and 61.75% compared to the baseline of 84.88%). Due to this fact, we must contribute the improvements achieved by model CM_2 (total error rate reduction of over 11%, Q_9) to the usage of perplexity vectors, indicating that low-quality sentences are detectable via features contained within them.

As for the task of machine translation detection (C_2) and the observed results on it (Q_4, Q_5, Q_6, Q_7), it is apparent that its difficulty is much higher. Two out of three standalone models failed to outperform the 50% accuracy mark, which can be attributed to random selection. The only standalone model that could even slightly differentiate between the expert and machine translations was the syntactic one (but with very low accuracy), which could mean that expert and machine translations differ mostly in the syntax used. However, model CM_1 which uses all three achieved better results (average accuracy of 51.71%) and the improvements were found to be statistically significant, indicating that the combination of syntax and semantics is a better indicator. Lastly, the results achieved by the CM_2 model (relative accuracy increase of 6.88% and error rate reduction of 7.13%, Q_9), despite the somewhat low achieved accuracy of 54.4%, indicate a high improvement through the usage of features extracted from perplexity vectors for this quite difficult task.

In conclusion, composite models are shown to improve on the accuracy of standalone models for classification tasks, with a composite language model based on a stacked classifier architecture that uses properties extracted from perplexity vectors as features being singled out as the best option for detection of both machine translations (low accuracy) and low-quality sentences (high accuracy). It should be noted that the drawback of composite models is higher training complexity and higher execution time. In future work, they should also be compared to bigger standalone models, i.e., whether the composition of a few smaller models is better than a large standalone model in terms of both training and execution speed, as well as in accuracy. If composite models are shown to be feasible, the research should focus on improving their quality through the improvement of the standalone models that they are composed of.

Perplexity vectors are shown to mitigate the main limitation of perplexity-based classification (the lack of dimensionality), but their limitations (aside from slightly higher execution time) are yet to be determined through future research. For example, features analysis should disclose the highest-value features of perplexity vectors, e.g., features extracted using RNN or features extracted from frequency-domain-based properties of perplexity vectors.

An inspection of further usages of both composite language models and perplexity vectors should be performed in order to expand on the idea of this research. Lastly, other methods should be tested for the examined tasks for the Serbian language, and a comparative study should be performed for a better understanding of both previously achieved and future results. Most prominently, BERT or a RoBERTa-based model for Serbian should be fine-tuned for the aforementioned tasks and tested on the prepared dataset.

Author Contributions: Conceptualization, M.Š. and R.S.; Data curation, M.U. and R.S.; Formal analysis, M.Š. and M.U.; Investigation, M.Š.; Methodology, M.Š. and M.U.; Project administration, R.S.; Resources, M.Š., M.U. and R.S.; Software, M.Š.; Supervision, M.U. and R.S.; Validation, M.U.; Visualization, M.Š.; Writing—original draft, M.Š.; Writing—review and editing, M.Š., M.U. and R.S. All authors have read and agreed to the published version of the manuscript.

Funding: The research is inline with the preparation for the TESLA project (Text Embeddings—Serbian Language Applications), Program PRIZMA, the Science Fund of the Republic of Serbia, grant number 7276.

Data Availability Statement: All of the data produced by this experiment as well as the complete code, which can be used to reproduce the results of the study, is publicly available as a repository at https://github.com/procesaur/composite-lang-models (accessed on 29 September 2023). All of the pre-trained models are available on the web: Baseline language model https://huggingface.co/procesaur/gpt2-srlat (accessed on 29 September 2023); Semantic language model https://huggingface.co/procesaur/gpt2-srlat-sem (accessed on 29 September 2023); Syntactic language model https://huggingface.co/procesaur/gpt2-srlat-synt (accessed on 29 September 2023).

Acknowledgments: The authors thank numerous contributors to the Serbian Corpora collection, especially the members of the Language Resources and Technologies Society JeRTeh.

Conflicts of Interest: The authors declare no conflict of interest. The funders had no role in the design of the study; in the collection, analyses, or interpretation of data; in the writing of the manuscript, or in the decision to publish the results.

Abbreviations

The following abbreviations are used in this manuscript:

ANN	Artificial neural network
BERT	Bidirectional Encoder Representations from Transformers
CLARIN	Common Language Resources and Technology Infrastructure
CNN	Convolutional Neural Network
ERR	Error rate reduction
GPT	Generative Pre-trained
LSTM	Long short-term memory
ML	Machine Learning
NLP	Natural Language Processing
PC	Personal computer
RAI	Relative accuracy increase
ReLU	Rectified linear unit function
RNN	Recurrent neural network

Appendix A. Implementation

Perplexity. The calculation of sequence (4) is based on the Equation (1) and implemented using the transformers Python library (https://huggingface.co/docs/transformers, accessed on 13 October 2023).

Perplexity vector. The calculation of sequence (5) is based on the Equation (3) and implemented using the transformers Python library (https://huggingface.co/docs/transformers, accessed on 13 October 2023).

GPT2 models. The training of the used language models was implemented using the transformers Python library (https://huggingface.co/docs/transformers, accessed on 13 October 2023). The training of all models was based on the GPT2 training configuration (https://huggingface.co/gpt2/raw/main/config.json, accessed on 11 November 2023), and the tokenization of the dataset was performed using the tokenizers Python library ((https://huggingface.co/docs/tokenizers, accessed on 11 November 2023).

Fully connected layers. All fully connected layers for this research (used for composite model CM_1, as well as neural network components NN_1 and NN_4 for composite model CM_2) are implemented using PyTorch library and torch.nn.Linear class (https://pytorch.org/docs/stable/generated/torch.nn.Linear.html#torch.nn.Linear, accessed on 13 October 2023).

Recurrent layer. A recurrent layer used for the component $NN2$ of the composite model CM_2 is implemented using PyTorch library and torch.nn.RNN class (https://pytorch.org/docs/stable//generated/torch.nn.RNN.html#torch.nn.RNN, accessed on 13 October 2023).

Convolutional layer. A (one-dimensional) convolutional layer employed in the component $NN3$ of the composite model CM_2 is implemented using PyTorch library, torch.nn.Conv1d class (https://pytorch.org/docs/stable//generated/torch.nn.Conv1d.html#torch.nn.Conv1d, accessed on 13 October 2023).

Max pooling layer. A (one-dimensional) max pooling layer is employed in the component $NN3$ of the composite model CM_2 is implemented using PyTorch library, torch.nn.MaxPool1d class (https://pytorch.org/docs/stable//generated/torch.nn.MaxPool1d.html#torch.nn.MaxPool1d, accessed on 13 October 2023).

Hyperbolic Tangent (Tanh) function. Tanh activation is used on the output of the recurrent layer in the NN_2 component and implemented using PyTorch library, torch.nn.Tanh class (https://pytorch.org/docs/stable/generated/torch.nn.Tanh.html, accessed on 13 October 2023).

Rectified linear unit function. After each non-terminal fully connected linear layer, as well as after each convolutional and max pooling layer, a rectified linear unit (ReLU) activation is implemented using PyTorch library, torch.nn.ReLU class (https://pytorch.

org/docs/stable//generated/torch.nn.ReLU.html#torch.nn.ReLU, accessed on 13 October 2023). The following layer use ReLU activation:

1. The sole layer NN_1 component;
2. Each layer of the NN_3 component;
3. The first layer of the NN_4 component.

References

1. Elman, J.L. *Finding Structure in Time. CRL Technical Report 9901*; Technical Report, Center for Research in Language; University of California: San Diego, CA, USA, 1988.
2. Elman, J.L. Finding Structure in Time. *Cogn. Sci.* **1990**, *14*, 179–211. [CrossRef]
3. Hochreiter, J.S. Untersuchungen zu Dynamischen Neuronalen Netzen. Master's Thesis, Institut für Informatik Technische Universität München, München, Germany, 1991. Available online: https://people.idsia.ch/~juergen/SeppHochreiter1991ThesisAdvisorSchmidhuber.pdf (accessed on 12 November 2023).
4. LeCun, Y.; Bengio, Y.; Hinton, G. Deep Learning. *Nature* **2015**, *521*, 436–444. [CrossRef] [PubMed]
5. Hochreiter, S.; Schmidhuber, J. Long Short-Term Memory. *Neural Comput.* **1997**, *9*, 1735–1780. [CrossRef]
6. Vaswani, A.; Shazeer, N.; Parmar, N.; Uszkoreit, J.; Jones, L.; Gomez, A.N.; Kaiser, Ł.; Polosukhin, I. Attention Is All You Need. In Proceedings of the 31st Conference on Neural Information Processing Systems (NIPS 2017), Long Beach, CA, USA, 4–9 December 2017.
7. Kenton, J.D.M.W.C.; Toutanova, L.K. BERT: Pre-Training of Deep Bidirectional Transformers for Language Understanding. In Proceedings of the NAACL-HLT 2019, Minneapolis, MN, USA, 2–7 June 2019.
8. Radford, A.; Narasimhan, K.; Salimans, T.; Sutskever, I. Improving Language Understanding by Generative Pre-Training. 2018. Available online: https://cdn.openai.com/research-covers/language-unsupervised/language_understanding_paper.pdf (accessed on 12 November 2023).
9. Lee, M. A Mathematical Interpretation of Autoregressive Generative Pre-Trained Transformer and Self-Supervised Learning. *Mathematics* **2023**, *11*, 2451. [CrossRef]
10. Peng, B.; Li, C.; He, P.; Galley, M.; Gao, J. Instruction Tuning with GPT-4. *arXiv* **2023**, arXiv:2304.03277.
11. Radford, A.; Wu, J.; Child, R.; Luan, D.; Amodei, D.; Sutskever, I. Language Models are Unsupervised Multitask Learners. *OpenAI Blog* **2019**, *1*, 9.
12. Bogdanović, M.; Tošić, J. SRBerta-BERT Transformer Language Model for Serbian Legal Texts. In Proceedings of the Analysis, Approximation, Applications (AAA2023), Vrnjačka Banja, Serbia, 21–24 June 2023.
13. Ljubešić, N.; Lauc, D. BERTić-The Transformer Language Model for Bosnian, Croatian, Montenegrin and Serbian. In Proceedings of the 8th Workshop on Balto-Slavic Natural Language Processing, Online, 20 April 2021; pp. 37–42.
14. Dobreva, J.; Pavlov, T.; Mishev, K.; Simjanoska, M.; Tudzarski, S.; Trajanov, D.; Kocarev, L. MACEDONIZER-The Macedonian Transformer Language Model. In Proceedings of the International Conference on ICT Innovations, Skopje, North Macedonia, 29 September–1 October 2022; Springer: Cham, Switzerland, 2022; pp. 51–62.
15. Šmajdek, U.; Zupanič, M.; Zirkelbach, M.; Jazbinšek, M. Adapting an English Corpus and a Question Answering System for Slovene. *Slov. 2.0 Empirič Ne Apl. Interdiscip. Raziskave* **2023**, *11*, 247–274. [CrossRef]
16. Singh, P.; Maladry, A.; Lefever, E. Too Many Cooks Spoil the Model: Are Bilingual Models for Slovene Better than a Large Multilingual Model? In Proceedings of the 17th Conference of the European Chapter of the Association for Computational Linguistics. Association for Computational Linguistics, Dubrovnik, Croatia, 2–6 May 2023; pp. 32–39.
17. Agichtein, E.; Castillo, C.; Donato, D.; Gionis, A.; Mishne, G. Finding High-Quality Content in Social Media. In Proceedings of the 2008 International Conference on Web Search and Data Mining, Palo Alto, CA, USA, 11–12 February 2008; WSDM '08; Association for Computing Machinery: New York, NY, USA, 2008; pp. 183–194. [CrossRef]
18. Vajjala, S.; Majumder, B.; Gupta, A.; Surana, H. *Practical Natural Language Processing: A Comprehensive Guide to Building Real-World NLP Systems*; O'Reilly Media: Newton, MA, USA, 2020.
19. Jurafsky, D.; Martin, J.H. *Speech and Language Processing*, 3rd ed.; Draft; Pearson; Prentice Hall: Hoboken, NJ, USA, 2023.
20. Fernández-Pichel, M.; Prada-Corral, M.; Losada, D.E.; Pichel, J.C.; Gamallo, P. An Unsupervised Perplexity-Based Method for Boilerplate Removal. *Nat. Lang. Eng.* **2023**, 1–18. [CrossRef]
21. Toral, A.; Pecina, P.; Wang, L.; Van Genabith, J. Linguistically-Augmented Perplexity-Based Data Selection for Language Models. *Comput. Speech Lang.* **2015**, *32*, 11–26. [CrossRef]
22. Gamallo, P.; Campos, J.R.P.; Alegria, I. A Perplexity-Based Method for Similar Languages Discrimination. In Proceedings of the Fourth Workshop on NLP for Similar Languages, Varieties and Dialects (VarDial), Valencia, Spain, 3 April 2017; pp. 109–114.
23. Jansen, T.; Tong, Y.; Zevallos, V.; Suarez, P.O. Perplexed by Quality: A Perplexity-based Method for Adult and Harmful Content Detection in Multilingual Heterogeneous Web Data. *arXiv* **2022**, arXiv:2212.10440.
24. Lee, N.; Bang, Y.; Madotto, A.; Fung, P. Towards Few-Shot Fact-Checking via Perplexity. In Proceedings of the 2021 Conference of the North American Chapter of the Association for Computational Linguistics: Human Language Technologies, Online, 6–11 June 2021; pp. 1971–1981.

25. Kalchbrenner, N.; Grefenstette, E.; Blunsom, P. A Convolutional Neural Network for Modelling Sentences. In Proceedings of the 52nd Annual Meeting of the Association for Computational Linguistics (Volume 1: Long Papers), Baltimore, MD, USA, 22–27 June 2014; pp. 655–665.
26. Stanković, R.; Škorić, M.; Šandrih Todorović, B. Parallel Bidirectionally Pretrained Taggers as Feature Generators. *Appl. Sci.* **2022**, *12*, 5028. [CrossRef]
27. Škorić, M.; Stanković, R.; Ikonić Nešić, M.; Byszuk, J.; Eder, M. Parallel Stylometric Document Embeddings with Deep Learning Based Language Models in Literary Authorship Attribution. *Mathematics* **2022**, *10*, 838. [CrossRef]
28. Škorić, M.D. Kompozitne Pseudogramatike Zasnovane na Paralelnim Jezičkim Modelima Srpskog Jezika. Ph.D. Thesis, University of Belgrade, Belgrade, Serbia, 12 November 2023. Available online: https://nardus.mpn.gov.rs/handle/123456789/21587 (accessed on 12 November 2023).
29. Costa-jussà, M.R.; Cross, J.; Çelebi, O.; Elbayad, M.; Heafield, K.; Heffernan, K.; Kalbassi, E.; Lam, J.; Licht, D.; Maillard, J.; et al. No Language Left Behind: Scaling Human-Centered Machine Translation. *arXiv* **2022**, arXiv:2207.04672.
30. Landauer, T.K.; Dumais, S. Latent Semantic Analysis. *Scholarpedia* **2008**, *3*, 4356. [CrossRef]
31. Grace Winkler, E. *Understanding Language*; Continuum International: Danbury, CT, USA, 2008; pp. 84–85.
32. Andonovski, J.; Šandrih, B.; Kitanović, O. Bilingual Lexical Extraction Based on Word Alignment for Improving Corpus Search. *Electron. Libr.* **2019**, *37*, 722–739. [CrossRef]
33. Perisic, O.; Stanković, R.; Ikonić Nešić, M.; Škorić, M. It-Sr-NER: CLARIN Compatible NER and GeoparsingWeb Services for Italian and Serbian Parallel Text. In Proceedings of the Selected Papers from the CLARIN Annual Conference 2022, Prague, Czech Republic, 10–12 October 2022; Linköping University Electronic Press: Linköping, Sweden, 2023; pp. 99–110. [CrossRef]
34. Perišić, O.; Stanković, R.; Ikonić Nešić, M.; Škorić, M. It-Sr-NER: Web Services for Recognizing and Linking Named Entities in Text and Displaying Them on a Web Map. *Infotheca—J. Digit. Humanit.* **2023**, *23*, 61–77. [CrossRef]
35. Hinrichs, E.; Krauwer, S. The CLARIN Research Infrastructure: Resources and Tools for eHumanities Scholars. In Proceedings of the Ninth International Conference on Language Resources and Evaluation (LREC'14), Reykjavik, Iceland, 26–31 May 2014; Calzolari, N., Choukri, K., Declerck, T., Loftsson, H., Maegaard, B., Mariani, J., Moreno, A., Odijk, J., Piperidis, S., Eds.; European Language Resources Association (ELRA): Reykjavik, Iceland, 2014.
36. Škorić, M. Text Vectorization via Transformer-Based Language Models and N-Gram Perplexities. *arXiv* **2023**, arXiv:2307.09255. [CrossRef]
37. Amari, S.I. Learning Patterns and Pattern Sequences by Self-Organizing Nets of Threshold Elements. *IEEE Trans. Comput.* **1972**, *100*, 1197–1206. [CrossRef]
38. Waibel, A.; Hanazawa, T.; Hinton, G.; Shikano, K.; Lang, K.J. Phoneme Recognition Using Time-Delay Neural Networks. In *Backpropagation*; Lawrence Erlbaum Associates Inc.: Hillsdale, NJ, USA, 2013; pp. 35–61.
39. Rabiner, L.; Gold, B.; Yuen, C. Theory and Application of Digital Signal Processing. *IEEE Trans. Syst. Man, Cybern.* **1978**, *8*, 146. [CrossRef]
40. Yamaguchi, K.; Sakamoto, K.; Akabane, T.; Fujimoto, Y. A Neural Network for Speaker-Independent Isolated Word Recognition. In Proceedings of the ICSLP, Kobe, Japan, 18–22 November 1990.
41. Kingma, D.P.; Ba, J. Adam: A method for stochastic optimization. *arXiv* **2014**, arXiv:1412.6980.
42. Bouckaert, R.R.; Frank, E. Evaluating the Replicability of Significance Tests for Comparing Learning Algorithms. In Proceedings of the Pacific-Asia conference on knowledge discovery and data mining, Sydney, Australia, 26–28 May 2004; Springer: Berlin/Heidelberg, Germany, 2004; pp. 3–12.
43. Student. The Probable Error of a Mean. *Biometrika* **1908**, *6*, 1–25. [CrossRef]

Disclaimer/Publisher's Note: The statements, opinions and data contained in all publications are solely those of the individual author(s) and contributor(s) and not of MDPI and/or the editor(s). MDPI and/or the editor(s) disclaim responsibility for any injury to people or property resulting from any ideas, methods, instructions or products referred to in the content.

Article

Leveraging Zero and Few-Shot Learning for Enhanced Model Generality in Hate Speech Detection in Spanish and English

José Antonio García-Díaz, Ronghao Pan * and Rafael Valencia-García

Facultad de Informática, Universidad de Murcia, Campus de Espinardo, 30100 Murcia, Spain; joseantonio.garcia8@um.es (J.A.G.-D.); valencia@um.es (R.V.-G.)
* Correspondence: ronghao.pan@um.es

Abstract: Supervised training has traditionally been the cornerstone of hate speech detection models, but it often falls short when faced with unseen scenarios. Zero and few-shot learning offers an interesting alternative to traditional supervised approaches. In this paper, we explore the advantages of zero and few-shot learning over supervised training, with a particular focus on hate speech detection datasets covering different domains and levels of complexity. We evaluate the generalization capabilities of generative models such as T5, BLOOM, and Llama-2. These models have shown promise in text generation and have demonstrated the ability to learn from limited labeled data. Moreover, by evaluating their performance on both Spanish and English datasets, we gain insight into their cross-lingual applicability and versatility, thus contributing to a broader understanding of generative models in natural language processing. Our results highlight the potential of generative models to bridge the gap between data scarcity and model performance across languages and domains.

Keywords: hate speech detection; zero-shot learning; few-shot learning; fine-tuning; large language models; natural language processing

MSC: 68T50

Citation: García-Díaz, J.A.; Pan, R.; Valencia-García, R. Leveraging Zero and Few-Shot Learning for Enhanced Model Generality in Hate Speech Detection in Spanish and English. *Mathematics* 2023, 11, 5004. https://doi.org/10.3390/math11245004

Academic Editor: Florentina Hristea

Received: 9 November 2023
Revised: 11 December 2023
Accepted: 14 December 2023
Published: 18 December 2023

Copyright: © 2023 by the authors. Licensee MDPI, Basel, Switzerland. This article is an open access article distributed under the terms and conditions of the Creative Commons Attribution (CC BY) license (https://creativecommons.org/licenses/by/4.0/).

1. Introduction

Online social networks have evolved into vast interconnected communities that function as communication platforms, facilitating the exchange of information and social discourse. While these virtual spaces undoubtedly enhance global connectivity, they also raise a troubling concern: the spread of hate speech. Hate speech encompasses a range of discriminatory and biased behaviors, including homophobia, misogyny, racism, transphobia, and other forms of intolerance, which affect individuals as well as online communities and platforms that strive to create inclusive and safe environments. Identifying and mitigating instances of hate speech on social media platforms is critical to protecting the digital sphere from the harmful effects of prejudice, hostility, and harassment.

In the ongoing fight against hate speech in online spaces, the field of Natural Language Processing (NLP) has evolved significantly in recent years. Traditional methods of hate speech detection, often based on statistical approaches and conventional machine learning classifiers, have been outpaced by advances in deep learning. In particular, Automatic Document Classification (ADC) using Transformers has emerged as the new frontier in the fight against online hate. These powerful models, with their ability to learn complex patterns in language and context, have achieved unprecedented accuracy and efficiency in distinguishing hate speech from benign content. Their success has led to a paradigm shift in how we approach this multifaceted problem.

While Transformers have undoubtedly demonstrated exceptional performance in controlled and simulated environments, their effectiveness has faced notable challenges when applied to the unpredictable and dynamic landscape of real-world online social networks. The discrepancy between idealized laboratory conditions and the complexity of the online ecosystem has raised concerns about the generalizability of the models. These discrepancies call for a deeper examination of their adaptability to diverse and evolving hate speech contexts. However, the latest approaches in NLP, such as Large Language Models (LLMs), have the ability to directly handle a wide range of NLP tasks and domains, and they possess Zero-Shot Learning (ZSL) and Few-Shot Learning (FSL) capabilities. Thus, the central motivation of this research is to evaluate the potential of ZSL and FSL approaches, which are specifically designed to address the very issue of generalization and adaptability. By subjecting generative models such as BLOOM [1] or LLAMA [2] to a battery of real-world Spanish and English hate speech datasets, we seek to uncover whether these models exhibit improved generalization and robustness in the fight against hate speech compared to traditional fine-tuning approaches.

In this case, the evaluation of the datasets for English and Spanish was chosen because English is the most spoken language and Spanish is the fourth [3], even though both are typologically different languages, one belonging to the Germanic languages and the other to the Romance languages [4].

To evaluate the performance of ZSL and FSL capabilities compared to fine-tuning strategies, we defined the following research questions:

- RQ1. Do ZSL and FSL strategies improve the performance of fine-tuning an LLM for hate speech detection?
- RQ2. Are current ZSL and FSL models equally good at detecting hate speech in English and Spanish?
- RQ3. What are the best generative LLMs for performing ZSL and FSL classification in hate speech detection?
- RQ4. Are the same models equally valid for ZSL and FSL in hate speech detection?

The rest of the manuscript is organized as follows. First, in Section 2 the reader will find the state-of-the-art in hate speech detection and different strategies for performing ZSL and FSL experiments. Next, Section 3 describes the evaluated dataset and the pipeline for performing the comparisons between ZSL and FSL in comparison with fine-tuning approaches. Next, Section 4 presents the results which are evaluated in Section 5. Finally, the conclusions of the paper as well as and promising lines of research can be found in Section 6.

2. State-of-the-Art

Hate speech can be defined as the use of language that promotes discrimination, hostility, or violence against individuals or groups based on their race, ethnicity, religion, gender, sexual orientation, disability, or other protected characteristic [5]. Hate speech can take many forms and is often targeted at specific groups, resulting in types such as racism, xenophobia, homophobia, misogyny, transphobia, and more. These types of hate speech are characterized by their specific prejudices and discriminatory attitudes, highlighting the diversity of groups that may be targeted or marginalized by such expressions. Hate speech is an important social and ethical concern because it can contribute to real harm, perpetuate stereotypes, and undermine inclusivity and tolerance in society.

Hate speech detection has undergone a paradigm shift, driven by the evolution of NLP. Transformer-based models, which are the building blocks of Large Language Models (LLMS), exemplified by BERT, RoBERTa, and their multilingual counterparts, have become the focus of modern hate speech detection systems. Their ability to capture contextual linguistic information has revolutionized the field. In contrast, earlier methods relied on statistical features such as TF–IDF or non-contextual word embeddings such as GloVe [6] or fastText [7].

In a survey published in 2018 in [5], the authors highlighted the lack of hate speech detection systems for non-English languages. Since then, a few datasets have been published on this topic, especially those published in shared tasks in workshops. However, in recent surveys, such as the one published in [8], in which the authors evaluate the most important datasets published in recent years on the topic of hate speech, the authors conclude that several datasets in the bibliography do not have sufficient examples and are therefore not reliable for hate speech detection. In Spanish, the authors of [9] evaluated which features and which feature integration techniques are most effective for hate speech detection. They focus mainly on transformers and linguistic features, and two strategies for combining the features: knowledge integration and ensemble learning. The evaluation was carried out on four Spanish datasets on different types of hate speech. Two of them were published in workshops as shared tasks. They were the shared tasks (1) AMI 2018 [10], held at IberEval 2018 and which focused on the detection of misogyny; and (2) HatEval 2019 [11], held at SemEval 2019 and which focused on the detection of hate speech against immigrants and women. The other two datasets are (3) the full Spanish MisoCorpus 2020 [12], which focused on misogyny; and (4) HaterNET [13], a binary dataset compiled from Twitter. The authors concluded that the integration of linguistic features with the transformers using the knowledge integration strategy outperformed other approaches in identifying hate speech in Spanish.

Zero and Few-Shot Learning

In recent years, many studies have addressed the problem of so-called low-resource languages and the possibilities of using multilingual approaches based on LLMs. In [14], evidence was found that Multilingual BERT (mBERT), a multilingual masked language model based on transformers, is capable of zero-shot cross-lingual transfer. Furthermore, in [15], the ability of this model to transfer syntactic knowledge between languages was investigated by examining whether and to what extent syntactic dependencies learned in one language are maintained in others. In [16,17], the compressibility of the BERT model was verified, specifically its ability to capture linguistic knowledge in word representations.

In particular, some have focused on the transfer of specific knowledge or phenomena into phylogenetically different languages by ZSL and FSL of LLMs. For example, the authors of [18] explored the problem of multilingual transfer in unseen languages where no unlabeled data are available for pre-training a model. A sentiment analysis task in 12 languages, including 8 unseen languages, was used to analyze the effectiveness of different few-shot learning strategies. Another similar paper [19], where the ability of the pre-trained BERT neural model in Italian to embed syntactic dependency relations in its layers by approximating a dependency parse tree was investigated. For this purpose, a structural probe, a supervised model capable of extracting linguistic structures from a language model, was trained using the contextual embeddings of BERT layers.

Regarding the evaluation of novel ZSL and FSL strategies in deep learning, the work described in [20] measures the reliability of using state-of-the-art generative LLMs to build knowledge graphs. In this sense, the authors propose a novel strategy for asking different LLMs to extract the data to build the knowledge graph. This strategy is based on ZSL, since no requirements are needed to guide the prompts. Another work evaluating ZSL capabilities is [21], in which the authors propose ChatIE, which combines ZSL strategies and ChatGPT for a question-answering task. The evaluated task is divided into several subtasks, including the extraction and recognition of entities and their relations. The authors evaluate a total of six datasets written in two languages. Their proposed model outperforms models trained in the traditional way (i.e., full-shot models).

The paper published in [22] comes closest to our proposal. Among other research objectives, the authors evaluate the ZSL performance of different LLMs and hate speech using the HatEval 2019 dataset [11]. Five LLMs posing as different human annotators are evaluated. While the results are promising, the authors conclude that human annotation is still needed. The main differences with our work are that no few-shot learning capabilities are evaluated and that hate speech is only evaluated in one dataset.

3. Materials and Methods

This section describes the experiments conducted to answer the proposed research questions regarding the performance of ZSL and FSL in detecting hate speech. Therefore, this section is divided into two parts. The first, Section 3.1, describes the datasets evaluated in our proposal. These datasets are in Spanish and English. Next, Section 3.2 describes the pipeline for carrying out the experiments. This pipeline includes three strategies: fine tuning of an LLS, defined as baseline, and ZSL and FSL.

3.1. Datasets

This section describes the datasets used to evaluate the performance of the ZSL and FSL features. In order to select the datasets that help us answer the RQs defined in this work, we focus on hate speech datasets in two languages: Spanish and English. Another goal is to cover different subtopics of hate speech, such as the detection of sexist or misogynistic content, or racism, transphobia, and homophobia.

In order to make the results comparable across datasets, we focused on a unique task: binary hate speech detection. That is, we select datasets that allow us to identify which texts contain hate speech and which do not. It is worth noting that most of the selected datasets come from shared tasks in workshops that defined a binary classification task. However, there are a few datasets that we have adapted to meet this requirement. Another important point is that not all datasets published in the workshops had the gold labels published. In these cases, we reorganized the dataset to create a new test set from the training split. Therefore, the results in these cases are not comparable to those published in the official task rankings.

The selected datasets are described below, but a summary can be found in Table 1, which includes their publication year, language, hate speech subdomain, and size.

- **EXIST** (EXIST 2021-es, EXIST 2022-es, EXIST 2022-es, EXIST 2022-en): These are a series of shared tasks focused on identifying sexism in Spanish and English. There are editions of EXIST in 2021 [23], 2022 [24], and 2023 [25] in different international workshops such as CLEF or IberLEF. The challenges proposed to the participants usually consist of a binary classification of sexist comments and multi-classification problems to explain why the comments are sexist. In this work, we focus on the binary classification task of 2021 and 2022, with the datasets of Spanish and English separately. The golden labels are not published for these datasets, so we have chosen a custom split for testing in this work.
- **HaterNet 2019** (HaterNet). The HaterNet 2019 dataset [13] contains 6k documents annotated as hateful and non-hateful. The dataset can be accessed at 8 November 2023 (https://zenodo.org/record/2592149#.YNBqJGj7SUl). This dataset is unbalanced, since only about 1.5k documents are annotated as hateful. The original evaluation of the dataset focuses on the F1 score of the hateful class. This dataset has the gold labels of the test split.
- **HatEval 2019** (HatEval). The HatEval [11] shared task took place in SemEval 2019, and is about detecting hate speech against immigrants and women. The dataset is in two languages: Spanish and English, and it was collected from Twitter. In our work, we focus on the first subtask of the competition, which is about binary classification to detect hate speech. This dataset has the gold labels of the test split.
- **Spanish hate speech detection in football** (Football) [26]. In this paper, the authors published a dataset for hate speech detection in Spanish, consisting of almost 7.5k football-related tweets. These tweets were manually categorized as aggressive, racist, misogynist, and safe. In the work, the authors proposed a multi-label approach, and achieved a macro F1 score of 88.713% with the combination of LLM features within the same neural network. This dataset has the gold labels of the test split.
- **Spanish MisoCorpus 2020** (MisoCorpus). The Spanish MisoCorpus 2020 dataset [12] focuses on the binary identification of misogyny. This dataset is almost balanced. It can be downloaded in the full version or divided into three splits regarding different categories. The first one focuses on the violence against relevant women; the second one is about the messages from Spain and Latin America to understand cultural and background differences; and the last one is about general characteristics related to misogyny. This dataset has the gold labels of the test split.

- **Explainable Detection of Online Sexism** [27] (EDOS). This shared task was conducted in SemEval 2023 and focused on detecting and explaining sexism in English. The dataset was collected from Gab and Reddit. In this paper, we focus on the first subtask, binary sexism detection. This dataset has the gold labels of the test split.
- **Hate Speech and Offensive Content Identification in Indo-European Languages, 2020** (HASOC). The HASOC shared task was conducted in FIRE 2020, and it contains documents in English, German, and Hindi for the identification of hateful, offensive and profane content. This dataset has the gold labels of the test split.

It is worth noting that these datasets were selected based on their relation to hate speech, rather than other common datasets for understanding assessment such as GLUE [28]. Furthermore, the selected datasets have been used in international workshops such as IberLEF or CLEF.

Table 1. Year, language, hate speech subdomain, and size of the datasets.

Dataset	Year	Language	Domain	Size
EXIST-2021-es [23]	2021	Spanish	Sexism	3436
EXIST-2022-es [24]	2022	Spanish	Sexism	6233
HaterNet [13]	2019	Spanish	Hate	6000
HatEval [11]	2019	Spanish	Hate	6599
Football [26]	2023	Spanish	Hate	8026
MisoCorpus [12]	2020	Spanish	Misogyny	8390
EXIST-2021-en [23]	2021	English	Sexism	3106
EXIST-2022-en [24]	2022	English	Sexism	6170
HatEval [11]	2019	English	Hate	13,000
EDOS [27]	2022	English	Hate	20,000
HASOC	2020	English	Hate	5124

3.2. Pipeline

3.2.1. Baseline: Fine-Tuning Models

For a fair comparison of the ZSL and FSL capabilities of generative models with fine-tuning LLMs, we established a strong baseline by fine-tuning several popular LLMs based on different architectures (BERT, RoBERTa) and different optimization strategies (distillation) and focusing on a specific dataset or multilingual.

Fine-tuning an LLM for an ADC task involves the process of adapting a model, such as BERT, to a specific classification objective. This is achieved by taking a well-trained LLM and further training it on a labeled dataset containing documents annotated with labels. During this fine-tuning process, the parameters of the LLM are adjusted to learn the patterns and features relevant to the classification task. The goal is to optimize the model's performance in accurately categorizing new documents into predefined labels. Fine-tuning LLMs is a powerful approach that leverages the model's pre-trained language understanding capabilities for ADC tasks such as sentiment analysis, topic categorization, spam detection, and more.

Below is a comparison of the LLMs evaluated.

- **Mono-lingual Transformers**. The two most popular monolingual transformer architectures are BERT (Bidirectional Encoder Representations from Transformers) [29] and RoBERTa (a Robustly Optimized BERT Pre-training Approach) [30]. These models were trained on English data.

  BERT is pre-trained on large amounts of text data to understand the contextual nuances of language. BERT's bidirectional architecture allows it to capture relationships between words and their environment, making it highly effective for various NLP tasks, from sentiment analysis to question answering and more. RoBERTa is an evolution of the original BERT model. It has been trained on a larger and more diverse dataset, using a longer training period and a dynamic masking strategy. Unlike BERT,

RoBERTa does not use the Next Sentence Prediction (NSP) task during pre-training. It also uses a larger vocabulary and incorporates additional training techniques, all of which contribute to its superior performance and robustness in various natural language understanding tasks. Both general-purpose models can be adapted to solve other tasks through a form of transfer learning called fine-tuning. In this process, a pre-trained model is retrained on specific datasets and tasks, and the model's parameters are adjusted to perform well on these new tasks.

There are two LLMs in Spanish, MarIA and BETO. MarIA [31], on the one hand, is trained with the RoBERTa architecture and BETO [32], on the other hand, is trained with the BERT architecture.

We are also evaluating lightweight models: ALBERT [33] and DistilBERT [34]. AL-BERT (*A Lite BERT*) is an optimized variant of the BERT model designed to improve computational efficiency without sacrificing performance by significantly reducing the number of parameters. DistilBERT, on the other hand, is a distilled version of the BERT model. It achieves compactness and computational efficiency by using distillation. Distilling involves compressing and simplifying its architecture to create a lighter version while retaining its essential knowledge. The process typically involves training a smaller model (known as the student) to mimic the behavior of the larger, pre-existing model (the teacher). These models have also been adapted to Spanish [35].

- **Multi-lingual Transformers**. Multilingual LLMs are models that have been trained on text from multiple languages, giving them the ability to understand and generate text in different linguistic contexts. Some advantages are that these models facilitate cross-lingual knowledge transfer because they can apply their understanding from one language to another, reducing the need for language-specific models. Second, they are resource efficient, allowing multiple languages to be handled by a single model, thereby reducing computational overhead. In some scenarios, multilingual LLMs require less labeled data to achieve competitive performance on some tasks. However, dedicated monolingual models typically outperform multilingual models.

In this paper, we evaluate multilingual BERT, one of the first multilingual models, but also two newer models: DeBERTa [36], and TwHIN [37]. DeBERTa stands for Decoding-enhanced BERT with Disentangled Attention. It is a model that improves BERT by enhancing its decoding capabilities and disentangling attention mechanisms, resulting in better performance on various natural language processing tasks. TwHIN is trained on 7 billion microblogging posts from Twitter, making it suitable for short, noisy, and user-generated text often found in hate speech.

To obtain the best result for each dataset and language model, we perform a hyperparameter tuning step to perform the fine-tuning process. For this, we use the RayTune library [38]. This step is as follows. For each dataset and language model, we train a total of 10 models. Each model has different parameters to be evaluated. The hyperparameters are as follows: (1) the training batch size, where 8 or 16 are the only alternatives; (2) the weight decay, with values between 0.0 and 0.3 following a uniform distribution; (3) the warm-up steps, with step values of 0, 250, 500, or 1000; (4) the number of epochs (between 1 and 5); and (5) the learning rate, with values between 1×10^{-5} and 5×10^{-5} following a uniform distribution. The algorithm for selecting the next pair of hyperparameters is based on HyperOptSearch, with the Tree of Parzen Estimators (TPE) and the ASHA scheduler. The goal is to maximize the macro-weighted F1 score.

3.2.2. Generative Models

In terms of text generation models, we have conducted experiments with five state-of-the-art fine-tuned instruction LLMs based mainly on three architectures: (1) T5 with an encoder—decoder, (2) Llama-2, and (3) BLOOMZ. We specifically chose these five models because they have extensive fine-tuning across a wide range of instructions, making them the most representative of each architecture category. The selected models are described below.

- **Flan-T5**. It is the instruction fine-tuned version of T5 [39] that has achieved strong few-shot performance, even compared to much larger models like PaLM 62B. It has been fine-tuned on over 1000 tasks and covers 60 languages. For this study, we used the XL version of Flan-T5, which contains a total of 3 billion parameters [40].
- **Flan-alpaca**. It is an encoder–decoder model based on T5 [39] and has been fine-tuned with the Alpaca instruction dataset and GPT4ALL [41].
- **mT0**. It is a model belonging to the BLOOMZ and mT0 family, a group of models capable of understanding human instructions in dozens of languages through zero-shot learning [42]. Specifically, these are fine-tuned models derived from BLOOM and mT5 over a mixture of multilingual tasks. For this paper, we used the large version, which has a total of 1.3 billion parameters.
- **Llama v2**. It is a family of pre-trained LLMs, fine-tuned over a range of 7B to 70B parameters, capable of generating text and summarizing or rewriting existing text [2]. In this case, we used the Stable Beluga 7B and Stable Beluga 13B models, based on Llama-2 with 7B and 13B parameters, fine-tuned with the Orca-style dataset [43]. Note that due to hardware limitations, the Llama-2 13B is loaded with a 4-bit quantization and this fact usually reduces the performance of the model.

3.2.3. ZSL and FSL Prompting

A prompt is a type of input or instruction that is inserted into an LLM to generate a desired response. It can be a sentence, a phrase, or even an entire paragraph, and serves as a starting point or guide for the language model to generate text. Therefore, the proper design and customization of prompts can have a significant impact on the performance of LLMs in specific tasks, such as sentiment analysis.

For ZSL in T5-based models (Flan-T5 and Flan-alpaca), we have defined a prompt in the form of a paragraph consisting mainly of two parts: an instruction to the LLM and the text to be analyzed. In the LLM instruction, to ensure that the models always return one of the classification classes, we introduced a kind of control sequence, as shown in Figure 1. We considered the classification of the aforementioned datasets from a binary perspective. Thus, for the mT0 model, the best performance was achieved with a prompt like *"Is this a sexist tweet?"* and the answer will always be yes or no. Instructed models of Llama-2 require prompts to be constructed with specific fields: "system", "user", and "assistant". The "system" field is used to specify the instruction or guidance to the system, "user" contains the instance to be classified, and "assistant" is the output indicator.

For the FSL approach, we randomly selected five examples of each label and included them in the prompt using the *Stormtrooper* (https://github.com/centre-for-humanities-computing/stormtrooper/tree/main/stormtrooper(accessed at 8 November 2023)) tool approach, which consists of including the examples in the instruction part of the LLM with the following format: "Please respond with a single label that you think fits the document best. Here are some examples of labels given by experts: examples". The "examples" part is where the randomly extracted examples from the dataset are inserted.

Despite the inclusion of a control sequence in the model, there are still a few cases where the model returns an unrelated response. In these cases, we replaced the response with the most common label in the dataset.

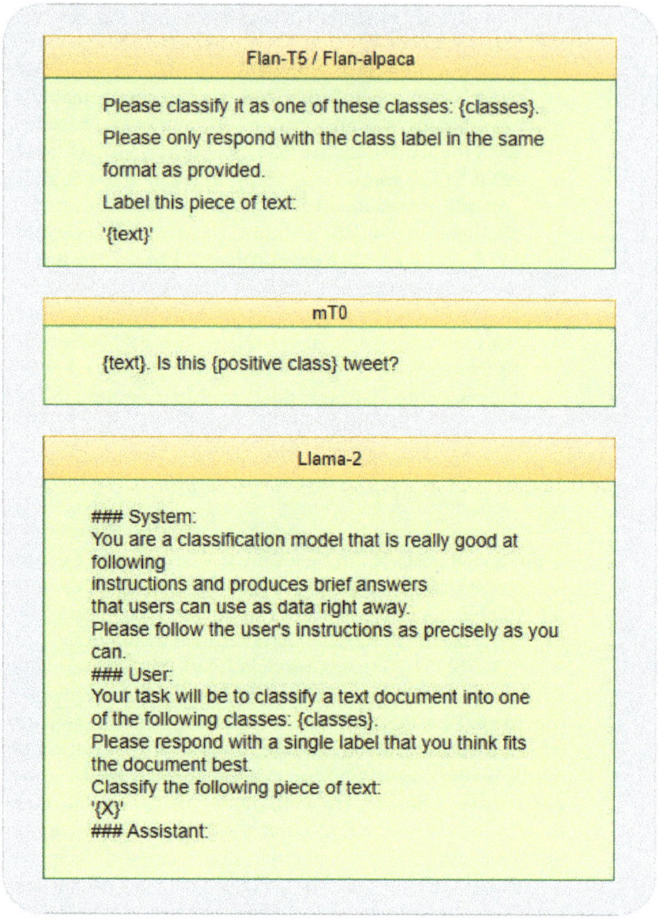

Figure 1. Instructions formulated for ZSL in our study of LLMs for each classification task. The "classes" part indicates the possible labels of the dataset and the "text" part is where the text to be parsed is inserted.

4. Results

In this section, we present the results obtained for the comparison between the fine-tuning and generative models. The results are divided into Spanish (see Section 4.1) and English (see Section 4.2) datasets.

Since we only consider hate speech classification from a binary perspective, the comparison of all models is based only on the hate speech class, including precision, recall, and F1 score. In this sense, we ignore the relevance of the class imbalance between the datasets in our benchmark.

In terms of hardware resources, all experiments are performed on a GeForce RTX 4090 (24 GB). As mentioned earlier, the Llama-2 13B model is evaluated with 4-bit precision due to hardware limitations.

4.1. Spanish Datasets

First, we report the results obtained with the Spanish split of the EXIST dataset in Table 2 for 2021 (left) and 2022 (right) for the positive class (i.e., a document annotated as sexist). Note that this evaluation is performed with a custom validation split, as the gold labels were not released for this shared task. Looking at the results obtained with the fine-tuning strategy, we can see that the two multilingual models, DeBERTa and TwHIN, achieved very good performance on the 2021 dataset. On the other hand, these models obtained more limited results in 2022, where DistilBETO obtained the best F1 score for the sexist label (2022). In this sense, multilingual DeBERTa obtained an almost perfect recall but very limited precision in 2022, which in binary classification indicates that the model is not reliable, as it always predicts that all documents are sexist. It is worth noting that EXIST 2022 is almost twice the size of EXIST 2021. However, monolingual LLMs such as BETO and MarIA give consistent results in both 2021 and 2022, with MarIA slightly better in both cases.

In terms of ZSL, the 7B version of the Llama-2 model achieved the best results in both EXIST 2021 and EXIST 2022 datasets, with F1 scores of 69.883% and 69.872%, respectively. Contrary to the zero-shot scenario, the FSL inference (five shots in our experiments) shows that the performance of Flan-Alpaca, Flan-T5, and 13B Llama-2 did not improve in EXIST 2021 and even worsened due to the introduced examples being poorly correlated with the training data of these models. In the FSL of EXIST 2022, we can see that the five examples selected for each label have improved the performance of Flan-T5, Flan-Alpaca, and Llama-2 13B. The largest absolute gains are obtained with mT0, with an improvement of about 28%.

Table 2. Benchmark of the fine-tuning, zero, and few-shot learning of Spanish datasets of EXIST 2021 (left) and 2022 (right) with the positive class. The results are calculated with a custom validation split. The best results for each metric are shown in bold.

		2021			2022		
	LLM	Precision	Recall	F1 Score	Precision	Recall	F1 Score
Fine-tuning	ALBETO	78.4530	80.2260	79.3296	**79.0484**	75.3927	77.1773
	BETO	80.5882	77.4011	78.9625	77.7597	83.5951	80.5719
	DistilBETO	80.3815	83.3333	81.8308	78.0309	83.6823	**80.7579**
	MarIA	80.5479	83.0508	81.7802	78.0130	83.5951	80.7077
	mBERT	73.2240	75.7062	74.4444	73.4459	83.5078	78.1543
	mDeBERTa	**81.9718**	82.2033	82.0874	50.2413	**99.9127**	66.8613
	TwHIN	78.4615	**86.4406**	**82.2581**	50.0323	67.5393	57.4824
Zero-shot	Flan-T5	**67.1598**	64.1243	65.6069	**64.0981**	63.8743	63.9860
	Flan-alpaca	61.8943	79.3785	69.5545	60.8696	79.4066	68.9133
	mT0	63.2653	8.75671	15.3846	58.6538	10.6457	18.0207
	Llama-2	64.8910	75.7062	**69.8827**	55.2178	**95.1134**	**69.8718**
	Llama-2 13B	72.3684	62.1469	66.8693	70.0397	61.6056	65.5525
Few-shot	Flan-T5	**69.8305**	58.1912	63.4823	**67.7686**	64.3979	66.0403
	Flan-alpaca	51.3828	**99.7175**	**67.8194**	53.6176	**97.6440**	**69.2236**
	mT0	51.8868	77.6836	62.2172	52.2752	41.0995	46.0186
	Llama-2	69.2547	62.9944	65.9763	64.1658	56.7190	60.2131
	Llama-2 13B	71.2871	61.0169	65.7534	65.1969	72.2513	68.5430

Next, we evaluate the Spanish split of the HatEval 2019 shared task for discriminating between documents labeled as hateful to immigrants and hateful to women. The results are shown in Table 3. In this case, the performance is obtained with the test set, as the gold labels were released. For the fine-tuning strategy, the best performance for the hateful comments is achieved with DistilBETO, with an F1 score of 76.237%. Looking at the result of the other lightweight model, ALBETO, its performance is also very competitive for detecting hateful comments, with a performance of 75.334%. In general, all the fine-tuned LLMs achieve a similar range of values. The most limited result is obtained with multilingual BERT (70.240%). Nevertheless, the performance of the other multilingual models, mDeBERTA and

TwHIN, is very promising, as they both outperform the monolingual model BETO, although the result of MarIA is slightly better (75.912%). Finally, to compare the performance with the official results of the shared task [11], the overall macro averaged F1 score is 73% and our best macro averaged F1 score (not shown in the table) is 78.45%, also with DistilBETO.

In the ZSL of the hate speech detection models, we can see that Llama-2 from the 7B version achieved the best result with an F1 score of 65.369%, followed by Llama-2 from the 13B version with an F1 score of 64.100%. Regarding the FSL, the examples included in the prompt did not improve the performance of the models. We suspect that this is because the examples have little correlation with the test set, introducing noise into the hate speech prediction. Nevertheless, the 13B version of the Llama-2 model improved its performance by about 2%, achieving an F1 score of 66.283%, surpassing the best ZSL result.

Table 3. Benchmark of the fine-tuning, zero, and few-shot learning of Spanish datasets of HatEval 2019 with the positive class. The results are calculated with the test split. The best results for each metric are shown in bold.

	LLM	Precision	Recall	F1 Score
Fine-tuning	ALBETO	70.2490	81.2121	75.3338
	BETO	66.4216	82.1212	73.4417
	DistilBETO	70.5806	82.8787	**76.2369**
	MarIA	71.2766	81.2121	75.9207
	mBERT	65.6992	75.4545	70.2398
	mDeBERTa	67.2393	**83.0303**	74.3051
	TwHIN	**72.8324**	76.3636	74.5562
Zero-shot	Flan-T5	**65.8228**	55.1515	60.0165
	Flan-alpaca	50.8961	86.0606	63.9640
	mT0	46.3177	79.0909	58.4219
	Llama-2	53.5266	83.9394	**65.3687**
	Llama-2 13B	47.8358	**97.1212**	64.1000
Few-shot	Flan-T5	**74.8428**	36.0606	48.6708
	Flan-alpaca	47.7702	95.7576	63.7418
	mT0	41.2874	**96.2121**	57.7798
	Llama-2	58.3110	65.9091	61.8777
	Llama-2 13B	53.4323	87.2727	**66.2831**

The next evaluated dataset is the Spanish MisoCorpus 2020, the results of which are shown in the Table 4. This dataset is about misogyny detection with tweets containing hatred towards women with responsibility charges, tweets from different Spanish speaking countries and tweets with different misogynistic characteristics. The strategy of fine-tuning LLMs for the binary classification task yields very high results in terms of precision, recall, and F1 score for the positive label, regardless of the language model. In fact, the difference between the best (mDeBERTa) and the worst (multilingual BERT) is only 1.808% of the F1 score. Regarding ZSL in text generation models for the classification of misogyny texts, we can see that the best result is obtained with the 13B version of Llama-2, with an F1 score of 69.60%. Furthermore, inference with few shots (five shots in our experiments) shows an improvement in all models except mT0. This draws our attention to the large performance loss compared to fine-tuning with ZSL and FSL. Especially in models such as Flan-T5 in ZSL and FSL, or mT0 in FSL, with very limited recall, there is a suggestion that these models give random predictions.

Table 5 shows the results obtained for the detection of hate speech in the football dataset. In this sense, if we observe the results of the fine-tuning strategy, we can see that the best precision and F1 score is obtained with the monolingual model MarIA (87.535% of precision, 85.175% of F1 score), while the multilingual DeBERTa achieved the best recall (85.302%). Multilingual BERT achieved the lowest F1 score (80.926%), but this result is surpassed by another multilingual model, TwHIN, with an F1 score of 83.974%). The lightweight models ALBETO and DistilBETO also achieved very good results, with F1 scores of 84.888% and 84.375%, respectively. This table also shows the performance of different text generation models in a ZSL and FSL scenario. The best result was achieved with the 13B version of

Llama-2, with an F1 score of 72.326% in ZSL. However, we can see that the examples selected for FSL did not improve the performance of the models due to their quality, since FSL models depend heavily on the composition and quality of the test set.

Table 4. Benchmark of the fine-tuning, zero, and few-shot learning of Spanish datasets of Spanish MisoCorpus 2020 with the positive class. The results are calculated with the test split. The best results for each metric are shown in bold.

	LLM	Precision	Recall	F1 Score
Fine-tuning	ALBETO	90.1389	88.5402	89.3324
	BETO	90.3581	89.4952	89.9246
	DistilBETO	89.9587	89.2224	89.5890
	MarIA	89.8649	**90.7230**	90.2919
	mBERT	89.1185	88.2673	88.6909
	mDeBERTa	**90.6849**	90.3138	**90.4990**
	TwHIN	90.6207	89.6316	90.1235
Zero-shot	Flan-T5	**68.0581**	51.1596	58.4112
	Flan-alpaca	51.6817	85.9482	64.5492
	mT0	51.1530	33.2879	40.3306
	Llama-2	51.8270	**94.8158**	67.0203
	Llama-2 13B	57.3959	88.4038	**69.6026**
Few-shot	Flan-T5	**72.0247**	63.5744	67.5362
	Flan-alpaca	46.5176	**99.3179**	63.3594
	mT0	42.6172	83.0832	56.3367
	Llama-2	64.2005	73.3970	68.4914
	Llama-2 13B	62.0619	82.1282	**70.6988**

Table 5. Benchmark of the fine-tuning, zero, and few-shot learning of Spanish datasets of Hate Football Corpus 2023 with the racist class. The results are calculated with the test split. The best results for each metric are shown in bold.

	LLM	Precision	Recall	F1 Score
Fine-tuning	ALBETO	85.0	84.7769	84.8883
	BETO	85.2632	85.0394	85.1511
	DistilBETO	83.7209	85.0394	84.3750
	MarIA	**87.5346**	82.9396	**85.1752**
	mBERT	84.1360	77.9528	80.9264
	mDeBERTa	80.0493	**85.3018**	82.5921
	TwHIN	84.7594	83.2021	83.9735
Zero-shot	Flan-T5	**80.2548**	33.0709	46.8401
	Flan-alpaca	57.8829	67.4541	62.3030
	mT0	48.1061	66.6667	55.8856
	Llama-2	50.9874	74.5407	60.5544
	Llama-2 13B	64.3892	**82.4934**	**72.3256**
Few-shot	Flan-T5	87.3016	14.4357	24.7748
	Flan-alpaca	54.9729	**79.7900**	65.0964
	mT0	26.3636	15.2231	19.3012
	Llama-2	**88.3041**	39.6325	54.7101
	Llama-2 13B	65.5629	78.7798	**71.5663**

Finally, for the Spanish datasets, we report the results of HaterNET 2019 in Table 6. Regarding the fine-tuning strategy, the multilingual model DeBERTa achieved the best performance with an F1 score of 68.858% with the positive (hateful) class. These results outperform the experiments carried out when the dataset was compiled, which had an F1 score of 61.1% [13] based on a neural network combining Long–Short Term Memory (LSTM) and MultiLayer Perceptron (MLP) architectures with features related to words, emoticons, and embeddings enriched with TF–IDF. Similar to other Spanish experiments (see Tables 2 and 3), the most limited results are obtained with multilingual BERT, with an F1 score of 58.519%. In these experiments, we also observed that most models achieve better precision than recall, with the multilingual models DeBERTa and TwHIN being the most notable exceptions. For ZSL on the HaterNET dataset, we can see that the best model is Llama-2 from the 13B version, which achieved an F1 score of 50.741%. Regarding FSL, we can see that it did not improve the performance of the Flan-T5 and mT0 models due to the fact that the example set is poorly correlated with the training set of these models. However, with the same examples, it improved the performance of Flan-Alpaca and both the 7B and 13B versions of Llama-2, obtaining the best results in FSL with an F1 score of 56.350%, surpassing the best results in ZSL.

Table 6. Benchmark of the fine-tuning, zero, and few-shot learning of Spanish datasets of Spanish HaterNET 2019 with the positive class. The results are calculated with the test split. The best results for each metric are shown in bold.

	LLM	Precision	Recall	F1 Score
Fine-tuning	ALBETO	64.8649	54.3689	59.1549
	BETO	**72.7612**	63.1068	67.5910
	DistilBETO	67.4193	67.6375	67.5283
	MarIA	67.9054	65.0485	66.4463
	mBERT	68.3983	51.1329	58.5185
	mDeBERTa	66.6666	**71.1974**	**68.8576**
	TwHIN	66.0436	68.6084	67.3016
Zero-shot	Flan-T5	**42.0245**	44.3366	43.1496
	Flan-alpaca	33.5535	82.2006	47.6548
	mT0	36.7925	50.4854	42.5648
	Llama-2	30.5328	**96.4401**	46.3813
	Llama-2 13B	35.5383	88.6731	**50.7407**
Few-shot	Flan-T5	**54.0541**	6.4725	11.5607
	Flan-alpaca	36.1613	84.1424	50.5837
	mT0	17.0683	27.5081	21.0657
	Llama-2	42.0382	**85.4369**	**56.3501**
	Llama-2 13B	37.0656	93.2039	53.0387

4.2. English Datasets

In this section, we report the results for the English datasets on the identification of hate speech.

The first experiments use the English splits of the EXIST 2021 and 2022 datasets. The results are shown in the Table 7. Regarding the fine-tuning strategy, BERT is the model that achieves the best results in both datasets, reaching an F1 score of 79.769% in 2021 and 79.682% in 2022. In 2021, BERT also achieves the best precision, but not the best recall, while TwHIN achieves the best precision in 2022. In both cases, the best recall is obtained by the multilingual model DeBERTa, but the low precision obtained indicates that the multilingual DeBERTa always predicts the positive class, making this model useless compared to the others. The lightweight models ALBERT and DistilBERT achieve very competitive results, as well as the multilingual model TwHIN. Looking at the results of ZSL and FSL, we notice that these results are much better than those obtained with the Spanish splits of EXISTS (see Table 2). In fact, Llama-2 (13B) achieves 74.240% of the F1 score in 2021 and 73.962% in 2022 with ZSL. These results are 5.529% below BERT in 2021 and 5.72% in 2022. The performance of FSL is slightly worse in most of the evaluated models, except in the case of mT0.

The next evaluated comparison is with the HASOC 2019 dataset, the results of which are shown in Table 8. Regarding the fine-tuning model strategy, the best performance is achieved by the multilingual model TwHIN, with an F1 score of 86.760% and an almost perfect recall of 93.609%; however, TwHIN is not the model with the best precision, as DistilBERT achieves a precision of 84.754%. All the fine-tuned LLMs achieve similar performance, but as observed with the Spanish datasets (see Section 4.1), the most limited result is obtained with multilingual BERT. From the results obtained in ZSL, we can see that the models perform better in classifying hate speech in English, achieving an F1 score above 70% in all models. Regarding FSL, the performance of Flan-Alpaca has improved, surpassing the best ZSL result with an F1 score of 84.602%.

Table 7. Benchmark of the fine-tuning, zero, and few-shot learning of English datasets of EXIST 2021 (left) and 2022 (right) with the positive class. The results are calculated with a custom validation split. The best results for each metric are shown in bold.

		2021			2022		
	LLM	Precision	Recall	F1 Score	Precision	Recall	F1 Score
Fine-tuning	ALBERT	73.0337	78.7879	75.8017	73.9726	82.1109	77.8296
	BERT	76.24309	83.6364	**79.7688**	74.8038	85.2415	**79.6823**
	DistilBERT	74.4505	82.1212	78.0980	74.6479	80.5903	77.5054
	mBERT	70.0831	76.6667	73.2272	73.8731	79.1592	76.4249
	mDeBERTa	48.0349	100.0	64.8968	49.4681	**99.8211**	66.1529
	RoBERTa	71.9895	83.3334	77.2472	74.7026	84.2576	79.1929
	TwHIN	73.9612	80.9091	77.2793	**75.6869**	81.3059	78.3959
Zero-shot	Flan-T5	**67.1642**	81.8182	66.7643	**81.5742**	73.4300	73.7705
	Flan-alpaca	61.2159	**88.4848**	72.3668	61.0234	**86.4043**	71.5291
	mT0	55.3672	29.6970	38.6588	61.7094	32.2898	42.3958
	Llama-2	64.3373	80.9091	71.6779	56.2698	95.5277	70.8223
	Llama-2 13B	65.8080	85.1515	**74.2404**	65.3187	85.2415	**73.9620**
Few-shot	Flan-T5	**73.6059**	60.0000	66.1102	**70.4825**	66.6369	68.5057
	Flan-alpaca	54.1176	**97.5758**	69.6216	54.7379	**97.1377**	70.0193
	mT0	47.9279	80.6061	60.1130	49.0061	57.3345	52.8442
	Llama-2	67.1598	68.7879	67.9641	66.5081	62.5224	64.4537
	Llama-2 13B	67.5978	73.3333	**70.3488**	64.2755	80.1431	**71.3376**

Table 8. Benchmark of the fine-tuning, zero, and few-shot learning of English datasets of HASOC 2021 with the positive class. The results are calculated with the test split. The best results for each metric are shown in bold.

	LLM	Precision	Recall	F1 Score
Fine-tuning	ALBERT	81.0872	89.7243	85.1874
	BERT	82.6037	89.8496	86.0744
	DistilBETO	**84.7539**	88.4712	86.5726
	mBERT	80.7474	89.3484	84.8305
	mDeBERTa	82.4074	89.2231	85.6799
	RoBERTa	83.4313	88.9724	86.1128
	TwHIN	80.8442	**93.6090**	**86.7596**
Zero-shot	Flan-T5	**81.1180**	81.8296	81.4722
	Flan-alpaca	74.3665	**95.6140**	**83.6623**
	mT0	64.6825	81.7043	72.2038
	Llama-2	70.6767	94.2356	80.7734
	Llama-2 13B	72.4521	89.9749	80.2683
Few-shot	Flan-T5	**90.2527**	31.3283	46.5116
	Flan-alpaca	76.9231	**93.9850**	**84.6024**
	mT0	59.7484	83.3333	69.5971
	Llama-2	74.2553	87.4687	80.3222
	Llama-2 13B	72.5198	91.6040	80.9524

The results with the EDOS 2023 dataset are shown in Table 9, where monolingual BERT achieves the best performance for the fine-tuning strategy, with an F1 score of 73.795%. It also achieves the best recall (75.773%), but not the best precision, which is achieved by DistilBERT (77.203%). The most limited result is achieved by ALBERT (70.049% of the F1 score), followed by multilingual BERT (70.192% of the F1 score). Compared to BERT, RoBERTa also achieves a good performance with an F1 score of 71.680%, but the multilingual TwHIN surpasses this result with an F1 score of 72.083%. The text generation models for classifying sexist text in the EDOS dataset performed best in the ZSL scenario, with Flan-T5 achieving an F1 score of 53.12%. In the FSL scenario, it improved this result by about 8%, achieving an F1 score of 61.57%.

Table 10 shows the results of HatEval 2019 with the English dataset. Regarding the fine-tuning strategy, the best result is obtained with the multilingual TwHIN, with an F1 score of 67.977% over the positive class. However, the precision of all the LLMs is very limited for the positive class since the recall is almost perfect in every case. This behavior is not observed in the Spanish part of the HatEval 2019 dataset, where the recall is around 75% and 83%. However, the maximum result obtained in the official ranking for the English dataset was a macro average F1 score of 65.10% [11]. Regarding the ZSL and FSL strategies, the performance of the models is very similar, as almost all models achieve limited precision but high recall, but this suggests that these models also always predict the positive class. However, Llama-2 is the best performer for both ZSL and FSL. Specifically, the best overall result is achieved with Llama-2 for FSL, when the highest overall performance is achieved (F1 score of 67.083%).

Table 9. Benchmark of the fine-tuning, zero, and few-shot learning of English datasets of EDOS 2023 with the positive class. The results are calculated with test split. The best results for each metric are shown in bold.

	LLM	Precision	Recall	F1 Score
Fine-tuning	ALBERT	74.3917	66.1856	70.0491
	BERT	71.9178	**75.7732**	**73.7952**
	DistilBERT	**77.2033**	67.7320	72.1581
	mBERT	72.8381	67.732	70.1923
	mDeBERTa	75.1412	68.5567	71.6981
	RoBERTa	74.2541	69.2783	71.68
	TwHIN	72.8421	71.3402	72.0833
Zero-shot	Flan-T5	**37.2007**	92.8866	**53.1250**
	Flan-alpaca	31.7258	94.9485	47.5600
	mT0	31.1571	49.6907	38.2996
	Llama-2	28.5887	**97.3196**	44.1948
	Llama-2 13B	33.0914	93.8272	48.9270
Few-shot	Flan-T5	**50.1622**	79.6907	**61.5691**
	Flan-alpaca	27.3882	**97.8351**	42.7959
	mT0	24.1716	91.7526	38.2631
	Llama-2	39.9890	74.7423	52.1020
	Llama-2 13B	40.0659	75.1029	52.2548

Table 10. Benchmark of the fine-tuning, zero, and few-shot learning of English dataset of HatEval 2019 with the positive class. The results are calculated with test split. The results are calculated with test split. The best results for each metric are shown in bold.

	LLM	Precision	Recall	F1 Score
Fine-tuning	ALBERT	42.7975	97.6190	59.5065
	BERT	47.0161	97.5397	63.4486
	DistilBERT	45.6329	97.8571	62.2413
	mBERT	45.3933	96.1905	61.6794
	mDeBERTa	45.9650	**98.0952**	62.598
	RoBERTa	46.1831	96.5079	62.4711
	TwHIN	**47.5988**	97.5397	**63.9771**
Zero-shot	Flan-T5	**45.0873**	98.3333	61.8263
	Flan-alpaca	42.8523	99.6825	59.9380
	mT0	44.6973	91.9841	60.1609
	Llama-2	44.8768	**99.7619**	**61.9059**
	Llama-2 13B	44.2918	**99.7619**	61.3470
Few-shot	Flan-T5	50.8132	91.7460	65.4031
	Flan-alpaca	42.1546	1.000000	59.3081
	mT0	42.1414	97.4603	58.8404
	Llama-2	**62.3891**	72.5397	**67.0826**
	Llama-2 13B	48.4294	96.6667	64.5298

5. Discussion

Tables 11 and 12 present a comparison showing the best results obtained by different datasets and approaches for the Spanish and English datasets, respectively. In general, we can observe that the fine-tuning approach for transformer models in classification has achieved better performance than ZSL and FSL, but at a higher computational cost.

These results answer RQ1, which asks whether zero and few-shot improve the results of fine-tuning for hate speech detection. In the ZSL approach to hate speech classification in Spanish, the models achieved competent results even though they were not explicitly trained for it, as in the case of the fine-tuning approach. The best model for ZSL was Llama-2 in its 7B and 13B versions.

Regarding FSL, we experimented with a prompt-based FSL using five random examples for each label, and we inserted them into the prompts of the text generation models to guide the model towards better performance. However, based on the results obtained, we can see that the FSL approach did not improve the performance of ZSL, and this is largely due to the quality of the selected few-shot dataset and its relationship with the pre-trained data of the models. Furthermore, finding a set of examples that generalize the concept of hate speech is quite challenging [44]. In this paper [45], an additional retrieval module based on sentence transformers was used to maximize the few-shot performance in clinical and biomedical tasks. However, there are still cases where few-shot learning has worsened the performance of ZSL. Therefore, it would be convenient to select the examples using some kind of heuristic or a method to search for phrases that are more related to a certain class.

If we compare the results obtained for the Spanish and English datasets, we can see that the results obtained by the three strategies evaluated (fine-tuning, ZSL, FSL) are more similar for the English datasets, but greater for the Spanish ones. For example, in EXISTS 2021, there is a 12.402% decrease in performance between the fine-tuning and ZSL strategies in Spanish. However, this difference is only 5.529% in English. Moreover, if we look at the results comparing monolingual and multilingual approaches to fine-tuning, we see that there is a tie in Spanish, as DistilBETO and MarIA are the best performing models in three datasets, while TwHIN and DeBERTa, two multilingual LLMS, achieve the best results in the other three Spanish datasets. In the case of the English datasets, English BERT performed best in both EXISTS 2021 and 2022 and in EDOS, and TwHIN performed best in HatEval and HASOC. In the case of ZSL and FSL, all evaluated models are multilingual. It was therefore expected that the difference in performance would be the same in both languages. Since the results show the opposite, we answer RQ2 (are current ZSL and FSL models equally good at detecting hate speech in English and Spanish?) that ZSL and FSL are better at detecting hate speech in English than in Spanish. However, this comparison must be made with caution, as English and Spanish are typologically different languages with different roots.

With regard to RQ3, which asks about the best generative LLMs for performing ZSL and FSL classification in hate speech detection, we observed that Llama-2 13B is the model that obtained a better result in five of the evaluated datasets for ZSL: three Spanish and two English. In the case of Spanish, the other evaluated version of Llama achieved the best performance in the rest of the evaluated datasets and only one other dataset in English. For the rest of the evaluated English datasets, Flan T5 and Alpaca performed best for EDOS and HASOC. In the case of FSL, Llama-2 13B also achieved the best results in three of the Spanish datasets (HatEval, Football and MisoCorpus), tying with ZSL in two of them (Football and MisoCorpus). Flan-alpaca achieved the best results for the two Spanish EXIST datasets, and Llama-2 for HaterNET. In the case of English, the same models that performed best on ZSL also performed best on FSL. This behavior was not observed for the Spanish datasets. Given these results, we can conclude that Llama-2 13B is the best performing model for zero and few-shot classification in hate speech detection, but this model is not a silver bullet, as there are six datasets where this model did not achieve the best results.

Finally, RQ4 asks whether the same generative LLMs are equally good for zero and few shots. The results show that only two of the Spanish datasets agree (Llama-2 13B in soccer and the MisoCorpus). In English, however, the same models are the best for both ZSL and FSL. So, in this case, the results suggest that the answer to this RQ4 is that it depends on the language. However, if we look at the results individually across all the datasets and generative models evaluated, the difference between ZSL and FSL is usually small, with ZSL performing better. There are exceptions. For example, mT0 shows a difference of 46.832% between FSL and ZSL in the Spanish EXIST 2021 dataset and a difference of 27.998% in 2022 (see Table 2). In other cases, there are strong differences between ZSL and FSL, both in Spanish and in English. This fact suggests that experiments are needed to evaluate which strategy is better depending on the dataset.

Table 11. Resume of the results of fine-tuning, zero, and few-shot learning for the Spanish datasets.

	Fine-Tuning		ZSL		FSL	
Dataset	F1 Score	Model	F1 Score	Model	F1 Score	Model
EXIST-2021-es	82.2581	TwHIN	69.8827	Llama-2	67.8194	Flan-alpaca
EXIST-2021-es	80.7579	DistilBETO	69.8718	Llama-2	69.2236	Flan-alpaca
HatEval	76.2369	DistilBETO	65.3687	Llama-2	66.2831	Llama-2 13B
HaterNET	68.8576	mDeBERTa	50.7407	Llama-2 13B	56.3501	Llama-2
Football	85.1752	MarIA	72.3256	Llama-2 13B	71.5663	Llama-2 13B
MisoCorpus	90.4990	mDeBERTa	69.6026	Llama-2 13B	70.6988	Llama-2 13B

Table 12. Resume of the results of fine-tuning, zero, and few-shot learning for the English datasets.

	Fine-Tuning		ZSL		FSL	
Dataset	F1 Score	Model	F1 Score	Model	F1 Score	Model
EXIST-2021-en	79.7688	BERT	74.2404	Llama-2 13B	70.3488	Llama-2 13B
EXIST-2022-en	79.6823	BERT	73.9620	Llama-2 13B	71.3376	Llama-2 13B
HatEval	63.9771	TwHIN	61.9059	Llama-2	67.0826	Llama-2
EDOS	73.7952	BERT	53.1250	Flan-T5	61.5691	Flan-T5
HASOC	86.7596	TwHIN	83.6623	Flan-alpaca	84.6024	Flan-alpaca

6. Conclusions and Outlook

In this research, we compare and contrast different strategies for detecting hate speech. In particular, we evaluate two alternatives based on prompting, known as zero and few-shot, against a fine-tuning strategy. Our main goal is to test the generalization ability of these models to detect hate speech in texts written in English or Spanish. Through rigorous evaluation on diverse hate speech detection datasets spanning different domains and languages, we uncovered key insights. The evaluation highlighted the robust generalization capabilities of generative models such as T5, BLOOMZ, and Llama-2, underscoring their potential to bridge the gap between data scarcity and model performance. However, the results are still more limited in performance compared to fine-tuning strategies, but with less time and hardware resources. Our research not only contributes to the evolving landscape of hate speech detection, but also underscores the ability of generative models to advance the fight against online intolerance and discrimination.

In order to unravel the potential of zero and few-shot learning strategies in the field of hate speech detection, a number of core research questions were defined. First and foremost, we investigated the impact of these strategies on fine-tuning language models (LLMs) to improve performance (RQ1). In addition, our research ventured into the cross-lingual landscape by investigating whether these strategies are equally effective for hate speech detection in English and Spanish (RQ2). We delved into the intricacies of generative LLMs to identify the best models for zero and few-shot classification in hate speech detection (RQ3). Finally, we questioned the versatility of these models by exploring whether they are equally valid in the context of zero- and few-shot learning for hate speech detection (RQ4). Our research efforts have been driven by these questions and have provided valuable insights into the evolving field of hate speech detection strategies.

The results show that the performance of models based on T5, BLOOMZ, and Llama-2 is still more limited than the fine-tuning of an LLM for hate speech detection, but the results are more stable with English datasets compared to Spanish. The results also show the potential of Llama-2 13B, which achieved the best performance in most of the datasets. Moreover, we observe a large variability in terms of precision and recall, which suggests that a deep experimentation is still needed for each case to determine which is the best performing model to perform ZSL and FSL. Another interesting finding is that FSL strategies usually do not outperform ZSL. These results may be due to a poor selection of examples used as input to the FSL models.

These results also suggest that the selection of the best strategy for hate speech detection is highly dependent on the dataset and the model. Therefore, further research should be conducted to find the similarities and differences of the evaluated linguistic models and strategies. In this sense, we propose to combine the use of linguistic features [46] and explicable machine learning tools, such as SHAP and LIME, [47] to analyze the results across datasets. In particular, we propose to compare the results in similar datasets, such as those of EXIST, which published a Spanish and an English variant in the same competition.

As a promising line of research, we propose to build a retrieval module based on Sentence Transformers to identify the subset that generalizes the concept of hate speech from the training set. The idea would be to fine-tune a Sentence Transformers model through contrastive learning [48] for extracting examples for prompt-based FSL, thus maximizing its performance. In this sense, we also propose to improve the quality of the prompts used and to evaluate different strategies for selecting the examples for FSL. Another line we propose is the use of hyperparameter optimization for text generation models. It is also worth noting that, due to hardware limitations, the 7B version of the Llama-2 model was loaded into the GPU with 8-bit precision, and the 13B version with 4-bit precision. In this sense, the comparison between the two models is unfair (although Llama v2 achieved better performance in most experiments). Therefore, we recommend evaluating both models with 8-bit and 4-bit precision.

Finally, we will also propose to evaluate FSL and ZSL capabilities in other domains. We propose two domains. The first one is author profiling, where the number of publications per author is quite large, so the capabilities of ZSL and FSL models will imply a large time saving of resources if the results have the same performance. In this sense, we will evaluate the generative models with the dataset published in [49], which contains demographic and psychographic traits of politicians and journalists from Spain. The second domain is subjective language. Therefore, we will evaluate these models with the Spanish SatiCorpus 2021 [50], which contains pairs of satirical and real digital news, in order to check which models are better suited to discriminate between them. We also propose to evaluate standard reference datasets for model evaluation, such as GLUE [28] and those similar.

Author Contributions: Conceptualization, J.A.G.-D. and R.V.-G.; data curation, R.P.; funding acquisition, R.V.-G.; investigation, R.P.; project administration, R.V.-G.; resources, R.V.-G.; software, J.A.G.-D. and R.P.; supervision, R.V.-G.; visualization, J.A.G.-D.; writing—original draft, all. All authors have read and agreed to the published version of the manuscript.

Funding: This work is part of the research project LT-SWM (TED2021-131167B-I00) funded by MCIN/AEI/10.13039/501100011033 and by the European Union NextGenerationEU/PRTR.

Data Availability Statement: Source code for training the zero and few-shot models is available at https://github.com/NLP-UMUTeam/mathematics-zsl-fsl-hate-speech (accessed on 8 November 2023). No new data are created in this research. Therefore it is necessary to request the datasets from the original authors of each paper evaluated in this work.

Conflicts of Interest: The authors declare no conflict of interest.

References

1. Scao, T.L.; Fan, A.; Akiki, C.; Pavlick, E.; Ilić, S.; Hesslow, D.; Castagné, R.; Luccioni, A.S.; Yvon, F.; Gallé, M.; et al. Bloom: A 176b-parameter open-access multilingual language model. *arXiv* **2022**, arXiv:2211.05100.
2. Touvron, H.; Martin, L.; Stone, K.; Albert, P.; Almahairi, A.; Babaei, Y.; Bashlykov, N.; Batra, S.; Bhargava, P.; Bhosale, S.; et al. Llama 2: Open Foundation and Fine-Tuned Chat Models. *arXiv* **2023**, arXiv:2307.09288.
3. Cong Khanh, L. English as a Global Language: An Exploration of EFL Learners' Beliefs in Vietnam. *Int. J. TESOL Educ.* **2022**, *3*, 19–33. [CrossRef]
4. Nichols, J. *Linguistic Diversity in Space and Time*; University of Chicago Press: Chicago, IL, USA, 2018.
5. Fortuna, P.; Nunes, S. A survey on automatic detection of hate speech in text. *ACM Comput. Surv. CSUR* **2018**, *51*, 1–30. [CrossRef]
6. Pennington, J.; Socher, R.; Manning, C.D. Glove: Global vectors for word representation. In Proceedings of the 2014 Conference on Empirical Methods in Natural Language Processing (EMNLP), Doha, Qatar, 25–29 October 2014; pp. 1532–1543.

7. Mikolov, T.; Grave, É.; Bojanowski, P.; Puhrsch, C.; Joulin, A. Advances in Pre-Training Distributed Word Representations. In Proceedings of the Eleventh International Conference on Language Resources and Evaluation (LREC 2018), Miyazaki, Japan, 7–12 May 2018.
8. Alkomah, F.; Ma, X. A literature review of textual hate speech detection methods and datasets. *Information* **2022**, *13*, 273. [CrossRef]
9. García-Díaz, J.A.; Jiménez-Zafra, S.M.; García-Cumbreras, M.A.; Valencia-García, R. Evaluating feature combination strategies for hate speech detection in spanish using linguistic features and transformers. *Complex Intell. Syst.* **2023**, *9*, 2893–2914. [CrossRef]
10. Fersini, E.; Rosso, P.; Anzovino, M. Overview of the Task on Automatic Misogyny Identification at IberEval 2018. *IberEval SEPLN 2018*, *2150*, 214–228.
11. Basile, V.; Bosco, C.; Fersini, E.; Debora, N.; Patti, V.; Pardo, F.M.R.; Rosso, P.; Sanguinetti, M. Semeval-2019 task 5: Multilingual detection of hate speech against immigrants and women in twitter. In Proceedings of the 13th International Workshop on Semantic Evaluation, Minneapolis, MI, USA, 6–7 June 2019; pp. 54–63.
12. García-Díaz, J.A.; Cánovas-García, M.; Colomo-Palacios, R.; Valencia-García, R. Detecting misogyny in Spanish tweets: An approach based on linguistics features and word embeddings. *Future Gener. Comput. Syst.* **2021**, *114*, 506–518. [CrossRef]
13. Pereira-Kohatsu, J.C.; Quijano-Sánchez, L.; Liberatore, F.; Camacho-Collados, M. Detecting and monitoring hate speech in Twitter. *Sensors* **2019**, *19*, 4654. [CrossRef]
14. Chi, E.A.; Hewitt, J.; Manning, C.D. Finding Universal Grammatical Relations in Multilingual BERT. In Proceedings of the 58th Annual Meeting of the Association for Computational Linguistics, Virtual, 6–10 July 2020; pp. 5564–5577. [CrossRef]
15. Guarasci, R.; Silvestri, S.; De Pietro, G.; Fujita, H.; Esposito, M. BERT syntactic transfer: A computational experiment on Italian, French and English languages. *Comput. Speech Lang.* **2022**, *71*, 101261. [CrossRef]
16. Jawahar, G.; Sagot, B.; Seddah, D. What Does BERT Learn about the Structure of Language? In Proceedings of the 57th Annual Meeting of the Association for Computational Linguistics; Florence, Italy, 28 July–2 August 2019; pp. 3651–3657. [CrossRef]
17. Hewitt, J.; Manning, C.D. A Structural Probe for Finding Syntax in Word Representations. In Proceedings of the 2019 Conference of the North American Chapter of the Association for Computational Linguistics: Human Language Technologies, Minneapolis, MI, USA, 2–7 June 2019; Volume 1: Long and Short Papers, pp. 4129–4138. [CrossRef]
18. Winata, G.; Wu, S.; Kulkarni, M.; Solorio, T.; Preotiuc-Pietro, D. Cross-lingual Few-Shot Learning on Unseen Languages. In Proceedings of the 2nd Conference of the Asia-Pacific Chapter of the Association for Computational Linguistics and the 12th International Joint Conference on Natural Language Processing, Virtual, 20–23 November 2022; Volume 1: Long Papers, pp. 777–791.
19. Guarasci, R.; Silvestri, S.; De Pietro, G.; Fujita, H.; Esposito, M. Assessing BERT's ability to learn Italian syntax: A study on null-subject and agreement phenomena. *J. Ambient. Intell. Humaniz. Comput.* **2021**, *14*, 1–15. [CrossRef]
20. Carta, S.; Giuliani, A.; Piano, L.; Podda, A.S.; Pompianu, L.; Tiddia, S.G. Iterative Zero-Shot LLM Prompting for Knowledge Graph Construction. *arXiv* **2023**, arXiv:2307.01128.
21. Wei, X.; Cui, X.; Cheng, N.; Wang, X.; Zhang, X.; Huang, S.; Xie, P.; Xu, J.; Chen, Y.; Zhang, M.; et al. Zero-shot information extraction via chatting with chatgpt. *arXiv* **2023**, arXiv:2302.10205.
22. Plaza-del Arco, F.M.; Nozza, D.; Hovy, D. Leveraging Label Variation in Large Language Models for Zero-Shot Text Classification. *arXiv* **2023**, arXiv:2307.12973.
23. Rodríguez-Sánchez, F.; Carrillo-de Albornoz, J.; Plaza, L.; Gonzalo, J.; Rosso, P.; Comet, M.; Donoso, T. Overview of exist 2021: Sexism identification in social networks. *Proces. Leng. Nat.* **2021**, *67*, 195–207.
24. Rodríguez-Sánchez, F.; Carrillo-de Albornoz, J.; Plaza, L.; Mendieta-Aragón, A.; Marco-Remón, G.; Makeienko, M.; Plaza, M.; Gonzalo, J.; Spina, D.; Rosso, P. Overview of exist 2022: Sexism identification in social networks. *Proces. Leng. Nat.* **2022**, *69*, 229–240.
25. Plaza, L.; Carrillo-de Albornoz, J.; Morante, R.; Amigó, E.; Gonzalo, J.; Spina, D.; Rosso, P. Overview of exist 2023–learning with disagreement for sexism identification and characterization. In Proceedings of the International Conference of the Cross-Language Evaluation Forum for European Languages, Thessaloniki, Greece, 18–21 September 2023; pp. 316–342.
26. Montesinos-Cánovas, E.; Garcia-Sánchez, F.; Garcia-Díaz, J.A.; Alcaraz-Mármol, G.; Valencia-García-Sánchez, R. Spanish hate speech detection in football. *Proces. Leng. Nat.* **2023**, *71*, 15–27.
27. Kirk, H.; Yin, W.; Vidgen, B.; Röttger, P. SemEval-2023 Task 10: Explainable Detection of Online Sexism. In Proceedings of the 17th International Workshop on Semantic Evaluation (SemEval-2023), Toronto, ON, Canada, 10–31 January 2023; pp. 2193–2210. [CrossRef]
28. Wang, A.; Singh, A.; Michael, J.; Hill, F.; Levy, O.; Bowman, S. GLUE: A Multi-Task Benchmark and Analysis Platform for Natural Language Understanding. In Proceedings of the 2018 EMNLP Workshop BlackboxNLP: Analyzing and Interpreting Neural Networks for NLP; Brussels, Belgium, 1 November 2018; pp. 353–355. [CrossRef]
29. Devlin, J.; Chang, M.W.; Lee, K.; Toutanova, K.N. BERT: Pre-training of Deep Bidirectional Transformers for Language Understanding. In Proceedings of the NAACL-HLT, Minneapolis, MN, USA, 2–7 June 2019; pp. 4171–4186.
30. Liu, Y.; Ott, M.; Goyal, N.; Du, J.; Joshi, M.; Chen, D.; Levy, O.; Lewis, M.; Zettlemoyer, L.; Stoyanov, V. Roberta: A robustly optimized bert pretraining approach. *arXiv* **2019**, arXiv:1907.11692.
31. Gutiérrez Fandiño, A.; Armengol Estapé, J.; Pàmies, M.; Llop Palao, J.; Silveira Ocampo, J.; Pio Carrino, C.; Armentano Oller, C.; Rodriguez Penagos, C.; Gonzalez Agirre, A.; Villegas, M. MarIA: Spanish Language Models. *Proces. Leng. Nat.* **2022**, *68*, 1–22.

32. Cañete, J.; Chaperon, G.; Fuentes, R.; Ho, J.H.; Kang, H.; Pérez, J. Spanish Pre-Trained BERT Model and Evaluation Data. In Proceedings of the PML4DC at ICLR 2020, Addis Ababa, Ethiopia, 26 April 2020.
33. Lan, Z.; Chen, M.; Goodman, S.; Gimpel, K.; Sharma, P.; Soricut, R. Albert: A lite bert for self-supervised learning of language representations. *arXiv* **2019**, arXiv:1909.11942.
34. Sanh, V.; Debut, L.; Chaumont, J.; Wolf, T. DistilBERT, a distilled version of BERT: Smaller, faster, cheaper and lighter. *arXiv* **2019**, arXiv:1910.01108.
35. Cañete, J.; Donoso, S.; Bravo-Marquez, F.; Carvallo, A.; Araujo, V. ALBETO and DistilBETO: Lightweight Spanish Language Models. In Proceedings of the Thirteenth Language Resources and Evaluation Conference, Marseille, France, 20–25 June 2022; pp. 4291–4298.
36. He, P.; Gao, J.; Chen, W. Debertav3: Improving deberta using electra-style pre-training with gradient-disentangled embedding sharing. *arXiv* **2021**, arXiv:2111.09543.
37. El-Kishky, A.; Markovich, T.; Park, S.; Verma, C.; Kim, B.; Eskander, R.; Malkov, Y.; Portman, F.; Samaniego, S.; Xiao, Y.; et al. Twhin: Embedding the twitter heterogeneous information network for personalized recommendation. In Proceedings of the 28th ACM SIGKDD Conference on Knowledge Discovery and Data Mining, Washington, DC, USA, 14–18 August 2022; pp. 2842–2850.
38. Liaw, R.; Liang, E.; Nishihara, R.; Moritz, P.; Gonzalez, J.E.; Stoica, I. Tune: A research platform for distributed model selection and training. *arXiv* **2018**, arXiv:1807.05118.
39. Raffel, C.; Shazeer, N.; Roberts, A.; Lee, K.; Narang, S.; Matena, M.; Zhou, Y.; Li, W.; Liu, P.J. Exploring the limits of transfer learning with a unified text-to-text transformer. *J. Mach. Learn. Res.* **2020**, *21*, 5485–5551.
40. Chung, H.W.; Hou, L.; Longpre, S.; Zoph, B.; Tay, Y.; Fedus, W.; Li, Y.; Wang, X.; Dehghani, M.; Brahma, S.; et al. Scaling instruction-finetuned language models. *arXiv* **2022**, arXiv:2210.11416.
41. Chia, Y.K.; Hong, P.; Bing, L.; Poria, S. INSTRUCTEVAL: Towards Holistic Evaluation of Instruction-Tuned Large Language Models. *arXiv* **2023**, arXiv:2306.04757.
42. Muennighoff, N.; Wang, T.; Sutawika, L.; Roberts, A.; Biderman, S.; Scao, T.L.; Bari, M.S.; Shen, S.; Yong, Z.X.; Schoelkopf, H.; et al. Crosslingual generalization through multitask finetuning. *arXiv* **2022**, arXiv:2211.01786.
43. Mukherjee, S.; Mitra, A.; Jawahar, G.; Agarwal, S.; Palangi, H.; Awadallah, A. Orca: Progressive Learning from Complex Explanation Traces of GPT-4. *arXiv* **2023**, arXiv:2306.02707.
44. Mozafari, M.; Farahbakhsh, R.; Crespi, N. Cross-Lingual Few-Shot Hate Speech and Offensive Language Detection Using Meta Learning. *IEEE Access* **2022**, *10*, 14880–14896. [CrossRef]
45. Labrak, Y.; Rouvier, M.; Dufour, R. A zero-shot and few-shot study of instruction-finetuned large language models applied to clinical and biomedical tasks. *arXiv* **2023**, arXiv:2307.12114.
46. García-Díaz, J.A.; Vivancos-Vicente, P.J.; Almela, A. Umutextstats: A linguistic feature extraction tool for spanish. In Proceedings of the Thirteenth Language Resources and Evaluation Conference, Marseille, France, 20–25 June 2022; pp. 6035–6044.
47. Nguyen, H.T.T.; Cao, H.Q.; Nguyen, K.V.T.; Pham, N.D.K. Evaluation of explainable artificial intelligence: Shap, lime, and cam. In Proceedings of the FPT AI Conference, Ha Noi, Vietnam, 6–7 May 2021; pp. 1–6.
48. Gunel, B.; Du, J.; Conneau, A.; Stoyanov, V. Supervised Contrastive Learning for Pre-Trained Language Model Fine-Tuning. *arXiv* **2020**, arXiv:2011.01403.
49. García-Díaz, J.A.; Jiménez-Zafra, S.M.; Valdivia, M.T.M.; García-Sánchez, F.; Ureña-López, L.A.; Valencia-García, R. Overview of PoliticEs 2022: Spanish Author Profiling for Political Ideology. *Proces. Leng. Nat.* **2022**, *69*, 265–272.
50. García-Díaz, J.A.; Valencia-García, R. Compilation and evaluation of the spanish saticorpus 2021 for satire identification using linguistic features and transformers. *Complex Intell. Syst.* **2022**, *8*, 1723–1736. [CrossRef]

Disclaimer/Publisher's Note: The statements, opinions and data contained in all publications are solely those of the individual author(s) and contributor(s) and not of MDPI and/or the editor(s). MDPI and/or the editor(s) disclaim responsibility for any injury to people or property resulting from any ideas, methods, instructions or products referred to in the content.

MDPI
St. Alban-Anlage 66
4052 Basel
Switzerland
www.mdpi.com

Mathematics Editorial Office
E-mail: mathematics@mdpi.com
www.mdpi.com/journal/mathematics

Disclaimer/Publisher's Note: The statements, opinions and data contained in all publications are solely those of the individual author(s) and contributor(s) and not of MDPI and/or the editor(s). MDPI and/or the editor(s) disclaim responsibility for any injury to people or property resulting from any ideas, methods, instructions or products referred to in the content.

www.ingramcontent.com/pod-product-compliance
Lightning Source LLC
LaVergne TN
LVHW070454100526
838202LV00014B/1722